Praise for *Eleven Presidents*

"Ivan Eland has done it again. In *Eleven Presidents* he looks at the history of the presidency from an entirely new perspective. Along the way, this well-written and thoroughly researched book persuasively challenges the conventional wisdom at every turn. Even when readers disagree with Eland's interpretations, he will make them think and ponder."

—**David T. Beito**, Professor of History, University of Alabama; author, *From Mutual Aid to the Welfare State: Fraternal Societies and Social Services, 1890–1967*

"In *Eleven Presidents*, Ivan Eland has deployed his encyclopedic knowledge of twentieth-century political history and his superb analytical ability—with groundbreaking results. Delivering even more than the title promises, this much-needed, liberty-minded work of scholarship gives us an objective comparative history of what we might call the limitations of limited government from the perspective of the White House over the last hundred years. Along the way, this fine book becomes no less than a political history of the last hundred years, as well as a trove of Eland's insights . . . and some surprises as well."

—**T. Hunt Tooley**, Professor of History, Austin College; author, *The Western Front: Battleground and Homefront in the First World War*

"Only rarely is a book needed more than *Eleven Presidents*. . . . As a tour de force in style and substance, *Eleven Presidents* should appeal to all reasonable readers regardless of persuasion in the vital debate between big versus limited government. . . . No other book on the American presidency speaks with such grace and clarity."

—**Charles W. Dunn**, former Chairman, U.S. J. William Fulbright Foreign Scholarship Board; Professor Emeritus of Political Science, Clemson University; author, *The Seven Laws of Presidential Leadership*, and editor, *The Future of the American Presidency*

"Political conservatism may or may not be out of ideas as some of its adversaries claim, but sincere small-government advocates like Ivan Eland in *Eleven Presidents* are continuing to stimulate debate in original and highly interesting ways."

—**Richard Shenkman**, Founder and Publisher, History News Network

"'All is not what it first appears to be in presidential history,' as the excellent volume *Eleven Presidents* makes painfully clear. The book offers a devastating critique of Republican presidents and their 'limited government hypocrisy.' Beginning with Herbert Hoover, GOP presidents have expounded on the benefits of smaller government but expanded it nonetheless. (Dwight Eisenhower gets credit for being the one Republican president who kept his promises.) 'Watch what they do, not what they say' is a lesson to be learned from this insightful volume. Carefully comparing promises with results, Eland shows how GOP presidents, from Hoover to George W. Bush, have been Big Government Republicans, despite their rhetoric about 'limited government.' *Eleven Presidents* turns historical assessments of U.S. Presidents upside down—and makes for a fascinating read. Eland makes a good case that Warren Harding and Calvin Coolidge, normally ranked low in presidential polls that prize presidential 'energy,' were in fact two of our greatest presidents when judged by keeping their promises to limit government, both here and abroad. The lesson here is that neither major political party is committed to limited government *in practice*. While there are episodes of deregulation (under Jimmy Carter) or restrained spending (Eisenhower, Clinton), government grows inexorably. So, what is to be done? Eland states that the 'continuing hypocrisy of promising limited government and then not delivering it should be penalized [by voters], not rewarded.' Whether there is any public will to hold presidents accountable or not is then a serious question for readers to ponder."

—**Jonathan J. Bean,** Professor of History, Southern Illinois University

"Ivan Eland's *Eleven Presidents* looks to be as indispensable as his last excellent book on the U.S. presidents, *Recarving Rushmore*. How well have American presidents since World War I done in keeping their promises to constrain government? Read this book!"

—**Ron Paul**, former U.S. Congressman and candidate for U.S. President

"Whatever prospects lie ahead for limited government, the rule of law, and authentic Constitutionalism, Americans first need to know their history. Leviathan did not emerge by accident. Democrats and Republicans alike have built the welfare-warfare state over the past century. Even self-described 'conservatives' have been complicit. In a moment when labels seem to be losing their meaning and once-familiar categories have been upended, Americans find themselves facing urgent questions about the political, economic, and social conditions necessary to a free society. In his important and well-written book *Eleven Presidents*, Ivan Eland unmasks the pretensions of power in Washington, D.C., and invites us to take a fresh and honest look at deeds more than words, at policy more than rhetoric."

—**Richard M. Gamble,** Anna Margaret Ross Alexander Chair
in History and Politics, Hillsdale College

"Ivan Eland sets out to puncture the widely held impression that Republicans acted as the party of limited government over the last 100 years. In the closely argued book *Eleven Presidents*, he succeeds very well. With the exception of Harding, Coolidge, and to some extent Eisenhower, the author shows that government spending and the national debt, measured against the nation's GDP, rose faster under Republican presidents than under Democrats. Some may disagree with Eland's view that this fact is unfortunate, but none can dispute the fact itself."

—**James H. Broussard**, Professor of History and Director,
Center for Political History, Lebanon Valley College

"Finally, with Ivan Eland's *Eleven Presidents* we have the much-needed book that deals directly with . . . the obsession with the notion that presidents can solve all of our problems from the White House by just raising the debt ceiling over and over again. The constant overpromising of presidents and presidential candidates has enshrined the panacea of government deliverance from all of our problems. . . . *Eleven Presidents* examines the counterpoint to the notion that presidents can stop the rise of the oceans with the assertion that presidents can return to limited government. Bill Clinton asserted in a State of the Union address that 'the era of big government, as we've known it, is over,' but since then the national debt has gone up by trillions, not merely hundreds of billions, of dollars. . . . The great promise to return to limited government, as Eland demonstrates, has met with little success. Republican presidents far outnumber Democrats in the promise of a return to limited government, but their rhetoric has far outweighed the reality of their accomplishments. This book is sobering and enlightening in showing the gap between the mostly Republican promise of limited government and the seemingly inexorable march toward the Leviathan state. The book is a welcome addition to the literature on the presidency. It reminds the reader of William Howard Taft's words: 'The President cannot make clouds rain or crops grow.' We can add to the list, that presidents, for the most part, seem incapable of scaling back the growth of the federal government and returning to some semblance of constitutional restraint."

—**Phillip G. Henderson**, Professor of Politics, Catholic University of
America; author, *Managing the Presidency: The Eisenhower Legacy—From
Kennedy to Reagan*; editor, *The Presidency Then and Now*

"Some idols deserve to be smashed, particularly when it comes to the American presidency. In *Eleven Presidents*, Ivan Eland sets about the task with a bracing iconoclasm, toppling alleged 'greats,' and elevating others—like Warren Harding and Jimmy Carter—who've never gotten the respect they deserve. 'All is not what it first appears to be in presidential history,' Eland writes; but readers of *Eleven Presidents* will get a clear-eyed view of which presidents gave lip service to limited government—and which actually delivered."

—**Gene Healy**, Vice President, Cato Institute; author, *The Cult of the Presidency: America's Dangerous Devotion to Executive Power*

ELEVEN PRESIDENTS

INDEPENDENT INSTITUTE is a non-profit, non-partisan, public-policy research and educational organization that shapes ideas into profound and lasting impact. The mission of Independent is to boldly advance peaceful, prosperous, and free societies grounded in a commitment to human worth and dignity. Applying independent thinking to issues that matter, we create transformational ideas for today's most pressing social and economic challenges. The results of this work are published as books, our quarterly journal, *The Independent Review*, and other publications and form the basis for numerous conference and media programs. By connecting these ideas with organizations and networks, we seek to inspire action that can unleash an era of unparalleled human flourishing at home and around the globe.

100 Swan Way, Oakland, California 94621-1428, U.S.A.
Telephone: 510-632-1366 • Facsimile: 510-568-6040 • Email: info@independent.org • www.independent.org

ELEVEN PRESIDENTS

PROMISES vs. RESULTS
in Achieving Limited Government

IVAN ELAND

INDEPENDENT
I N S T I T U T E

OAKLAND, CALIFORNIA

Independent Institute
100 Swan Way, Oakland, CA 94621-1428
Telephone: 510-632-1366
Fax: 510-568-6040
Email: info@independent.org
Website: www.independent.org

Cover Design: Barbara Genetin
Cover Image: Getty Images © Bettmann / Contributor

Library of Congress Cataloging-in-Publication Data Available

Contents

Acknowledgments

I WOULD LIKE to thank the team at the Independent Institute for their hard work bringing this book to life.

Thank you to director of acquisitions Roy M. Carlisle for his initial review of the manuscript and his helpful suggestions. Thank you to production editor Cecilia Santini and art director Barbara Genetin for overseeing production of the book. Thanks to Dawn Adams for her thorough copyedit. Finally, I'd like to thank David J. Theroux for his support throughout the project.

I

Popular Reputations
Depend on Political Rhetoric

SURPRISINGLY, POPULAR HISTORICAL reputations of presidents depend less on the actual policies they promulgated while in office than one might imagine. To a great extent, the public reputation of each president depends on rhetorical claims—while campaigning, governing, or otherwise—and a president's party label, which has its own reputation based on political rhetoric. In other words, despite being suspicious of politicians, the public, journalists, and even many historians take the carefully cultivated images of politicians as the basis for their evaluation of them, usually without carefully examining the policies these politicians actually instituted. In addition, a particular president's reputation is affected by the political climate at the time analysts are making the assessment—that is, assessment of the past depends on the present.

In an earlier book, *Recarving Rushmore: Ranking the Presidents on Peace, Prosperity, and Liberty* and its revised edition (published in 2009 and 2014, respectively), I evaluated all US chief executives on their actual policies rather than their rhetoric, intelligence, leadership styles, charisma, activism, service during a crisis, or other largely irrelevant attributes. I ranked them as the framers of the nation's Constitution might well have assessed them if the framers had been around to see them all—on the basis of whether each one stayed within the limited role that the framers intended the president to fulfill in the government.

In contrast, this discussion examines only certain chief executives who served during the last hundred years—the age of big government, which began with World War I and has lasted to the present—who promised to constrain government. It evaluates whether their actual policies matched their "limited government" reputations. Most of these presidents happened to be Republican, because during most of that timespan, Republicans cornered the market on "limited government" rhetoric, although two Democratic presidents, Jimmy Carter and Bill Clinton, also claimed such a goal.

Most Democratic presidents during that period—Woodrow Wilson, Franklin Delano Roosevelt (FDR), Harry Truman, John F. Kennedy (JFK), Lyndon B. Johnson (LBJ), and Barack Obama—never seriously claimed that objective and are thus not covered by this discussion. All of these blatantly big government Democratic presidents ranked very low in *Recarving Rushmore*—Wilson ranked the worst out of forty-one presidents evaluated, FDR ranked thirty-first, Truman fortieth, JFK thirty-sixth, LBJ thirty-second, and Obama thirty-fourth. Yet, none of them cultivated reputations for limiting government and then delivered the opposite. Thus, for the most part, with a few exceptions, our discussion is about "limited government" hypocrisy of Republican presidents in the last hundred years.

Why Is Limiting Government, Especially the Executive Branch, So Important?

The framers of the Constitution, reflecting the views of the vast majority of Americans at the time the document was signed and ratified, desired only a limited and strictly delegated role for the federal government. The fear of central government came as a result of the American colonies' experience with the British king and parliament.

Thus, the framers allowed the federal government to have rigidly enumerated powers in only certain areas—foreign affairs, deciding on war, funding the armed forces, calling forth the militia when needed, immigration, coining money, regulation of commerce among the states and with foreign lands, and the establishment of post offices and post roads. To highlight the strictly limited role the federal government was to play in the American system, the Tenth Amendment to the Constitution in the Bill of Rights directs that all powers not explicitly delegated to the federal government and not prohibited to the states are to be retained by the states and the people.

In other words, the framers' system was designed for the states to retain all other governmental functions not listed above—for example, education, social services, police powers, and the conservation of natural resources to name just a few. The state governments were favored in the system because they were closer to the people, knew their needs better, and were more responsive to them than the distant federal government. Said differently, the framers intended the states to be much stronger and the federal government to be much weaker than they are now.

The massive growth of the federal government, and particularly the executive branch within it, is the main story in this chronicle. It took this significant expansion of federal power to arrive where we are today. Much of what the federal government now does is unconstitutional—for example, federal law enforcement through agencies such the FBI and DEA, Social Security, Medicare, the federal Department of Health and Human Services, and the Departments of Education and Energy.

Even within the federal sphere, the framers, being suspicious of monarchical power, clearly intended Congress to be the most prominent branch of government, even delegating to the legislative body more powers than the executive branch in dealing with foreign nations and national security. Yet since World War I, and especially starting with the long Cold War, the executive branch has unconstitutionally usurped the powers of the other two federal branches, especially those of Congress. Thus, although the framers intended the states and Congress to be the strongest entities in a truly federal system, now the president and the Supreme Court dominate.

Some say that the Constitution is out of date in a complex, post-industrial world and thus needs to be regarded as a "living document." That term essentially means changing the document's meaning—through unconstitutional legislation, executive actions, or court rulings that set bad precedents—without going through the much harder process of formally amending the language. Conservatives criticize liberals for advocating a living Constitution, but they are also guilty of ignoring and misinterpreting the Constitution to further their own policy agenda.

These shortcuts violate the all-important rule of law critical to the success of a republic. Using them also makes the questionable assumption that more complicated, modern societies need bigger governments and stronger executives to be successful. Yet the more complex the society, the harder it is for the government and a strong chief executive to competently regulate it. Thus, limiting government is still a worthwhile endeavor in the modern era.

Limited Government Prior to the Last One Hundred Years

In the latter half of the 1800s, ending with the presidency of William McKinley, of the two major American parties, the Republican Party was the party of bigger government. The Republicans were for a more activist national government funded by high tariffs and sales of federal land, which would provide for a central bank, internal improvement projects (the nationally subsidized building of roads, canals, and railroads), programs to put people to work during hard times, and subsidies for business. In contrast, the Democrats were generally out to help the little guy (white only), usually by limiting intervention by national government, which traditionally had helped the moneyed classes. Also, the Democrats were for keeping more power at the state and local levels and lowering tariffs—regressive taxes hurting everyday consumers.

Then came the rise of progressivism and Republican presidents Theodore Roosevelt and William Howard Taft, both of whom wanted to regulate big business because it was already subsidized and protected via tariffs, primarily by prior Republican-run governments. In foreign policy, Roosevelt "stole fair and square" what would become the Panama Canal Zone through armed coercion and added the Roosevelt Corollary to the Monroe Doctrine, which paved the way for US military intervention in Latin American countries if they did not do what the United States wanted.

Taft is thought of as a conservative today, but that is only because his declared progressivism was more restrained and constitutional than that of the megalomaniacal Roosevelt. Yet despite Roosevelt's and Taft's efforts in trust busting and conservation, the era of big government was not yet at hand. A major crisis—in fact, US involvement in World War I—would be needed to transform the traditional American suspicion of central government into a permanent, latent acceptance of a greater role for the federal government in the American economy and society.

The Last Hundred Years of Big Government

Only during the presidency of Democrat Woodrow Wilson, chief executive after Roosevelt and Taft during the Progressive Era, did the Democrats flip from a party of small government to a big government, progressive party. Not only was Wilson a progressive domestically, but he embroiled the United States in the horrendous slaughter of World War I. During that war, the federal government penetrated the US economy and society to a greater extent than any time theretofore in American history (including the Civil War) and provided the blueprint for further government expansion during the subsequent New Deal, World War II, Cold War, and War on Terror.

Although he moderated his rhetoric during the 1912 campaign against Roosevelt and Taft, Wilson's views on expanding the presidency past the limits written into the Constitution were published for all to see in his 1908 book, *Constitutional Government in the United States*:

> The makers of the Constitution seem to have thought of the President as what the stricter Whig theorists wished the king to be: only the legal executive, the presiding and guiding authority in the application of law and the execution of policy. His veto upon legislation was only his 'check' on Congress—was a power of restraint, not of guidance. He was empowered to prevent bad laws, but he was not to be given an opportunity to make good ones. As a matter of fact he has become much more. He has become the leader of his party and the guide of the nation in political purpose, and therefore in legal action. The constitutional structure of the government has hampered and limited his action in these significant roles, but it has not prevented it. . . .
>
> Greatly as the practice and influence of Presidents has varied, there can be no mistaking the fact that we have grown more and more inclined from generation to generation to look to the President as the unifying force in our complex system, the leader both of his party and of the nation. To do so is not inconsistent with the actual provisions of the Constitution; it is only inconsistent with a very mechanical theory of its meaning and intention.[1]

In the book, Wilson concluded, "The trouble with the theory is that government is not a machine, but a living thing. It falls, not under the [mechanical] theory of the universe, but the theory of organic life."[2] Thus, Wilson believed in a living Constitution and an expanding presidency.

According to A. Scott Berg, author of the biography *Wilson*,

> In the middle of a period of great economic inequality—when the nation's richest 1 percent owned half its wealth—[Wilson] unveiled his Presidential program. His "New Freedom" worked honestly to protect the less favored 99 percent of his countrymen. In order to actualize his slate of progressive reforms, he brought a bold new approach to his office, one in which the executive and legislative branches co-operated the government. . . .
>
> "What I am interested in is having the government of the United States more concerned about human rights than about property rights," he insisted. Toward that end, he lost no time in creating the Federal Reserve Board, reducing excessive tariffs, reforming taxation, strengthening anti-trust laws, inaugurating the eight-hour workday, establishing the Federal Trade Commission, developing agricultural programs, improving rural life, and making corporate officials liable for the actions of their companies. He even offered the first government bailout of a private industry in distress—cotton. Without so much as a breath of scandal, his New Freedom served as the foundation for the New Deal [FDR] and Fair Deal [Truman] and New Frontier [JFK] and Great Society [LBJ] to come.[3]

Despite his pioneering for other unabashed expansionists of government, and the presidency in particular, Wilson is not covered in our discussion, because he, like most of the others Democratic chief executives of the last hundred years, did not try to hide his agenda from the public, Congress, or the press.

As a reaction to the carnage and costs—both human and material—of World War I and Wilson's ambitious domestic agenda, his Republican successors, Warren Harding and Calvin Coolidge, wanted to reduce the size of government.

Warren Harding inherited a country in disarray from a long distracted (spending months overseas negotiating the Versailles Treaty ending World War I) and then debilitated (incapacitated with a stroke during the last seventeen months of his presidency) Woodrow Wilson. The ill-advised US entry into the war had led to postwar economic ruin, labor unrest, race riots, and fear induced by terrorism from anarchists and the resulting excesses of Palmer Raids and government-sanctioned vigilante activity designed to combat that terrorism.[4] After campaigning on a "return to normalcy," Harding's inaugural address made that more specific by stating, "We can reduce the abnormal expenditures, and we will. We can strike at war taxation, and we must. . . . Our most dangerous tendency is to expect too much of government, and at the same time do for it too little." He also rejected joining the League of Nations and said America should have "no part in directing the destinies of the Old World. We do not mean to be entangled."[5]

In his annual messages to Congress, keeping the Tenth Amendment of the Constitution in mind, Calvin Coolidge, who took over as president when Harding died suddenly in 1923, regularly spoke of limiting the federal government from encroaching on the role of states and localities. Here is an example from his third annual message in 1925:

> The functions which the Congress are to discharge are not those of local government but of National Government. The greatest solicitude should be exercised to prevent any encroachment upon the rights of the States or their various political subdivisions. Local self-government is one of our most precious possessions. It is the greatest contributing factor to the stability, strength, liberty, and progress of the Nation. It ought not to be in ringed by assault or undermined by purchase. It ought not to abdicate its power through weakness or resign its authority through favor. It does not at all follow that because abuses exist it is the concern of the Federal Government to attempt their reform.[6]

Yet, as this discussion will demonstrate, the Harding/Coolidge period was one of the few times in Republican presidential history, since the party's origin in the mid-nineteenth century, that GOP chief executives matched their limited government rhetoric with actual deeds.

Coolidge's successor, Herbert Hoover, who nowadays is also thought of as a conservative in the popular mind, was one only when compared to the subsequent presidencies of Progressives Franklin D. Roosevelt and Harry Truman. President when the stock market crashed in 1929, the progressive Hoover took government beyond where it had gone before, unfortunately turning a mundane recession into the great economic cataclysm that was the Great Depression. In many instances, Hoover set the precedents for FDR's great expansion of government under the New Deal.

Yet, another reason for the erroneous popular perception that Hoover was a "do-nothing" conservative was his use of "limited government" rhetoric to hide precedent-setting and disastrous peacetime state intervention into self-regulating market mechanisms, which could have righted the economic downturn before it turned into the cataclysm of the Great Depression. An example of such deceptive rhetoric is the "associationalism"—which was supposedly designed to ward off pressure for government intervention—enunciated in Hoover's inaugural address:

> Our people have in recent years developed a newfound capacity for co-operation among themselves to effect high purposes in public welfare. It is an advance toward the highest conception of self-government. Self-government does not and should not imply the use of political agencies alone. Progress is born of cooperation in the community—not from governmental restraints.[7]

Yet Hoover's actual policies hypocritically went way beyond such associationalism and set undesirable precedents for government intervention in American society that his successor—the Democrat FDR—would take advantage of with blatant and reckless abandon.

Although FDR did criticize Hoover in the 1932 election campaign for being a tax-and-spend aristocrat, he also made it clear that he would stick up for the "forgotten man"—that is, the little guy. As Charles Rappleye summarized:

> As governor Roosevelt showed a lively interest in the plight of the unemployed and the elderly poor; the Depression seemed to warrant exploiting such themes on a national scale.

Entering the election season in earnest, Roosevelt moved to placate the isolationists of his party by repudiating U.S. participation in the League of Nations. But any notion he would close ranks with the old guard and battle Hoover for the political center Roosevelt erased with a national radio address in April [1932]. There he denounced Hoover's recovery program as a top-down strategy that did nothing to answer the privations afflicting "the little fellow." This was his "Forgotten Man" speech, where Roosevelt cast his lot with "the infantry of our economic army.". . .

In Hoover's single-minded focus in the salvaging [of] America's credit apparatus, Roosevelt found "a national administration which can think in terms only of the top of the social and economic structure. It has sought temporary relief from the top down rather permanent relief from the bottom up.". . .

After all, Roosevelt had for years hewed to Hoover's line that relief for the unemployed was a strictly local affair; only now was he endorsing federal intervention. . . . .

In March [1932], [James] MacLafferty [President Hoover's liaison with Congress] was pleased to report [to Hoover] that Roosevelt was gaining strength among what he termed Progressives and radicals. "They are more and more proclaiming him as their leader," MacLafferty told the president, "and that will scare even the small home-owner to death."[8]

Although FDR's first inaugural address did mention reducing the cost of government, the speech—putting forth a blatant big government program—promised to "put people to work" through government employment, controlling prices, nationalizing the transportation and communication industries, and controlling credit, banking, and speculation.[9] He even proposed to use the war model to fight the Great Depression at home through a vast expansion of executive power.

I am prepared under my constitutional duty to recommend the measures that a stricken Nation in the midst of a stricken world may require. These measures, or such other measures as the Congress may

build out of its experience and wisdom, I shall seek, within my constitutional authority, to bring to speedy adoption.

But in the event that the Congress shall fail to take one of these two
courses, and in the event that the national emergency is still critical, I
shall not evade the clear course of duty that will then confront me.
I shall ask the Congress for the one remaining instrument to meet the
crisis—broad Executive power to wage a war against the emergency, as
great as the power that would be given to me if we were in fact invaded
by a foreign foe.[10]

In addition, by this point in American history, neither FDR nor the Democratic Party had a reputation for limiting government. In the end, FDR
blatantly and massively increased the penetration of the federal government
into the American economy and society through his New Deal program during the Great Depression and also in World War II—using Wilson's World
War I model, but vastly exceeding it.

After FDR died, Harry Truman billed his "Fair Deal" policies as a continuation of FDR's expansion of government domestically. During the 1948
campaign for his own full presidential term and in his 1948 and 1949 State
of the Union addresses, Truman transparently advocated for a vast expansion of government programs. The list includes national health insurance,
more conservation of natural resources, welfare for farmers, federal assistance
for education and housing, a war on poverty, an increase in the minimum
wage, and Keynesian meddling with the business cycle.[11]

According to presidential author Brion McClanahan,

Truman was his own man, but it is difficult to divorce his administration from that of Roosevelt, largely because Truman's own domestic
and foreign policy initiatives were, at times, indistinguishable from
Roosevelt's. What Roosevelt imagined in 1944—"the Second Bill of
Rights"—Truman attempted to put into practice during his almost
eight years in office. By the end of his second term, Truman had become the most progressive president in American history to that point.[12]

Truman also created a costly informal American Empire overseas to police
the world, which lasted throughout the Cold War and even after the Cold

War ended. This empire resulted in large increases in defense spending and the creation of a new permanent military-industrial complex and national security state.

Although Dwight Eisenhower did not try to repeal the significant FDR/Truman governmental expansion, he can only be faulted so much, because the Republican Party had already bought into many of their wildly popular, but ineffectual and even counterproductive, programs. According to historian Richard V. Damms,

> Domestically, although [Eisenhower] resisted calls from some Republican Party leaders to roll back the previous two decades of democratic social welfare and economic reforms, he believed that it was necessary to "hold the line" against any further expansion of federal powers and responsibilities. . . .
>
> Like most conservatives, President Eisenhower took seriously the view that the framers of the Constitution had deliberately sought to avoid an overcentralization of power by specifying that powers not explicitly assigned to the federal government should be reserved to the states or to the people themselves. Under the guise of responding to national emergencies at home and abroad, Ike believed, New Dealers in the federal government had abused the powers of national taxation to impoverish the states and enhance the central government's role over citizens' lives, thereby undermining the principle of federalism. Wherever possible, Eisenhower preferred that state and local authorities, not the national government, take responsibility for addressing citizens' needs. He argued that these governmental bodies would be more attuned to local circumstances and would be more fiscally responsible given their limited powers.[13]

Despite his limited "hold the line" mentality against the further expansion of government, Ike was one of only two presidents since Harry Truman to reduce government spending as a proportion of US economic output (gross domestic product or GDP).

In his speech accepting the presidential nomination at the Democratic convention in 1960 at the Los Angeles Memorial Coliseum, John F. Kennedy—trying to be vibrant in contrast to the perceived stodginess of the existing Eisenhower administration—proposed a "New Frontier" program at home and abroad in the following way:

> Woodrow Wilson's New Freedom promised our nation a new political and economic framework. Franklin Roosevelt's New Deal promised security and succor to those in need. But the New Frontier of which I speak is not a set of promises—it is a set of challenges. It sums up not what I intend to offer the American people, but what I intend to ask of them. It appeals to their pride, not to their pocketbook—it holds out the promise of more sacrifice instead of more security.
>
> But I tell you the New Frontier is here, whether we seek it or not. Beyond that frontier are the uncharted areas of science and space, unsolved problems of peace and war, unconquered pockets of ignorance and prejudice, unanswered questions of poverty and surplus.[14]

Translated, JFK assumed the presidency with intentions for bold initiatives to increase competition with the Soviets, including in space, and to end poverty. But the New Frontier really was designed to do much more.

The New Frontier significantly expanded the federal government's role in the social and economic spheres. Programs sold to fight poverty consisted of aid to blighted areas, resurrecting food stamps for the poor, more school lunches, housing and transportation assistance for cities, increases in unemployment insurance and the minimum wage, and an expansion of Social Security benefits, including retirement at age sixty-two for men.

JFK also doled out benefits to other special interests. He attempted to raise farmers' incomes with the most comprehensive farm legislation since the Great Depression (only no such economic catastrophe existed during JFK's term). The Water Pollution Control Act threw a bone to environmentalists. More money also went to build libraries and hospitals.

After President Kennedy was assassinated, Lyndon Baines Johnson (LBJ), the new Democratic president, skillfully used Kennedy's "martyrdom" to get the rest of JFK's legislative program through Congress and added many of his own initiatives to it. To keep JFK's name associated with the War on Poverty, LBJ named Sargent Shriver, JFK's brother-in-law, to head it. On March 15, 1964, the day before LBJ sent the first bill in that war to Congress—the Economic Equal Opportunity Act (EOA), which established the Job Corps and VISTA, a domestic Peace Corps—he told CBS news correspondent Eric Sevareid that he was a "prudent progressive." Shortly thereafter, on May 22, he used the term "Great Society" for the first time in a commencement speech at the University of Michigan in Ann Arbor. To reach that high societal plateau, LBJ said Americans would need to reconstruct their cities from urban decay by creating efficient transportation and modern dwellings, to preserve the nation's environment, and to build school systems across the country that would eliminate poverty.

LBJ's Great Society program was the largest expansion of the federal government since the New Deal and World War II. Yet when given the task of being the chief general on the War on Poverty, Sargent Shriver famously sarcastically quipped, "Now you tell me how I abolish poverty." But he was eager, as was LBJ, to throw money at the problem. Shriver also notably said, "This will be my first experience in spending a billion dollars, and I'm quite excited about it." LBJ approached the vast expansion of government under the Great Society umbrella in much the same cavalier and unfocused way, betting that if the programs he proposed did not work, they would be difficult for opponents to terminate and eventually could be transformed.[15] Such cockiness on the part of LBJ is a major indication that he in no way was hiding his big government agenda.

The next Republican president, Richard Nixon, had a prior reputation as an anti-Communist conservative and as an admirer of limited government,[16] but when in office he ran economic, social, and foreign policies that were starkly different than this tack. Nixon's "New Federalism" slogan implied that power would devolve from the federal government back to the states and localities by eliminating federal grants for specific projects, such as road building, while distributing federal tax receipts to state and local governments through "revenue sharing" that could then be used with more flexibility.[17] Yet this moniker proved to be a mirage, as the federal government attached bureaucratically byzantine mandates that states and localities had to satisfy to get the federal money. Brion McClanahan best sums up Nixon's "New Federalism" chicanery:

Nixon's domestic policy differed very little from Johnson's "Great Society." The "New Federalism" was an ingenious smokescreen for continued unconstitutional expansion of the federal government into areas where it had no legal authority.[18]

In fact, prior to the election of Barack Obama, Nixon was the last progressive president.

Gerald Ford, the only unelected president in American history, had only a short time in office after Nixon resigned because of the Watergate scandal, but he can be categorized as merely a carryover from Nixon, who also did not challenge the entrenched system of an activist federal government. Although Ford never had a formal plan or agenda, he continued the policies of the moderate wing of the Republican Party since World War II (read: the general acquiescence to big government). After Vietnam and Watergate, Congress began to somewhat reassert its constitutionally given powers. However, Ford pushed back in the name of executive power. For example, he allowed the CIA to meddle in the Angolan civil war while Congress was investigating the intelligence community and excluded Congress from the military intervention during the Mayaguez incident in 1975, despite the recently passed War Powers Resolution of 1973, which required congressional involvement.[19]

Curiously, the first president who began leading the march back toward limiting government was southern Democrat Jimmy Carter. Carter biographers Burton I. Kaufman and Scott Kaufman describe the political environment after Vietnam and Watergate in election year 1976 and why an obscure Democratic governor of a relatively small, southern state did well enough to become president:

> A revolt against Washington was what the election was all about. American voters, most polls showed, felt that government was far too meddlesome and intrusive, that it was unmovable and overbureaucratized, and that it was out of touch with the American people and insensitive to their ability to manage their own affairs. . . .
>
> The counterculture, so often identified with the 1960s, actually burgeoned in the 1970s, represented in every manner from long, shaggy hair to outrageous fashions and challenges to traditional sexual mores. Alongside this counterculture were a libertarian ethic, a renewed faith in the marketplace, the evangelical Christian movement that Carter had successfully tapped into, and a renascent conservative political

movement—all manifested in Ronald Reagan's nearly successful bid
for the Republican presidential nomination as well as Carter's own
campaign for president.[20]

During the campaign of 1976, the evangelical Protestant Carter was one of
the most conservative Democratic candidates. He advocated welfare reform,
promised to deregulate American industries, argued that then President Ford's
détente policy of easing relations with the Soviet Union had gone beyond
prudence, offered that he might back a federal law limiting abortion, and
pledged to cut back federal spending and balance the budget.[21]

In office, Carter cut the federal budget deficit as a portion of GDP, deregulated four major industries, and appointed Paul Volcker as chairman of the
Federal Reserve. Volcker conducted a "monetarist experiment," which bled
the high inflation out of the economy and ushered in a long prosperity. Carter
also restrained governmental activism overseas, severely limiting unneeded
American military action, and thus carried out one of the best foreign policies of the twentieth century. In many ways, Carter set precedents in limiting
government for which Ronald Reagan later received excessive credit.

A litany of speeches exist in which Reagan warned of the dangers of big
government and expressed his desire to limit it. For example, this excerpt is
from a speech given by Reagan in Westminster in 1982:

> [T]here is a threat posed to human freedom by the enormous power
> of the modern state. History teaches the dangers of government that
> overreaches—political control taking precedence over free economic
> growth, secret police, mindless bureaucracy all combining to stifle
> individual excellence and personal freedom.[22]

Well said, but Ronald Reagan's championing of limited government was
mostly rhetorical, as our discussion will demonstrate. Most of his major policies did not succeed in achieving that goal. He actually increased the size of
the federal government as a percentage of GDP (unlike Ike and Bill Clinton),
added the second most nonmilitary federal bureaucrats as a percentage of
the American population of any president since Truman, presided over the
largest debt accumulation as a proportion of GDP of all presidents during
that period, had deregulation policies outmatched by Democrats Carter and

Clinton, and had the smallest tax cuts as a percentage of GDP among post–World War II Republican presidents. Most important, Reagan's illegal and unconstitutional secret war in Nicaragua, in direct contravention of congressional prohibition and unlawfully funded by the proceeds from illegal arms sales to a terrorist-sponsoring nation, led to the worst political scandal in American history to date: the Iran-Contra affair. The scandal was a result of Reagan eviscerating the system of checks and balances in the US Constitution by executive branch aggrandizement of Congress's most important remaining power—the power of the purse. Finally, if Reagan had any role in ending the Cold War, it was because he negotiated with the reform-minded Soviet leader Mikhail Gorbachev—a dovish policy compared to his earlier dangerously harsh anti-Soviet rhetoric.

Reagan was hawkish at the beginning of his stint as president—inadvertently almost starting a nuclear war with the Soviets in late 1983—but his successor, George H. W. Bush, who had the popular reputation of being a "wimp," was even more hawkish and also more suspicious than Reagan about Gorbachev's intentions.

Bush, like Reagan, was strong on the antigovernment rhetoric, famously declaring during the 1988 campaign, "Read my lips, no new taxes."[23] This pledge was disingenuous, because at the time he made it Bush had surmised that once he took office he likely would need to raise taxes to close the massive federal budget deficit he had inherited from Reagan. However, Bush did contribute to the reduction of Reagan's red ink by cutting spending and raising taxes, although fewer times than Reagan increased taxes.

Bush's challenger in the 1992 election, Bill Clinton, had in 1990 become the national chairman of the Democratic Leadership Council (DLC), an organization of conservative Democrats from right-leaning states. On May 6, 1991, Clinton became the favorite of the southern wing of his party and vaulted himself into the top tier of Democratic candidates by addressing the DLC national convention in Cleveland with these words:

> Too many of the people who used to vote for us, the very burdened middle class we are talking about, have not trusted us in national elections to defend our national interests abroad, to put their values into our social policy at home, or to take their tax money and spend it with

discipline. We've got to turn these perceptions around or we can't continue as a national party.[24]

In office, Clinton did take actions to limit government. For example, he had been advocating welfare reform long before he was president and achieved it as chief executive. He also shepherded the North American Free Trade Agreement (NAFTA) to congressional ratification, eliminating governmental trade barriers between the United States, Canada, and Mexico. Clinton, the champion of post-Truman presidents in federal budget reduction as a portion of GDP, also was the only president during that period to actually reduce federal spending per capita. Although he was unnecessarily aggressive militarily in minor wars overseas, he learned from his mistakes and avoided a large foreign quagmire on the ground.

The same cannot be said about Republican George W. Bush, who landed the United States in two exhausting and costly—in lives and dollars—nation-building sinkholes in Afghanistan and Iraq. And Bush was not only a big spender militarily but also domestically; he spent more on domestic programs than any president since Lyndon B. Johnson.

These policy realities differed from his campaign rhetoric. In a campaign speech at the Citadel military academy in South Carolina in September 2000, Bush rejected Bill Clinton's numerous military interventions overseas—designed to achieve nation-building and humanitarian ends—for a humbler US foreign policy.

> Sending our military on vague, aimless and endless deployments is the swift solvent of morale. . . . The problem comes with open-ended deployments and unclear military missions. In these cases we will ask, "What is our goal, can it be met, and when do we leave?" . . . We must be selective in the use of our military, precisely because America has other great responsibilities that cannot be slighted or compromised. And this review of our deployments will also reduce the tension on an overstretched military.[25]

Domestically, although Bush's "compassionate conservatism" did pledge more federal involvement in education and the shifting of government resources to religious charities, it also hoped to control federal spending, reform

Social Security, significantly cut taxes, and be softer on illegal immigrants—all implying the limiting of government.[26]

Despite his administration's generally "limited government" program, as Benjamin A. Kleinerman writes, expanding the power of the presidency was not just the means to achieve other policy objectives for Bush but an end itself:

> Presidents typically assert their constitutional authority in the context of attaining their own political goals. By contrast, Bush seemed to go out of his way to assert the constitutional powers of the presidency, in a manner almost divorced from his own political agenda. In fact, Bush's advocacy and behavior as president revealed the establishment of a strong presidency itself as one of his most important political objectives. As former head of the Office of Legal Counsel Jack Goldsmith later wrote, Bush pursued a constitutionally strong presidency with an almost "theological" zeal, which sometimes conflicted with his other political ambitions.[27]

Bush's vice president, Dick Cheney, with his "unitary theory of the executive," somehow had gotten the impression that—instead of being slightly diminished toward the more limited, constitutional role intended by the nation's founders—the post-Vietnam and Watergate presidency had been severely harmed and eroded, thereby requiring restoration. Cheney's view seems to have also driven Bush's thinking. Bush's pursuit of Goldsmith's "constitutionally strong presidency" vaulted an already imperial presidency into the unconstitutional stratosphere.

Although Barack Obama, unlike George W. Bush, did not claim the president's right, as commander-in-chief, to ignore congressionally passed laws in time of emergency or assert the right to illegally torture people, he certainly took advantage of many of Bush's unconstitutional expansions of executive power and added some of his own. However, Obama is one of the big government presidents not included in this volume because, as an unashamed progressive, he did not promise to limit government.

Among other things, Obama promised to undo Bush's tax cuts for the wealthiest Americans, to undertake more federal intervention in the banking sector after the economic meltdown, to give assistance to people having trouble with their mortgages, to increase federal intervention in education by giving states grants for adopting federal education standards, to give tax credits for college, to heavily subsidize renewable energy in his massive economic stimulus plan, to promote international climate change agreements, to get high-speed Internet access for 98 percent of the US population, and, as a long-term goal, to achieve high-speed rail access for 80 percent of Americans.[28]

Although Obama reduced George W. Bush's massive deficit through spending cuts and tax increases, he also expanded government intervention into the healthcare market, socialized two of the three American automakers, drastically increased the regulation of the financial system, and enacted a huge "stimulus" bill of pork spending, justified in the name of saving the country from Bush's Great Recession. In foreign policy, Obama was more restrained than Bush but failed to get the United States out of potential quagmires in Afghanistan and Iraq, enmeshed it anew in Syria and Libya, and accelerated unconstitutional US drone wars in the Middle East and Southwest Asia.

Hypocrisy During the Last One Hundred Years of Big Government

In sum, Republican presidents in the last hundred years have often failed to limit government. Only three of them during that time—Warren Harding, Calvin Coolidge, and Dwight Eisenhower—had much of a record of doing so, thus making these few out of step with most of their party's presidential history since the 1860s. And in contrast to the history of the Democratic Party in the 1800s, which advocated limited government, all but two Democratic presidents in the last hundred years—Jimmy Carter and Bill Clinton—could be labeled as barefaced big-government "progressives." Those two exceptions—both southern Democrats—were unsurprisingly more moderate than the rest of the Democrats. On the other hand, six out of nine Republican presidents in the last hundred years—Herbert Hoover, Richard Nixon, Gerald Ford, Ronald Reagan, George H. W. Bush, and George W. Bush—pursued policies that did not fit with their popular reputations that have come down through history. Even the three Republican presidents who actually limited government—Harding, Coolidge, and Eisenhower—have been mischaracterized as "conservatives" when they should have been labeled proto-libertarians (the first two) or libertarianesque (the last). Jimmy Carter and Bill Clinton, being

Democrats, actually have not received enough credit for their efforts to limit government.

In fact, when analyzing the completed terms of post–World War II presidents, Democrats have actually restrained the growth of government spending as a portion of GDP significantly more than Republicans. Democrats have also reduced federal budget deficits as a percentage of GDP and federal debt as a portion of GDP, whereas the Republicans have increased both. Perhaps that is why economic growth—measured in annualized change in net real GDP growth (the change in real GDP per capita minus the change in real debt per capita)—has been substantially higher in Democratic administrations than during Republican ones.[29] All such statistics defy the popular conventional wisdom.

Thus, the divergence between many Republican presidents' rhetoric and their actual policies is what makes studying them so interesting. Studying Carter and Clinton on the Democratic side is also fascinating because they had a surprising number of less popularly heralded policies that limited government. As noted, Democrats Woodrow Wilson, Franklin D. Roosevelt, Harry Truman, John F. Kennedy, Lyndon B. Johnson, and Barack Obama are not in my discussion because although they were guilty of rapidly expanding government, they were not at all surreptitious and hypocritical about doing so—thus providing a less interesting story.

Classifying the Presidents

I am classifying the presidents based on the delta of policy changes they made while chief executive relative to expectations about the size and proper functions of the federal government when they took office. For example, the federal government was much smaller during Herbert Hoover's time in office than it was during Dwight Eisenhower's tenure, yet Hoover is labeled a progressive and Eisenhower as libertarianesque. This is the case because Hoover was a pioneer, even before FDR, in enlarging the functions of the federal government, while Eisenhower cut an already large government's size relative to GDP and also reduced its debt-to-GDP ratio.[30] In other words, a president has to be evaluated in his time in history.

The eleven presidents of the last hundred years who promised small government can be classified in three groups:

Proto-Libertarian or Libertarianesque

Warren G. Harding
Calvin Coolidge
Dwight D. Eisenhower
Jimmy Carter
Bill Clinton

Moderately Progressive

Herbert Hoover
Richard M. Nixon/Gerald Ford

Big Government Hawks

Ronald Reagan
George H. W. Bush
George W. Bush

The reader may be surprised by the categorizations of some presidents who have very different popular historical reputations. However, public memory of presidents and actual historical facts about their policies often diverge.[31] In an especially egregious example of such divergence, the current myth surrounding Ronald Reagan depicts him as a small government Republican but his actual policies tell a much different tale. Hopefully, the subsequent discussions about each president will explain and justify the above classifications and explode some of the myths surrounding these chief executives.

In sum, considering the presidents of the last hundred years—that is, those serving in the era of big government beginning with World War I—most chief executives, both Democratic and Republican, have not limited government. On the Democratic side, only Carter and Clinton out of eight presidents were better than expected at effectuating policies limiting government. Similarly, only three of nine Republicans who served during that same time period—Harding, Coolidge, and Eisenhower—lived up to the expectations of their "small government" popular reputations. Thus, in the last hundred years, neither major party has had a good record in limiting the federal government's growth.

An argument can be made that most of the five presidents who had some success in limiting government did so only because a major war had ended before they took office. Of the five, however, Coolidge did not take office until almost five years after World War I had ended, and Jimmy Carter did not take office until about four years after the Vietnam War had ended. Also, Truman and Ford had less success in limiting government, despite their presidencies being after World War II and the Vietnam War, respectively, had ended. Even Harding, Eisenhower, and Clinton (although they had the advantage of serving just after World War I, the Korean War, and the Cold War, respectively, had ended) could have simply redirected defense resources to domestic programs instead of limiting government. They did not. Harding even reduced domestic spending.

As Thomas Jefferson said, "The natural progress of things is for liberty to yield, and government to gain ground." So the few instances in which presidents have limited or even reversed the government's growth should be celebrated under any circumstances. This chronicle tries to do that without regard to personality, party, or other irrelevant factors.

2

Years of Normalcy and Restraint

WARREN HARDING (PRESIDENT from 1921 to 1923) and Calvin Coolidge (president from 1923 to 1929) seem dull by today's standards of assessing presidential performance, which value activism both at home and abroad. Even Harding's sex scandals have been overshadowed by the even more salacious ones of John F. Kennedy and Bill Clinton. Coolidge was simply dull, period.

After the bipartisan Progressive Era of Theodore Roosevelt, William Taft, and Woodrow Wilson and its unnecessary involvement of the United States in the bloody World War I—leading to a steep US economic downturn and social unrest—the exhausted country was ready to get back to "normalcy," as Warren Harding and his running mate, Calvin Coolidge, put it in the 1920 election. In his campaign, Harding famously eschewed more activism, at home and abroad, by declaring,

> America's present need is not heroics, but healing; not nostrums, but normalcy; not revolution, but restoration; not agitation, but adjustment; not surgery, but serenity; not the dramatic, but the dispassionate; not experiment, but equipoise; not submergence in internationality, but sustainment in triumphant nationality.[1]

Rhetoric by politicians is often unhelpful in evaluating what they actually did, but for the most part, the policies of Harding and Coolidge comported well with this campaign pitch.

To Harding and Coolidge, "normalcy" meant peace, economic stability, and less uncertainty for business. Conservatives at this time realized, but have long since forgotten, that war is the principal cause of big government, both at home and abroad. Harding shrunk Wilson's still war-bloated government by more than half.[2] After Harding died, Coolidge continued Harding's restrained foreign policy and budget-cutting ways. At the end of the Coolidge administration in 1929, the federal budget was in surplus.

Unfortunately for the country, a second progressive era, again of bipartisan presidents, followed during the presidencies of Herbert Hoover, Franklin D. Roosevelt, and Harry Truman. Especially key to this re-intrusion of big government into the domestic economy during the Great Depression and beyond was Woodrow Wilson's precedent-setting government control of the wartime economy during World War I. An even bigger war during this second progressive era—World War II—established a precedent for deeper government penetration of the civilian economy in the armed peace that followed during the Cold War.

However, in between these two Progressive eras and their huge wars lies the halcyon days of the 1920s, when peace, prosperity, and liberty reigned.

A More Restrained Foreign Policy

Almost everything that happened during the Harding/Coolidge period was a reaction to the Progressive Era—foreign policy was no exception. Coming after probably the most interventionist president in American history—Woodrow Wilson—Warren Harding wanted to return to the traditional US foreign policy of staying out of most foreign wars. The nation's founders realized that such noninterventionism was a luxury afforded by the country's great intrinsic security arising from being oceans away from the centers of world conflict. During his presidential campaign, Harding cogently said, "[M]ost questions which are settled by armed force are never permanently settled. . . ."[3]

Harding wanted to stay out of Wilson's League of Nations because he thought it would drag the United States into another war. Article Ten of the Versailles Treaty required member nations to assist any other member who was the victim of aggression. Agreeing to this provision would have undermined Congress's constitutional power to decide whether or not the nation went to war and also would have likely involved the United States in more overseas wars, large and small.[4] Congress had rejected the Versailles Treaty and the League of Nations, so Harding reached a separate peace treaty with Germany in 1921.

And the American public also was ready to renew what, with a few notable exceptions, was the restrained foreign policy that lasted from George Washington to William Taft. The public recoiled at the severe carnage of World War I and the cynicism of Woodrow Wilson in allowing US wartime allies Britain and France to expand their colonial empires with territories taken from the war's losers, especially in the Middle East—so much for Wilson's advocacy of national self-determination in his Fourteen Points and the "war to make the world safe for democracy."

In the Middle East, instead of following even Wilson's rhetorical promotion of national self-determination, Harding preferred only to protect US interests. Also, Harding did not share one of Wilson's principal goals in the Middle East—promoting the activities of American Christian missionaries.

When Christian Greece invaded Muslim Turkey and the Turks turned the tide and advanced on Smyrna, American Christian groups pressured Harding to send US troops to prevent the massacre of Christians. However, Harding wisely told his Secretary of State Charles Evans Hughes, "Frankly, it is difficult for me to be consistently patient with our good friends of the Church who are properly and earnestly zealous in promoting peace until it comes to making warfare on someone of the contending religion. . . ." Publicly, Hughes properly condemned the "barbaric cruelty" of the Turks but noted that the Greeks had invaded Turkey, not vice versa, and had burned towns and committed "general devastation and cruelties" too. In other words, Hughes concluded that both sides in the conflict had committed atrocities. Thus, Hughes rejected US intervention, noting that the United States had not been party to the conflict and that if its wartime allies, who were more closely connected to the situation, did not intervene, neither should the United States.[5]

This wise advice should be followed more often by US policymakers today, who regularly worry more about "crises" in faraway regions of the world than do nearer countries who should care more about them, thus leading to much unneeded, expensive, and counterproductive American military meddling abroad.

First US Arms Control Treaty

Because the US Senate had rejected the Treaty of Versailles and the League of Nations, which would have usurped Congress's power to declare war, the United States undertook a series of multilateral treaties designed to secure peace—including Harding's Washington Naval Treaty of 1922 and Coolidge's Dawes Plan in 1924 to deal with war reparations and the Kellogg-Briand Treaty to outlaw war in 1928.

Even after World War I had ended, Wilson ordered a naval buildup before leaving office. This policy shows how bigger government in wartime continues into peacetime. Harding attempted to return to "normalcy" in the foreign policy area by achieving a lasting peace among the great powers through reversing Wilson's naval expansion into a peacetime reduction, setting limits on the size of nations' navies, and resolving potential conflicts in the Asia/Pacific region—all at the Washington Disarmament Conference. The conference was designed to lessen military power as an instrument of statecraft in the world and substitute economic forces, which would take the lead in reconstruction from the Great War.[6]

Harding invited a number of important countries to this first ever disarmament conference and then made startling proposals for actually cutting the size of navies. To avoid a costly arms race in battleship construction, the signatories to the Washington Naval Treaty agreed that the United States, Great Britain, and Japan would cut naval tonnage to end up with a ratio of 5–5–3, respectively. Harding realized that the United States would need to cut its naval forces more deeply than the other nations to get such an agreement; America scuttled ships amounting to 845,000 tons, versus 583,000 tons by Great Britain and 480,000 tons by Japan. During the subsequent Coolidge administration, the Navy was shocked to learn that it would not be able to build warships even up to the treaty's reduced limit because of Coolidge's deep budget cuts—needed to shrink the ballooned national debt as a result of US involvement in World War I.[7]

As it covered only capital ships (battleships), the treaty applied to only 30 percent of the naval tonnage of the signatory nations, thus allowing unlimited building of smaller ships.[8] Although the United States also failed to keep up with the building of the other treaty signatories in these smaller categories, it had a better strategic position—far from the centers of world conflict—than even the island nations of Japan and Britain.

To attempt to avoid conflict among the great powers in Asia, the conference also continued the traditional Open Door policy in China, whereby all of the great powers had equal access to exploitative trade with China. Harding then did what Wilson could not do with the Treaty of Versailles and the League of Nations: use his political skills to get the Washington treaties ratified by the US Senate.[9] The Washington Conference is still studied by political scientists as a model for a successful disarmament conference.

However, the conference has been criticized by modern-day interventionists for allowing Japan's rise into the aggressive power of World War II. The Japanese did violate the treaty in a quest for an empire such as Great Britain, France, the Netherlands, and the United States already had in Asia. Treaties are mere scraps of paper unless countries fulfill their commitments to them. The treaty still allowed the United States and Great Britain a naval edge over Japan and reiterated the Open Door policy as an attempted constraint to Japanese expansion into China. The treaty did initially restrain Japan but ultimately failed to restrict Japan's expansionist desires.[10] Nonetheless, the pact was not a naïve treaty; it was the first international arms control agreement and set a precedent for attempting to reduce arms, establish limits on them, and thus avoid an arms race—all of which would be imitated in the future.

Who Allowed the Rise of the Axis Powers?

More generally, the Harding and Coolidge presidencies have been criticized, again in hindsight, for "not staying involved in Europe and the world," thus allowing the rise of the aggressive Axis powers of World War II. But the popular revulsion in America at the carnage and allied double-dealing in World War I—much more pronounced than after World War II—was so great that Harding and Coolidge could not have kept a large US military presence overseas, as American presidents did in the post–World War II era. Also, after World War II, the looming perceived threat of the Soviet Union made the American people more accepting of such overseas military commitments. Harding's attempt to dampen the chance of war by naval disarmament and by trying to solve potential conflicts in Asia were the limits of what American public opinion at the time would allow.

Besides, such Monday morning quarterbacking is done retrospectively through the lens of the Munich syndrome. In today's American foreign policy, so much is seen through Neville Chamberlain's failed attempt to appease Adolf Hitler concerning Czechoslovakia in 1938. The lesson that has been taken from that episode is that every threat, no matter how small, must be nipped in the bud before it snowballs into cataclysmic aggression. Taking this lesson from Munich is debatable, however, because Chamberlain's appeasement probably saved Britain—Britain was behind Germany in its military buildup and needed time to augment the air defenses that ultimately saved the country from Luftwaffe bombardment. But the real problem with this analysis is ignoring what came before Munich.

During the Wilson administration, the unnecessary US entry into World War I tipped the balance in the war to Germany's defeat and humiliation, laying the seeds of World War II and the Cold War. The Kaiser's Germany, which did not want a general European war and was no more at fault for it than other European powers, was not bent on taking most of Europe (as Hitler later was in World War II). This limited orientation was demonstrated by the Kaiser's prewar proposal that if Britain would remain neutral in World War I, Germany would not take any of France but only some of her colonies. Britain should have taken this offer but unwisely refused; even in victory, she was so spent that her empire eventually began to decline.

Without American entry into the war, an exhausted Germany would have won a fifteen-round decision and only modestly altered the boundaries of Europe. The economic depression in Germany caused by the war, Allied demands from Germany for heavy war reparations, and Wilson's insistence on the abdication of Kaiser Wilhelm II paved the way for the rise of Adolf Hitler and World War II. Also, Wilson, with his allies, cajoled and bribed the new post-czar Provisional Government in Russia with aid to stay in the bloody war, which led to the Bolshevik Revolution, a harebrained US and Allied invasion of Russia to help the Bolshevik's domestic enemies, and thus bad US-Soviet relations until the end of the Cold War.

An argument exists that even after Wilson's entry into World War I planted the seeds for the rise of Hitler and World War II, Harding and Coolidge should have "done something"—that is, made the United States stay in Europe to prevent the second cataclysm. Yet foreseeing Hitler's rise to the German chancellorship in 1933 and the Japanese invasion of Manchuria in 1931 would have been extremely difficult for Harding and Coolidge during the 1920s. Therefore, they should not be criticized for not having clairvoyance.

In fact, after World War I, the Harding and Coolidge administrations went overboard in trying to help European nations with big war debts get some relief. In 1923, the Foreign Debt Commission negotiated agreements with allied nations that owed war debt to the United States to covertly write off 43 percent of those loans, while making it seem like repayment was being made. Congress and Harding administration officials knew of this subterfuge—designed to avoid public outrage in America at the United States forgiving the debt of countries that it had already bailed out of the stalemated World War I.[11]

In 1924, Coolidge actually tried to lessen the burden of war reparations on the German economy through the Dawes Plan. The plan encouraged private American lenders to make loans to an economically devastated Germany so that it could pay the reparations owed to Britain and France, and they in turn could pay back their war loans to the United States. This unstable self-paying scheme was never revealed to the American public.[12] Harding wisely stayed out of France's postwar invasion of the German Ruhr in 1923 to enforce reparations payments, and Coolidge used Allied debt owed to the United States to pressure the French to end their occupation of the Ruhr.[13]

However, in 1929 and 1930, France proposed European integration that would have been similar to the post–World War II economic unification that led to the European Union. This post–World War I integration was, as was the latter more successful form, designed to hug Germany and prevent it from rising again. However, the British rejected the French proposal, making it easier for Germany to reject it.[14] France's proposed model was based on inclusion of the war's loser into the European system—like the successful paradigm established at the Congress of Vienna after the Napoleonic Wars, which prevented a European-wide conflagration for almost one hundred years. Had the proposal been adopted, it might have gone some way toward ameliorating Germany's anger over stiff reparations and the "war guilt" clause in the Versailles Treaty, which unfairly blamed Germany for World War I. At any rate, the proposal shows that there were higher-probability ways of avoiding another cataclysmic European war than retaining US forces in Europe after World War I—which was an impossibility anyway, given the American public's postwar disgust with getting involved in European conflagrations.

The blame for World War II should not be laid at the feet of Harding and Coolidge for doing too little to prevent it, but rather at the feet of Wilson for doing too much to cause it. Contrary to the conventional historical narrative, the best way to have prevented World War II (really World War I, Part Two) was for America to have stayed out of World War I, thus avoiding tipping the balance in the war toward victory by the Allies (Britain and France), which ended up trampling over defeated nations (Germany, Austria-Hungary, and Ottoman Turkey) and stealing their empires. Even if the results of World War I were a given, Allied behavior after the war, during the Harding and Coolidge administrations, was much more to blame for the rise of Hitler and World War II than US "isolationism"—which was really a return to the American founders' policy of military restraint abroad. This episode also shows that unnecessary wars merely lead to more wars and revolutions.

More Restraint Was Needed in Latin America

Although Harding and Coolidge both tried to return to the traditional US foreign policy of military restraint, both presidents could have done more to curb the policy of excessive US military intervention in Latin America, which had evolved from the promulgation of the Monroe Doctrine in 1823. Charles Evans Hughes, the secretary of state for Harding and Coolidge, did make some attempt to lessen US meddling in the region. American businessmen and some government officials—such as Herbert Hoover, secretary of commerce for Harding and Coolidge—came to regard US "dollar diplomacy," based on US political and military interference in Latin America, especially the long-term US military occupations of Haiti and Nicaragua, as harmful to American economic interests. Yet under Harding and Coolidge, those occupations continued. Thus the presidencies of Herbert Hoover and his successor FDR had wiser "good neighbor" policies toward Latin America than Harding and Coolidge. However, President Hoover made important exceptions to Harding's commendable blanket ban on US arms sales abroad, which began in 1923. This policy change had the inadvertent effect of stoking revolutionary activity in Latin America.

Shrinking Government and Restoring Prosperity

The stark economic downturn after World War I—the gross domestic product (GDP) plummeted 15 percent from 1920 to 1921[15]—was Harding's first priority, and he approached it, unlike George W. Bush and Barack Obama after the 2008 financial crisis, by cutting government spending. This spending reduction also helped battle the substantial war-induced inflation of the day. He was, therefore, able to lower wartime levels of debt and taxation.

Although Harding threw a bone to Herbert Hoover, his secretary of commerce, and Hoover's fellow progressive Republicans by sponsoring the President's Conference on Unemployment in 1921, he did not help get its stimulative relief and recovery recommendations through Congress.[16] Such proto-Keynesian countercyclical government intervention could very well have interfered with the economy's natural ability to right itself, as it did later when President Hoover messed with market recovery forces during the Great Depression, including by "jawboning" businesses to keep wages artificially high. Thus, the unemployment conference had little adverse effect on the economic recovery that began in 1922.

Instead, Harding allowed flexible market prices and wages to restore prosperity; prices had plummeted during the recession of 1920 to 1921, so wages also had to decline to restore market equilibrium.[17] By 1923, Harding, by merely cutting federal spending from wartime levels and returning scarce resources to the private sector, had turned the economy from recession to prosperity.

As economist John A. Moore concluded, "Harding started a revolution in economic policy upon taking office in 1921."[18] Coolidge continued that revolution after Harding's death. Moore further noted that during the 1921 to 1929 period, such enlightened policies were wildly successful in turning around the nation's bad post–World War I economy into sustained prosperity.

The nation's economic success during this period can be measured in several ways. Production, as measured by real GDP per capita, sharply increased. Real wages rose strongly. The unemployment rate fell, remaining below 5 percent after 1924. Federal government costs were greatly reduced and income taxes were lowered. Yet the national debt, accumulated during the war, shrank because of resulting government budget surpluses.[19] From 1922 to 1927, gross national product (GNP) rose 40 percent.[20]

Harding Spurs the Economy with His Fiscal Policies

To control and reduce federal spending, Harding created the first budget bureau in the executive branch. As requested by Harding, the Budget and Accounting Act of 1921 created a new Bureau of the Budget in the Department of the Treasury, but the Bureau reported directly to the president, not the secretary of the treasury. Previously, executive departments had negotiated their budgets with their respective congressional committees, thus giving the president no central control over the federal budget. Also, in 1921, Harding recruited Charles Dawes to come to Washington for a year to cut the budget. Harding instructed him to slash $1 billion from the federal budget. When Dawes left the government in 1922, he had cut $1.77 billion. (Back then, that was a lot of savings.) From 1920 to 1923, annual federal spending dropped by more than half. Harding reduced discretionary spending to roughly prewar levels;[21] this accomplishment has been a rarity in American history.

Harding was ardent in his desire to pay down the national debt, which had ballooned during World War I to the highest level in memory,[22] but the Senate wanted to pass a popular bonus bill for the war's veterans that would have increased the debt and nixed Harding's plans for a tax cut. In 1921, Harding went to the Senate chamber to confront that body over the bonus bill, in what John W. Dean calls "one of the defining moments of his presidency." Harding noted that thirty-eight states had already passed bonus bills, and extensive compensation, insurance claims, vocational training, and rehabilitation programs were already being given to veterans. Although tremendous pressure still existed for an additional federal bonus, Harding was successful in beating back the bonus bill, thus saving his debt reduction and tax cut. However, the next year, in 1922, Congress passed the bonus bill by wide margins. Going against the conventional wisdom, in September of that year, Harding courageously vetoed it shortly before a bi-election, thus incurring short-term political damage. Yet

Dean correctly concluded that Harding's holding the line on the budget helped create the booming economy of the 1920s.[23] In 1924, Congress again passed the bonus bill and Coolidge vetoed it, but his veto was overridden.[24]

As for taxes, Woodrow Wilson had hiked them substantially during the war (the highest marginal income tax rate was raised from 7 to 77 percent[25]), but in an example of emergency wartime policies continuing into peacetime, Wilson did not lower them after the war, desiring to take advantage of the added revenues to pursue a progressive agenda. Secretary of the Treasury Andrew Mellon and Secretary of Commerce Herbert Hoover had convinced Harding that a tax cut would stimulate the economy out of its postwar recession. Harding proposed cutting the excessive profits tax and corporate tax rates but leaving personal income tax rates the same. Mellon wanted to recoup the lost revenues by increasing the charge for sending postcards and by taxing cars and bank checks. Congress agreed with the administration tax reduction proposals, except for cuts in the corporate tax rate (which they actually raised instead of lowering).[26] By late December 1922, the economy had recovered, demonstrating that cutting the federal budget, and therefore taxes, spurs economic growth by transferring resources from the inefficient public sector to the more efficient private sector.

As for regulation, Harding appointed conservatives to regulatory agencies that the progressives had set up during the war.[27] In the latter years of his administration, Coolidge relaxed enforcement of antitrust laws against business.

Coolidge Continues Harding's Fiscal Policies

Coolidge continued Harding's frugality and reaped the reward of a growing economy until 1929. Like Harding, Coolidge was one of the four presidents that actually limited government during the twentieth century (noting that Bill Clinton and Dwight Eisenhower were the others, while, despite the conventional wisdom, Ronald Reagan was not). Coolidge cut real federal expenditures slightly, after Harding's massive spending cuts, and continued to reduce the national debt, but roughly maintained tax revenues after Harding's dramatic reduction in such receipts.[28] Coolidge cut the surtax on people who made more than $100,000, reduced the estate tax to 20 percent, and terminated the gift tax but increased the corporate tax. As historian Lewis Gould noted, however, Coolidge's tax policy, spending cuts, and reduction of the national debt was not a 1920s version of Reagan's supply-side doctrine of the 1980s.[29]

Coolidge courageously vetoed much popular, but expensive legislation—bonuses for Mexican War, Civil War, and World War I veterans, raises for postal workers, and price supports for farmers twice (in this last regard, Coolidge was better than Harding, who subsidized farmers too much during the postwar farm depression of the 1920s).[30] Congress overrode Coolidge's veto of veterans' bonuses but twice sustained his vetoes on farm price supports.

Overall, the Harding-Coolidge years from 1921 to 1929 were the only time during the twentieth century that the federal government reduced its absolute level of nonmilitary spending.[31] At the end of the Harding-Coolidge period in early 1929, the budget was in surplus and the national debt reduced.[32]

If only George W. Bush and Barack Obama had been as fiscally responsible during the financial meltdown that began at the end of the Bush administration—instead, they followed the Keynesian path of spending more public money on corporate and financial bailouts and pork-filled stimulus programs, adding to the budget deficits and ballooning the national debt. The economy was dragged by this huge debt, and consequently, the recovery from recession was slow. In contrast, Harding and Coolidge realized that the economy would right itself naturally, with the market pruning the dead wood of failed businesses, if the government just got out of the way.

The Resurrection of the Framers' Original Limited Conception of the Executive Role

For most of his time in office, Harding stuck with his campaign pledge to take a "hands off" approach to Congress. The framers of the Constitution had intended that Congress be the dominant branch of the American government and that the president merely execute the laws it passed. Activist progressive presidents, such as Theodore Roosevelt and Woodrow Wilson, had deviated from this intention, with Woodrow Wilson even thinking of himself as an American prime minister who would—and did—push an ambitious legislative program through Congress. In fact, Harding had campaigned on restoring representative government, which was juxtaposed against Wilson's autocratic style. Both Harding and Coolidge did have the advantage that both houses of Congress were solidly Republican during their tenures, but that did not prevent the legislative body from trying to dole out subsidies to Republican constituency groups, such as farmers and veterans.[33]

Because the twentieth century—with a Great Depression, two world wars, and a Cold War—was so rife with presidents taking advantage of such crises to aggrandize power far beyond what the Constitution's framers had envisioned, Harding's attempt to restore a more limited, constitutional role for the executive was refreshing. H.L. Mencken, a writer who surprisingly had more disdain for Harding than other presidents, once said of him, "No salient piece of legislation bears his name. He led no great national movement. He solved no great public problem."[34] Maybe so, but judged by the framers' conception of a restrained executive, Harding would get fairly good marks.

As would Coolidge, who voluntarily imposed a term limit on himself by leaving the presidency after only one full elected term, even though he could have probably been reelected because the country enjoyed peace and prosperity and the opposition Democratic Party was divided. Few chief executives in American history have adhered to such a self-imposed limit on their power. However, although Coolidge, along with Harding, believed that the Constitution limited the role of the federal government in regulating the economy, Coolidge also curiously believed that restricted federal powers included building the moral character of citizens.[35] In the latter case, at the time the Constitution was framed, state sumptuary laws existed, but nowhere in the Constitution was this listed as the purview of the federal government. In this case, Coolidge's view shows that not only progressives can read excessive federal powers into the Constitution.

Less objectionable, but a portent of future executive behavior, was Coolidge's mastery of image-enhancing techniques that came to be associated with Franklin D. Roosevelt. Coolidge was excellent on the radio, held frequent press conferences, and relied on the First Lady to increase popular support for his administration.[36]

Four Supreme Court Picks

Although he served less than two and a half years as president, Harding made four Supreme Court selections. Most of his picks were highly regarded and created a majority for narrowly delineating the power of government. One was former President William Howard Taft as chief justice, who was a better head of the court than he had been chief executive of the government. Taft had always wanted that job more than he had wanted the presidency. Another of Harding's Supreme Court appointees, Edward T. Sanford, wrote the landmark opinion in *Gitlow v. New York,* which allowed the federal government to use the due process clause of the Constitution's Fourteenth Amendment to keep states from infringing on the rights of freedom of speech and freedom of the press.[37]

In contrast to Harding, who appointed judges primarily based on their judicial philosophy, Coolidge was more pragmatic. Guiding his appointments were the Justice Department's assessment of potential nominees' experience and abilities, the degree of unanimity among political and bar leaders in the judicial district or circuit about such qualifications, and nominees' representation from states in the circuit. However, in these sorts of nominations, Coolidge tried to avoid senatorial courtesy.[38]

Healing the Nation's Wounds in a Postwar World

Harding wanted to heal the wounds of war and return the nation to a state of "normalcy." As soon as Germany ratified its separate peace with the United States in 1921, technically ending a state of war between the two countries, Harding commuted the prison sentence of Socialist Party Leader Eugene Debs, who had been jailed for opposing US involvement in World War I and urging young men not to comply with conscription. Harding then hosted Debs for an Oval Office meeting. Harding wanted to give clemency to others who had been jailed during the war and reviewed their cases individually. Harding also freed labor leaders and socialists jailed in Wilson's war-induced 1919 Red Scare.

Coolidge continued Harding's policy of post–World War I reconciliation. Coolidge, against the advice of his attorney general, issued more than 30 pardons for people who had criticized US involvement in World War I before the pardons were even requested.

World War I was not the only war that had created wounds in America that needed healing. In 1924, Coolidge presided over the granting of citizenship to all Native Americans, whose populations had been decimated and their lands stolen during America's westward migration in the 1800s. Citizenship did not end their plight, but such recognition was long overdue.

Woodrow Wilson, a virulent racist with southern upbringing, re-segregated the federal workforce during his administration by ousting African-Americans, replacing them with whites, and then extending civil service protection so that the new officeholders could not be removed. Although Harding reversed Wilson's segregationist policies in the federal government, it was difficult for him to return African-American employment in the federal government to pre-Wilson levels. However, Harding did make active efforts to find more positions for blacks, including high-level positions. One of the first things Harding did after coming to office was to urge the passage of an anti-lynching law, which was filibustered in the Senate by southern Democrats although it did pass the House of Representatives. After his backing of the failed anti-lynching bill, Harding's enemies advanced the rumor that he had secretly become a member of the Ku Klux Klan.[39] Ironically, such rumors existed alongside the longstanding rumors that Harding had black ancestry. DNA tests have recently disproven the latter claim.

Finally, in a courageous and risky move at the time, Harding went to Birmingham, Alabama, and preached equal opportunity for African-Americans in politics, economic endeavors, and education.[40] He reiterated this message in two other speeches. Although Harding's efforts may seem meager by post–Civil Rights era standards, they were greater than those of presidents who came before and soon after him. Not since Ulysses S. Grant had a president called for national action to improve race relations. In contrast to Theodore Roosevelt, who made his Progressive (Bull Moose) Party lily white so as not to put off southern white voters, Harding actively sought African-American votes for the Republicans.[41] However, Harding could have done more to use the bully pulpit against the rising power of the Ku Klux Klan.

Terms Better than Most

Harding is often regarded by many historians as one of the worst presidents in American history, if not the worst, because of scandals involving his administration. Curiously, Harding died in early August 1923, about two and a half years into his term, as a very popular president who was perceived as having been a successful chief executive. He was seen as having successfully returned the nation to "normalcy" after the cataclysmic world war and as having kept the nation at peace thereafter. He only became perceived as a poor president posthumously, because the scandals did not become widely public until after he died.

Scandals

Despite the more serious scandals involving some of his appointees sticking money in their pockets, Harding's reputation as president was truly ruined by posthumously revealed personal scandals involving alleged affairs with women. One woman's story about fathering a child with Harding was disputed until DNA evidence recently showed her claim to be likely true. Today's views of Harding focus on his personal scandals rather than his presidency.[42] But these personal scandals had nothing to do with Harding's performance as president and should not even be considered when evaluating it.

In addition, progressive writers and journalists who had supported Woodrow Wilson, Harding's predecessor, attacked Harding's legacy during the decade after his death.[43] Fictional accounts portraying Harding as a president too weak to rein in his out-of-control crooked appointees—such as F. Scott Fitzgerald's play *The Vegetable* in 1923, the year of Harding's death—were taken by the public as fact and have forever tainted Harding's reputation. Harding's family and friends abetted such fiction-to-fact "history" by hiding documents about his presidency. Harding's bad reputation became carved in stone before these papers became available. It was finally realized that First Lady Florence Harding had not destroyed all of Harding's papers after his death, and that the Harding Memorial Association withheld them from the public for a considerable period of time.[44] A more balanced view of the Harding administration arose after scholars got access to Harding's presidential papers in 1964. However, by then the unfavorable public perception of Harding's administration had become too entrenched to change.[45]

Harding, like Ulysses S. Grant, had no personal role in the scandals involving the petty graft of subordinates (unlike Richard Nixon's and Ronald Reagan's personal culpability in the more serious constitutional Watergate and Iran-Contra scandals, respectively). However, Harding selected, as Grant also did, men for official positions who ultimately betrayed his trust. Curiously, Calvin Coolidge, Harding's successor, seems to have escaped any blame for these scandals, even though he left some of the main players in them—Attorney General Harry Daugherty and Secretary of the Navy Edwin Denby—in the cabinet even after Harding died.[46]

Of course, Harding also selected some very good people—for example, Charles Evans Hughes for secretary of state, Andrew Mellon for secretary of the treasury, Henry C. Wallace for secretary of agriculture, and Herbert Hoover for secretary of commerce (Hoover performed better in this job than he did later as president).

As for the bad apples, Charles Forbes, the head of Harding's new Veterans Bureau, which was created out of several agencies and rapidly expanded to deal with the large number of veterans returning from World War I,[47] took kickbacks for land purchases, building contracts for new hospitals, and the sale of government hospital supplies at artificially low prices. While Harding was investigating Forbes for the sales of supplies, the president told him to stop the sales, which Forbes did not. Harding demanded Forbes resign for insubordination and then let him slip off to Europe to quit. Yet, at this time, Harding knew for certain only of Forbes's insubordination, not his corruption. Not until after Harding died did the extent of Forbes's graft come out. Forbes was later convicted of plundering as much as $2 million from the bureau. In the meantime, Harding's new appointee to be director of the bureau very effectively righted the sinking ship.[48]

In the most famous scandal of the Harding presidency, Secretary of the Interior Albert Fall was eventually convicted of taking bribes to lease federal oil fields in Teapot Dome, Wyoming, and Elk Hills, California, to oilmen who were his friends or employers, even though the oilmen were acquitted of bribing him. (One of the oilmen was convicted of contempt of court and contempt of the Senate and was imprisoned.) Fall was the first cabinet member in American history to be sentenced to prison for illegal conduct in office.[49] Secretary of the Navy Denby, who had previously approved transfer of the oilfields from the Navy Department to Fall's Interior Department, also had to resign because of the scandal. Although Harding wrote a letter vouching for the transfer, Harding did not know of Fall's illegal activities.

Similarly, Harding's Justice Department was said to be rife with corruption—concerning presidential pardons, violations of Prohibition, and property seized by the government during the war.[50] Harding's Attorney General Harry Daugherty was accused of taking bribes not to prosecute accused criminals and was indicted for receiving money in the illegal seizing of a German-owned US subsidiary by an American syndicate under provisions remaining from World War I—but Daugherty was never convicted of any crime.[51]

Harding, as with the Forbes case in the Veterans Bureau, may have eventually discovered the corruption in the Justice Department. Shortly before Harding went on his trip to Alaska, from which he never returned, he had confronted Jess Smith, Daugherty's top political operative, about his actions at the department. Smith promptly burned his papers and committed suicide. According to Herbert Hoover in his post-presidential memoir, on the Alaska trip, an unnerved Harding asked then Secretary of Commerce Hoover what he would do if he uncovered a "great scandal" in the administration—publicize it for the good of the country and party, or bury it.[52] Because of Harding's death soon thereafter, the answer about what he would have done will never be known, but judging by Harding's framing of the question, perhaps he would have exposed the corruption himself. Also, before this last trip to the West, Harding famously told journalist William Allen White, "My God, this is a hell of a job! I have no trouble with my enemies. I can take of my enemies all right. But my damn friends, my God-damned friends, White, they're the ones that keep me walking the floor nights."[53]

In sum, Harding had some inkling of the Veterans Administration and Justice Department scandals before he died, but not the most important scandal—Teapot Dome. Harding had no personal involvement in any of these scandals. Historians have concluded that Harding did his best and was personally honest.[54]

Implications of the Scandals

Certainly, any administration with some government officials making money at taxpayers' expense should come under criticism, but many historians do not dish out such criticism uniformly—for example, significant corruption in the historian-favored Truman administration is usually swept under the rug. More important, petty corruption scandals in the Grant and Harding administrations tore the fabric of the American republic far less than the shredding of the Constitution in Nixon's Watergate and Reagan's Iran-Contra scandals (see their respective chapters in this volume for a delineation of why their constitutional scandals were so bad).

As Harding administration scandals surfaced after the president's death, Calvin Coolidge, his successor, restored confidence in government and the presidency by cooperating with congressional investigation of the corruption, by partially cleaning house, and by prosecuting corrupt officials.[55] Coolidge signed a joint congressional resolution requiring the appointment of two special counsels to investigate the Teapot Dome scandal, because Attorney General Harry Daugherty had been implicated. Unlike Presidents Grant and Nixon, Coolidge actually let the counsels do their work instead of firing them. But Coolidge eventually did fire Daugherty for failing to obey his order to comply with a congressional investigation.[56]

Because the Justice Department's Bureau of Investigation (later to become the Federal Bureau of Investigation or FBI) had also been implicated in corruption during the Harding administration, J. Edgar Hoover was put in charge of the bureau during the Coolidge administration in 1924. Hoover would serve 48 years until 1972 during the Nixon administration. He hated Communists and took the bureau's surveillance, legal and illegal, much farther than ever before. Hoover repeatedly violated the Constitution to spy on Americans, including other public officials, and even carried out unlawful dirty tricks against domestic groups he saw as a threat. By gathering dirt on other politicians, he developed a potent independent power base and was feared by other government officials.

Suspect Policies

On policy, Harding did not advocate for a completely laissez-faire free market approach,[57] but he was pro-business, as was his successor Coolidge. Coolidge reversed few of Harding's policies.[58] However, they were both in favor of limiting government and compare well to the economically interventionist mentality of most other US presidents. But Harding and Coolidge both made some policy mistakes.

Immigration

Harding called for a new immigration law and got a draconian one passed, the Emergency Quota Act, which reduced the sizeable and valuable influx of new ambition, talent, and ideas that came with immigration to only a trickle. Immigration traditionally had been appreciated in America as making society and the economy stronger. The new law established the first general restrictions on immigration in American history (although immigrants from specific countries earlier had been targeted). After the great conflagration of World War I, which was fought against other countries, foreigners who came to US shores raised suspicions among a newly nationalistic public, which also believed they were taking American jobs during the post-conflict economic trough. Enacted in 1921, the new law slashed annual immigration quotas to only 3 percent of the population of any nationality in the United States as of the year 1910. Harding agreed with the law but believed it had to be enforced humanely and made generous exceptions, thus disappointing avid proponents of strong enforcement.[59]

In 1924, during the Coolidge administration, Congress went beyond even the draconian Emergency Quota Act to enact the Johnson-Reed Act, which dramatically reduced immigration quotas on Southern and Eastern Europeans and banned Asian immigrants.[60] The obviously discriminatory law showed the long-term effects of World War I on America's traditional openness as a society.

Economic Policy

The signature issue for the Republican Party in the last half of the nineteenth century and in the early twentieth century was tariffs. Tariffs on imports impair free trade, while free trade makes most people, both producers and consumers, more prosperous by making US firms stronger and more efficient, forcing them to compete on the world stage, and by reducing prices for consumers. Although tariffs tend to be a regressive tax on the less well-off, because they need to spend more of their income consuming than wealthier people, certain narrow societal factions do benefit from these taxes.

Important Republican constituencies—agriculture and manufacturing—wanted high tariffs. After the war, the US farm economy, which had made a significant amount of money exporting crops to feed Europe during the conflict, was now forced to compete with a resurgent European agriculture, thus pitching it into depression. US manufacturing also now had to compete worldwide. To satisfy these constituencies, Harding unfortunately raised the tariff. However, the Fordney-McCumber Tariff, passed in mid-1921, applied to only 8 percent or less of US imports, cut imports as a percentage of GDP only from 5.5 percent to 4.8 percent, and so did not impair the rebound of the American economy.[61] US interest rates were reduced to help a war-devastated Europe attract more investment, but the higher US tariffs on European exports to satisfy American interest groups mitigated the charitable effect.

Although the money supply was kept largely in check during the Harding administration, Coolidge may bear some culpability for causing the economic bubble that burst in 1929 and later became the Great Depression. Many blame Coolidge for not dampening speculation in stocks,[62] which ultimately led to the market crash in 1929, but the real cause was the loosening of the money supply by the relatively new Federal Reserve banks (thus reducing interest rates); the extra money fueled the stock bubble. Even Herbert Hoover, Coolidge's progressive secretary of commerce, warned the administration as early as 1924 that the easy money policies of the Fed were fueling easy credit and excessive speculation in stocks. Hoover unsuccessfully implored Coolidge and Secretary of the Treasury Andrew Mellon to intervene with the Fed to dampen the credit binge.[63]

Harding and Coolidge, however, get too much blame for causing the Great Depression. Harding deserves little blame at all, because the money supply did not increase that much while he was president. The more substantial money supply increases under Coolidge probably did help cause the stock bubble that led to the 1929 market crash, but Coolidge's successors as president—Herbert Hoover and Franklin D. Roosevelt—most likely converted what would have been an ordinary recession into the Great Depression. They arrived at this unfortunate end by artificially propping up the economy using government intervention, rather than letting natural market forces right the economic ship.

Also, Harding resisted pressure from the farm bloc, traditionally a Republican supplicant, to do something about the postwar depression in agriculture. However, he did provide some help to farmers—for example, farm cooperatives were exempted from antitrust law by passage of the Capper-Volstead Act; farm land banks got more capital and were permitted to lower interest rates; the passage of the Grain Futures Trading Act and the Packers and Stockyard Act restricted competition by regulating speculation in the former industry and mandating "fair practices" in the latter; and the War Finance Corporation, which had subsidized industries deemed crucial to the war, lived on after the war and was used to help agriculture. All of these measures are an example of an industry benefiting from government intervention during a war and successfully extending it into peacetime. They all violate the Constitution's provision that government money should provide for the "general welfare"—in other words, not be used to help only specific groups in society.

However, Presidents Calvin Coolidge and Herbert Hoover were less friendly to such farm assistance than Harding.[64] Congress twice passed export subsidies for farmers in the McNary-Haugen bill, which would have created a federal export corporation to buy up surplus agricultural commodities from farmers and sell them overseas. This would have artificially raised domestic farm prices, increased future overproduction, and fostered demands from other industries for similar handouts. Coolidge vetoed the bill twice.[65] Thus, Coolidge foiled a resumption of unconstitutional agricultural price fixing to control agricultural production, which the Wilson administration and Congress had undertaken during World War I.[66]

However, Coolidge, with the Cooperative Marketing Act of 1926, and Hoover, with the Federal Farm Board, developed a system of government-sponsored "voluntary" agricultural marketing cooperatives, which also provided government standardization of agricultural product quality through certification. Even so, restraining largesse from the government toward agriculture was one of the few areas in which Coolidge and Hoover did better than Harding.

Without getting rid of federal regulations on business (a la Jimmy Carter), Coolidge weakened enforcement of them by starving industrial regulatory agencies of funds and by appointing top officials who would weaken those federal agencies or allow businesses to self-regulate[67] (an approach similar to that later taken by Ronald Reagan). The problem with loosening enforcement, without getting rid of regulations, is that the next president could simply tighten enforcement again. Yet, despite Coolidge's aversion to federal power in the economic and social realms, Coolidge subsidized and then, as part of the bargain, regulated the relatively new industries of broadcasting and commercial aviation.

During the Harding administration, Secretary of Commerce Hoover set up guidelines for the new broadcasting industry that favored large companies operating radio stations over smaller ones by giving the larger companies choice broadcasting frequencies, thus leading to monopolistic trends.[68] However, the industry had lobbied for subsidization but got none until Coolidge took office. Coolidge believed that broadcasting was in a state of anarchy, with radio stations using overlapping frequencies. In the first ever regulation of radio broadcasting, Coolidge signed the Radio Act, which made the broadcast spectrum public property, thus subjecting it to the power of Congress to oversee. A Federal Radio Commission was set up in the Commerce Department in 1927 to grant licenses to broadcast and assign frequencies. Like most licensing arrangements, this one helped a few large businesses keep out potential competition.[69]

In aviation, Coolidge wanted to create an air force. Therefore, he convinced Congress to fund experiments in designing and building aircraft, to allow the Commerce Department to regulate civil aviation, to establish the first two commercial air routes, and to study subsidizing airmail.[70]

Unfortunately, Coolidge also accepted and even promoted legislation for "internal improvements" (federal infrastructure projects that violated the "general welfare" clause of the Constitution by benefiting specific groups), although he did veto federal money for the Muscle Shoals power plant to provide electric power to rural Tennessee and Alabama.[71]

Social Issues

Under Harding, farmers were not the only group to get welfare. The Sheppard-Towner Maternity and Infancy Act, signed by Harding, gave funding to states to subsidize medical care for expecting women and new mothers and for prenatal and child healthcare clinics. These efforts may have been laudable but should have been done entirely by the states; the Constitution does not allow a federal role in such areas.

Teddy Roosevelt had set bad precedents for getting the government heavily involved in labor management disputes. Although Harding tried to exhibit restraint in this area by remaining neutral and working behind the scenes to—ultimately unsuccessfully—mediate strikes in the coal and railroad shop industries, occasionally, he would take stronger action, sometimes to the benefit of labor and sometimes to the advantage of management. Most famous, however, was the nationwide injunction sought by his administration that resulted in a violent conclusion of the many strikes of 1922. Harding probably should have avoided all of these actions; the Constitution does not mandate a role for the federal government in solving labor management issues. In contrast, just after Coolidge replaced Harding, an anthracite coal strike broke out in Pennsylvania, and the new president was able to avoid federal intervention, instead letting the governor of Pennsylvania settle the matter.[72]

In 1923, Harding's activist, progressive Secretary of Commerce Herbert Hoover, arbitrarily picked the steel industry and converted it from a standard twelve-hour day to an eight-hour day, without even garnering any federal legislation. Hoover did so by using the power of the government publicity apparatus, coercing the steel companies by regularly berating them publicly.[73] Although the Constitution enumerates a federal role in regulating interstate commerce in general, it does not provide for the government singling out and regulating a specific industry involved in both intrastate and interstate commerce; thus Hoover violated at least the spirit of the document. Also, the progressive Hoover seemed ignorant that market forces would likely compensate for his artificial intervention in the industry. The steel companies partly nullified the financial losses of the shorter workday by hiring more Hispanic and African-American workers at below average wages rather than by bringing on more expensive white workers. Thus, employment among Hispanics and African-Americans increased but this laudable, inadvertent outcome was realized in a very inefficient and discriminatory way.

During a time of economic downturn, Harding encouraged state and local governments to undertake make-work public works projects. Even after the economy recovered, he advocated federal-state partnerships to undertake irrigation, conservation, and reclamation projects. Coolidge also sprang for some public works projects.

Unlike Democrat Grover Cleveland in the late 1800s, who had vetoed federal relief for victims of a Texas drought because he correctly felt the federal government had no constitutional authority to provide such assistance, Coolidge, who also thought disaster aid was the constitutional purview of state and local governments, nevertheless provided the largest amount of federal disaster relief ever for the victims of the Mississippi River flood of 1927—until George W. Bush outdid him in the next century for Hurricane Katrina.[74] Coolidge's legislation expanded the power of the commerce clause of the Constitution considerably more than the document's framers had intended.[75] To help flood victims and repair dikes, Coolidge provided federal credit and relief assistance and also encouraged the provision of private credit and the raising of private relief funds.

Herbert Hoover, Coolidge's progressive secretary of commerce, attempted to take advantage of the crisis to expand the role of the federal government (a time-tested Washington trick). In this case, Hoover attempted to divide up flooded plantations and sell the small land plots to tenants and sharecroppers and to insert the federal government into nationwide flood control (not an enumerated power mentioned for it in the Constitution). Hoover failed in his first goal and was only partially successful in the latter objective, because President Coolidge and the Congress were too frugal. However, Hoover was able to establish a federal responsibility for flood control on the Mississippi and Colorado rivers (in the latter case, by building the Boulder Dam). Hoover also got the Coolidge administration to increase spending on other public works projects. Coolidge's public works program included a massive building program in Washington for an expanding federal bureaucracy.[76] Also, with the Oil Production Act of 1924, Coolidge battled oil pollution from offshore dumping along the American coastline.[77]

Coolidge believed the US Constitution restricted federal power in the economic and social spheres, which were the purview of the states and private individuals, but curiously and questionably believed that the federal government should have a role in developing the general moral character of Americans. Coolidge wanted Congress to establish a federal department to promote individual character development and education. Coolidge also proposed constitutional amendments to establish a minimum wage for women and restrict child labor.[78] He seemed to characterize the latter two amendments as developing general moral character—even though these proposed federal measures benefited very specific groups, thus violating the nation's founders' clear intent in the Constitution that the federal government should promote only the general welfare and therefore leave such matters to the states. Fortunately, Congress realized that the Constitution had said nothing of a federal role in building moral character and demurred on all such proposals.

Foreign Policy

Harding's foreign policy was generally good, but his revulsion for war in the wake of World War I did lead him to try to guide the nation into the World Court, the judicial arm of the League of Nations, even though he had rejected joining the League. Although Harding's attempt to diminish the chances of war by using an international judiciary to solve transnational problems was laudable, the court would have undermined US sovereignty, and the standards of justice in such international bodies rarely attain the same high level of those in the United States. Thus, Coolidge made the right decision by refusing to negotiate with other nations over conditions the US Senate had stipulated for American entry into the court, thus killing US participation.

However, Coolidge also had his spate of idealism. He got the Kellogg-Briand Pact—which outlawed war as a way to settle international disputes and which he and his secretary of state had spearheaded—ratified by the Senate and forty-seven other nations. Although the treaty had no sanctions for violations and was thus unenforceable, it did indicate the world's revulsion at the carnage of World War I and Coolidge's own desire to run a more restrained foreign policy. The treaty did not cause the rise of Adolf Hitler, and like US entry into World War I, US financial aid to the British—rather than peaceful neutrality—resulted in American involvement in World War II.[79]

However, although pilloried nowadays as naïve, the Kellogg-Briand Treaty had a major beneficial side effect. After World War II, the Nazis were prosecuted at Nuremburg not for war crimes, crimes against humanity, or genocide, but for violations of the peace as stipulated by the Kellogg-Briand Pact.[80]

Although by recent standards both Harding and Coolidge used the US military only sparingly, Coolidge was slightly more interventionist than Harding. Coolidge intervened in Panama in late 1925 when strikes and riots motivated him to land six hundred American soldiers to keep order and protect American interests. And although US forces were in and out of Nicaragua from 1926 until 1933, the United States occupied the country to protect American interests in the wake of a military coup, which had triggered revolutionary activity. Both of Coolidge's interventions were designed to ensure that no one would build canals in those two countries except the United States. The United States also remained involved in Mexico's chaotic situation, which threatened American oil interests with expropriation.[81]

Unfortunately, the Washington Treaty continued the Open Door policy of long-term exploitative trade at gunpoint with China by the United States and Western powers. And the Harding and Coolidge administrations contributed to Western enforcement of that policy. However, although the US ambassador in China advocated ousting the Chinese government and replacing it with a pro-Western international agency, fortunately Harding refused to send a large US force to do it. In contrast, in 1927, Coolidge helped the British respond to a Chinese Nationalist (Guomindang) push to take Shanghai and other Chinese cities. When riots broke out after the Nationalists occupied the city, the British and American navies shelled the city of Nanjing, inflicting heavy casualties on the inhabitants. Today such indiscriminate action might probably be classified as a war crime. The United States put the brakes on military action when Chiang Kai-shek purged the Communists from the Nationalist Party. A year later, in 1928, after the Nationalists had taken Beijing, the United States recognized Chiang's government in Nanjing, allowing the Chinese the power to establish their own tariffs—a longstanding goal of Chinese nationalism.[82]

After the Wilson administration had sent an invasion force to help the anti-Bolshevik cause in the post–Russian Revolution civil war, the Harding administration used surplus American agricultural production to provide assistance to feed the starving Soviet Union from 1921 to 1923—the effort led by Herbert Hoover, the master food aid facilitator. Although reducing the US surplus may have helped American farmers and some of the White Russian rebels, the Bolshevik regime merely exploited this aid for its own survival during these crucial civil war years.[83] While getting food aid from abroad, the Bolsheviks exported grain to earn money to revive Soviet industry—at the expense of their starving people.

Conclusion

Despite some bad policies, it is what Harding and Coolidge did not do that made them good presidents. They were for limiting government, mostly promoted free markets, restrained their actions as chief executives, and reined in much of the foreign interventionism of the Wilson era. Had the Constitution's framers been able to evaluate Harding and Coolidge, they likely would have lauded them for maintaining peace, prosperity, and liberty and for trying to stay within the limited role for the executive enshrined in the Constitution.

If conservatives want a model for the ideal presidency, that model should be these two traditional conservatives or proto-libertarians, not the big government conservative, Ronald Reagan, who waged war (overtly and covertly) and almost caused a nuclear war with overheated rhetoric, ballooned budget deficits by cutting taxes while increasing government spending as a portion of GDP, and dangerously expanded executive power by unconstitutionally funding a secret war against a congressional prohibition.

Harding, Coolidge, and Reagan cut taxes, but only Harding and Coolidge also cut federal spending. In contrast, Reagan increased federal spending absolutely and as a portion of GDP by increasing both domestic and defense spending. In fact, as a tradeoff to get his unneeded peacetime defense spending increases, Reagan had to accept even greater hikes in domestic spending. The one thing that Harding and Reagan had in common was a propensity to delegate too much authority to subordinates, which backfired on both of them when subordinates misbehaved. Yet Reagan likely had more knowledge of the activities of underlings in the constitutionally serious Iran-Contra scandal than Harding had about the petty corruption among officials in his administration.

Many conservatives have long forsaken Harding and Coolidge. Today, Coolidge is making somewhat of a comeback among this crowd—for example, Amity Shlaes has written an admiring biography and Reagan, as president, had a photo of Coolidge in the Oval Office—but perhaps conservatives also should take another look at Harding, despite the scandals of his administration. Reagan was certainly no match for either Harding or Coolidge in creating a favorable presidential model for those appreciating limited government in all aspects.

3

Domestic Troubles
But No Foreign Entanglements

TODAY, HERBERT HOOVER (president from 1929 to 1933)
is regarded by most of the public as a conservative who fiddled while Rome
burned, doing too little to remedy the Great Depression. At the time he took
office, however, the country had low income taxes centered on the wealthy,
almost no social programs, and a modest defense structure, which made up
most of the then small federal government. Also, seemingly strange now,
most citizens did not expect the federal government to ensure prosperity and
employment, as it had not throughout American history up to that point. The
Great Depression and the Hoover administration changed this expectation.

In fact, at the time, Hoover was regarded, unlike his predecessors Warren
Harding and Calvin Coolidge, as a moderately progressive Republican and
so regarded himself: "I emerge . . . an unashamed individualist. But let me
say also that I am an American individualist. For America has been steadily
developing the ideals that constitute progressive individualism." He also said
that he was for "regulated individualism." Six months after leaving office,
Hoover wrote, "I see a consistent effort on the part of our opponents to entirely misrepresent my position as being the advocate of nineteenth-century
laissez-faire and other long-forgotten social theses."[1] Essentially, like other
progressives of the day, Hoover believed in partially regulated capitalism.

One reason that Hoover is regarded as a reactionary today is because after
three years of grinding depression, in the 1932 election campaign Franklin D.
Roosevelt (FDR) painted Hoover as a president who opposed providing direct
federal relief to citizens—relief for which the country was then clamoring.
Although Hoover had initiated a revolutionary big government program to
right the economy, people were so desperate they wanted even more.

As a former mining engineer, Hoover adopted the progressive belief that scientific planning by experts could successfully modify market forces. Also like most progressives, Hoover did not believe in the nationalization of production or distribution of goods or services—the textbook definition of socialism—but did believe in government cooperation with business (associational corporatism), provision of information and guidance to business, arbitration among private economic interests, and regulation of markets to prevent domination or unfair industrial practices, just as Theodore Roosevelt and Woodrow Wilson had.[2] As the depression worsened and the presidential election neared, Hoover went further, as Wilson had in the economy during World War I, and brought back Wilson's war model, thus supplanting his associationalism. Therefore, contrary to conventional wisdom today, Hoover likely turned a mundane business cycle recession into the Great Depression by undertaking too much, not too little, intervention by the federal government.

Presidential Activism Made the Economic Downturn Worse

Hoover believed that private economic interests could operate independently without government help, except in times of emergency. But of course, the stock market crash and ensuing deep economic downturn brought pressure on Hoover to recognize that such a dire situation had arrived.

Economic Policy Which Was Revolutionary and Unfortunate

By the end of 1931, the gross national product (GNP) had declined by 30 percent.[3] Over his four years as president, Hoover presided over an average annual decline in real gross domesetic product (GDP) per capita of about 10 percent, worse than any president who followed.

The United States had never seen an economic collapse like this one. It would shock Americans today, but prior to the Hoover presidency, American citizens expected their government to provide for their physical security, but not for their economic well-being. And the reason for this was that up until that time, the country had generally prospered with very little government interference in the economy, with the few hard patches overcome by letting market forces restore economic equilibrium.

However, instead of letting the market automatically right itself, which it had so many times before—for example, as Harding did in the post–World War I recession of the early 1920s—Hoover tried many new and innovative government stimuli to spur the economy but ended up making the economic situation worse. He rejected the view of some in his government and party that the economy would naturally recover from the downturn, and he feared the political consequences of being seen as too passive.

According to Hoover biographers Edgar Eugene Robinson and Vaughn Davis Bornet:

> In the crisis, his program as president was nevertheless a radical departure from the policy—or lack of policy—of his presidential predecessors faced with similar crises. It was not the old Republican conservatism that he brought to bear upon the situation, relying on big business to carry the nation through the emergency. Big business—perhaps, more accurately, big finance—had failed the nation. Yet under Hoover, it was not big government that came directly to the rescue, but government at every level as an indirect agent of economic arbitration and economic stimulation.
>
> [President Hoover's proposals and activities] produced sharp criticism from those who still felt that it was not a proper function of the president to attempt to determine the economic climate in which private business should be carried on. Many Americans had been shocked into a realization of the precariousness of the American financial and industrial system, but they still thought in political terms and of a simple economic order rooted in "capitalism." To them, an inactive president was desirable except as he exerted himself in "politics." Some felt that Hoover, in his usual approach to economic problems, was exceeding his powers as president, for, as [journalist] William Allen White judged, he was proposing "economic and financial legislation which in normal times would be regarded as revolutionary."[4]

Similarly, historians Charles A. and Mary Beard concluded:

> Though [Hoover's] program, as a matter of course, came within the framework of his experience and social philosophy, it was none the less

radical in its implications, for it marked a departure from the renun-
ciation [of government intervention] of his predecessors. It accepted a
responsibility on the part of the Federal Government for breaking the
clutches of the crisis and for seeking ways and means of overcoming
the violent fluctuations of such cyclical disturbances.[5]

Despite his modern-day image of having done too little to cure the depression, Hoover took much more government action to counter an economic
downturn than any prior president in American history had undertaken.
Only when compared to the subsequent massive New Deal of FDR did
Hoover's efforts look weak; FDR's continuation and augmentation of Hoover's
precedent-setting government efforts did not help and once again prevented
market forces from restoring the economy's natural equilibrium.

Hoover's informal or associational corporatism, in which the government
encouraged large businesses to cooperate through the formation of oligopo-
listic trade associations, only looks meager in retrospect when compared to
FDR's subsequent statist corporatism, in which industry cartels were formally
sanctioned by the state. Hoover believed that markets unfettered by at least
temporary government intervention had "destructive competition," too much
unemployment, some people who made too much money, and economic instability, including price instability. For example, Hoover encouraged the Cotton
Textile Institute's associational attempts to end destructive competition. Yet
Hoover refused an entreaty from the US Chamber of Commerce to suspend
antitrust laws for two or more years. Unlike FDR later, Hoover wanted to
limit the cooperation between companies in industrial trade associations and
encouraged the Justice Department's Antitrust Division to prosecute associations that went over the line into being semi-cartels. This task had to be a
judgment call and thus had to result in some arbitrary prosecutorial outcomes,
much as Teddy Roosevelt's earlier trust-busting crusade had given the nation.
This "cooperation-but-don't-go-too-far" policy created much uncertainty in
business, thus exacerbating the economic crisis.

With associationalism, Hoover essentially was on the road to bringing back wartime practices during peacetime. Under associationalism, the
government would encourage businesses in the same industry to share information on price, production, and standardization practices, and the government would bring informal and indirect pressure on business to solve the

problems of business cycles, unemployment, sick industries, foreign trade, insufficient housing, industrial waste, and agricultural overproduction.

As the Great Depression deepened after the stock market crash in 1929, accepting no solution that would lead to a decline in America's standard of living, Hoover successfully pressured business and labor leaders to voluntarily pledge to maintain current production, employment, price, and wage levels and to avoid strikes. Thus, wages and farm prices in the United States were held 30 to 40 percent higher than in the rest of the world.[6] He also encouraged state and local governments to speed up their public works construction to maintain employment levels, provided more federal funding for public works, and created the Unemployment Relief Organization. All of these policies interfered with natural forces in the market that would have automatically restored prosperity and economic growth.

Simply speaking, a recession or depression occurs when the supply of goods and services exceeds the demand for them. To restore market equilibrium between supply and demand, levels of production, employment, prices, and wages must all decline in the short-term. Hoover (and later FDR) prevented this economic rebalancing and thus extended the severe economic slowdown. In fact, because wages and farm prices were held higher in the United States than those in the rest of the world, this prevention of the restoration of market equilibrium may explain why the American depression lasted longer than the economic downturns of other countries.

According to Joan Hoff Wilson, author of *Herbert Hoover: The Forgotten Progressive*, Hoover even rivaled FDR in artificially stimulating the economy:

> [Hoover in June 1930] proclaimed that his administration had already done more than any other in American history to combat deflation. Expansion of public works, he said, marked a "new experiment in our economic life" and an "advance in economic thought and in service to our people." Modern statistics partially confirm these statements. Through Hoover's numerous conferences and exhortations about voluntarism to state and local governments and to business and labor leaders, plus increased federal expenditure for public works, and the authorizing by Congress (over the president's veto) of payment up to 50 percent on veterans certificates, the net stimulation of federal fiscal policy was larger in 1931 than in the next ten years, except 1934,

1935, and 1936. Moreover, the total fiscal stimulation at all levels of government—federal, state, and local—was larger in that year than in any other of the decade. From 1929 through 1930 beyond any doubt Hoover was the most active national leader dealing with the depression.[7]

Wilson concluded that, "for partisan reasons, Hoover's innovative actions to relieve the Great Depression have long been ignored, while those of the Roosevelt administration have been exaggerated."[8] Thus, astoundingly, more than any other president, including FDR, Hoover was to blame—through excessive economic stimulation, not inaction—for turning a run-of-the-mill downturn in the business cycle into the worst economic cataclysm in American history. In late 1931, two years after the stock market crash and just after the European financial collapse and Britain's exit from the gold standard, the severe economic downturn turned into the Great Depression.[9]

Associationalism and Beyond

As secretary of commerce, Herbert Hoover's associationalism already had failed in the three sickest industries of the 1920s—textiles, agriculture, and soft coal—and miscarried even more as the Great Depression unfolded while he was president. An example of the latter was Hoover's Agricultural Marketing Act of 1929, which developed a system of "voluntary" marketing cooperatives for farmers and created the Federal Farm Board, which supported artificially high farm prices by providing federal loans to the cooperatives, guaranteeing government purchases of agricultural surpluses, and allowing government standardization of agricultural product quality by certification. One of the board's functions was to withdraw agricultural production from marginal lands, which had begun cultivation during World War I to feed Europe, but which were unneeded as European farm production resumed after the war. Manufacturers had been compensated for overproduction, and Hoover felt that farmers deserved the same. The board for the agricultural industry was supposed to be similar to the Interstate Commerce Commission for the transportation industry and the Federal Reserve for the banking industry. However, the board was barely set up when the stock market crash began the economic slowdown, during which the board impaired economic recovery by acting as an emergency relief organization to "stabilize" farm prices—that is, to keep them artificially high.[10] The board was not really designed to deal with a financial crisis and economic downturn; it incurred massive monetary losses to provide welfare for a narrow industry, while raising food prices for down-and-out consumers during America's worst depression; and it did not really solve the farm problem.

In addition, Hoover provided government assistance in the form of capital to modernize American agriculture. In short, even slavish defenders of Hoover—Edgar Eugene Robinson and Vaughn Davis Bornet—admit that Hoover's farm program failed because the depression changed the basis on which it was formulated.[11] Yet even without the depression, the federal government providing welfare for specific industries violates the US Constitution (the document allows the federal government to provide only for the "general welfare") and hurts the consuming and tax-paying public.

In 1931, Hoover initially tried to forestall a domestic banking panic in response to Britain's scrapping of the gold standard. He set up the National Credit Corporation (NCC) and pressured private banks through this organization to "voluntarily" lend to other banks that were not eligible for assistance from Federal Reserve banks. Leading bankers were unhappy with this coercive solution and instead wanted government subsidization. The NCC saved seven hundred sick banks, which were deadwood in the economy and should have been allowed to go under to help reestablish market equilibrium by distributing their assets to more efficient actors.[12] Hoover said about the financial policy of his administration, "We determined that if necessary we should lend the full credit of the Government thus made impregnable, to aid private institutions to protect the debtor and the savings of our people."[13]

In a desperate bid to stimulate the sagging economy toward the end of his term to enhance his prospects for reelection, Hoover abandoned the voluntary approach used under the NCC, directly increasing loans to banks through the Federal Reserve banks and motivating Congress to create the Reconstruction Finance Corporation (RFC) in 1932. The RFC—modeled after the War Finance Corporation (WFC) during World War I and headed by the same chairman and senior staff—issued bonds to fund loans to troubled large firms in what were regarded as key industries—banks, land banks, railroads, insurance companies, and agricultural credit corporations. Thus, the organization further stunted the process of regaining market equilibrium by preventing the elimination of sick firms from the economy.

The RFC was precedent-setting, because it was a major turn away from private solutions for economic downturns.[14] Therefore, Hoover's administration became the first in American history to use federal power to intervene directly in the economy during peacetime. This important precedent resulted in much more direct federal economic intervention in subsequent presidential administrations. That Hoover had readopted a wartime mentality during peacetime is reflected in his rhetoric, which noted that combating the depression was like war, because "it is not a battle on a single front but on many fronts."[15] And despite being initiated during the calamity of the Great Depression, like many government efforts, the RFC had its roots in the war and lasted long after the economic crisis had passed.

As Coolidge's secretary of commerce in the late 1920s, Hoover had unsuccessfully warned Coolidge that excessive credit by the Fed was fueling excessive speculation in stocks. Yet after becoming president, he first supported the Fed in tightening loans for stock speculation, but after the stock market crashed in October 1929 and the Great Depression ensued, he became aggravated by the tight money policies of the Federal Reserve Board and wanted unwisely to insert more credit into the economy in a vain attempt to fight fear and boost business and public confidence. The Fed complied with Hoover's pressure for a reversal toward easy money, which eventually made the Great Depression worse. Hoover, again with the goal of expanding credit, urged Congress to pass the Glass-Steagall Act of 1932, which allowed more assistance to banks by the Federal Reserve and made government gold available for use by private business. The law also unwisely walled off consumer and investment banking from each other. Hoover infused money into Federal Land Banks and created Home Loan Banks, also expanding credit. All economic indices temporarily went up during the summer of 1932, just before the election.[16]

These examples show that when politicians are desperate to get reelected, they throw their principles—in this case, Hoover's voluntary associationalism and preference for tight monetary policy—to the wind in a frantic bid to use federal power to remain in office. But it did not work; Hoover was not reelected.

Yet in the fall of 1932, the sugar rush of easy money from the Fed was abandoned, leading Hoover to urgently prod President-elect Franklin D. Roosevelt to make a pledge to again turn on the spigot or to have the government guarantee bank deposits, neither of which FDR would do. FDR told Hoover's Secretary of State Stimson that he was fortunate to come into office when the crisis was so bad that the public and Congress would do anything he said. The abandonment of the addictive artificial stimulus led to the bank panic of March 1933, which caused the new president to close the banks for a time just after he took office.[17]

However, unlike FDR, who bested him in the 1932 election, Hoover did not win reelection during the Great Depression; Hoover was an administrator who had a tin ear for politics and the plight of the individual citizen. Hoover had given radio addresses in which he refused to identify with the common person's suffering during bad economic times and ineffectively used the war metaphor to "attack" the economic downturn (later FDR was a master of both techniques). But like his successor, the Progressive Hoover, who believed in conferences of experts more than in constitutional and republican processes, was secretive about crises he was dealing with and many of his responses to them, so as not to spook the public.

Hoover increased government spending on infrastructure—waterways, dams, highways, hospitals, and military bases—in a failing attempt to goose the economy. Curiously, however, Hoover regarded the Garner bill to create more post offices nationwide as a "pork barrel project," rather than as a reliever of unemployment, and properly vetoed it.[18]

Increased Taxes

To help pay for all of the added spending, balance the budget, and curb the international run on gold reserves, Hoover increased taxes in the middle of a drastic economic downturn—raising the income, gift, and luxury taxes. This tax hike at the end of 1931 was a bad precedent, because it was the first time in American history that taxes were increased during a severe depression. (Earlier in his administration, he had instituted a progressive tax cut, with lower incomes getting a much bigger reduction than upper incomes, much to the dismay of Andrew Mellon, his secretary of the treasury.) Despite the tax increase, however, Hoover, a rhetorical advocate of balanced budgets, ended up running budget deficits because of the Depression and the added government spending. The increased taxes or public borrowing required to pay for a public works program three times the normal size—to artificially boost employment with government make-work jobs—took money away from more productive private investment, as Hoover even admitted himself.[19] In a further nod to Progressives, Hoover—in a gross violation of privacy—published, over the objections of Secretary of the Treasury Mellon, large government refunds to taxpayers of estate, gift, and income taxes.[20]

Hoover also raised taxes in another way. Instead of doing away with the tariff to help consumers in the midst of the Depression, as he knew to be the right policy, Hoover (being a Republican and acting like one on the party's seminal issue) supported a flexible tariff—pegged to equalize the domestic cost of production with its foreign counterpart and adjusted by a semi-judicial tariff commission with expanded powers.[21] Because the Constitution gives the power of setting the tariff to Congress, not a tariff commission of individuals appointed and removed by the president, the role of the expanded commission was unconstitutional.

In June 1930, Hoover signed the Smoot-Hawley tariff—which imposed the highest tariff rates in American history with flexible rates and the empowered commission to adjust them—despite protests from more than one thousand economists, as well as international business interests and tens of countries. Hoover favored the high tariffs mainly to help the depressed agricultural sector (an important Republican electoral constituency),[22] and he could have limited tariff increases to that sector but did not.

The increased tariffs of Smoot-Hawley, also benefiting certain American businesses by disadvantaging foreign competitors, raised government revenue but sparked an international trade war, which exacerbated the already war-disrupted world trade patterns. Many foreign countries retaliated against Smoot-Hawley by hiking their own tariffs, which deepened the economic downturn worldwide.[23] Yet, contrary to the consensus of economic thought and data at the time, Hoover, in defending the high tariffs, unconvincingly maintained that world trade would not be adversely affected, even during a depression.

Moreover, even if the high tariff helped special interests in agriculture (although some farmers in the West did not think this was the case) and business, it hurt the average consumer by raising prices during a depression. Finally, Smoot-Hawley was unconstitutional, because the Constitution allows tariffs to generate government tax revenues but not to protect certain industries. Protective tariffs violate the general welfare clause of the document, which requires that such duties provide for citizens' general well-being, not protect particular interests.

The European Financial Crisis of 1931

When his domestic program of associational corporatism failed to end the Depression, Hoover became convinced that the origin of—and therefore, solution to—the Depression was overseas. He was actually right that the roots of the Great Depression lay in both World War I and the punitive settlement imposed on the Germans at Versailles in 1919[24] (the roots of World War II also lay in this first war). The inflation and economic dislocation of the Great War in Europe took a long time to negatively affect the then fairly self-sufficient American economy.[25] Yet, Hoover was not oblivious to the root cause of the dangerous situation in Europe. He said of the collapse of the European financial system in 1931:

> When . . . the financial systems of Europe were no longer able to stand the strain of their war inheritances and of their after-war economic and political polices, an earthquake ran through forty nations. Financial panics; governments unable to meet their obligations; banks unable to pay their depositors; citizens, fearing inflation of currency, seeking to export their savings to foreign countries for safety; citizens of other nations demanding payment of their loans; financial and monetary systems either in collapse or remaining only in appearance.[26]

This cataclysmic European financial crisis of 1931 stemmed from the after-effects of World War I. The Young Plan of 1929 during the Hoover administration, which was similar to the Dawes plan in 1924 during the Coolidge administration, loaned money to Germany to prevent default on war reparations payments to France and Britain, America's World War I allies, who in turn owed war debt payments to the United States. So the Germans were paying reparations to the Allies with American money, and the Allies were then paying back the United States with the same money. Yet the Hoover administration never admitted this unstable self-paying scheme to its taxpaying public.

Hoover's welfare for domestic business was compounded by welfare for former war allies who had dragged the United States needlessly into World War I. The European credit market, especially in Germany, began to deteriorate in 1931 because US wartime allies irresponsibly called in short-term loans from banks in the defeated powers of Austria and Germany as a political punishment in response to the two countries creating a customs union. The collapse of the Austrian bank Kredit-Anstalt created a chain reaction in the German financial system.

Hoover got Congress to approve a one-year moratorium postponing payments of Allied war debts to the United States in exchange for a similar Allied moratorium on German payments of war reparations. The agreement came too late to avoid a banking panic in Germany, and the freezing of short-term credit to that country, which Hoover's debt payment moratorium was designed to avoid. However, Hoover then negotiated a London "standstill" agreement to stanch the further withdrawal of short-term credit from Germany.[27] In the face of a worsening economic depression, Hoover's moratorium and standstill agreement only delayed the inevitable—a repudiation of Allied debt to the United States, as well as German repudiation of reparations payments to the Allies in 1932.[28]

The European financial crisis of 1931 (German financial collapse and British abandonment of the gold standard) caused foreigners to withdraw massive amounts of gold from the United States and US citizens to withdraw deposits in currency and gold from their own banks, thus constricting credit and worsening the depression.[29] In 1931 and 1932, a hostile Congress made sure to give Hoover all of his proposed government interventions in the market, so if the measures failed it could hold him responsible—both of which happened. Both houses of Congress still had majorities of his fellow Republicans, but Hoover had alienated them. In any event, because of his mishandling of the economic crisis, Republican margins had declined to razor-thin majorities in both houses as a result of the 1930 off-year elections.[30] To keep the United

States, which was hemorrhaging gold, on the gold standard, Hoover got the Federal Reserve to raise interest rates.[31] This interest rate hike certainly did not help the moribund economy.

A Preference for Indirect, Rather Than Direct, Federal Aid

Interestingly enough, Hoover wanted to provide veiled welfare only for selected groups, such as businessmen, financiers, farmers, and labor while refusing philosophically to provide direct federal relief for down-and-out people. He thought the "dole" led to poor incentives for people and destroyed the American spirit. For example, after a drought hit various states in 1930 and 1931, Congress wanted loans to help the needy farmers buy seeds for crops, animal feed, equipment, food, and clothing. However, Hoover agreed that farm animals should be fed but disagreed with government loans for food for farmers and their families. Hoover prevailed in excising federal loans for farmers' food and clothing but permanently damaged his relations with Congress.[32] This odd state of affairs caused one Democrat from Arkansas to observe that the Hoover administration believed in feeding "jackasses but . . . not starving babies."

In practice, however, Hoover—unlike President Grover Cleveland in the late 1800s, who felt that such drought relief was the constitutional responsibility of state and local governments—did find creative ways to provide indirect federal help to drought victims: for example, extension of loans and credits to farmers through new Agricultural Credit Corporations, increased highway construction in the Emergency Construction Bill, and accelerated public building, including accelerated rivers and harbors work in drought-stricken states.[33]

Even then, Hoover made a distinction between emergencies such as drought and war. He believed that in war, voluntary mutual self-help was impossible, but in drought and general economic depression, it still was. Hoover thought that direct federal aid would sap the self-reliance of the American people.[34] He may have been right, but then he should have realized that his subsidies and assistance to businesses, besides looking bad in comparison, would have the same effect. Finally, when desperate to get reelected, Hoover partially relented and approved the Emergency Relief and Construction Act

(ERCA), which allowed the federal government to indirectly loan money to states to start public projects to provide employment. This arrangement at least kept the veneer that the federal government was not providing direct aid to people, which Hoover correctly believed was the responsibility of the states.

However, Hoover did believe that federally funded public works were indirect, rather than direct, relief. So he approved some federal public works projects and rejected others, which was a factor in costing him reelection in 1932.[35] In 1928, Hoover had received more than 58 percent of the popular vote, but in 1932, he got less than 40 percent (FDR, his opponent, got more than 57 percent).[36]

Setting Precedents for Government Action to Counter Economic Downturns

The onset of the Great Depression, with the stock market crash in October 1929, induced financial belt-tightening on Hoover's associational nirvana.[37] Yet as the depression continued, FDR's statist corporatism resorted to more heavy-handed regulation of commerce, replacing Hoover's subtler coercion of business under the guise of associational corporatism.

Hoover's naïve associational corporatism—demanding less materialism, more cooperation, and more voluntary social responsibility from business, labor, and farming interests—was a disaster. And although Hoover always remained in denial, his precedents with the Reconstruction Finance Corporation (RFC), Emergency Relief and Construction Act (ERCA), public works projects, and aid to the agricultural industry set a template for later and more intrusive government intervention in the economy. FDR's aide Rexford Tugwell much later acknowledged, "We didn't admit it at the time, but practically the whole New Deal was extrapolated from programs that Hoover started." Ironically, in today's world where big government is accepted, FDR is regarded as the innovator, for better or worse, in this regard. Yet, the fathers of permanent big government in the United States were Woodrow Wilson, who pioneered wartime government stewardship of the American economy during World War I, and Herbert Hoover, who reintroduced and adjusted that model for the crisis of the Great Depression.

The Best Foreign Policy of the Twentieth and Twenty-First Centuries

Hoover may have botched his attempt to bring the nation out of the Great Depression, but his foreign policy of "independent internationalism" was much more effective. Although Hoover had deplored the US "isolationism" induced by the horrors of World War I and although he had admired Teddy Roosevelt's aggressive foreign policy, in practice he avoided war and supported international arms limitation and defense cost-cutting at home. Hoover also feared American entanglements in Europe.

In general, Hoover wanted to avoid using force abroad, especially in Latin America and East Asia. Hoover wanted only limited US political and moral meddling in the world and controlled economic expansion. He thus eschewed the moralistic internationalism of Woodrow Wilson and the militant nationalism of Senators William Borah and Hiram Johnson.[38]

Better Policy Toward Latin America

One important area in which Hoover had better policy than Harding and Coolidge (and FDR) was in US relations with Latin America. As president-elect, he toured Latin America and proclaimed a "good neighbor" policy, later laudably reducing US military intervention in the region, formerly justified by the Monroe Doctrine. He rejected previous US policy in that region—"dollar diplomacy"—and rejected using force to "maintain contracts." He especially rejected Theodore Roosevelt's corollary to the Monroe Doctrine, which reserved the US right to use force to maintain order in Latin American countries, thus giving European powers no excuse to intervene in the Western Hemisphere.[39] Despite the Platt Amendment making Cuba a virtual US protectorate, Hoover avoided intervening militarily there even in the face of rising autocracy. In all, Hoover, for the most part, avoided intervening in the twenty rebellions in Latin American nations during his term and also did not intervene when such countries infuriated US bondholders by defaulting on their financial obligations.[40] Hoover restricted the activities of US Marines in Nicaragua and began to slowly end the long, expensive, and fruitless military occupations of that country and of Haiti. He successfully withdrew the marines from Nicaragua before he left office.[41] The previously noted adoption of the high Smoot-Hawley tariff, however, had a negative effect on intra-hemispheric relations.

As with many precedents set by Hoover, FDR, trying to win support in the Western Hemisphere against a rising Nazi Germany, continued Hoover's Good Neighbor policy during the 1930s and became famous for it. Hoover, however, refused to have the United States monitor elections in Latin America, which became common in FDR's administration in 1933 and thereafter.

Arms Sales and the Military-Industrial Complex

In making exceptions to Harding's blanket ban on government arms sales abroad (established in 1923), Hoover inadvertently allowed more arms sales in revolutionary situations, especially in Latin America. He intended to alter the anti-rebel bias in US arms policy. Hoover also altered Harding's general ban on US arms exports to allow the US military to export defensive weaponry. Thus, Hoover had a mixed record on curtailing US arms sales abroad and the militarization of the US economy at home.

Hoover's creation of a War Policies Commission in 1930 led to further mobilization of the economy for war, rather than fulfilling the congressional intent of lowering the possibility of war by reducing unneeded arms production through the taxation of industry profits. Hoover did, however, refuse to support federally funded munitions factories and tried unsuccessfully to get Congress to give him discretionary executive authority over arms sales abroad. The latter might have been unconstitutional, because the document gives Congress the power to regulate commerce with foreign naitons.

Even before the onset of the depression, Hoover attempted to battle the military-industrial complex and minimize spending on defense. He noted that the United States, at the time, had the largest spending on the army and navy in the world, despite fewer threats to peace than at any time in more than half a century.[42] Hoover tried to garner savings by achieving an international agreement to further limit naval arms (building on Harding's successful efforts at the Washington Conference in 1922) and attempted to create a "pocket" budget—spending for the War Department, the Navy Department, veterans, and interest on the debt—that was more honest about the costs to the country for military spending. In 1931, such spending was 72 percent of the projected federal budget. Although the US military was unhappy about this transparency, the pocket budget did not reduce military appropriations until the depression forced cuts.[43]

In the London Naval Treaty of 1930, Hoover plugged gaps in the Naval Treaty of the Washington Conference by reaching an arms control agreement on ships smaller than the capital ships (battleships) controlled in the 1922 pact. Although the London agreement actually resulted in the United States increasing its cruiser tonnage because it had not built as many such ships as Japan and Britain had since 1922, the treaty commendably reduced naval tonnage worldwide by 12 percent.[44] For the first time, all naval weapons of Japan, Britain, and the United States were restricted. Although Hoover believed that "parity" with Japan and Britain was a diplomatic, rather than military, doctrine, he somehow bought into the increase in cruisers only to keep up with the Joneses—this despite the fact that the United States had an even better intrinsic security position away from world centers of conflict than even the island nations of Japan and Britain.

During the 1932 Disarmament Conference, Hoover tried to abolish selected "aggressive" (offensive) arms and reduce by one-third land armies in excess of the levels needed to preserve internal order. Although Germany, Italy, and the Communist Soviet Union accepted the idea, the conference failed because US wartime allies—Britain and France—refused to go along. Had they done so, Germany likely would have been constrained by treaty to a smaller army and less offensive capability after Hitler took over as German chancellor as Hoover left office in early 1933.

Dealing with Japanese Empire-Building

In 1929, in a Sino-Soviet dust-up, the Hoover administration made it clear that the United States would not intervene militarily in such crises. The Japanese invasion of Manchuria in 1931, Japan's establishment of a protectorate there in 1932, and Japanese withdrawal from the League of Nations in 1933 undermined the Nine-Power Treaty, originally signed at the Washington Naval Conference of 1921 to 1922, which had pledged that signatories would honor the territorial integrity of China.[45] Hoover actually thought Japan's military intervention was justified because of chaos in China and Bolshevik influence there. At any rate, the Stimson Doctrine of nonrecognition of territorial aggrandizement (a moral sanction) and an unofficial lending ban by the United States toward Japan may have prevented a full Japanese takeover of China in 1931. (Hoover also adroitly used this doctrine of nonrecognition in Latin America as a moral sanction to avoid military intervention when rebellions and invasions of other countries by neighboring nations occurred there.[46])

France and Britain were unwilling to impose economic sanctions on Japan, either unilaterally or through the League of Nations. Thus, Hoover, his cabinet, the Department of Commerce, and key senators were also unwilling to impose such ineffective unilateral economic sanctions during a depression; other countries would have just traded with Japan, to the disadvantage of American businesses. But Britain and France did follow the US nonrecognition of Japan's actions; Japan did halt its attack on central China and withdraw from some occupied areas there but did not pull out of Manchuria.[47]

Hoover made it clear to Secretary of State Stimson that he would not use force to enforce either the Stimson Doctrine or the Kellogg-Briand Pact, which had outlawed war. In short, Hoover correctly saw a contradiction in using force to preserve peace.[48] More specifically, although he approved of Calvin Coolidge's Kellogg-Briand Pact of 1928, Hoover refused to use economic sanctions or military action to enforce it. Hoover had seen the suffering economic sanctions had caused during World War I and also cogently argued that economic sanctions led to war and that world peace should not be based on military force or coercion. Hoover was certainly right that economic sanctions would lead to war, as his successor Franklin D. Roosevelt demonstrated—FDR strangled the Japanese economy by cutting off its oil and supplies of key metals in an effort to prevent it from acquiring an Asian empire similar to those already possessed by Britain, France, the Netherlands, and the United States. The resulting economic paralysis led Japan to use its military to grab oil overseas, eventually leading to the desperate Japanese attack on Pearl Harbor.

Some analysts have criticized Hoover for not drawing a line in Manchuria in 1931, arguing that he gave a green light to potential aggressors in Japan,

Germany, and Italy. However, Hoover was bent on withdrawing US forces from long-term occupations in Haiti and Nicaragua and certainly did not want to send them to China to fight Japan. Besides, with the horrors of the unpopular World War I only just over a decade in the background, the American public, battered by the Great Depression, would not have permitted such a war with Japan at that time. Even FDR thought that "old Hoover's foreign policy has been pretty good."[49]

Hoover did say that one way to bolster the Kellogg-Briand Pact was for the United States to join the World Court, which was associated with the League of Nations, to provide an arena for the peaceful settlement of disputes among nations. Although Hoover did negotiate and present a Court Protocol to the Senate for ratification, he then laudably slow-rolled it by only providing half-hearted support.[50] Such judicial bodies are usually politicized and rarely live up to the high standards of American justice. Also, the American people were fearful that joining the World Court would be a stepping stone to membership in the League of Nations. Nevertheless, more acceptably, Hoover reached seventeen treaties of conciliation and twenty-five arbitration treaties with specific nations.[51]

Hoover believed in using moral sanctions, instead of economic sanctions, and had thus adopted the Stimson doctrine of nonrecognition. The doctrine was appropriately used to deny moral acceptance of territorial aggression by foreign nations, such as Japan's takeover of Manchuria in 1931. However, Hoover perpetuated the foolish nonrecognition policy toward the Bolshevik regime in Russia from the administrations of Woodrow Wilson, Warren Harding, and Calvin Coolidge. Wilson had even sent troops, in conjunction with US allies in World War I, to overthrow the new Bolshevik government, thus souring relations with that regime for a long time to come. However, despite Hoover's unnecessary perpetuation of bad relations with the Soviet Union by nonrecognition of mere internal developments (rather than external aggression), he curiously supported indirect US government financing of exports to that country by providing credit to sick US businesses through the Reconstruction Finance Corporation (RFC). For purposes of negotiation and peace, recognition of the USSR would have been a good policy, but subsidizing the totalitarian regime to provide welfare for America businesses was beyond the pale.

Another one of Hoover's unenlightened policies was his stance on Philippine independence. He vetoed a congressionally passed bill granting just that, although his veto was then thankfully overridden by Congress.[52]

To add insult to injury, after Hoover had been defeated for reelection, a member of his own party introduced an impeachment resolution, based on Hoover's alleged incompetence in dealing with the economy and foreign policy. However, the resolution was resoundingly defeated in the House of Representatives 361 to 8.[53] Hoover had been incompetent in dealing with the economy but laudably had the most restrained foreign policy of the twentieth century (and so far, more restrained than the foreign policy of any administration in the twenty-first century).

Political and Economic Liberties

Hoover had a mixed, but generally poor, record on civil and economic liberties.

Hoover Used the Military Against Veterans

To save public money, Hoover got Congress to pass a law that consolidated the Pension Bureau, the Veterans Bureau, and the Soldiers' Homes into one agency—what is the modern-day Veterans Administration. However, Hoover vetoed a bill aiding disabled veterans and got Congress to pass a substitute bill with even more broad and generous benefits—the most anyone had proposed.[54] So much for saving taxpayer dollars.

Hoover did laudably, but unsuccessfully, veto a bill that would have allowed the politically powerful World War I veterans to borrow up to 50 percent of the value of their 1924 veterans certificates that did not come due until 1945, courageously saying that "the country should not be called upon . . . either directly or indirectly, to support or make loans to those who can by their own efforts support themselves."[55] However, Hoover seemed callous when he used Army troops, commanded by Douglas MacArthur, against World War I veteran demonstrators who, because of the hard economic times, were lobbying in Washington in 1932 to get 100 percent of their promised government bonuses immediately.

Hoover initially ordered the provision of tents, blankets, cots, rolling kitchens, medical care, and shelter in vacant federal buildings to the bonus marchers. The mainly middle-class bonus army had overstayed their welcome and had some incidents of disorderliness, but federal authorities wanted the protesters out because they were holding up the construction of federal buildings. Hoover ordered buildings and parks cleared of the veterans. Violence occurred between local police and the demonstrators, which led to two veterans' deaths, police injuries, and a call to federal authorities for assistance. Hoover ordered the Army only to assist local authorities in enforcing the law. The main protesters' camp was across the Anacostia River, and Hoover ordered the Army not to cross the waterway. Although Hoover took full responsibility for MacArthur's assault on the veterans' camp, MacArthur had deliberately disobeyed Hoover's orders to merely contain the camp and instead attacked it. The Army and the protesters burned the camp. Although the protesters and some dependents fled, none died in MacArthur's attack.[56]

Although Hoover should not have called out the military for any reason against the largely peacefully protesting veterans, he nevertheless should have gone public with MacArthur's insubordination (Harry Truman would later have the same problem with MacArthur in the Korean War) and fired him. Instead, at the time, Hoover latched onto nonsensical allegations by MacArthur and the secretary of war that the protesters were Communist subversives leading an insurrection against the government. Yet Hoover laudably refused to issue a declaration of insurrection or institute martial law.[57] On another occasion, Hoover, although an opponent of Communism, refused to break up peaceful demonstrations by Communists in front of the White House or give government support for proposed "red hunts" for Communists.[58] Therefore, the Communists ended up getting better treatment than the veterans.

Reluctance to Ease Prohibition

The Eighteenth Amendment—prohibiting the manufacture, sale, and transportation of alcohol—had passed in 1919 and had taken effect in 1920 during the Wilson administration. Hoover came out against repealing it, as many Republicans had, even though the government's attempt to impose the religion-driven morality of some of its citizens on the whole country had long been unpopular and an abject failure. Hoover's reasons against repeal reflected his Progressive values. Bizarrely, he supported Prohibition and its destruction of an industry without government compensation (violating the Constitution) because he believed it was morally the right thing to do, allowing Americans to transcend materialism and respect for property rights. He claimed that Prohibition increased agricultural prices and made American families richer. But scholar Joan Hoff Wilson noted that Hoover was oblivious to the fact that the higher price of illegal liquor was taking money out of those same families' wallets. She also concluded that resisting the repeal of Prohibition did not help Hoover at election time.[59]

In fact, Hoover tightened enforcement of the already failed policy, which led to an increase in crime, especially organized crime. Hoover even admitted in 1932 that despite increasing fines, confiscations, and the population in jails, illicit trafficking in alcohol had increased. He acknowledged that even the original zealously "dry" states refused to help federal authorities enforce Prohibition, but nevertheless, because most Republicans were "drys," Hoover cynically recommended that the Republican national platform keep the ban on commerce in alcohol and turn enforcement over to the states. FDR, the Democratic candidate in the 1932 election, had run on a platform of repealing Prohibition. In the interregnum period between FDR's election victory and his inauguration, Congress repealed the alcohol ban. President Hoover had nothing to do with this legislative action and the states ratified the Twenty-First Amendment, repealing the Eighteenth Amendment, by December 1933.[60] (Americans today could learn from this attempt at prohibiting the production and sales of alcohol, since most still advocate enforcing the equally costly War on Drugs, removing the right of adults to decide what to put in their bodies and causing substantial increases in violent crime and the prison population.)

Record on Other Civil Rights and Liberties

Hoover did have a few accomplishments concerning other civil rights and liberties issues, by the standards of the time. Hoover, ignoring the protests of southern segregationists, allowed his wife to entertain an African-American woman at the White House. Also, Hoover commuted the sentence of a black man convicted of murder without receiving legal due process and recommended that the new federal parole board have members proportionally representing populations of blacks and women in prison. Finally, Hoover proposed an increased budget for Howard University, a black institution of higher learning in the District of Columbia. Hoover also almost doubled funding of the Indian Bureau between 1928 and 1933, which aimed at increasing health and educational services among Native Americans.[61]

Hoover replaced William Howard Taft, retiring chief justice of the Supreme Court, with Charles Evans Hughes. Hughes presided over the court's shift in its primary role from a defender of property rights to a defender of civil liberties, writing landmark opinions on freedom of speech and the press. Hughes also opposed Franklin D. Roosevelt's court packing scheme.[62]

In labor relations, Hoover signed the Norris-La Guardia Anti-Injunction law of 1932, which prevented courts from ending peaceful worker protests with injunctions, prohibited employers from interfering in the right of labor unions to organize workplaces, and made illegal yellow dog contracts—which workers had to sign, pledging not to join a union before being given a job.

Economic Rights

Responding to the Teapot Dome scandal earlier in the 1920s, which was still playing out when he took office, and trying to throw a blanket over the issue to get it out of public attention, Hoover reviewed existing private leases of federal oil-laden lands but then overreacted by revoking all permits that had not yet been drilled and by halting all future exploring or leasing of such areas. In oil lands not owned by the federal government, which were constitutionally governed by state regulation, Hoover wanted regional agreements among states to control physical and economic waste in oil drilling. Yet his own Federal Oil Conservation Board deemed such compacts to be a violation of the federal Sherman Antitrust Act. So Hoover wisely backed off on both federal regulation and those regional agreements.[63]

Hoover's desire to conserve the nation's oil reserves is in stark contrast to today's government preference to produce more oil domestically to reduce US imports of foreign oil. Given the fact that in the twenty-first century, America is still producing much petroleum and is now even increasing its oil production to again be the largest oil producer in the world, Hoover's conservation policy was a prime example of the government getting it wrong. Perhaps the best federal energy policy is none at all.

More generally, similar to Teddy Roosevelt before him, Hoover wanted to use federal authority to conserve the nation's natural resources for future generations and improve the nation's waterways through public works projects. Even before the stock market crash in late 1929 and ensuing depression, Hoover was pushing for huge increases in public works spending, including flood control on major American rivers such as a section of the Mississippi River that had flooded in 1927. Hoover settled disputes to permit the construction of a dam—approved during the Coolidge administration—on the Colorado River in the southwest United States that now bears his name; Hoover also started the Reclamation Service bureaucracy to work on the Grand Coulee Dam on the Columbia River in the Pacific Northwest. Hoover loved to have the federal government build dams when the private sector or local government allegedly could not or would not construct them, but did not think the federal government should be competing with private utility companies in selling the power generated by dams built with government assistance; he felt that the federal government should remain only in a regulatory role in electricity. However, Congress wanted the government to sell power in the expansion of the Muscle Shoals Dam under the Tennessee Valley Authority. Hoover lost this battle. In general, all of the above federal economic activity was likely to impinge on the economic rights of many US citizens that had traditionally been observed.

Conclusion

Herbert Hoover, contrary to conventional wisdom, was a revolutionary in economic policy by doing too much, not too little, to counter the Great Depression. By not letting natural market forces restore economic equilibrium, through excessive government action, he deepened and prolonged what would have probably been an ordinary periodic market correction. Franklin D.

Roosevelt, his successor, ran with Hoover's precedents for federal action in the economy and did not help matters.

Despite his abysmal economic policy, Hoover had the best foreign policy of any president in the twentieth century and so far, in the twenty-first century—restricting US military intervention abroad, bringing American troops home, and reaching an agreement with other major powers to limit the building of warships. He began a less interventionist policy toward Latin America, called the "Good Neighbor Policy," for which FDR usually gets the credit.

Hoover had a mixed, but generally poor, record in preserving political and economic liberties. He needlessly used military force to put down a protest by veterans, increased enforcement of the long-failed policy of Prohibition, and had a checkered record on economic rights.

4

Smaller Government
at Home and Abroad

ALTHOUGH EVEN HISTORIANS believed that Dwight D. Eisenhower (popularly known as Ike; president from 1953 to 1961) was a passive, disengaged, and even lazy president, much new information has come to light that he was far more on top of things than many had previously thought. He cultivated this vacationing, golf-playing image merely to disguise his constant behind-the-scenes maneuvering.[1] Although he was Progressive in some respects—he not only did not dismantle Franklin D. Roosevelt's New Deal but thought parts of it should be expanded (for example, Social Security)—overall, he was a budget hawk. Next to Bill Clinton, Eisenhower has the best fiscal record of any post-Truman president in cutting federal spending as a portion of gross domestic product (GDP); they were the only presidents to do it. Eisenhower also limited overt US government military interventions overseas and cut the defense budget. Ike did, however, rely too much on covert operations to overthrow foreign leaders he did not like, even democratically elected ones, and also built up the US nuclear arsenal from what was needed to deter attacks into a preemptive first-strike capability against the Soviet Union. In sum, as far as post–New Deal presidents go, Eisenhower has a reasonably good record in limiting government, both domestically and abroad.

"New Look" at National Security
Permitted Cuts in the Defense Budget

Although Eisenhower had made his reputation overseas as a general, he realized—unlike many other recent presidents, especially Richard Nixon, his vice president and future chief executive—that foreign policy was supposed to protect the domestic population, territory, political and economic system, and way of life. According to historian Daniel J. Sargent:

> New presidents bring their own priorities, and domestic issues often predominate. Even Eisenhower, unequaled in international experience, appears to have been concerned as president mainly with guarding American society against the political consequences of unwarranted militarism.[2]

Ike was afraid that the Cold War would convert the United States into a garrison state. Therefore, Eisenhower foresaw a long Cold War against Communism, believed time was on America's side because the Soviet Union would weaken and moderate over time, and thus was for containment of the USSR, US economic growth, covert action, arms control, and, in general, American perseverance.[3]

Budget Cuts, Including Defense

Upon taking office, Eisenhower wanted a rapid conversion from a wartime to a peacetime economy. He worried that the large budget deficit Truman had used to fight the Korean War would weaken the US economy. From mid-1952, before he took office, until the fall of 1953, an inflationary boom afflicted the country. Ike deflated the inflationary balloon by reducing the Truman deficit through the cutting of federal spending, especially defense spending. In 1953, the Department of Defense spent at least 70 percent of the federal budget— or up to 90 percent of it, if the interest payments on the national debt were included. He slashed the budget of the Army, his own former service, by a third, and also cut the Navy budget; only the Air Force expanded its budget, because of its prominent role in nuclear deterrence against the Soviet Union. Even here, Ike opposed the Air Force's planned high-altitude B-70 bomber.

Ike's frugal budget policies actually led to federal surpluses in three different years and inflation averaging only a remarkable 1.5 percent over his eight years in office, thus leading to robust economic growth for most of his tenure. Ike was one of the more successful post–World War II presidents in average annual growth in net real GDP per capita (growth in real GDP per capita minus the growth in real debt per capita), coming in at almost 2 percent.[4] However, as other presidents have done, Ike did occasionally deviate from frugality and pressure the supposedly independent Federal Reserve to loosen the money supply before elections to ensure he and his party had a better chance to win.[5]

Eisenhower's general thriftiness, and the resultant economic growth, sliced the national debt from 100 percent of GDP in 1953 to 60 percent of GDP in 1960, thus reducing drag on the economy. Ike's success achieving robust prosperity by focusing on fiscal frugality should be an antidote to the anemic economic growth resulting from federal fiscal stimulus plans—such as the stimulus packages of the George W. Bush and Barack Obama presidencies.

And remarkably for a former general, Ike realized that a weak economy over the long term in the Cold War would impair the US ability to counter Communism. He also correctly concluded that excessive military spending would undermine investment in the civilian economy, which underpinned US military, political, diplomatic, and cultural power. According to historian Geoffrey Perret, Eisenhower was prescient: "Possessions, not weapons, won the Cold War, because Eastern Europeans and Russians finally grasped the true nature of Communism—it not only made people poor, but would keep them in poverty forever."[6] It is unfortunate that other American presidents did not have Ike's confidence that the capitalist system could be used as a model to ultimately defeat Communism, instead of conducting military spending on a vast scale to "contain" Communism over three more decades.

The "New Look" Strategy

In the wake of the North Korean invasion of South Korea, Harry Truman had adopted NSC-68, a national strategy that called for marshalling "preponderant power" for waging a Cold War against the Soviet Union by massively expanding US conventional and nuclear forces. The US defense budget had soared from $13 billion in 1950 to $73 billion in 1953.[7]

However, Ike refused to accept the strategic orientation of NSC-68 or its exorbitant cost. NSC-68 envisioned countering the Soviet threat everywhere in the world. Ike wanted to defend only America's permanent "interests"— that is, Western Europe, Japan, South Korea, Taiwan, and Israel. (If he had limited American defense to only securing US vital interests—defined as areas of the world with great potential economic power and advanced technology—only the first two would have required defense in the 1950s.) In general, Ike thought that defending Europe was more important than defending Asia but believed that collective security was the only affordable defense. He and Pentagon officials had never contemplated a permanent presence of US ground troops in Europe. Eisenhower appropriately asked why 200 million Americans should defend 250 million Europeans. Yet although Germany had rearmed, six American divisions remained in Europe. German rearmament and NATO's forward defense strategy led the Soviet Union and its Eastern European allies to create a counter alliance called the Warsaw Pact in 1955.

Ike's rhetoric spoke of rolling back Communism from countries already under its sway rather than just containing it. Yet in reality, like George Kennan, who during the Truman administration originated the policy of US containment of the USSR, Eisenhower believed that the Soviets would moderate over time and that the United States should negotiate with them.

At the same time, Ike ruled out preventive war but nevertheless geared US nuclear strategy, forces, and weaponry toward a dangerous preemptive atomic first strike against the Soviet Union, if US intelligence picked up warning of an imminent Soviet strike.[8] However, to his credit, Eisenhower refused the advice of his aides to use nuclear weapons on two occasions without provocation or imminent threat, reinforcing an important no-first-use precedent.[9] (Truman had also nixed Douglas MacArthur from using nuclear weapons in the Korean War.) Yet, being a consummate bridge player, Ike was willing to bluff about using nuclear weapons to keep the United States out of World War III. Eisenhower's Secretary of State John Foster Dulles crowed that Ike had bluffed Communists about using nukes three times to get them to back down.[10]

Although Secretary of State Dulles gave a speech calling for "massive retaliation," implying that the United States would launch nuclear weapons only after it had been attacked by the Soviet Union, the speech had been written mostly by Ike himself and masked the real US doctrine of preemptive first strike. Eisenhower's famous speeches on "Atoms for Peace," bringing most fissionable nuclear material under international control, and "Open Skies," opening up both the Soviet Union and United States to surveillance of their nuclear facilities, were propaganda ploys to enable the United States to maintain its preemptive first-strike advantage and more easily allow the open American society to spy on the closed Soviet society to get targets for a first strike. The Soviets did not have as much fissionable material to spare as the Americans and also did not want to show their weakness by signing up for the increased surveillance of Open Skies. Predictably, the Soviets were not thrilled with either initiative and nothing much happened on them. In fact, during his presidency, Ike never got what he wanted most—a disarmament agreement with the USSR.

To develop that nuclear preemptive strike, even though Eisenhower had been an Army general, the Air Force received first priority in his "New Look" defense posture. The Navy got the second priority to supplement the Air Force's preemptive force but also to project power into backwater areas of the world—a dubious goal for a republic and more appropriate for an empire. Relying more on air power, nuclear weapons, and new missile technology, the New Look replaced manpower with technology and permitted the reduction of ground forces and post–Korean War defense budgets from $43 billion in 1954 to $37.5 billion in 1955. Eisenhower's Army chief of staff, Maxwell Taylor, argued for the doctrine of "flexible response"—that is, that any future war with the USSR would be limited and involve conventional forces, especially Army infantry. Ike rejected this paradigm and believed that even in limited wars, the Army would provide only a few infantry and artillery battalions to train local forces and to guard air and naval bases, which would be used by the US Air Force and Navy to support the client state's ground forces.[11] Ike correctly believed that the doctrine of "flexible response" would drag the United States into more nonstrategic brushfire wars that could escalate.[12]

When Eisenhower encountered complaints from congressional leaders that the preemptive strategy would undermine the constitutional requirement for Congress to declare war, he said that if faced with an atomic Pearl Harbor, he would act to protect the nation.[13] This congressional complaint ignored that under the original conception of the Constitution's framers, as elucidated in the debate at the Constitutional Convention, under emergencies when Congress could not take rapid action to declare war, the president could take military action to defend the country. Nevertheless, the framers believed that Congress should later validate the president's emergency actions with such a declaration. Because as commander-in-chief, the president has always commanded the US armed forces during war, the advent of nuclear weapons challenged this constitutional framework less than the congressional leaders thought—although theoretically, during the nuclear age, a greater chance might exist that rapid presidential emergency action would be needed. Fortunately, so far that has not proven to be the case. In fact, Congress did more than Ike ever did to undermine its constitutional power to declare war by setting an unfortunate precedent during the Korean War when it failed to insist that Truman request a congressional declaration.

Ike tried to tamp down the national hysteria following the Soviet launch of Sputnik on an intercontinental ballistic missile (ICBM) into the Earth's orbit in 1957 by correctly saying that it did not increase the threat to the United States (the Soviets did not yet have an operational ICBM that could hit US targets). By early 1956, Eisenhower knew that the United States had enough bombers and hydrogen bombs to destroy the USSR, even if the Soviets were the first ones to launch a surprise attack. However, he eventually was forced by the unrelenting public pressure to put priority on missile programs, create NASA, and reluctantly sign the National Defense Education Act of 1958, which subsidized graduate school education—but for nonscientific degrees as well as scientific ones.

When the press erroneously began imagining bomber and missile gaps, with the United States trailing the USSR, Ike and the CIA refused to debunk them to protect secret U-2 spy plane flights over Soviet territory and National Security Agency (NSA) snooping activities.[14] Eisenhower knew that the U-2 overflights were a provocative act that could result in war with the USSR (Ike realized the likely severe US reaction if a Soviet spy plane were shot down over American territory) or the public embarrassment if one were shot down, but he regarded the intelligence information gained as so valuable that they were worth the immense risk. Because Democrats in Congress were pressing for much more funding for added B-52s to close the bomber gap, Eisenhower needed evidence to prove the gap was illusory,[15] which the overflights provided.

An American U-2 was shot down over the Soviet Union and the pilot captured, leaving egg on Ike's face after he had earlier lied and denied that U-2 flights were taking place. He refused, however, to apologize to the Soviets for the incident, but did promise not to overfly their territory anymore. Ike's lies violated what was later to be the first law of crisis management during Washington scandals: tell the truth and tell it early.[16] Other presidents have also forgotten this rule—Richard Nixon during Watergate, Ronald Reagan during Iran-Contra, and Bill Clinton during the Monica Lewinsky affair.

In reality, the United States was ahead of the Soviets in intercontinental- and intermediate-range missiles. By the end of his second term, Eisenhower and Congress had created an enormous, invulnerable triad of bombers and long-range land-based and submarine-based missiles, far before the Soviets could create a respectable long-range land-based missile force. Eisenhower, however, did tell lawmakers that the Cold War was going to be long, that time was on the US's side, that the United States had to pace itself in buying weapons, and he asked repeatedly, "How many times do we have to destroy Russia?"[17] Although he always privately argued against the bureaucratic and political impetus to spend more on weapons, he should have been stronger and more public in his condemnation of such waste. It was not until his farewell address that he warned of the military-industrial complex.

Although Eisenhower's top priority was a US-Soviet arms control agreement, he never got one, because the Soviets realized that it would lock in vast superiority for the United States in nuclear weapons.[18] Yet after Joseph Stalin's death in 1953, his successors in the USSR dropped the Marxist-Leninist belief in the inevitability of war with capitalism in favor of peaceful coexistence, largely because they realized the power of nuclear weapons to incinerate the world.[19] So Ike essentially was at least partly responsible for his own failure in arms control. However, he did establish a voluntary, informal moratorium with the Soviets on nuclear tests, which later turned into the Partial Nuclear Test Ban Treaty during John F. Kennedy's administration; that treaty banned the testing of nuclear weapons in the atmosphere, underwater, and in outer space.[20]

The excessive buildup of nuclear weapons past a minimum force needed to deter nuclear and conventional attacks against an intrinsically secure United States was the result of the insidious military-industrial complex that Eisenhower complained about in his famous farewell address. But Ike had not dismantled that complex or the sizeable military forces that it provisioned, both of which Truman had created during the Korean War. After that war, during Ike's tenure, even with his defense budget reductions, the United States retained a large peacetime military for the first time in its history. That large force in turn justified the continuation of the military-industrial complex about which Eisenhower later complained. Ike's alerting the country to the dangers to liberty and the republic of the "unwarranted influence" of such a complex was a step in the right direction, but he could have done more to combat it during his two terms in office.

Overseas Restraint Except Covertly

Although Ike rejected the laudable philosophy of overseas restraint propounded by Senator Robert Taft's wing of the Republican Party, he did have a more restrained view of fighting the Cold War than Democrat Harry Truman did. Eisenhower said, "I hate war as only a soldier who has lived it can."[21]

An End to the Stalemated Korean War

As he took office, Eisenhower discovered that Mark Clark, the US commander in Korea, and South Korean dictator Syngman Rhee wanted to re-escalate the Korean War to invade North Korea. Douglas MacArthur, the ex–US commander there who had been defrocked by Truman, suggested to Ike going even further and bombing targets in China or spreading radioactive waste along the Chinese–North Korean border to trap Chinese forces that were in Korea. Ike sympathized with these hawks but said that the exhausted American public would not support more war, and he laudably ended the stalemated war with an armistice. He did so by a carrot-and-stick approach. For the carrot, in mid-April 1953, Eisenhower gave a "Chance for Peace" speech directed at the Soviets after Joseph Stalin had died earlier in the year. Stalin had been using the intractable Korean War to bleed the West of resources, but after Stalin's death, new Soviet leaders wanted a settlement of the conflict to better relations with the United States.[22]

For the stick, in May 1953, Eisenhower told China, via an Indian diplomat, that if the Chinese did not rapidly negotiate an armistice in the Korean War, the United States would launch nuclear attacks on China. The next month, the armistice talks made rapid progress. Yet, journalist Evan Thomas believed that Ike's conventional bombing of civilian targets—dams, hydroelectric plants, and irrigation canals—to create famine by flooding rice crops devastated and demoralized North Koreans and their sponsors into ending the war.[23] (Some would just call such bombing a war crime.)

The final hurdle to settlement of the war was Rhee of South Korea, who said that he could not accept any agreement that did not end with a united Korea. Ike gave Rhee a choice of a mutual defense treaty with the United States, including the stationing of US forces there, and generous military and economic aid if he accepted a divided Korea. If Rhee did not, he faced American withdrawal of its military forces. Rhee then saw the light and accepted a divided peninsula, and this sweet deal for South Korea largely endures to this day—decades after the war has been over and long after the South Korean economic miracle has given the South approximately thirty-five times the GDP of the North.

Restraint in Other Hot Spots in the Developing World

After getting out of Korea, Eisenhower wanted to avoid unimportant brushfire wars, yet put the USSR and China on notice that he would respond strongly to any significant real threat to US security.[24]

Ike laudably confirmed Truman's decision to withdraw the US Navy from the waters between the Chinese mainland and Taiwan, which Truman had deployed there during the Korean War. This move made it less likely that Chiang Kai-shek, the ruler of Taiwan, could drag the United States into a war with Communist China. Yet Chiang kept trying to do so. He had 58,000 troops on the small islands of Quemoy and Matsu just off the Chinese coast. In 1955, the Chinese began shelling them. During the dust-up, Eisenhower asked Congress in advance for the authority to act militarily without a declaration of war, which they provided. (Ike's action was at least better than what is often done now, which is unilateral presidential warfare without any congressional approval.)

Eisenhower then threatened the use of tactical nuclear weapons and urged Chiang to transfer the provocative troops from the islands to help defend Taiwan. Ike was trying to avoid war and was not really going to use the nuclear weapons unless China took the islands and used them to mount an extremely difficult, and therefore unlikely, amphibious assault over 150 miles of water to attack Taiwan. The French and the British, however, became alarmed, because they astutely did not want a nuclear war with China over some offshore rocks.

But Ike's needlessly risky nuclear brinksmanship did lead to US-Chinese direct negotiations, thus ending the crisis. Nevertheless, Eisenhower unfortunately signed a treaty with Taiwan to provide its defense.[25]

In 1958, China shelled the islands again and Chiang this time sent 100,000 troops there, but Ike's views on nuclear weapons had evolved, because the Soviets now had many more such arms; he did not threaten to use them again.[26] Eisenhower negotiated a diplomatic solution in which China would stop shelling and Taiwan would reduce its troops on the islands.[27] In reality, Eisenhower should have quietly told Chiang he was on his own, thus avoiding a risky and nonstrategic alliance and lessening the chance of a nuclear war over mere granite outcroppings in the sea.

In 1954, Eisenhower commendably refused to provide much assistance to the beleaguered French colonial garrison of Dien Bien Phu in Vietnam, avoiding what could have become a US quagmire. Ike felt that the real problems were China and Russia, and if they could not be attacked directly, the United States would be forced into fighting a series of limited wars that would drain the US military and ruin the American economy.

Unfortunately, however, Eisenhower's subsequent policies in Vietnam helped lead to the future American bog there during the Johnson and Nixon administrations. Ike did not sign the Geneva accords ending French involvement in Indochina, which were supposed to temporarily partition Vietnam until a nationwide election could be held in 1956 that would elect a government for all of Vietnam. Fearing that the popular Communist Ho Chi Minh would win such an election, Eisenhower supported South Vietnamese violation of the accord by not holding one. Because the North Vietnamese could not take all of Vietnam by vote, they tried to take it by force.

Ike had already begun aiding the new South Vietnamese government of Ngo Dinh Diem (which even he admitted lacked popular legitimacy), including the provision of money, arms, training, and US military advisers. This small US troop presence was later escalated into more than 500,000 US combat troops in the 1960s. Although Truman had made the initial mistake of trying to help the French reassert control of their restive Indochinese colony after World War II, Eisenhower essentially took over French colonialism when the French left in 1954. Ike saw "falling dominoes" in Southeast Asia, as the

Communists might conquer a country and use it as a base to take over another neighboring nation, with the process repeated.

To bolster these nations against the Communist threat, Ike formed the Southeast Asian Treaty Organization (SEATO), another one of his entangling Pax Americana alliances around the world designed to check Communism. The SEATO alliance would drag the United States into a ground quagmire in Vietnam that would last many years and cost 58,000 American and many more Vietnamese lives.

But the United States did not always side with colonialism. To woo the Egyptian dictator, Gamal Abdul Nasser, the United States, Britain, and the World Bank agreed to help him build the Aswan Dam. However, Nasser, committed to remaining unaligned with any bloc during the Cold War, rejected a US requirement to form a mutual defense alliance in order to buy US weapons to counter Israel. Nasser instead decided to buy arms from Communist Czechoslovakia and recognized Red China diplomatically. Ike saw Nasser jumping in bed with the Reds, and Congress effectively killed Nasser's dam project. In retaliation, Nasser nationalized the Suez Canal, which was owned and operated by France and Britain and allowed them to transport their oil from the Persian Gulf. Britain approached the Eisenhower administration about using force to liberate the canal—as it had done before the successful 1953 US-British coup against President Mohammad Mossadegh in Iran, after the Iranian government expropriated Britain's economic assets. Eisenhower rejected the British offer, however, and warned the British against taking military action.

Then the British lied to Ike and conspired with the French and Israelis to use force to take back the canal. Israel invaded Egypt through the Sinai, but before it got to the canal, the British and French used the Israeli invasion as a pretext to launch airborne and amphibious landings to "protect" the canal from the Israeli-Egyptian fighting. Britain intervened under the 1954 Anglo-Egyptian Treaty allowing Britain to intercede if the canal was threatened. In the end, the plan was that Nasser would be replaced by a government friendlier to the West and Israel.

The British expected Eisenhower to delay or block any action in the United Nations that would complicate the effort to get rid of Nasser. However,

Eisenhower did not believe that Egypt's nationalization of the canal provided adequate justification for war. Ike, who had orchestrated coups in Iran in 1953 and Guatemala in 1954 when Western economic interests had been nationalized, shocked the British by introducing, with the support of the Soviets, a UN resolution for an immediate ceasefire with the invaders just miles short of the canal. Ike gained leverage on the British and French to comply with the resolution, halt the fighting, and withdraw their forces by interrupting their oil supplies, threatening financial pressure on the British by driving down the value of the pound, and providing international loans to Britain only if it complied with US demands. Also, the Soviets threatened to intervene militarily on the Egyptian side, leading to a speedy resolution of the crisis with Nasser still in control of the canal.[28] Both Nasser and the Soviets gained strategically in the Middle East after this crisis.

Ike and most Americans disapproved of imperialist interventions by other powers but never saw their interventions in the same way (this view holds true to this day). In the 1956 Suez Crisis, although Eisenhower's advisers warned him that his decisions would adversely affect his reelection chances a few days later, he bravely aligned against Israel, believing that the United States should honor its obligations under the Tripartite Agreement of 1950 to guarantee existing borders between Israel and the Arab countries. Ike even contemplated using US forces to stop the Israelis if they failed to halt their advance. Yet Ike's attempt to take the moral high ground in the crisis won him few friends in the developing world because of prior US imperialistic behavior. And Ike—who had previously had a more distant relationship to Israel than Truman, the president who was instrumental in creating that state—had to promise the Israelis long-term economic and military support to get them out of the Egyptian Sinai. Also, US intervention did not stop Nasser from trying to establish a pan-Arab state; in fact, it emboldened him. But the American people concurred with Eisenhower's actions, reelecting him by a large margin.[29]

At the same time as the Suez Crisis of 1956, the Hungarians revolted against Soviet power, returned ousted Hungarian premier Imre Nagy to power, and announced Hungary's withdrawal from the Warsaw Pact. The Soviets invaded Hungary to put down the revolt.[30] Although the CIA had encouraged the Hungarians in their revolt and they were begging for American help, Ike was not going to aid a rebellion in the sphere of influence of a rival nuclear superpower, either overtly or covertly, which would have risked escalation to nuclear war.

However, Eisenhower did want preapproved congressional authority to cooperate with Middle Eastern countries whose independence was threatened and to provide military aid or US troops to these nations if they requested them (the Eisenhower Doctrine).[31] The only time in eight years in office that Eisenhower used the US military to directly attack or invade another country was his overt intervention in Lebanon in 1958 to support his doctrine. This intervention in the affairs of a small, unimportant country was strange for a noninterventionist like Ike and may have been done merely to answer his more interventionist critics. With Soviet support, and encouraged by US intervention in the Suez Crisis against Israel, Britain, and France, Nasserites were trying to collapse pro-Western governments in the Middle East and establish a pan-Arab state. Pro-Nasser Iraqi Army officers murdered the royal family in Iraq. Camille Chamoun, the Christian president of Lebanon, took advantage of the coup in Iraq to appeal for American help to counter what he asserted was an imminent pro-Nasser Syrian invasion. Yet Chamoun was really trying to deal with Muslim street mobs howling about his attempt to remain in power using unconstitutional means. Although the United States had no vital interests in Lebanon, the Saudis wanted Ike to demonstrate his commitment to allies in the Middle East, a region that Eisenhower believed was more strategic to the United States than East Asia was.[32]

As US troops hit the beach in Lebanon—in an intervention beget by Ike's intervention in the Suez Crisis two years before—the only resistance they met was quizzical looks from startled sunbathers. Also, US naval forces were sent to the Persian Gulf to protect oil-producing Kuwait, and the British sent paratroopers to protect Jordan's King Hussein from a feared coup.[33]

The Overuse of Covert Action

In general, Eisenhower was an artist at downplaying international crises to avoid overt American military intervention, thus avoiding escalation with the Soviets. Yet at the same time, he overused the CIA in trying to covertly topple governments while also escaping such escalation. When the popularly elected Iranian Prime Minister Mohammed Mossadegh threatened British oil interests in Iran, Britain organized an international boycott of Iranian oil and began to plot a coup against him. Although Mossadegh pleaded for additional US assistance to counter the British boycott, the CIA helped the British overthrow him in 1953 and reinstate the more compliant Shah Reza Pahlevi. The autocratic Shah then brutalized his people to such an extent that he was finally overthrown by an Islamist revolution in the late 1970s. Because the Shah was a client of the United States, bad relations have ensued with the Islamist Iranian government down to the present. Therefore, the ramifications of Ike's coup have lasted to today.[34]

The success in overthrowing Mossadegh in Iran led Eisenhower to overuse covert action as a tool of foreign policy more generally. Similar to the situation in Iran, a popularly elected leader in Guatemala, Jacobo Arbenz, had begun nationalizing economic Western interests in the early 1950s. In a land reform program, Arbenz began expropriating much of the American corporation United Fruit Company's property holdings. Dictators in neighboring Nicaragua and Honduras were also unnerved by Arbenz's precedent. Eisenhower had visions of toppling dominoes to Communism in Latin America and thus authorized the CIA to train a rebel army to overthrow Arbenz. This force was much like the insurgent force that Ike later authorized the agency to train to overthrow Cuba's Fidel Castro, which later led to the Bay of Pigs fiasco during the administration of John F. Kennedy.

Yet Eisenhower had overestimated the likelihood of a Communist take-over in Guatemala; it was the anti-Communist Guatemalan Army that held the bulk of the power in the country, not Arbenz. Communists were few in number in the country. Ike had ham-handedly reversed the "Good Neighbor" policy of Herbert Hoover and Franklin D. Roosevelt in Latin America and gone back to the blunt interventionism that the United States had practiced in the region from the Spanish-American War to the Great Depression. The Guatemalan Army was afraid of direct US military intervention and refused to back Arbenz. The United States passed over leaders more popular with Guatemalan citizens and installed a US quisling. Ike also had a role in over-throwing Patrice Lumumba in the Congo after he flirted with the Soviets.[35]

Unlike Harry Truman, however, Ike laudably did not let the CIA launch covert operations on its own authority, bringing them under the control of the White House's National Security Council and establishing the Foreign Intelligence Advisory Board to provide independent oversight.[36]

Miscellaneous Foreign Policy

In addition to an excessive reliance on CIA covert action, Ike also attempted to battle Communism by using copious amounts of foreign aid. Yet such aid distorts economies of recipient countries, creates unneeded dependence and corruption, and insulates such nations from the need to make free market economic reforms that would strengthen their economies. The United States should have supported countries' ability to stand on their own economically as barriers to Communist subversion, but Ike's policy merely increased such dependence.

In pushback to FDR's wartime executive agreements with Joseph Stalin (especially at Yalta), which Roosevelt did not allow the Senate to ratify, the Bricker Amendment, supported by most Republicans and some Democrats in the Senate, specified that if Congress did not ratify an international agreement, it had to be approved by all the state legislatures before it would bind the United States. Ike was not thrilled with what FDR had done, but he believed FDR's actions were well within the president's powers as commander-in-chief during wartime and tried to stop the amendment.[37] The nation's founders would have probably disagreed with Eisenhower, because they originally construed the commander-in-chief role only narrowly as commanding troops on the battlefield, but they probably also would have regarded the Bricker Amendment as unconstitutional. The founders intended all arrangements with other countries to be ratified by the Senate as treaties; no alternative mechanisms for approval, solely by the president or by the states, were mentioned in the Constitution. At any rate, the Bricker Amendment was fortunately defeated, principally because of Ike's efforts.

Slight Expansion of the State

Eisenhower turned his immense popularity into legislative success. Despite the Democrats controlling Congress after the 1954 election,[38] he got 80 percent of his proposed legislation passed, a postwar high. Ike even pushed a progressive domestic program through a Republican Congress during the first two years of his presidency. Despite the expansion of domestic programs, Ike's cuts in defense eventually led to a reduction in federal spending as a percentage of GDP. Along with Clinton, who bested Ike's spending reduction as a portion of GDP, Eisenhower was one of only two presidents since Truman to achieve this laudable outcome.[39]

Beyond the New Deal

Eisenhower did not want to roll back the New Deal, which he thought would be political suicide for Republicans, but intended to improve management of the welfare state and, in some areas, expand it. Although Ike was the first Republican president after the long twenty-year FDR/Truman period, he can be blamed for some expansion of the New Deal, but it is probably a stretch to blame him for not rolling it back. First, in the American political system, which works like a ratchet, once bad laws are passed they are hard to repeal. A majority of both houses of Congress must vote to rescind a law, and a minority of Senators can filibuster a repeal (or the president can veto the same, requiring a two-thirds majority of both houses to override it).

Second, long before Ike's presidency (as early as the Republican Party's platform in 1936)—for reasons of political expediency, because the New Deal was wildly popular during the Great Depression—the Republican Party had accepted in principle some key New Deal programs, including Social Security, the regulation of business practices, and the right of labor to organize. In fact, by 1944, the Republican Party had actually endorsed an expansion of Social Security to all employees not already covered. The party had also learned that the public objected to rolling back the New Deal when the Republicans had temporary second thoughts and promised to roll back portions of it, thus ensuring long-term Republican support for it. In other words, the party had long bought into the welfare state before Ike even came on the scene.[40] Thus, in general, Ike sought to merely "hold the line" against more New Deal–like programs, but exceptions existed to this status quo orientation.

In keeping with the Republican Party's willingness to expand Social Security, Eisenhower enlarged the program and created a new department of Health, Education, and Welfare (HEW) to administer it. Ike wanted people who had never paid into the Social Security System to get benefits—for example, those who retired before the advent of the system in 1935 or shortly after it was enacted. Although his new secretary of HEW criticized this expansion as "a criminal raid on the Social Security Trust Fund," Eisenhower ignored her and added ten million beneficiaries to the system.

The congressional Republican leadership correctly pointed out to Ike that the Constitution did not say anything about the federal government undertaking the functions of health, education, and welfare and had therefore left them to state and local governments; Ike did not care and pushed the legislation creating the new department through Congress anyway. Jimmy Carter's later ill-advised creation of the Departments of Energy and Education was not quite as bad as Ike's selected expansion of government, because the federal government was already doing these unconstitutional functions before Carter took office.

Truman and Ike both tried and failed to enact varying inefficient schemes for the government to ensure that those not covered by health insurance got it. Also, Ike provided federal "vocational rehabilitation" for people with physical disabilities but then stretched it to include many more people. Furthermore, Eisenhower expanded federal aid for public housing that had begun during World War II—an inefficient means to provide dwellings for people who could not afford them. Most important, he initiated the largest public works program in American history—an interstate highway system that was financed by a gas tax—and helped initiate the St. Lawrence Seaway project, which built locks so the Great Lakes region would have access to the Eastern Seaboard.[41] Ike justified the interstate highway system as a way to evacuate people from cities after a nuclear war.[42] Lastly, Ike launched urban renewal for blighted cities.

In addition, Eisenhower thought that eliminating labor laws and governmental agricultural programs would be political suicide.[43] So he did not hesitate to mess with the imperfect markets for labor and farm products. In fact, he increased the minimum wage by a third[44] and expanded it to cover millions more workers. Counterintuitively, any minimum wage hurts the poorest people, because as the price of labor goes up, businesses demand less of it, and thus throw the least skilled into the unemployment line. Yet, in general, as Europe was nationalizing industries, Eisenhower was abolishing wartime wage and price controls.[45]

Although his secretary of agriculture regarded the government's providing support for minimum prices to farmers as welfare and complained about farmers "feeding at the public trough," agriculturalists were an important Republican constituency, and like FDR, Ike believed any farm recession would migrate to the cities. Thus, Eisenhower massively increased agricultural subsidies, resulting in more than half of farmers' net income being provided by the federal government. Farmers also got Public Law 480, which compensated them for any losses when exporting their crops; such agricultural "dumping" abroad hurt agricultural industries in poor developing countries and soured relations with developed allied nations.[46] Furthermore, most of the money involved in such welfare programs went and still goes to the biggest, wealthiest farmers.

The Expansion of the Imperial Presidency

Ike added to the imperial presidency by appointing the first White House chief of staff, Sherman Adams, and creating a staff secretariat to support Adams. Adams later had to resign for taking gifts from a favor-seeking friend. Also, Eisenhower elevated the profile of the National Security Council, which Truman had established, and created the post of Special Assistant to the President for National Security Affairs (known today as the national security advisor).

Like Truman, Eisenhower unfairly ruined the careers of thousands of people accused of being disloyal, security risks, or Communists. One of Eisenhower's victims was Robert Oppenheimer—the scientist who was the driving force behind the atomic bomb (A-bomb)—for his opposition to the development of the much more potent hydrogen bomb (H-bomb), which Oppenheimer believed was so powerful that it would be used to destroy cities instead of military targets. Truman and Eisenhower both tried to take unjustifiable preemptive actions to root out "subversives" so they would not be criticized as being soft on Communism. However, unlike Democrat Truman, Ike refused to publicly oppose popular Senator Joe McCarthy, the anti-Communist crusader and demagogue, for fear of losing the support of the conservative wing of the Republican Party. Eisenhower said that he preferred to undermine McCarthy from behind the scenes.

In 1954, when Joe McCarthy went after the Army for coddling Communists, Ike got the attorney general to rule that he could order the Army not to respond to McCarthy's congressional subpoenas. Eisenhower then stretched the ruling to cover the entire executive branch. Although George Washington had even dubiously claimed some limited authority to withhold information from Congress, no mention of such executive privilege is made in the Constitution. Since Andrew Jackson's presidency, discussion between a president and his staff personnel or cabinet members had been questionably privileged from Congress to shroud what orders he gave them and what information he received from them. The purpose of this limited form of executive privilege was to ensure that the president got frank advice from his closest advisers. Yet Ike made the ambitious and unconstitutional claim that this executive privilege allowed the entire executive branch to decline to give Congress testimony or documents.

Although Eisenhower invoked this broader claim of executive privilege for the understandable reason of protecting the Army and other executive agencies from a raging and dangerous congressional demagogue, Eisenhower's act created the unconstitutional doctrine of modern executive privilege, which would be partially overturned during the Watergate scandal almost two decades later. Ike got away with it because McCarthy failed to sue in federal court. In spite of Ike's victory on executive privilege, it was unneeded; McCarthy's repellant televised rant against the Army vindicated the Army and was the end of his threat to the republic. The Senate censured McCarthy for his shabby conduct.[47] McCarthy had gone too far and had begun to attack fellow Republicans.[48]

A Mixed Record on Civil Rights

On civil rights, Ike had a mixed record. He wanted slow progress, so as not to provoke riots, lynchings, or even civil disobedience. In 1953, Eisenhower ended segregation in Washington, DC, and ensured implementation of Truman's lagging 1948 directive to desegregate the military, ordering an end to resistance to racial integration in the Navy.

However, in 1954, Ike enraged Earl Warren, his own appointee for chief justice of the US Supreme Court, by his ham-handed attempt to influence the Supreme Court's coming ruling in *Brown v. Board of Education* that the "Equal Protection" clause of the Fourteenth Amendment to the Constitution (states are required to provide equal protection under the law for everyone) required the desegregation of public schools. Eisenhower's attempt to limit desegregation contradicted his own Justice Department, which filed a brief in the *Brown* case supporting desegregation.[49] Chief Justice Warren also criticized Eisenhower for not endorsing the Court's decision, but Ike felt he should not under the Constitution's separation of powers. However, Ike should have considered the separation of powers rationale when he was trying to mitigate the court's likely ruling in advance.

Ike, however, did appoint Earl Warren as chief justice in the first place—a man who struck a major blow for civil rights in the *Brown v. Board* ruling by writing for the court, "We conclude that in the field of public education the doctrine of 'separate but equal' has no place. Separate education facilities are inherently unequal." Yet in 1956, when the admission of an African-American student to the University of Alabama caused rioting and the university suspended the student, allegedly for her own safety, Eisenhower refused to send troops and the school remained segregated for another seven years.[50] In sum, Ike did little to support desegregation during his first term.[51]

However, in 1957, although Ike did not believe coercive force was the best path toward desegregation, he reversed his policy at the request of the mayor of Little Rock, Arkansas. To enforce the equal protection clause of the Fourteenth Amendment and snuff out Arkansas's defiance of federal courts, Eisenhower sent regular Army troops there and federalized the Arkansas National Guard to quell violence and enforce federal desegregation at the high school, as commanded by the Supreme Court's *Brown v. Board* decision. He took such actions in the face of a defiant Arkansas governor Orval E. Faubus, who had called out the state's National Guard forces to prevent desegregation. At this point, Ike was not facing reelection, but his action did impair for a while the inroads Republicans were making into a solidly Democratic South.

In the end, as the children returned to school, the Supreme Court ruled against further delays of desegregation. In retaliation, Governor Faubus closed all Arkansas public high schools for the 1958 year.[52] Therefore, Eisenhower's use of federal troops may have been initially counterproductive. Furthermore, technically, the governor or state legislature of an affected state, according to the Constitution, must request the militia to be sent—not a city mayor—and Congress—not the president—should have been the one to call forth the militia—not federal troops.

In addition, Ike signed the first civil rights bill since post–Civil War Reconstruction. The bill was designed to enforce the Fourteenth and Fifteenth Amendments to the Constitution but was weakened as it went through Congress. The final federal law negated state laws and practices that had effectively denied African-American voting rights guarantees under the Fifteenth Amendment. All such aforementioned federal action was generally justified, because the Fourteenth and Fifteenth Amendments previously were not being enforced in the South.

More generally, Eisenhower appointed four judges on what became the historic Warren Court, which incorporated the Bill of Rights under the due process and equal protection clauses of the Fourteenth Amendment, thereby requiring states to safeguard the same rights that the federal government had to guarantee under the Bill of Rights.[53] However, Ike said that his two biggest mistakes were appointing liberals Earl Warren and William Brennan to the Supreme Court.[54]

Conclusion

Eisenhower was mildly progressive on domestic issues, but conservative on spending, including the cutting of defense spending. He called himself a "responsible progressive" and believed that the government should redistribute wealth to the less fortunate.[55] Essentially he cut defense spending and transferred part of it to social programs and used the rest to cut Truman's budget deficit. Overall, he and Clinton were the only post-Truman presidents to cut federal spending as a portion of GDP. Despite his Progressive tendencies in the social sphere, this reduction of federal spending as a percentage of GDP and his restrained foreign policy (at least overtly) make him one of the best post–World War II presidents.

To cut the defense budget, Ike bought cheaper nuclear weapons instead of more expensive conventional arms, but the nuclear buildup was much more than the minimum nuclear force needed for deterring a nuclear or conventional attack on the United States. Also, Ike avoided intervening abroad directly with US combat forces (except in the bizarre case of Lebanon in 1958) but overused CIA covert operations to overthrow unfriendly governments, some freely elected, in the developing world.

In other ways of attempting to counter Communism, Eisenhower ratcheted up foreign aid and created a Pax Americana alliance system around the world. The latter essentially gave the United States a globe-girdling informal empire, which was costly, unneeded for US security, and overextended American power and foreign policy.

Yet historian Stephen E. Ambrose summarized Eisenhower's strong suit—handling crises during the Cold War:

> What Eisenhower had done best was managing crises. The crisis with Syngman Rhee in early 1953, and the simultaneous crisis with the Chinese Communists over the POW issue and the armistice; the crisis over Dien Bien Phu in 1954, and over Quemoy and Matsu in 1955; the Hungarian and Suez crises of 1956; the Sputnik and Little Rock crises of 1957; the Formosa Resolution crisis of 1958; the Berlin crisis of 1959, the U-2 crisis of 1960—Eisenhower managed each one without overreacting, without going to war, without increasing defense spending, without frightening people half out of their wits. He downplayed each one, insisted that a solution could be found, and then found one. It was a magnificent performance.[56]

5

Watergate and a More Restrained Foreign Policy

ACCORDING TO CONSERVATIVE Brion McClanahan, "[Richard] Nixon has an undeserved reputation as an admirer of limited government—not to be confused with originalism. His fight for executive privilege during the Watergate scandal betrayed his firm commitment to a more substantial role for the executive branch."[1] The Vietnam War and Watergate, however, spurred the large Democratic majorities in Congress to at least temporarily push back, both at home and aboard, against the ever-expanding imperial presidency.[2]

Although Nixon (president from 1969 to 1974) resigned in disgrace for illegal acts, which has been his main legacy, he also had some foreign policy successes that somewhat offset this corruption. Although he had always marketed himself as an anti-Communist hawk, as president he astutely played China and the Soviet Union, bitter Communist rivals, against one another by creating a diplomatic opening to an isolated China and establishing an easing of relations (détente) with the USSR. By creating this more benign international environment, Nixon could more indirectly assist countries in fighting Communism instead of relying on US forces (the Nixon Doctrine).

Corruption

During the 1968 presidential campaign between Richard Nixon and Democratic candidate Hubert Humphrey, Nixon became nervous that sitting Democratic President Lyndon B. Johnson (LBJ), by halting the bombing of North Vietnam, was going to get the North Vietnamese to participate in peace talks to end the Vietnam War, thus adversely affecting Nixon's chances to get elected president. The bombing halt did not lead to peace talks, however, because South Vietnam would not negotiate with the North, as a result of the Nixon campaign using a back channel to tell the South Vietnamese that they would get a better deal if he became president. To find out what Nixon was up to, LBJ used wiretaps to spy on his campaign, thus leaving Nixon a bad precedent for doing similar things when he became president.[3] Nixon's near treasonous act also gave a hint to his ruthless and paranoid character.

As early as 1969, the paranoid Nixon ordered illegal wiretaps on reporters and White House aides, and repaying the favor that John F. Kennedy and Lyndon B. Johnson had done to him and the right wing, Nixon used the Internal Revenue Service to audit the tax returns of leftist groups, journalists, and Democratic critics. The White House staff even coordinated efforts to disrupt Democratic political campaigns.[4]

Nixon's legacy will always be clouded by his resignation, which was necessitated by his illegal and unconstitutional use of federal power to attempt to cover up the Watergate scandal—dirty tricks done in the 1972 presidential campaign despite a very weak Democratic challenger.[5]

Nixon had lost the 1960 presidential election narrowly and won the 1968 election in the same way; in the 1972 contest, he did not want any more close calls.[6] In 1971, after Daniel Ellsberg, a whistleblower, leaked the Pentagon Papers—a secret Pentagon history of US involvement in Vietnam that did not paint the US in a favorable light but also did not reflect poorly on the Nixon administration—the administration had contracted with a team of former CIA operatives to plug further government leaks and gather intelligence on the Democrats, earning the group the nickname the "plumbers."

The plumbers were caught breaking into the offices of the Democratic National Committee at the Watergate hotel and office complex in Washington, DC.[7] After the burglary, Nixon was recorded in June 1972 on his Oval Office taping system obstructing justice by agreeing to tell the FBI that the break-in was a national security operation that should not be investigated. When this "smoking gun" tape became public in 1974 as a result of the efforts of the Watergate Special Prosecutor, Nixon was forced to resign or face certain impeachment by Congress.[8] Nixon's illegal and unconstitutional behavior in the Watergate scandal was so severe and demonstrable with the smoking gun evidence that he had no choice but to resign or be eventually ousted.

Eminent legal historian Raoul Berger has noted, "Executive privilege—the President's claim of constitutional authority to withhold information from Congress—is a myth." Chief Justice Warren Burger agreed, "[T]here is not a scintilla of evidence in the constitutional records of a design to curtail the historical scope of legislative inquiry or to authorize executive withholding of *any* [emphasis in original] information from Congress." Nevertheless, Nixon tried to use executive privilege to shield the White House tapes from Congress and the public, although he was not the first president to invoke the doctrine. Under the Constitution, the president is charged with executing the laws, and thus Congress, which passes the laws, must have all information about how the chief executive is doing so.[9] The Supreme Court did not go this far in its ruling against the president in *United States v. Nixon*, but said executive privilege did not apply to obscuring potential illegal wrongdoing by the president.

In October 1973, Nixon plotted to get Vice President Spiro Agnew to resign, which Agnew did after pleading "no contest" to income tax violations related to bribes he took during his tenure as Maryland's governor; he was still committing illegal acts as vice president. Forty-eight hours later, Nixon announced he was nominating House Minority Leader Gerald Ford to be the new vice president.[10] Nixon resigned in August 1974, making Ford president.

The most important decision that Gerald Ford made as president (he held the office from 1974 to 1977) was whether or not to pardon Richard Nixon. Seeming to reverse the position he took during his Senate confirmation hearing for vice president, in which Ford stated, "I do not think the public would stand for it,"[11] he granted the pardon a month after becoming president in 1974. Ford's press secretary quit in disgust, and Ford's approval rating in the polls plummeted from 71 percent to 50 percent in the week after the pardon was announced.[12] Some accused Ford of trading the pardon to Nixon for the presidency. Nixon had chosen Ford for the vice presidency less than a year before Nixon resigned the presidency during the summer of 1974. As the minority leader in the House of Representatives, Ford had a reputation for integrity and was thus acceptable to Democrats for the vice presidency.

By late 1973, Nixon was in trouble over Watergate, and everyone knew Ford, when selected for vice president, could eventually be president. The Democratic Speaker of the House Carl Albert even said, "Congress made Jerry Ford president." According to Albert, he and Democratic Senate Majority

Leader Mike Mansfield gave Nixon only one choice for vice president—Gerald Ford.[13] Nixon also thought Ford would be a good choice for vice president, because Congress would be less likely to impeach him and install an untrained man in the White House. However, Nixon's choice boomeranged, because as his criminality was increasingly exposed in 1974, Ford's perceived integrity acted as a safety net for a Congress that was inclined to push out Nixon.[14]

Although a shady deal between Nixon and Ford exchanging the presidency for a pardon seems unlikely, Ford's pardon did undermine the republic. The US Constitution gives the president the unconstrained power to grant pardons for "Offences against the United States." To be an "offence" under the US judicial system, which presumes innocence until guilt is proven, one has to be convicted of a crime before one can be pardoned. Yet Ford's unconstitutional early pardon on Nixon's terms essentially gave the ex-president immunity from any humiliating trial and sentencing, thus putting the former president above his fellow citizens and the law. At the time, the American public realized this reality, destroying much of the residual public trust in government that Watergate had already greatly shrunk and making the pardon so unpopular that it helped lead to Ford's defeat by Jimmy Carter in the 1976 presidential election.[15] Yet this negative view was short-lived, and Ford's narrative—that he was selflessly trying to heal the country by ending the national nightmare of Watergate—has prevailed over time. At the time of Ford's funeral in 2006, historians and journalists largely parroted Ford's original narrative in citing the healing as his major presidential accomplishment.

Yet a closer inspection would reveal more selfish motives for and more adverse consequences from the pardon. To have any chance of winning the presidency on his own in 1976, Ford had to put Watergate behind him and his party quickly. Having Nixon's trial during an election campaign would have been a political disaster. Also, Ford did not want a Watergate trial to suck the oxygen out of any new policy agenda that he might propose (for the same reason, Barack Obama declined to prosecute George W. Bush administration officials for torture and other illegalities in the "war on terror").

Finally, in a republic, pardoning the president for illegal acts before he is convicted does put him above the law, and that is a very bad outcome. Although a trial of Nixon might have extended the "national nightmare," the republic would have been better off in the long-term by holding the chief executive accountable for unlawful behavior. Deterrence of bad behavior by future chief executives likely would have been enhanced. Sometimes living in a republic is not easy.

A Surprising Domestic Liberal

Although Nixon purported to be a conservative, his use of federal power for such corrupt ends seems the antithesis of a small government philosophy; in fact, Nixon was mainly a political opportunist. His conservative rhetoric belied a leftist policy record, and before Barack Obama, Nixon was the last progressive president.

Nixon had the most comprehensive environmental initiatives of any president—policies that would have been constitutional for states to implement but not for the federal government. He signed the National Environmental Policy Act, which required environmental impact statements for federal projects and created the Council on Environmental Quality to enforce them. He signed the Clean Air Act of 1970, which regulated vehicle and power plant emissions. He directed the Interior Department, by executive order, to establish almost 650 new national parks.[16]

Nixon created the Environmental Protection Agency (EPA), by unconstitutional executive order, to increase regulation of business as it related to the environment, and the Occupational Safety and Health Administration (OSHA), which strangled businesses with added workplace regulations. The EPA and OSHA violated the Constitution's separation of powers by including legislative, executive, and judicial functions in single agencies.[17]

Nixon also created the Office of Economic Opportunity in the White House to monitor the hiring of minority groups. Affirmative action to give preferential hiring to minorities started during his administration, and Nixon enforced the Supreme Court's "forced busing" of schoolchildren to achieve racial integration. However, the quotas to achieve racial balance in both busing and affirmative action likely violated the Civil Rights Act of 1964. Congress passed and Nixon signed the Education Amendments of 1972 ending future school busing and mandating Title IX equality in educational programs, including sports, despite the Constitution's failure to specify a federal role in education.

Laudably, more schools were desegregated in 1970 than in any year since the Supreme Court's *Brown v. Board of Education* decision in 1954 requiring it. In fact, Nixon really ended public school segregation in the South, contradicting his reputation as a conservative. However, an ambitious government effort to encourage black capitalism produced scant results.

The Family Assistance Act, which replaced government welfare for the poor with a guaranteed annual minimal income, and a radical comprehensive health insurance reform plan both got stuck in Congress. Yet, Nixon still spent at a greater rate on social programs than Lyndon Johnson, the architect of the Great Society. In fact, Nixon and Ford annually increased money spent on social programs more than any other post-Truman presidents.[18]

In sum, Nixon was a liberal activist on welfare, environmental protection, and Native American rights.[19] Finally, Nixon ended the military draft, creating the volunteer army of today—a great stride for liberty and military efficacy, but again not in line with his conservative reputation.

Progressive Economics

Economically, Nixon became a "progressive." Beginning in 1970, the country experienced stagflation—high inflation combined with high unemployment. It was caused by the Vietnam War, increased domestic spending under Nixon and his predecessor Johnson's Great Society program, and printing lots of money, which Nixon had pressured the Federal Reserve to do to lower interest rates and goose economic growth—thereby enhancing his reelection chances in 1972. Despite the stagflation, Nixon intimidated Arthur Burns—his handpicked chairman of the Federal Reserve, an agency supposedly independent of political meddling by the executive branch and Congress—to increase the money supply to pump up the economy in exchange for the president adopting wage and price controls to try to constrain inflation.[20] The government controls tried to artificially control only the end result—rising wages and prices—and did not deal with the aforementioned underlying causes of the inflation.

Growing the government domestically also allowed Nixon to hand out more favors to aid his reelection effort. To justify the increased government largesse, Nixon declared himself to be a "Keynesian"—formerly the stance of liberal Democrats—and thus proposed a "full employment budget" with a built-in budget deficit to allegedly encourage growth.

Also contributing to the high inflation was Nixon's inadvertent, but radical, step in 1971 of collapsing the international monetary order by taking the United States off what remained of the gold standard, thus devaluing the dollar. At the time of Nixon's policy change, because of lower US interest rates from the printing of money, foreign capital was fleeing the United States and the dollar. Foreign central banks then wanted to cash in their surplus dollars for gold—as was permitted under the Bretton Woods international monetary system, which had fixed exchange rates, with the dollar pegged at a rate of $35 per ounce of gold—thus resulting in hemorrhaging US gold reserves. To stanch the flow of gold, Nixon suspended the US government's exchange of dollars for gold, yet this action could have been constitutionally taken only by Congress. The dollar and the international financial system would no longer be in any way tied to the price of gold. Yet the principal problem that caused the crisis in the first place continued—excessive federal spending on both guns and butter, with the Federal Reserve printing bucketloads of money to pay for it, thus increasing inflation and eventually dragging the economy.[21]

Nixon's goal was not to unencumber financial globalization from the controls of the existing Bretton Woods system—Nixon actually did not want to scrap that international monetary order but did want to fulfill his personal and nationalist goals of devaluing the dollar to make US exports more competitive overseas and imports more expensive at home. Increasing American exports would put people back to work and enhance Nixon's chances of reelection.

Wealthy US allies under the American defense shield, such as Japan and West Germany, had export-driven economies and regularly undervalued their currencies to help their exports. In 1971, the United States ran its first trade deficit since 1893—that is, imports exceeded exports. From World War II to the early 1960s, current account (trade balance plus net income on foreign investments plus net cash transfers) surpluses had almost equaled US military spending overseas and outflows from American investments overseas. By the mid-1960s, the current account had deteriorated and overseas military spending remained a drain on the US balance of payments (as it does today). No thought was given to drastically reducing US military spending overseas, and in fact, Nixon wanted to liberate his cherished foreign policy, through monetary policy, from constraints imposed by periodic US balance-of-payments crises and by weaknesses in the international financial system. Thus, a nationalist response to the precipitous erosion of US balance of payments from 1969 to 1971 and a continuance of overextended American foreign and defense policies motivated Nixon's radical action, not a love for financial deregulation and allowing market forces to predominate.

However, one unintended positive result of destroying the Bretton Woods monetary system, a framework of regulated capitalism, was that eventually (in 1973) the market began to determine foreign exchange rates using floating, rather than fixed, exchange rates and thus greatly reduced pernicious efforts by the governments of industrial countries to manage the world economy collaboratively, including by manipulating exchange rates. Floating exchange rates would allow financial globalization to coexist with national monetary autonomy (which admittedly could allow abuse by politicians to print more money). The Nixon administration capped its reluctant and incoherent march toward open capital markets by commendably eliminating capital controls in January 1974. Yet, although Nixon had been reluctant to go down this route, international financial globalization may have made the scrapping of the overly rigid Bretton Woods system inevitable.

One intended positive consequence of Nixon's new policy of going off the gold standard—along with the Nixon Doctrine that replaced direct US military intervention with military and economic assistance to the developing world—was to somewhat lessen the costs of the US overseas empire. To preserve the empire up to that point, the United States had accepted that its wealthy Western allies would protect their domestic markets from US exports and that the US dollar would be overvalued to help Americans afford exports from the allies.[22] In effect, the United States was unwisely paying its allies to let it protect them from the Soviet Union. Thus, Nixon wanted US allies and friends to do more for themselves and thus lessen the economic and security burden on the United States. Devaluing the dollar by going off the gold standard was one way to do that. Although laudable, this burden-sharing was not sustained down to the present or even for the remainder of the Cold War, as Jimmy Carter, Ronald Reagan, and later George W. Bush hiked US defense spending instead of letting US allies pick up more of the load.

Curiously, stagflation at the time was blamed on the Arab embargo of oil to the United States and production cuts and concomitant worldwide petroleum price increases—all in response to US support for Israel in the 1973 Yom Kippur War in the Middle East. Later, economists debunked this notion, saying that government monetary loosening was primarily to blame for the inflation even before the oil crisis hit.[23] Yet, at the time, the TV images of people at gas stations waiting in lines to get insufficient supplies of fuel were seared forever into the American psyche. These gas lines, however, resulted from government price controls on oil that constrained price increases that would have efficiently allocated supplies to users willing to pay more and caused conservation among those who were not. Japan did not have any price controls and did not have any gas lines. Nixon did remove quotas on imported oil and replace them with tariffs, increasing the quantity of imported oil but making the system somewhat more efficient. In fact, industrial economies are very resilient to higher fuel prices, as long as market forces are allowed to work.

Nixon ineffectually battled the stagflation that he helped cause by resorting to very unconservative and unprecedented wage and price controls during peacetime, which merely artificially and temporarily constrained wages and prices while distorting the economy. At the same time that he was trying to control prices with these draconian measures, he slapped a 10-percent surcharge on imported goods, thus increasing their prices.

Nixon also meddled in agricultural markets. In 1972, a Soviet-US trade agreement allowed the Soviet Union to buy huge quantities of subsidized grain from the United States, thus raising domestic US food prices. The episode was dubbed "The Great Grain Robbery." As an example of one foolish government intervention leading to another, Nixon, to compensate for the first fiasco and to lower domestic food prices, instituted controls on exports of food—thus spreading the hurt overseas.[24] In fact, one of the few fiscally conservative things Nixon did domestically was cut NASA's space program.[25]

Despite all of his liberal social programs, from time to time Nixon also appeased the big government desires of conservatives. As part of a "get tough on crime" program, Nixon started the disastrous 1970s "war on drugs," which began the era of mass incarceration.[26] The war on drugs creatd new and longer prison sentences that were handed down for actions that should not even have been illegal—adults should have the right to control what goes into their own bodies, as long as they are not harming anyone else. More people were also jailed for committing crimes to pay rising prices for drugs; the increase in costs resulted from the war on drugs. All of this new law enforcement, prosecution, and expanded prison sentencing cost taxpayers bucketloads of money. Furthermore, overcrowded prisons became crime factories, where many nonviolent drug offenders learned how to become hardened, violent criminals. Nixon's war on drugs was—and still is—a costly failure, in terms of lives lost and the waste of massive government expenditures that have made the situation worse.

In sum, according to Brion McClanahan, "Nixon expanded several Great Society programs and initiatives; in fact, Nixon was responsible for more of the growth in unconstitutional federal regulation than Johnson himself."[27] In conclusion, much like Reagan later on, Nixon's rhetoric against big government and bureaucracy was belied by many of his actual policies.

Confused Conservative Domestic Policy

Ford inherited Nixon's stagflation and sky-high interest rates. Ford chose to run a "voluntary" campaign called "Whip in Inflation Now," which became the butt of many comedians' jokes. First, Ford asked Congress to cut spending and raise taxes to battle inflation. Perhaps more important, he laudably left the Federal Reserve alone to its natural tight money inclination.[28]

To combat the severe recession, Ford avoided the Keynesian remedy of hiking federal spending but then flip-flopped his prior tax policy, advocating a tax cut. Knowing that he would try to get elected on his own in 1976, Ford switched in 1975 from whipping inflation—which he had not succeeded in doing anyway—to stimulating economic growth. Thus, in 1976, the US economy grew by more than 5 percent. Yet, Keynesian economists were flummoxed by such stimulus initiatives in the mid-1970s, because they spiked inflation without reducing unemployment.[29]

Because Keynesian economists failed to successfully combat the recession of 1974 to 1975, advocates of free markets were emboldened. Ford had sympathy with such free marketers, but this sympathy was undermined by the influence of the "pragmatic" Secretary of State Henry Kissinger, who gave priority to politics over economics, although he did not know very much about economics in the first place. For example, Kissinger wanted to expand the US overseas food aid program and help create an international food bank to release food in times of scarcity. He advocated these policies not for humanitarian reasons, but to get geopolitical advantage. Kissinger said in a cabinet meeting, "I don't give a damn about Bangladesh or humanitarian grounds. I want it for foreign policy." Food, he said, "was useful in weaning India away from the Soviet Union" (curiously, under Nixon, Kissinger had not seemed to care much about driving a wedge between India and the USSR).[30]

Kissinger's food aid program ran afoul of domestic farmers and food consumers—the former because increased food production would lower farm prices and the latter because increased food exports would pit domestic consumers against foreign buyers for supplies. Kissinger had not learned from Nixon's previous attempts to meddle in agricultural markets, which gave the country the Soviet "Great Grain Robbery" previously mentioned.

However, the Ford administration should be given credit for ending the government requirement that farmers "set aside" land for the specific purpose of *not* being planted—the goal of these set asides was to artificially hike farm prices above market levels by lowering supply. Ending the set asides did lower world food prices by increasing supply.[31]

Congress increased Ford's tax cut, while trashing his enlightened energy program of increasing production and conservation by decontrolling oil and natural gas prices. To the dismay of economic conservatives, Ford went along with the congressional revisions.[32] (This was back in the pre-Reagan days when being a fiscal conservative meant paying for the government you had rather than passing tax cuts that were ultimately fraudulent because they were not accompanied by cutting federal spending as well.) Initially, Ford and Kissinger wisely decided to try to increase oil conservation and to substitute alternative non-petroleum-based fuels by decontrolling oil prices, the opposite of Nixon's price controls. Yet Ford went too far and meddled in the market the other way by proposing to increase oil prices even more by imposing a tax on imported oil. Kissinger even wanted the government to establish a floor price for oil, below which the price could not go. Congress fortunately nixed the plan.

Nixon's exit from the gold standard in 1971 and the world moving to floating currency exchange rates (informally in 1973 and formally in 1976) collapsed the rules-based Bretton Woods world monetary system and made it harder for the governments of leading industrial nations to collude to "manage" the global economy, including their manipulation of exchange rates. Nevertheless, Kissinger used the energy "crisis" of 1973 to try to unify the West—not only in terms of coordinating energy consumption but also to informally manage the world economy—thus rerouting Cold War alliances to new objectives. This new informal group of Western countries was later called the G-7 nations. Also, the dollar remained as the world's reserve currency, meaning that dollars stored in foreign central banks were essentially an indefinite interest-free loan for the United States, becoming a factor in excessive US borrowing and debt.

Although Ford initially threatened to veto a federal bailout for New York City's imminent insolvency, he caved in after the state of New York passed a tax increase to help the city financially.[33] However, Ford's skittishness may be explained by the fact that in only two and a half years as president, Ford tied with Harry Truman, who served as president far longer, in numbers of vetoes overridden by Congress, a total of twelve. After Nixon resigned while impeachment proceedings were underway, the post-Watergate Democratic Congress was reasserting itself somewhat; Ford got the brunt of this new legislative confidence. (Democrat Andrew Johnson, who was impeached by an equally cantankerous Republican Congress during Reconstruction, is the all-time leader in American history, with fifteen vetoes overridden.)

Nixon's Foreign Policy: Revolutionary Means to Maintain the American Empire

During the Vietnam War era, Nixon saw a declining United States with a populace less inclined to bear the costs of empire overseas. He therefore designed policies to sustain the American Empire on the cheap.

End the Vietnam War Slowly

In foreign policy, Nixon planned to end the Vietnam War by playing North Vietnam's rival Communist backers, China and the Soviet Union, against each other to get them to pressure the North Vietnamese into a negotiated settlement of the conflict. Although they were competing with each other for North Vietnam's favor by supporting its war effort, China and the USSR both did try to push Hanoi to a negotiated settlement but failed. The North Vietnamese remained intransigent. Meanwhile, Nixon gradually withdrew US troops and handed the ground war over to the South Vietnamese ("Vietnamization").[34] In the end, after promising in his first presidential campaign to end the Vietnam War, Nixon prolonged American involvement in a vain attempt to salvage some US credibility and prestige ("peace with honor"). He actually lost both peace and honor by escalating the conflict before Congress essentially forced him to close it down by threatening to cut funding in late 1972.

In the meantime, during Nixon's presidency, another 22,000 American soldiers were killed from January 1969 until 1973. Thirty-six thousand had been killed during the Johnson administration. Many more Vietnamese met the same fate, and countless American and Vietnamese resources were wasted to perpetuate a losing quagmire. The Vietnam War was not really about Vietnam, a poor country that was irrelevant to the United States strategically, but about the very imperial goals of maintaining US superpower credibility worldwide as an ally and deterring Soviet adventurism in other places. Yet this reasoning was based on a flawed concept; academic political science research is nearly unanimous that countries usually do not base their assessments of another nation's threats to go to war on that nation's past behavior but on the situational balance of power between the particular antagonists and the intensity of the nation's interests in a specific situation. For example, the Soviets did not seem to think that US credibility to defend Western Europe had been compromised by the American exit from Vietnam.[35]

While turning over the ground war to the ineffectual South Vietnamese military, Nixon started secret wars in Laos and Cambodia (eventually leading to a resumption of massive student antiwar protests in the United States) and carpet-bombed those two countries and North Vietnam, killing many civilians, to allegedly facilitate the US withdrawal. Nixon even ordered a secret nuclear alert to push the Soviets to pressure the North Vietnamese at the peace table, but even this gambit failed.[36] After a successful 1972 reelection campaign in which Nixon painted his weak Democratic opponent George McGovern as out of the mainstream for wanting to rapidly get out of the Vietnam conflict, Nixon then heavily bombed North Vietnam to get negotiating leverage. However, in the end, he got only a face-saving peace agreement that allowed North Vietnam to take over South Vietnam after a decent interval subsequent to US withdrawal, which occurred in 1973.

Overall, during the Johnson and Nixon years, massive destruction was inflicted on Vietnam because of the war. Echoing William Tecumseh Sherman's March to the Sea during the Civil War, the US military used heavy-handed tactics during the war, for example, forcibly moving Vietnamese into "strategic hamlets," then torching their villages and destroying their crops so that they could not be used by the Communist Viet Cong guerrillas. In General Colin Powell's memoirs, he described his earlier military career in operations against the Viet Cong: "We burned down the thatched huts, starting the blaze with Ronson and Zippo lighters. . . . Why were we torching houses and destroying crops? Ho Chi Minh had said the people were like the sea in which his guerrillas swam. . . . We tried to solve the problem by making the whole sea uninhabitable. In the hard logic of war, what difference did it make if you shot your enemy or starved him to death?"[37] (Perhaps because torching houses and crops also made civilians suffer?)

American search-and-destroy missions—which entailed US reconnaissance teams on the ground baiting Communist forces into the open to be hit by airstrikes or artillery fire—became a program of indiscriminate destruction that did not distinguish between enemy combatants, Viet Cong sympathizers, and ordinary Vietnamese civilians. In what one historian called "a scale of chemical warfare unseen since World War I," the United States defoliated jungles using Agent Orange and other toxic chemicals to expose enemy hideaways and supply paths. The League for the Rights of Man accused all sides in the Vietnam War of violating human rights, including the perpetration of torture, assassination, and systematic terror.[38]

Strangely, American counterinsurgency warfare doctrine—from the Philippines at the turn of the twentieth century, continuing through the Nixon years in Vietnam, and used most recently in Afghanistan and Iraq—has followed wanton violence and scorched earth tactics with foreign aid.[39] In the end, American credibility and prestige would have been better served by Nixon exiting the nonstrategic and already lost war more rapidly—the ill-fated US effort was engendering protests around the world as a result of these outrages on the battlefield.

Abuse of the War Power

After Nixon unilaterally expanded the war into Cambodia, Congress banned ground operations by US troops but ignored ongoing US air operations. In 1973, when Congress realized that Nixon had continued his secret war in Cambodia, it passed the War Powers Resolution (WPR). The resolution required that the president consult with Congress before inserting US forces into hostilities or situations in which hostilities are imminent and that within forty-eight hours after the president commits troops, he must notify Congress. He also must withdraw the troops within sixty days (with an additional thirty-day withdrawal period) if Congress has not authorized the operation or declared war. Some argue that the WPR is unconstitutional because the nation's founders, at the Constitutional Convention in 1787 and subsequent state ratifying conventions, had allowed for the president as commander-in-chief to repel sudden attacks, but otherwise required congressional authorization before US forces were committed to any military operation—especially those overseas.[40]

In late 1973, Congress passed the WPR over Nixon's veto. This override was one of the rare instances in which Congress overturned a presidential veto in the foreign affairs realm.[41] The resolution, passed while Nixon was politically weak from the Vietnam War and Watergate scandal, limited any president's ability to keep troops committed overseas in an emergency without congressional approval.[42] The resolution has not seriously limited subsequent presidents' military adventures, however, because Congress has usually been too scared to enforce it by cutting off funding for any unapproved or haywire military interventions—as it had threatened to do in late 1972 during the Vietnam War.

Nixon believed that foreign policy should be made in secret by the White House, thus marginalizing the State Department's influence. In general, in a republic, such secrecy is bad—for example, running a secret war in Cambodia beginning in 1970 without the knowledge of Congress or the American people goes against the intention of the Constitution's framers in giving Congress, as representatives of the people, the power to decide whether or not the country goes to war. Nixon, however, used the Gulf of Tonkin Resolution as an excuse. The vague and broad congressionally approved resolution, passed in 1964 during Lyndon Johnson's administration, authorized the president to "take all necessary measures to repel any armed attack against the forces of the United States and to prevent further aggression" and "to take all necessary steps, including the use of armed force, to assist any member or protocol state of the Southeast Asia Collective Defense Treaty requesting assistance in defense of its freedom."[43]

Although South Vietnam and Laos were protected under that treaty and Cambodia was not, Nixon could claim that Cambodia was a sanctuary for Communist forces attacking South Vietnam. In other words, Nixon could claim that Congress's willing abdication of its war power through the purposefully open-ended Gulf of Tonkin Resolution had already authorized his secret war in Cambodia. Thus, Nixon's clandestine war in Cambodia was not as clearly illegal as Ronald Reagan's flagrant secret violations of the congressionally passed Arms Export Control Act, National Security Act of 1947, and the second Boland Amendment during the Iran-Contra scandal. Congress eventually repealed the Gulf of Tonkin Resolution in January 1971, after the Cambodian warhorse had already left the barn. Nixon signed this repeal but simply continued to run military operations in Southeast Asia under an unconstitutionally broad interpretation of the president's authority as commander-in-chief. Unlike Reagan's secret flouting of congressional direction, however, Nixon did so in the open during this last part of the war in Southeast Asia.

One of the few episodes in which Nixon's secrecy in foreign policy might have had a positive effect was when US intelligence discovered in 1970 that the Soviets were building a submarine base in Cuba. Secret diplomacy resolved the crisis without a public loss of face.[44]

Easing Relations with Communist Powers

Because the American public was tired of years of being bogged down in the Vietnam War, in parallel with Vietnamization, Nixon formulated the Nixon Doctrine—really Vietnamization writ large—which provided military and economic assistance to countries fighting Communists instead of using direct US military intervention. In short, all US allies would need to pick up more of the burden for their own defense and security.[45] Although this policy was not the much-needed drastic reassessment of the US role in the world, it did move the United States toward a more intelligent and restrained "balancer-of-last-resort" role (at least until the end of the Carter administration). The Nixon Doctrine thus scaled back the expansive and burdensome Truman Doctrine—restated by John F. Kennedy that America would "bear any burden" in the global Cold War against Communism.[46] The new doctrine also allowed Nixon to reduce the US defense budget, a trend that lasted throughout the 1970s until 1980 under Jimmy Carter.

Given the actual border war between China and the Soviet Union in 1969, which eliminated the possibility of collusion between the two countries in attacking both Europe and Asia simultaneously, the United States could reduce its military force posture from being able to fight two and a half wars (one major conflict in Europe, one in Asia, and one regional conflict, such as the Vietnam War) to one and a half wars (one major conflict in Europe and one regional conflict). However, Nixon was able to beat back Senator Mike Mansfield's laudable amendment that would have cut back the disproportionate US burden in the NATO alliance by halving American force commitments in Europe, thereby requiring the now wealthy, but still freeloading, allies to do more in their own defense. Yet under pressure to cut the budget, Nixon also had to cut security assistance and foreign developmental assistance, undermining the Nixon Doctrine.[47]

In order to exploit the split between China and the Soviet Union, Nixon opened US relations with the isolated Communist China and began easing tension, normalizing trade relations, and limiting nuclear arms with the Soviet Union, which was called détente. He was attempting to alter the balance of power by aligning a perceived-to-be-declining United States with the more radically Communist China against the less rabid Soviet Union. Nixon skillfully made America the key linchpin in a competition between China and the Soviets to each better relations with the United States.

During the Vietnam War period, Nixon designed both the policies of better relations with Communist adversaries and the Nixon Doctrine as maneuvering tactics to sustain—rather than reduce—US commitments abroad and as a counter to what he believed to be the decline of relative US power and a reduced willingness of the American people to bear the political and financial costs of American global primacy and empire (Pax Americana). Although Nixon self-identified with realism, he believed, like his favorite president, the idealistic Woodrow Wilson, that only continued American internationalism (read: at least some American interventionism) could create a world order in which democracy would be safe.

Nixon believed, likely ignoring US military advantages, that the Soviet Union was approaching parity with the United States as a military power and that America had lost its post–World War II economic dominance.[48] Thus, he essentially ran a policy of "managed decline" but did so in order to keep America from becoming what he deemed "a second-rate power." The Nixon Doctrine and openings to the Communist powers for better relations were a revolutionary way to maintain the status quo of US global preeminence under what Nixon believed were less favorable military and economic conditions. Of course, the United States would have done better then, as now, to drastically reduce overseas commitments and military spending and renew itself economically—a healthy economy is the root of all military, cultural, and diplomatic power—but Nixon's policies were a distinct improvement over prior Cold War overextension.

Under his relaxed policy toward the Communist powers, the anti-Communist Nixon made history by initiating a celebrated diplomatic opening in 1971 toward a Communist regime in China that was more radical and reclusive than the Soviet Union. Also, Nixon reached the historic first nuclear arms limitation with the Soviet superpower rival (1972), which limited destabilizing anti-ballistic missile defense systems and froze the number of offensive nuclear weapons in both countries' arsenals.[49] Critics focused on the Soviets' higher number of intercontinental ballistic missiles, but the United States led in bombers, invulnerable submarine-launched missiles (the ultimate survivable deterrent), and missile technology, including accuracy and the ability to put multiple warheads on missiles.[50] Although the United States still retained a technological edge, this SALT I agreement was designed to lock in strategic nuclear parity in the wake of a rapidly expanding Soviet nuclear arsenal.[51]

Although Nixon failed to get the Communist powers to successfully pressure North Vietnam to come to the peace table (he finally got a face-saving settlement to end the US war using a massive bombing campaign of the North), he did attenuate the danger of the Cold War, and concomitant risk of nuclear war, by improving relations with the USSR and China, which lasted until the end of the 1970s and the late 1980s, respectively. The state of general relations between nuclear powers can lower the chances of nuclear war as much or more than quantitative limits on nuclear weapons. The Doomsday Clock of the *Bulletin of Atomic Scientists* rated the détente period as one of the two times during the Cold War when the threat of nuclear war was lowest (the other time frame was the post–Cuban Missile Crisis era from 1963 to 1968).[52]

Middle East

While Israel has started or provoked most of the Arab-Israeli wars, in 1973, Anwar Sadat, the president of Egypt, decided to attack Israel to regain some of the Arab prestige and territory lost to Israel in Israel's attack on the Arabs in the 1967 Six-Day War. Sadat later said that he "went to war to make peace." Although the Arabs eventually lost the war militarily to Israel, they did well enough to restore some of their lost prestige, which allowed Sadat to make his dramatic peace initiative to Israel that led to peace between the two nations in the late 1970s, mediated by Jimmy Carter at Camp David. The Camp David Accords of 1979 and the Egypt-Israeli peace treaty have ensured a lasting peace between the Middle East's two most important military powers, but not without cost to the United States.

In the 1973 Yom Kippur War, for diplomatic gain, Henry Kissinger, Nixon's secretary of state and national security advisor, at first slow-rolled Israel's desperate request for supplies but then relented after a panicked Israel, suffering large initial losses, put its nuclear forces on alert and threatened to take its case to the American public. Nixon then began a massive resupply effort to compete against the Soviet resupply of Egypt and Syria, and Israel began winning the war.[53] A US-sponsored ceasefire was arranged by the UN Security Council, but Nixon and Kissinger cheated on it and allowed the Israelis to keep pounding the Egyptian military. The Soviets became angry that Israel broke a second UN ceasefire and sent the United States a proposal that US and Soviet forces be sent to jointly enforce the ceasefire, threating to intervene unilaterally if the United States did not accept the proffer.

Ostensibly in response to this threat, but really to deflect domestic attention from Watergate, Kissinger raised the alert level of US nuclear forces from DEFCON 4 to DEFCON 3 and also raised the alert level on some conventional rapid reaction forces. Shockingly, Nixon was likely drunk and did not even participate in this dangerous decision; he was out of action because of stress and the Watergate scandal. Kissinger, really assuming the role of acting president, admitted that raising the alert level was a deliberate overreaction and told the Soviets privately that it was for domestic reasons. Nevertheless, the Soviets dropped their threat of unilateral action, and this may have been a bluff anyway.[54] Even so, the US cheating on the ceasefire, thereby riling the Soviets, and then raising the nuclear alert level for purely domestic reasons was very dangerous and bad policy. Without the president in the decision loop for raising the alert level for US nuclear and other forces, it seems that the massive American administrative state was (and still is) out of control.

Kissinger did use the 1973 war to ease the Soviets out of the Middle East and receive the defection of Egypt, under President Anwar Sadat, from the Soviet to the US camp. To do this, however, Kissinger undertook the dubious role of Middle East peacemaker between Israel and the Arabs—a role that subsequent US presidents have continued, usually with frustration or at high monetary cost to the United States.

American brinksmanship with the Soviet Union during the 1973 war undermined Nixon's new détente policy with the Communist powers, and US support of Israel in the conflict triggered Arab oil production cutbacks and an embargo against the United States. Although these actions sent oil prices skyrocketing and the embargo seemed successful, it was actually a failure.

Many historians believe high oil prices led to stagflation, yet stagflation existed before the Arab actions. Also, economists now think that Nixon's immense pressure on the Federal Reserve to print money in order to get himself reelected might have had more to do with stagflation than merely raising the price of one commodity did. If people have budget constraints, when the price of oil goes up, they spend less on other things, lowering the prices of those items and thus keeping inflation (increases in the general price level) in check. The lingering effects of all the added government spending on the Vietnam War and the Great Society likely had something to do with stagflation too.

As for the Arab embargo significantly reducing oil imports to the United States, that is impossible when a worldwide market will simply reorder itself—the United States will buy from other sellers and other buyers will start buying Arab oil. The Arab production cutbacks did increase the oil price by temporarily reducing world oil supply, but the economies of industrial nations proved more resilient than many thought to such price shocks. In addition, higher oil prices caused the long-term demand for OPEC (Organization of Petroleum Exporting Countries) oil to decline because conservation was spurred, people sought alternative fuels, or consumers simply bought more oil from non-OPEC producers. Oil is usually a much greater percentage of exports for Arab oil-producing countries than it is of imports for oil-consuming industrial nations. Indirect evidence demonstrates the failure of the Arabs' use of oil as a punitive weapon: since 1973, there have been other Arab-Israeli wars in the Middle East, but the Arabs have never imposed another embargo.

As an overreaction to the oil embargo, Nixon criticized US dependence on foreign sources of oil and instituted the dubious goal of gaining energy independence by 1980 through conservation, exploration, and alternative energy sources. He also was instrumental in creating a new international bureaucracy, the International Energy Agency, which coordinated oil-consuming nations' energy policies and created a coordinated system of oil reserves—both inefficient deviations from letting market forces deliver oil at the cheapest price possible. Some of these nonmarket measures, which made little economic sense, were designed to show Western solidarity against the vastly overstated "OPEC threat"—a response to the loosening Western alliance as continuing détente attenuated the threat from the Soviet Union. Unsurprisingly, all the coordination of industrial consuming nations' energy policies did not bring down the price of oil, which was determined mostly by supply and demand, or bust the largely feckless OPEC cartel.

In reality, with a worldwide market for the product, oil—or energy in general—is no different from any other good or commodity. Protectionism in energy is no less inefficient than protectionism in any other product. Essentially, Nixon started the canard that dependence on foreign oil was a terrible national security problem, a misconception that politicians of both parties have gleefully and erroneously rallied to ever since—mainly because it allows them to get government subsidies for various types of energy for their states or congressional districts. Yet, overall, eliminating US dependence on imported oil or energy would be very expensive, because the United States is usually a high-cost producer relative to other countries. As for national security, the United States only needs to produce enough oil to fuel its military during wartime—which it did several times over, even before domestic production rapidly increased from fracking—and only then if the war cuts off all outside sources of imported oil, which would be unlikely.

Nevertheless, as part of this energy independence program, the Nixon administration established a nationwide maximum highway speed limit of 55 miles per hour. Speed limits traditionally had been the purview of the states. This ill-advised measure harmed the economy and conserved far less fuel than originally projected. Only in 1995 did Congress pass, and Bill Clinton sign, a bill abolishing this national limit, properly returning the authority to set speed limits to the states.

Support for Dictators in the Developing World

Nixon, in pursuit of advantage against Communism during the Cold War, routinely supported autocratic governments with abysmal human rights records—for example, Pakistan in its 1971 attempt to crush the desire for Bengali independence in East Pakistan (now Bangladesh). Thus he rarely supported humanitarian concerns—the case of the civil war in Nigeria over Biafra was an exception.[55]

Despite openings to the two most important despotic Communist regimes in order to pull Maoist China further away from the Soviet Union, Nixon sided with Pakistan, in part for sentimental reasons, and thus missed the chance to pull Pakistan's archrival, democratic India, away from aligning with the Soviets. In 1971, despite Nixon's realization that the two distant parts of Pakistan, on either side of the massive Indian territory, could be held together only by force, he supported Yahya Kahn, the Pakistani dictator, even as Pakistan stood accused of genocide by the international community. Nixon could have condemned Pakistan's aggression and cut off military and economic assistance to the country, but instead he only deferred deliveries of "death-dealing" military equipment. Then Nixon illegally sent lethal US weapons to Pakistan that were first in the possession of third countries. The revelation of such illegal arms sales to Pakistan prompted Congress to terminate all military assistance to the country.

When India signed a treaty of friendship and cooperation with the Soviet Union, it confirmed to Nixon that his pro-Pakistani tilt was correct. Yet if

Nixon had not been as supportive of Pakistan in a lost cause—the much more powerful India defeated Pakistan after the latter attacked western Indian air bases in 1971, leading to the birth of the new nation of Bangladesh where East Pakistan once stood—India might not have been driven further into the arms of the USSR. Even after Nixon knew saving a united Pakistan was a fruitless effort, he sent a US aircraft carrier battle group into the Bay of Bengal to bully the Indian government. Even worse, the United States encouraged China, also an adversary of India, to send troops to the Sino-Indian border and offered to back China in any war with the Soviet Union.[56] In his desire to burnish American credibility by backing the obviously losing cause of US ally Pakistan, Nixon threatened to turn a regional war into what could have been a dangerous global conflict among nuclear powers. Thus, Nixon's diplomacy was not always adroit.

Following the Nixon Doctrine, to keep Soviet influence at bay in the Middle East, the Nixon administration relied on the "twin pillars" strategy of backing the twin despotic regimes of Iran and Saudi Arabia. Both regimes used their oil money to buy huge quantities of US arms and cooperated with each other to defend the Gulf from the Soviet threat. During the Carter administration, this policy fell apart as angry Iranians overthrew the Shah, who had one of the worst human rights records in the world. Zbigniew Brzezinski, Carter's national security advisor, then used the ouster of the Shah as an excuse to reverse the Nixon Doctrine and begin a direct US military role in "safeguarding" Persian Gulf oil supplies for the United States and its allies. Ronald Reagan converted Carter's modest force into the massive US Central Command, which carried out countless US military interventions in the Gulf and surrounding areas in subsequent years.

Also, to counter socialist inroads in the Western Hemisphere and in support of the Monroe Doctrine, Nixon worked to destabilize the left-leaning government of Salvador Allende, who was democratically elected in Chile in 1970. Augusto Pinochet, the head of Chile's armed forces, successfully launched a US-backed coup in 1973, leading to many years of human rights violations but also to an economic renaissance. In response to Pinochet's human rights abuses, Congress banned military aid to his regime and imposed a ceiling on other aid.

Ford's Foreign Policy: Less Interventionism

Although Ford only served as president two and a half years, he was less interventionist than most presidents. Of recent presidents, only Carter was probably more restrained militarily than Ford. Both presidents were constrained by the "Vietnam Syndrome," which inhibited the desire of the American people to engage in long-term overseas quagmires. Yet although the United States had withdrawn from Vietnam in 1973 before Ford took office, he did request emergency aid to help the South Vietnamese stave off a final assault by North Vietnam. A reluctant Congress, speaking for an exhausted public, would have none of it.

The Minor Mayaguez *Incident*

In May 1975, two weeks after Saigon ignominiously fell to the North Vietnamese and Ford's administration was at its low point, the brutal Communist Khmer Rouge, who had taken over neighboring Cambodia, seized the US merchant ship *Mayaguez* and held its sailors hostage. To show the United States was tough in the wake of the Communist takeover of part of Southeast Asia and to burnish his own strong leadership credentials for reelection, Ford first needlessly exaggerated the gravity of the situation and then went overboard in the one direct US military intervention during his brief presidency. Previous administrations had negotiated for the release of captured ships, but Ford escalated the crisis by calling the capture an act of piracy and publicly demanding the release of the crew and ship—making it harder for the Cambodian Communists to free the hostages without seeming to back down.

In trying to prevent the Khmer Rouge from taking the hostages by boat to the Cambodian mainland, where many US military options would have been foreclosed, a case can be made for Ford's aggressive strafing and bombing from the air near their boats to deter them from doing so—although this use of air power did injure some of the hostages. However, Ford then ordered an amphibious assault on an island to which the United States erroneously thought some of the hostages had been taken and also punitively bombed the Cambodian mainland. The latter two actions could have gotten hostages killed, because at the time US intelligence thought that some of them had been taken to the island and some to the mainland.

As it happened, the Cambodians released the *Mayaguez* crew, even after the Americans had sunk some of their boats, but savagely fought the misdirected Marine amphibious assault, killing forty-one US military personnel, wounding fifty, and downing seven of eight Marine helicopters. In short, the amphibious assault was a disaster. Furthermore, Ford ordered the punitive airstrikes on the Cambodian mainland, which might have ended in the death of the hostages, even after Cambodia announced on the radio that the captives were free to go. Kissinger wanted the United States to look "ferocious."

Afterward Ford crowed that the attack had been a psychological boost to the nation and claimed that the gloomy national mood from the fall of part of Southeast Asia to Communism was fading. But that national "feel macho" moment cost the United States forty-one service personnel in trying to free forty *Mayaguez* crew members, who were freed by their captors anyway. Lt. General Brent Scowcroft, Ford's blunt deputy national security advisor at the time, later admitted that the freeing of the hostages resulted from luck. An independent General Accounting Office report later said that China had helped secure the release of the hostages by putting pressure on its Cambodian ally.

To enhance his image for the 1976 election, Ford had put the hostages' lives in danger. Scowcroft indirectly admitted that Ford took actions in the crisis to save his own political neck. Journalist and historian Michael Bohn concluded that this appointed president overreacted in the *Mayaguez* incident in 1975 to show he had the credibility to be elected in his own right in 1976.[57] Even then, Ford did not get elected, but this botched military mission did increase his popularity.[58] After the recent loss of the Vietnam War, the American public was grasping for any military heroics it could find. The public did not seem to care that Ford had violated the recently congressionally passed War Powers Resolution[59]—which tried to reassert that legislative body's constitutional role in authorizing military action—by not even notifying Congress of the military operation until it was over.[60]

Although during his short term in office, Ford generally exhibited at least some restraint militarily, it did not keep his administration from blustering with the threat of war when useful. After OPEC raised oil prices again in

October 1975, word leaked out of the administration that military action was being considered. Yet the futility of such military threats was clearly demonstrated, as OPEC kept increasing oil prices anyway.

Ford did have one major intervention for peace. After the 1973 Middle East war, Kissinger helped the Israelis and Egyptians reach the Sinai Interim Agreement (Sinai II) in September 1975. The agreement demilitarized the Sinai Peninsula, and both parties pledged to settle disputes peacefully.[61]

Détente Begins to Erode

Conservatives compared Ford's signing of the Helsinki Accords in 1975 with Franklin Delano Roosevelt's alleged sellout of Eastern Europe at Yalta. The Accords, the high water mark of détente, conceded to the Soviet Union recognition of existing boundaries in Europe and respect for sovereignty in exchange for a Soviet pledge to respect human rights.[62] Today, in retrospect after the fall of the Eastern Bloc, conservatives see the Helsinki Accords in a different light—as having undermined the legitimacy of Communist systems.

Détente began to crumble when Senator Henry Jackson, a hawkish Democrat, effectively nixed a 1972 agreement to normalize US-Soviet trade relations by demanding, in the Jackson-Vanik amendment, that so-called Most Favored Nation (MFN) trade status be contingent on free emigration of citizens from nonmarket economies. Affirming Kissinger's correct notion that private approaches to the Soviet Union on human rights generated better returns than such public posturing, the Soviets then retracted their request for MFN status. Nixon had cogently said, "We cannot gear our foreign policy to transformation of other societies."[63] Jackson, a pioneering neoconservative, was not only trying to transform Communist countries but to also undermine détente. By late 1974, US-Soviet relations were at their worst since 1968; congressional Democrats were destroying détente, and the Ford administration was powerless to stop the erosion.[64]

Nixon signed the aforementioned first Strategic Arms Limitation Treaty (SALT I) and the Anti-Ballistic Missile (ABM) Treaty with the Soviets, and Ford signed SALT II, which equalized the number of strategic nuclear delivery vehicles. SALT II ratification by the Senate was stalled during the Ford and

Carter administrations because of the demise of détente, although the treaty's limits were followed informally by both countries.[65]

Nixon/Ford détente—merely an attempt to get the Soviet Union to behave as a status quo power within the existing global order and lessen the chance of nuclear war—had largely succeeded. According to historian Daniel J. Sargent, the United States got most of the advantages from détente—stabilizing US leadership and the Cold War balance of power in a time of declining US military and economic resources—and the Soviets provided most of the concessions, including looking the other way when Nixon bombed North Vietnam "to smithereens" (Kissinger's words) and accepting his attempt to muscle the Soviets out of the Middle East during and after the 1973 Arab-Israeli war. By signing the Helsinki Accords, the Soviets indicated that in Europe, the most important theater in the Cold War, a "revolutionary" power had accepted existing borders and a conservative interpretation of the international order.

Détente eventually eroded, concluded Sargent, not because the Communists were all that effective in spreading revolution—they still tried in the developing world—but because the American people were idealistic crusaders. Instead of the Cold War status quo, Americans wanted to poke the Soviet Union on human rights, and they did not want to be relegated to alleged military parity, if not inferiority, with the Soviets.[66] Unfortunately, this strand of "armed missionary" action in US foreign policy has deep roots in American history.

In contrast, Ford took a hard line against Eurocommunism. More moderate Communist parties had a renaissance in Western Europe. The Italian Communist Party won one-third of the seats in the Italian parliament in the 1975 and 1976 elections. The party reached a deal with the mainstream Christian Democrats, but Kissinger took a hard line against it—declaring that any government with Communists in it could not remain in the NATO alliance and, as in the late 1940s, interfering with elections in allied countries by funneling cash to anti-Communist parties.[67]

Similarly, Ford and Kissinger started the Angolan civil war that occurred after the Portuguese left in 1975. Against the good advice of the State Department's African Bureau not to intervene on the grounds that the United States had no irrevocable commitment of US power and prestige in Angola,

Ford and Kissinger, without telling Congress or the American people, initiated CIA aid to non-Communist forces in violation of the Alvor Accord and encouraged South Africa to intervene on the United States's behalf. When Congress found out about this covert operation—emboldened by its actions to end the war in Vietnam and seeing another potential US quagmire on the horizon—it then wisely decided to cut off US aid, which caused the South Africans to pull out and the Communists to win.

This shutdown of a covert action was the first time Congress had ever nixed such an operation. This debacle also motivated Ford to issue an executive order initiating a significant revamp of intelligence gathering and oversight, including an intelligence oversight board and a ban on assassinations by US government personnel.[68]

Yet the Communists in Angola proved not to be the Soviet puppets that Kissinger had assumed. Even if they had been, Ford and Kissinger never asked what strategic value this faraway developing country had for the United States. As it also failed to do in Vietnam, Laos, and Cambodia, the United States should have let the Soviets, without superpower opposition, acquire another corrupt, economic basket case for a client state. Then the USSR would have had to pay all of the costs in aid, reconstruction, and administration—with the idea being to weaken the Soviet Empire by financial overextension, not direct or indirect military competition.

The reality was different. Angola showed that although things had stabilized in the core of the Cold War system—Europe—the superpowers were still vying for advantage in the developing world. The Soviets sought advantage in southern Africa and the United States in the Middle East.[69]

However, to nix any possible Soviet attempt to take advantage of black nationalism in Africa, Ford and Kissinger laudably reversed support for minority white regimes in South Africa and Rhodesia, which was on the verge of a full-blown race-based civil war. By throwing its weight behind a gradual route to majority rule in South Africa and an immediate one in Rhodesia, the Ford administration created the framework for a peace process that led to a peaceful transition in Rhodesia to majority rule within three years.[70] Majority rule in South Africa ultimately worked out much better than the decades of despotism and economic ruin in Zimbabwe (formerly Rhodesia) under dictator Robert Mugabe. But at least in Zimbabwe, the majority earned the right to try and fail at governing itself.

In the mid-1970s, the growing push to include human rights promotion in American foreign policy led to a congressional prohibition in 1975 on US developmental aid to countries abusing human rights and the cutoff in 1976 of US military assistance to nations with rights issues (with a presidential waiver in extraordinary circumstances when US national interest required the provision of such aid). Congress also mandated that the State Department keep track of the human rights records of countries receiving US military assistance and send the legislature reports on it. The Ford administration did not like these commendable developments but went along with them. The administration instead dubiously argued that supporting autocratic regimes at times served the US national interest, such as Iran in the Middle East and Indonesia, the Philippines, and South Korea in East Asia.[71]

Conclusion

Neither Nixon nor Ford were conservative in their policies, and in fact their presidencies can be classified as moderately progressive domestically. The Watergate scandal and its aftermath were central to both administrations. The Watergate scandal was comparable to the later Iran-Contra scandal during the Reagan administration; they were the two worst scandals in American history because of Nixon's and Reagan's abuses of the Constitution. After implying that he would not pardon Nixon during his confirmation hearing for vice president, Gerald Ford reversed field and unconstitutionally did so when he became president.

In foreign policy, in contrast to hawkish Democrats Harry Truman, John F. Kennedy, and Lyndon B. Johnson, Republicans Nixon and Ford took the more dovish position of easing tensions with the Communist powers. Both pursued a policy of détente with the Soviet Union. Nixon even initiated a diplomatic opening to radical, isolated Maoist China to use it as a counterweight to the USSR. During and after the Vietnam War, Nixon tried to reduce the costs of the American empire by substituting US assistance to countries battling Communism in place of direct intervention using American forces.

Yet Nixon conducted secret wars in Southeast Asia; horrifically carpet-bombed North Vietnam, Cambodia, and Laos; and was slow to fulfill his campaign promise to end the Vietnam War. Ford intervened militarily only once during his presidency: the minor fiasco to rescue hostages from the ship *Mayaguez* using the risky and needless use of force against Cambodian hostage-takers.

6

Limited Government Starts to Return

IT MIGHT SEEM like it's stretching it to say that a president who gave us two new federal departments—Education and Energy—was a champion of limited government. The key is in what your point of comparison is for Jimmy Carter's policies. If you compare them to Harding/Coolidge's policies, they may be found wanting. However, comparing them to other, more recent presidents, Carter edges out Dwight Eisenhower for being the best post–World War II chief executive and surprisingly bests Ronald Reagan, whose "small government" rhetoric was largely fraudulent marketing.

The Work of Limiting Government

Most conservatives might laugh at the idea of putting Carter (president from 1977 to 1981) ahead of their hero Reagan in limiting government. But many conservatives define limited government selectively. They do not consider some policies to be "big government," such as spending excessive money and lives to "defend" an intrinsically secure country or to conduct profligate armed interventions and military social work overseas. Yet warfare is the biggest cause of expanding government—including government intervention at home—in human history and in American history. Reagan conducted a massive, and largely unnecessary, peacetime military buildup, began ramping up overseas military interventions after a post-Vietnam lull under Gerald Ford and Carter, and almost started a nuclear war with the Soviet Union because of his overheated anti-Soviet rhetoric. Finally, conservatives seem to dismiss Reagan's flagrant violation of a core principle of the US Constitution in the worst constitutional scandal in American history: the Iran-Contra affair.

Reagan gave us an expanding federal government, even in terms that conservatives accept: being the second worst post–World War II presidential administration in increasing civilian federal employees per capita and in hiking government spending, both absolutely and as a percentage of gross domestic product (GDP). Ronald Reagan did deregulate the economy to some extent, but Carter was really the pioneer here, and experts consider Reagan's efforts less ambitious than those of Carter.

In general, Carter was much less prone to use military force unnecessarily than Reagan and deregulated, partially or fully, four sectors of the economy: transportation, communication, finance, and energy. Carter advocated limiting government, fiscal austerity to reduce inflation, cutting the deficit and balancing the budget, slashing both pork spending and taxes, a greater role for local government (federalism), and personal responsibility. As Carter did when he was governor of Georgia, as president he regularly disregarded politics and made decisions that stuck a knife into vested interests, especially in the Democratic Party—the main reason he faced a Democratic primary challenger and did not get reelected. Carter opposed interest group politics, federal funding for abortion, and the welfare state because he thought it discouraged work and the traditional family. Carter stated, "Government cannot eliminate poverty or provide a bountiful economy or reduce inflation or save our cities or cure illiteracy or provide energy." Tip O'Neill, the Democratic Speaker of the House of Representatives, once opined, "When it came to the politics of Washington, DC, [Carter] never really understood how the system worked. . . . [He] did not want to learn about it, either."[1] Although both houses of Congress were controlled by substantial Democratic majorities, Carter's goring of such Democratic pork made him wildly unpopular, even within his own party.[2]

Similarly, against the advice of his advisers, who wanted him to say he would lead the nation out of inflation, a sluggish economy, and high energy prices, he had the temerity to tell the American people the truth—that their problems were caused by a "crisis of spirit."[3] Even though Carter never used the word "malaise," the American people never want to be told that in a democracy the fault ultimately lies with the people who are supposed to be in charge of the politicians. In the modern welfare state, the people expect the president and Congress to be father and mother figures and lead the country out of government policy–induced doldrums for which the people are ultimately responsible. Needless to say, Carter's speech was not well received by the public or the media.

In short, Carter was the first conservative president in the almost fifty years since Calvin Coolidge passed the baton to the more progressive Herbert Hoover in 1929. Although most conservatives admire Ronald Reagan and disdain Jimmy Carter, Carter set the precedents for much of Reagan's conservative agenda, which turned out to be largely rhetorical. (Carter was even the first president to identify himself as an evangelical Christian.[4]) However, Reagan was much better at sunny, optimistic public relations than Carter, who has thus suffered at the hands of historians, political scientists, and journalists, most of whom are unduly mesmerized by rhetoric and who do not take the time to examine actual policies.

More Restrained Foreign Policy

The US failure in Vietnam taught Carter what subsequent presidents have forgotten: limits to American power exist, and the United States alone cannot solve all of the world's problems.[5] Carter pledged that "we will not behave in foreign lands so as to violate our rules and standards."[6] For the most part, with a couple of glaring exceptions, Carter lived this philosophy while in office. He was an anti-interventionist, especially in the developing world; for a change, he wanted the United States to treat other nations as equals with their own interests. Subsequent chief executives should have memorized, but did not, this summary of Carter's truth-telling in foreign policy:

> A strong nation, like a strong person, can afford to be gentle, firm, thoughtful, and restrained. It can afford to extend a helping hand to others. It's a weak nation, like a weak person, that must behave with bluster and boasting and rashness and other signs of insecurity.[7]

Iranian Hostage Crisis

The seeds of the famous Iran hostage crisis during Carter's administration took place when Eisenhower approved a CIA coup that overthrew the elected government of Iran's Prime Minister Mohammad Mossadegh and reinstated the despotic Shah, who created the brutal SAVAK secret police that kept his regime in power through murder and torture. William Sullivan, the US ambassador to Iran from 1977 to 1979, said that from the late 1960s to the early 1970s, the Shah conducted "a reign of terror in Iran."[8] The United States was seen by Iranians as propping up this dictator.

Carter continued Nixon's premise that Iran was one of two pillars safeguarding US interests in the oil-rich Persian Gulf (Saudi Arabia was the other pillar). Oil-producing Iran had influence in the OPEC (Organization of Petroleum Exporting Countries) cartel, it sold oil to Israel, and its strong military served as a bulwark against Soviet expansion in the Gulf. So Carter ignored the increasing brutality of the Shah's regime and his own human rights orientation in foreign policy to keep selling the Shah huge quantities of weaponry, including riot control equipment.[9] Although Carter's actions merely continued longstanding US policy, that edifice came tumbling down when Iranians overthrew the Shah; a fundamentalist Shi'i regime under the radical Islamist Ayatollah Ruhollah Khomeini then seized power.

Carter, given his emphasis on human rights, earlier should have distanced himself publicly from the Shah and cut off arms sales; he did not do that. However, by the late 1970s, when Carter was president, after decades of close US association with the despised Shah, this distancing might not have spared the United States the venom of an anti-American Iranian revolution in 1978 and 1979, which resulted in the takeover of the US embassy by mobs supported by the new Islamist government.

In retrospect, Carter is portrayed as so restrained in foreign policy that he was naïve. Yet Carter presciently disagreed with the rest of his administration in his belief that admitting the recently deposed and critically ill Iranian Shah into the United States for medical treatment might endanger the US embassy in Tehran. Iranian officials, when advised by the United States of the administration's intended invitation to the Shah, predicted an adverse reaction in Iran but guaranteed the protection of US embassy personnel. So unfortunately, Carter reluctantly let his advisers talk him into admitting the Shah.

The protesting students then overran the embassy, and Ayatollah Ruhollah Khomeini, Iran's new supreme leader, despite Iranian officials' prior guarantees, threw up roadblocks to the hostages' release and played the "Great Satan" (external enemy) card to consolidate his power.[10] Specifically, in November 1979, breaking a pledge by the Iranian government that no retaliatory action would be taken if the United States admitted the Shah for treatment, Khomeini—to get rid of Iranian moderates, including Prime Minister Bazargan—told the students to disregard Bazargan's order to give up the overtaken US embassy and free the hostages. In early 1980, Abolhassen Bani-Sadr, Iran's first freely elected president, agreed that UN representatives could come to Iran to hear its complaints and then the hostages would be freed; but Khomeini again told the militants holding them not to turn them over to the new government. As a result of all this Iranian duplicity, Carter reluctantly decided to launch what turned out to be an unsuccessful military rescue attempt—instead of a more belligerent military action that might have resulted in the hostages being killed.

Under Carter's restrained foreign policy, when the US embassy in Iran was overrun and US diplomats taken prisoner—embassies are technically American soil and diplomats are supposed to have immunity from foreign persecution and prosecution—instead of militarily attacking Iran, Carter attempted to negotiate the hostages' release and tried and failed at a long-shot military mission to rescue the hostages. During the rescue mission, Carter, like Gerald Ford in the failed attempt to militarily rescue sailors from the ship *Mayaguez* in 1975, failed to follow the War Powers Resolution of 1973.[11] That resolution required the president to consult with Congress before sending US forces into hostilities or situations in which hostilities are imminent and to report to Congress within forty-eight hours of sending the forces.[12] However, Carter had a better excuse than Ford did for not doing so. The Constitutional Convention intended for the president to be able to act if the United States is under attack, and an embassy overseas is technically US territory.

The mission had to be aborted when multiple helicopters malfunctioned and one later crashed into a US Air Force transport plane. Although even Jimmy Carter has said that he wished he had sent at least another helicopter on the rescue mission, Stuart Eizenstat, Carter's chief domestic adviser, claims that the military, at the time, cautioned against this option because greater numbers of helicopters would blow the secrecy of the mission.[13] In addition, the military had been inept in its maintenance of the helicopters and in its execution of the mission.

Although Carter probably had one of the few best excuses for attacking another country in American history and faced formidable primary and general election opponents in his bid for reelection in 1980, he courageously avoided taking military action that might have won him the election. However, an all-out attack on Iran probably would have resulted in the hostages being killed and in an inflamed Islamic world with added venom directed at the United States. Thus, like Dwight Eisenhower, who risked his reelection in 1956 by not supporting Israel in a Middle East war, Carter essentially sacrificed his chances in 1980 by not taking bold, but likely tragic, military action against Iran. The American public, frustrated by the long captivity of the hostages, voted him out of office. In an election year, the failed rescue mission was a disaster from which Carter never fully recovered politically.[14] After the election and on Reagan's inauguration day, Carter did eventually secure the hostages' release—by unfreezing Iranian assets in the United States that he froze after the hostages were taken. Contrary to conventional wisdom, the hostages were not released because of Iran's fear of the incoming Reagan administration.[15]

Ronald Reagan, who criticized Carter's policy of negotiation for release of the hostages, later traded American hostages for Arab prisoners held by the Israelis (in the TWA Flight 847 hijacking) and for arms sold to Iran (in the Iran-Contra affair). However, Reagan did learn from Carter's mistake of initially elevating the embassy hostage-taking into a national security "crisis," which the media latched onto voraciously, breathlessly counting the number of days the hostages in Iran had been held. Presidents, by their rhetoric, define situations to the public, whether as "crises" or as less urgent situations (Eisenhower was skilled at dampening them into the latter).

Thus, Carter inadvertently gave the Iranians helpful publicity and implicitly staked his presidency on getting the hostages released. But that release took over a year and did not come in time to win him reelection. (Similarly, it took Lyndon B. Johnson a year to negotiate with North Korea for the release of hostages from the USS *Pueblo*, but LBJ was not in the middle of a reelection campaign.[16]) In contrast, Reagan later pretended not to negotiate for the TWA hostages or for captives held by the Iranian-backed group Hezbollah in Lebanon in retaliation for his military intervention in that country (in the latter case, Reagan's arms exports to terrorist-sponsoring Iran violated the Arms Export Control Act, a criminal statute).

Professor Betty Glad, who studied Jimmy Carter's management of the hostage crisis, concluded:

> Carter . . . provided somewhat better management of the Iranian hostage crisis than he is given credit for. He did make mistakes in admitting the shah into the United States, hyping the issue for almost six months, and launching an ill-fated rescue mission. But he avoided the temptation for military action, and skillfully used the Iranian assets he froze in the United States as a bargaining chip to secure the hostages' release.[17]

Carter courageously avoided intense pressure from advisers and members of Congress, in an election year, to "do something, anything" about the situation—meaning, taking rash military action—so that he could remain dedicated to keeping the hostages alive.[18]

The Reduction of Overseas Holdings and Commitments

In general, Carter wisely tried to lessen US overextension in the world by shedding unnecessary overseas holdings and commitments. At great cost politically, Carter ended one of the longest and most egregious colonial episodes in American history. In a colonial grab similar to the US acquiring the Philippines, Cuba, and Puerto Rico during the Spanish-American War, Teddy Roosevelt "stole" the Canal Zone in Panama "fair and square," as one member of Congress put it much later.[19] Roosevelt had encouraged and aided an insurrection against an uncooperative Colombian government and then bought the canal right of way from the grateful Panamanian rebels.

In 1978, Carter signed and got Congress to ratify two treaties that would return the American-occupied Canal Zone to Panama after 1999. These actions revved up American jingoists who forgot all of this history—or did not choose to recognize it—and merely saw the policy as giving away a canal that the United States built and as weakening the Monroe Doctrine, by which the

United States had dominated Latin America since the early 1800s. The jingo-ists used the issue against Carter in the 1980 election. Yet the canal had lost much of its strategic value because the United States now had large separate Atlantic and Pacific fleets and its biggest ships, including US aircraft carriers, could not transit its narrow passage. Also, even without having operational control of the canal on a day-to-day basis, a second treaty stipulated that if needed, the US could defend the waterway against external threats—the most important thing.

In addition, Carter recognized that the US commitment to defend rap-idly prospering Taiwan negatively affected US relations with geostrategic heavyweight China. Following up on Richard Nixon's historic opening to the latter country, which had in the meantime stagnated, Carter, pushing back against a strong Taiwan lobby, unilaterally withdrew from the Sino-American Mutual Defense Treaty with Taiwan and established full diplomatic relations and normalized trade relations with China. This policy change should have been made years before. Carter asked Congress to approve his normalization of trade relations with China.[20]

Carter—taking advantage of Mao Zedong's death and a new, more prag-matic Chinese leadership under Deng Xiaoping that wanted to integrate into the global economy—completed Nixon's use of China to strategically bal-ance the Soviet Union. After normalization, the US-China entente against the USSR included limited American military sales to China and intelligence co-operation, including joint intelligence facilities in western China to monitor Soviet military activities. The American-Chinese rapprochement went so far as for Carter to actually provide China with intelligence when China invaded Vietnam, after the pro-Soviet Vietnamese had taken out the pro-Chinese genocidal regime of Pol Pot in Cambodia. Carter had muted his human rights promotion policy toward China, with its poor record on individual freedom.

Although the Constitution says that the president has the power to rec-ognize foreign powers and negotiate treaties with them, it is silent on what procedure needs to be followed to withdraw from an existing treaty.[21] So although Carter's policy in the normalization of China was good, a dispute arose over the US withdrawal from the treaty with Taiwan. To exactly fol-low the Constitution in abrogating a treaty, the president, with approval of two-thirds of the Senate, probably needs to pass a new treaty that nullifies the previous one and substitutes any new one in its place. (Similarly George W. Bush later unilaterally withdrew from the Anti-Ballistic Missile Treaty without any congressional action.)

Similarly, Carter, also based on a changed strategic situation, wisely tried to withdraw the 32,000 US troops stationed in South Korea. In 1950, at the time of the Korean War, South Korea was a poor, underdeveloped nation that was outgunned by North Korea. By the time Carter became president, the South Korean economic miracle had given that country a GDP many times that of North Korea. Thus, it was high time the South Koreans did more for their own defense. Carter believed that in any emergency, the United States could help out with air power and logistics. Nervous nellies in Congress and even the White House put so much pressure on Carter that he had to suspend implementation of the withdrawal. In a Harry Truman–like move to demonstrate civilian control over the military, Carter fired General John K. Singlaub for telling Congress that the troop withdrawal would mean war.[22]

The Cutting of Unneeded Weapons

Carter eliminated the development of the B-1 bomber, the closest to production that any major weapon has ever been killed. Ronald Reagan, as a symbol of his greater commitment to national security than Carter—even though Carter had ramped up US defense spending after the Soviets invaded Afghanistan—later reinstated the plane. Carter was proven prescient, because the flying white elephant had years of difficulty with its electronic warfare systems, thus limiting its use to being a flying truck to drop bombs only after enemy air defenses had been knocked down. Similarly, Carter terminated an aircraft carrier that the Navy did not need (the Navy is centered around these very vulnerable ships). Carter also killed the neutron weapon, a high-radiation tactical nuclear weapon designed to kill people but leave buildings standing. On the margins, the weapon made nuclear war more likely by making nuclear weapons easier to use without totally destroying society. Besides, with an arsenal already containing thousands of nuclear weapons, the United States hardly needed yet another type of warhead.

Regrettably, Carter had to accept increases in the defense budget and the procurement of the destabilizing nuclear-tipped MX missile, which was a first-strike long-range weapon, each one of which could carry ten warheads. He took these actions to try to get congressional support for the SALT II arms limitation treaty, which equalized the limit on total strategic warheads each country could have at between 10,000 and 12,000 but allowed one new missile system. This incremental reduction from SALT I limits kept each superpower to 2,250 nuclear delivery vehicles, with limits on categories of weapons, such as heavy intercontinental ballistic missiles (ICBMs) and the deployment of tactical bombers and cruise missiles.

The worst of all worlds eventually happened when Carter had to withdraw the treaty from Senate consideration in the wake of the Soviet invasion of Afghanistan (however, the treaty was informally observed thereafter by both sides), and his invulnerable racetrack basing mode for MX missiles later fell victim to domestic protests in the American West—protestors objected to the missiles traveling around the countryside on mobile launchers. Thus, Reagan, instead of cancelling the system, finally had to deploy the huge missiles in existing fixed silos. This decision deployed many warheads in each vulnerable hole, creating lucrative and tempting targets that could have acted as a lightning rod for a Soviet nuclear first strike to take them out.

Yet both Reagan, coerced by Congress, and the Soviets informally observed the limits of the SALT II Treaty, despite the fact that it remained officially unratified. Thus, while Ford and Carter effectively achieved a de facto major limitation of strategic nuclear arms, Reagan later passed up the chance to actually reduce such long-range weapons in order to retain his fanciful and unworkable Star Wars dream of strategic defenses. Reagan had to settle for an Intermediate-Range Nuclear Forces (INF) Treaty that banned an entire class of shorter intermediate-range nuclear weapons, which many conservatives, at the time, argued undermined the defense of Western Europe in the face of allegedly superior Warsaw Pact conventional forces. Moreover, Carter had made the INF Treaty possible by making the decision, in December 1979, to deploy US Pershing II intermediate-range ballistic missiles and Ground Launched Cruise Missiles (GLCMs) in Europe to offset the Soviet deployment of intermediate-range SS-20 missiles. Carter's deployment created an incentive for the Soviets to agree to Reagan's proposal to remove the entire missile class.

Rectifying Past Policy Failures

Like Warren Harding after the tragic and unnecessary US involvement in World War I, Carter courageously tried to heal the nation's wounds after US involvement in the long brushfire Vietnam War—and was heavily criticized for it. The day after his inauguration, he granted unconditional amnesty to 10,000 Americans who had been convicted, were being indicted, or went abroad to avoid being drafted by the government to fight an unpopular war. Ironically, these men had their liberty infringed by being shanghaied by their government to "fight for freedom." Unsurprisingly, this move angered veterans groups.

As a reaction to Richard Nixon's abuse of the CIA and FBI during Watergate, Carter restricted warrantless spying at home. Prior to Carter's tenure, it was apparently unclear to US intelligence agencies whether they could conduct warrantless physical searches inside the United States. Carter signed an executive order stipulating that if a judicial warrant was needed for snooping on someone in the United States for law enforcement purposes, it also was needed for intelligence purposes, unless the president and attorney general signed off on it and the attorney general concluded that there was probable cause to believe that the person was the agent of a foreign power. Because the Constitution's Fourth Amendment specifies no exemptions from judicial warrants for national security, any president's substituting his approval for the requirement is probably still unconstitutional. Nevertheless, Carter substantially restricted warrantless domestic spying by intelligence agencies. Also, Carter pushed Congress to pass the Foreign Intelligence Surveillance Act (FISA), which required judicial warrants from a FISA court for electronic surveillance of Americans for intelligence purposes. Finally, Carter expanded restrictions on the CIA's domestic role and tightened presidential oversight of covert operations.[23]

Hawks made a big deal about the discovery of a small brigade of Soviet troops in Cuba, which violated no agreement between the United States and the USSR and had been there since the 1960s. In an Eisenhower-like move, Carter defused the "crisis" by saying that no crisis existed (which was true) and augmented reconnaissance and US presence in the Caribbean.[24]

Carter redirected US support away from the white minority government in Rhodesia (now Zimbabwe) and worked with Britain to create a path toward black majority rule. Carter was able to take advantage of the election of the first black prime minister in Rhodesia to lift economic sanctions against that country. Although the sanctions had been against the prior racist white government, they had only hurt black Rhodesians, whom they were supposed to be helping.

Strong Foreign Policy but with Mixed Results

One of Carter's most celebrated foreign policies lent more stability to the volatile Middle East but also had some drawbacks.

The Israeli-Egyptian Peace Treaty

Through the Camp David negotiations, Carter—helped by the fact that he was less pro-Israel than other presidents—mediated a durable peace treaty between Israel and Egypt, Israel's most powerful neighbor, using sheer personal will in the face of Israeli intransigence. The two countries recognized each other and established diplomatic relations. But to get the deal, Carter agreed to provide billions in US military and economic aid ad infinitum to get both nations to sign the arrangement—essentially a bribe. Bribing countries to do what is in their best interest anyway is not optimal policy. Carter also failed to keep his promise of involving the Soviet Union in the negotiations—much as Kissinger had fenced out the Soviet Union from the Middle East during and after the 1973 Arab-Israeli war.

In addition, the final status of the West Bank and Palestinian autonomy were finessed in order to get the Israeli-Egyptian peace treaty. Even then, Israel violated the spirit of the agreement by building new settlements on the West Bank.[25] International law prohibits permanently settling territory acquired through war, but Israel is still doing it today. In 1980, after the signing of the Camp David Accords, Carter, in a gutsy move just before the New York primary, approved a US vote in favor of a UN resolution calling on Israel to dismantle settlements in occupied Arab territories. Twice before in 1979, the United States had abstained on similar votes. The large Jewish population of New York was infuriated and voted in droves for Kennedy, who won the primary—in which he earlier had been in trouble—by a large margin.[26]

Contrary to conventional wisdom on the part of the American public, the United States has no vital security interest in safeguarding either Israel or peace between that nation and the Arabs; the issue is given importance merely because of domestic politics in the United States. Furthermore, giving huge amounts of military and economic aid to a fairly wealthy country should be embarrassing. Still Carter accomplished what no other president has been able to achieve even by Herculean efforts: helping at least some entities in the Middle East find a stable peace. And he courageously did so by putting more pressure on Israel than has been brought before or since—aggravating yet another Democratic constituency before the election.

Emphasizing Human Rights Globally

Unlike George W. Bush and other US presidents who used military force to spread democracy and regard for human rights, Carter kept his support mainly to rhetoric. However, Carter was suspicious of grandiose moral pronouncements, because, as he admitted at the United Nations, "our own ideals in the area of human rights have not always been attained in the United States."[27] In general, Carter eschewed imposing economic sanctions on human rights-abusing countries and instead wanted to give them positive inducements for reforms in the long term. For example, Carter criticized the genocidal regime of Pol Pot but wisely avoided imposing economic sanctions. Sanctions imposed from outside can often make things worse for those abused by shoring up internal support for any despotic regime through the "rally-around-the-flag" effect and also can make the autocracy more vindictive against its opposition. Also, dictators can usually rechannel the economic pain of sanctions from pillars of the target regime—the security forces and supporters of the despot—to the oppressed people the sanctioning country is trying to help.

Yet spending taxpayer dollars to actively aid human rights-abusing nations is an entirely different matter. Shortly after taking office, Carter laudably reduced US aid to three nations that abused human rights.[28] Carter had set up a committee to review whether developmental aid should continue to countries that abused individual freedoms. Carter focused his human rights program on Latin America, because these countries were not believed to be as vital to US interests as were nations in other parts of the world (by sheer proximity to US territory, this belief was misplaced). Because of human rights concerns, Carter restricted military aid to Argentina, Uruguay, Chile, Brazil, Paraguay, and several Central American countries. Human rights violations decreased in Latin America from 1977 to 1981, but how much of this improvement was attributable to Carter's policy is in doubt. David Hawk, former director of Amnesty International, did give credit to Carter for improvements in human rights in a number of countries, including Chile and Argentina.

Carter, however, opposed a successful congressional initiative to make US votes in international financial institutions contingent on borrowing countries not having human rights problems. Even in this international lending arena, the United States concentrated its efforts on Latin American human rights, nixing twenty-two loans to Latin America but only seven to Africa and four to East Asia.[29]

Even Carter's restrained efforts to promote human rights sometimes may have been counterproductive, because many authoritarian countries resisted another country's, even a superpower's, public criticism of their internal policies. Some countries reacted in anger to US criticism by cracking down on local dissidents. For example, Carter set a precedent for Reagan's later heated rhetoric toward the Soviet and Eastern European governments by scolding their political and economic status, publicly complaining about their treatment of those who dissented politically, and openly reaching out to Soviet dissidents. In response to Carter's public remonstrations, the Soviets promptly clamped down on dissidents. Such public chastisement of the Soviet human rights record also undermined US-Soviet détente. Similarly, Carter also generated a crackdown on the South African opposition when he and his appointees publicly criticized the apartheid government's policies.

However, the US government can monitor the fate of foreign dissidents and democracy advocates in autocratic countries, and Carter did require the designation of "human rights officers" in every American embassy overseas, who were to have blunt discussions with foreign officials about their human rights issues and to meet with abused citizens of that country. However, Carter learned that American protests about human rights violations are best kept behind the scenes to avoid a backlash from those nations that would hurt the people the United States was trying to help. As Carter's presidential term matured, his advocacy of human rights, originating from his evangelical Christian beliefs, did become more pragmatic. For example, such moderation was evident in the administration's behavior toward dictatorships in Iran, Egypt, Saudi Arabia, Indonesia, South Korea, the Philippines, China, and Zaire—countries that were perceived as important to US security.

Carter was trying to reduce US forces on the front line of the Cold War in South Korea, a dictatorship at the time, so he put human rights on the back burner—even when South Korean leader Park Chung Hee was assassinated in December 1979 and Chun Doo Hwan, his successor, brutally repressed pro-democracy protestors in May 1980. Carter voted against loans from international financial organizations to South Korea while Park was still in office and quietly remonstrated to South Korean officials about human rights conditions. However, Carter did not make public appeals for fear of destabilizing the regime and did not ever link US military aid to South Korean improvement on human rights.[30] In the end, Carter failed to significantly reduce US military forces stationed there, and South Koreans eventually took matters into their own hands—the best way to get results—finally achieving democracy.

In Nicaragua, a country perceived to be less important to US interests than South Korea, Carter, during the Sandinista Revolution, took the opposite approach against a despotic government. He initially criticized both the human rights record of the right-wing Somoza regime and the Soviet and Cuban support of the Sandinista opposition, but as the Sandinistas gained more Nicaraguan public support and military power, Carter pressured Somoza to relinquish power by cutting off military and economic aid. He feared Somoza's reluctance to give up power would radicalize the opposition. After the

Sandinistas took power, Carter tried to work with the new government, while trying unsuccessfully to constrain it within a coalition government. However, the Sandinista government moved to the left and began supporting socialist opposition movements in other Central American countries, including El Salvador.

The Soviet Invasion of Afghanistan

The conventional wisdom is that Carter was naïve about the Soviet Union until it invaded Afghanistan in December of 1979. However, Carter prophetically believed that American values had a magnetic appeal around the world and that the Soviet system eventually would be doomed by obsolescence. Thus, Carter started his term emphasizing international economic interdependence instead of East-West hostility. Carter's faith in future American triumph over its superpower rival was regarded at the time as complacency.[31] Yet, in the long term, Kissinger's pessimistic détente—an attempt to manage US decline—was less prescient than Carter's more optimistic view.

Unfortunately, Carter eventually became spooked and drifted from this confident and correct position. His policy toward the USSR began to harden in early 1978, despite advances in arms control negotiations, because of Soviet subversion in Africa and its use of Cuban troops as proxies there. Carter, unlike Reagan, gave the cold shoulder to the racist apartheid government in South Africa, which Reagan later embraced as an ally in the fight against Communists in Angola, Namibia, and Mozambique. The Communists also seemed to be ascendant in Central America, with the seizure of power by the Sandinistas in Nicaragua and a similar Marxist guerrilla movement threatening the US-sponsored right-wing dictatorship in El Salvador. Carter initially cut off aid to the El Salvadoran government because of human rights abuses but then restored it in the wake of rebel gains and conservative complaints. Yet neither the poor nations of Africa nor Central America were strategic to the United States.[32]

US-Soviet relations had already deteriorated by mid-1978, in part because of Carter's restrictions on US-Soviet trade and cancellation of official US visits in response to Soviet trials of dissidents, and détente finally ended and the full Cold War resumed in 1979. After the Soviet invasion of Afghanistan in December 1979, Carter overreacted by increasing defense spending significantly, withdrawing from pending congressional ratification the prized SALT II arms control treaty negotiated with the Soviets, deciding that the United States would boycott the Olympics to be held in 1980 in the USSR, registering males for a possible future draft (no draft was ever proposed), and launching a unilateral US technology and grain embargo against the superpower rival. Otherwise, Carter did not have many policy options in response, because Afghanistan is geographically much closer to the USSR than it is to the United States and was also in the Soviet sphere of influence, thus ensuring that the Soviet Union would have local military superiority in any superpower dust-up over the country. Therefore, Carter's actions were mainly symbolic options to protest, short of launching a war against a nuclear-armed adversary.

The measures had little effect. In the case of the Olympics, Carter did not have the authority to prevent athletes from traveling to Moscow to compete or to prohibit the private US Olympic Committee from sponsoring them. Yet Carter won by coercion, threatening legal action against the athletes and the committee.[33] Regarding the embargoes, the Soviets merely bought their technology and grain from other countries, many of them friends and allies of the United States. If ineffective, the grain embargo was courageous, coming shortly before the Iowa political caucuses that Carter needed to win on the road to possible reelection in 1980. The people of Iowa, however, rallied to the president in a time of perceived international crisis, and Carter beat Ted Kennedy handily in the caucuses anyway.

Carter responded hyperbolically to the Soviet invasion, calling it "the most serious threat to the peace since the Second World War."[34] (Hardly; he obviously had forgotten the Cuban Missile Crisis, the Soviet blockade of Berlin, and the 1973 Middle East war, all of which could have escalated to a nuclear holocaust.) Also, Carter later exaggerated, saying that "a successful takeover of Afghanistan would . . . pose a threat to the rich oil fields of the Persian Gulf area and to the crucial waterways through which so much of the world's energy supplies had to pass."[35]

Yet the Soviets invaded Afghanistan for defensive reasons, not to get Persian Gulf oil or a warm water port. If they had wanted those prizes, they could have instead invaded Iran—Afghanistan is a land-locked nation relatively far from the Persian Gulf. The Soviets had been alarmed by the recent

Islamist takeover of Iran and worried that radical Islamism would infect their own Muslim regions. So they sent thousands of military advisers to shore up the Marxist government in Afghanistan. But then another Marxist tyrant overthrew their Marxist client ruler in that country, making the Soviets fear that the new leader would pull an Anwar Sadat–like about-face and go from their camp into the American camp, leading to US intelligence posts right on their border. This fear motivated their full-blown invasion of Afghanistan in December 1979.[36]

In fact, whether Carter believed his own hyperbole or not, his national security advisor, Zbigniew Brzezinski, had been wanting for some time to have a permanent US military role in the Persian Gulf to deal with his own imaginary "arc of crisis" from Yemen to Bangladesh. The first pillar of US strategy to ensure stability in the Persian Gulf region after the British left the Middle East in the late 1960s—the Shah of Iran (Saudi Arabia was the second)—was faltering in 1978 and early 1979 due to the Iranian revolution. Also, although the United States was the dominant oil producer in the world until the late 1960s, it became an oil importer in the 1970s and had to weather the overly hyped Arab oil embargo and production cuts that came in response to US aid to Israel during the 1973 Middle East war. These factors drove the US desire to have an imperial role in the Persian Gulf to rival its other two regions of intense strategic interest, Europe and East Asia. The Soviet invasion of Afghanistan in December 1979 was merely used to justify implementation of this preexisting desire for a permanent military role in the Gulf and to make Arab countries in the region more accepting of it.

In 1980, facilities were rapidly set up in Saudi Arabia to house US combat aircraft in time of crisis and also to permanently base American AWACS command and surveillance aircraft in the kingdom. Also, light US ground forces that could use strategic mobility via cargo aircraft were designated as a Rapid Deployment Force (RDF), which could be deployed quickly to the region during a crisis. Later, Reagan permanently assigned more American forces to the Persian Gulf and upgraded the RDF to the US Central Command. Yet, the imperial Carter Doctrine to defend Persian Gulf oil against "outside" powers, issued after the Soviets invaded Afghanistan, already had been largely predefined.[37]

However, the symbolic response to the Soviet invasion of Afghanistan was a better policy than aiding the Afghan mujahideen rebels to give the Soviets their own Vietnam—a policy the hawkish National Security Advisor Zbigniew Brzezinski also had started even before the Soviet invasion. This timing has led some to speculate about whether Carter was trying to actually lure the Soviets to invade Afghanistan in the first place. Ronald Reagan later greatly expanded this military assistance effort, not just attempting to bog down the USSR in Afghanistan but to defeat it there.

Although this policy of aiding the rebels seemed like a good idea during the Cold War, it is an example of how foreign interventions can have severe unforeseen consequences. The strengthened Islamist Afghan insurgents did cause the Soviets to withdraw from Afghanistan at the end of the 1980s but later morphed into al Qaeda—the most severe threat to the continental United States since the War of 1812. Although some proponents of this US intervention, including Brzezinski, later claimed that this brushfire war had a pivotal role in bringing down the Soviet Union and was thus worth the unfortunate side effects, it was, at best, only one of several factors leading to the USSR's collapse, and ultimately endangered American citizens at home. In reality, it was Carter's most important policy failure (and one of Reagan's greatest too). As previously noted, Carter tried to use the Chinese as a counterweight to the Soviet Union in the East by selling them weapons and high technology and giving them normalized trade relations, all of which the Soviets were denied.

If anything—because of the oil price spikes of the early and late 1970s, the second arising from Iranian petroleum production being taken off the world market because of Iran's revolution—the Carter administration was excessively energy crazy. The Soviet invasion of Afghanistan led to the Carter Doctrine, pledging that the United States would directly defend the Persian Gulf with military force—a dramatic change from prior policy. In his State of the Union address in early 1980, he bluntly told the Soviet Union, "An attempt by any outside force to gain control of the Persian Gulf region will be regarded as an assault on the vital interests of the United States of America, and such an assault will be repelled by any means necessary, including military force."[38]

This new doctrine was unfortunately a step beyond the Nixon Doctrine, which had relied on Iran and Saudi Arabia to stabilize the Persian Gulf region but which was now obsolete because Iran had become a hostile Islamist state. In my book, *No War for Oil: U.S. Dependency and the Middle East*, I explain why oil is no more strategic than other products and that, even if production in certain places is disrupted by war or revolution here or there, it is still just cheaper to endure higher oil prices in the world market for a time than to pay hundreds of billions of dollars to keep military forces in the Gulf to prevent a cutoff of oil supplies that will probably never happen. Oil is a valuable commodity, and people and countries have a tremendous incentive to sell it into the world market—even through or around wars. So the Carter Doctrine was unnecessary and helped lead to later fiascos, such as the two expensive wars against Iraq.[39] All in all, even Carter's hardline anti-Soviet advisor Brzezinski thought Carter overreacted to the Soviet invasion of Afghanistan.

Carter's concern with the Middle East and oil also was a factor in his policy toward the Horn of Africa. Somalia, a Soviet client state, invaded Ethiopia over irredentist claims on the Ogaden desert in southern Ethiopia. The Soviets tried to get the two countries to make peace, but the Somalian leader refused, abrogated his treaty of friendship with the USSR, and turned to the United States for help. The Soviets then provided military aid to Ethiopia and airlifted in 12,000 Cuban troops and 1,500 Soviet military advisers in the hope of pushing Somalia out of the Ogaden. Brzezinski wanted to make inroads in an area perceived to be strategic, because it was near the Middle East. He wanted an aircraft carrier sent to the region and to provide US support to defend Somalia if invaded during the successful counterpunch that Ethiopia was mounting with Soviet and Cuban assistance. Brzezinski essentially wanted the United States to support an aggressor, just because the country had soured in its relations with the Soviet Union. Although Carter should have stayed out of this fight entirely, because the region was less strategic to the United States than commonly perceived, he did use restraint and conditioned the provision of defensive weaponry to Somalia on that country withdrawing from the Ogaden. Ethiopia, in the end, did not invade Somalia.[40]

Deregulation in the Economy

The US economy was fundamentally different in 1970 versus what it is at present. Substantial portions of it were governed by government regulations covering prices, entry into and exit from the market, business practices, and information reporting to the government.[41]

Carter was a pioneer in fully or partially deregulating four major industries—transportation, communication, finance, and energy. In the transportation industry, Carter terminated federal price regulation of railroads, trucking, interstate buses, and airlines.[42] The deregulation of the transportation industry was the most high profile, and within that sector, airline deregulation has been paid the most attention. According to John Howard Brown, an economist at Georgia Southern University who has studied airline deregulation, Carter appointed as regulators economists who had studied regulation, including Alfred ("Fred") Kahn. Three decades of research since airlines were allowed freer entry into the marketplace and the power to set their own prices shows that Carter's deregulation policy brought substantial benefits for the economy (greater efficiency) and consumers (lower airline fares). Although Kahn administratively gave airlines more leeway in setting routes and prices, he then spearheaded the passage of the Airline Deregulation Act of 1978, so that future industry-captured regulators could not reregulate the industry. The act dissolved the industry-dominated Civil Aeronautics Board (CAB) and its bureaucracy. And Brown adds that:

> the deregulatory impulse of the Carter administration did not die with the passage of the Airline Deregulation Act. The Motor Carrier Act and the Staggers Rail Act, both passed in 1980, extended deregulation of entry and rate setting to trucking firms and railroads, respectively. Thus, the Carter administration's deregulatory policies transformed American transportation industries into markets where competition, profit maximization, and entry, not the judgments of government bureaucrats, determined prices and service levels in a large segment of the economy. The benefits of this transformation appear to continue to this day.[43]

According to economists Steven Morrison and Clifford Winston, airline deregulation benefited consumers to the tune of $28.6 billion (converted to 2012 prices) in fare reduction and increased numbers of flights.[44] Ironically, Carter unwound one of the few areas of the economy regulated by Calvin Coolidge.[45]

Carter also began to phase out federal price controls in the oil and natural gas markets. This action increased the efficiency of the markets, and higher fuel prices led to more conservation, increased production, and enhanced the prospects of environmentally friendly alternative fuels. Congress's compromise on natural gas deregulation would not have been possible without Carter's interjection. Although ultimately deregulation may lower the price of any product by allowing new competitors into the market, in the short run, the gutsy Carter was hurt politically by conspicuous rises in fuel prices at home during a time of high inflation and already elevated world oil price spikes resulting from the Iranian revolution.

However, for the government to take away some of energy companies' newfound profits from deregulation, an ill-advised windfall profits tax was established. Carter also emphasized energy conservation and created a new Department of Energy—even though the functions of the new department already existed in other parts of the government.[46] In addition, Carter wasted money on expensive synthetic fuel programs and gave tax incentives to promote solar energy and home insulation (it was better than out-and-out subsidies, but still interfered with the free market for energy). During the second oil "crisis," gas lines recurred in the United States only because Carter's decontrol of oil prices was being phased in. In 1979, the OPEC cartel raised oil prices and then the Iranian revolution took large quantities of oil off the world market. Oil prices doubled, but that was not nearly enough to bring supply and demand into equilibrium, as some continued price controls in the United States ensured that excess demand would result in shortages, thus leading to traumatizing lines at gas stations.

Overall, Carter's energy policy was a mixed bag.[47] Although that policy was somewhat inconsistent, it was primarily designed to achieve the dubious goal of US energy independence, which is inefficient and usually just means artificial nonmarket price increases to consumers (in contrast to the aforementioned legitimate price increases from energy market deregulation). In fact, although many presidents have pledged to work toward that questionable objective, of all post-Truman presidents, Carter was the only one to increase the nation's energy independence.[48]

More generally, Carter improved executive branch efficiency and centralized control in the White House of a federal regulatory process that was out of control. Congress approved Carter's plan to reorganize the executive branch, the first such reorganization since Franklin Delano Roosevelt's administration.

One of the reforms Carter made was to get Congress to pass the Paperwork Reduction Act, which established the Office of Information and Regulatory Affairs (OIRA) office in the President's Office of Management and Budget.[49] The office centralized control over a haphazard and chaotic federal regulatory process by requiring White House review of every new federal regulation. Given the title of the act and Carter's record on deregulation, it is obvious that the office was designed to reduce, rather than increase, federal regulation.

Although Carter's 320 executive orders over four years look excessive compared to those in the four years each of Reagan and Bill Clinton and the entire eight years of George W. Bush, most of them focused on improving White House and executive branch efficiency. In contrast, some presidents use executive orders (especially in their second terms) to bypass Congress, when it is stalling a particular president's agenda. Executive orders are more defensible if used to implement Congress's wishes.

Carter implemented congressionally passed civil service reform, which enacted Carter's proposals for a new merit system and made it easier to fire incompetent federal employees. He also imposed financial disclosure rules and limits on gifts for his political appointees, slowed the revolving door of former officials lobbying their old departments for federal goodies, and appointed departmental inspectors general to root out fraud, waste, and abuse. Although these were additional rules and oversight, they were not aimed directly at the private sector, but only to cut down on crony capitalism—private business trying to win favors from the government instead of competing in the marketplace.

Yet using executive orders, Carter had his lapses. When Congress refused his proposal to create a consumer protection agency (such government efforts rarely help consumers, because they increase prices), he used an executive order to create a Consumer Affairs Council that advocated for consumers. The Constitution provides no federal role in advocating for consumers, and consumer advocates, by proposing and lobbying for more regulations and restrictions, do not in the end help consumers (again because such regulations increase prices).

One area where Carter largely stayed away from formal regulation but nevertheless caused problems was his "voluntary" wage and price "guidelines." Carter had not caused the sluggish economy and bad and worsening inflation. Johnson and Nixon had done this, even before the oil shocks of the 1970s, during the Vietnam War with "guns and butter" policies, and Nixon had printed money profligately to get reelected in 1972. Still, Carter was under immense pressure to do something about it.

Nixon's mandatory wage and price controls had failed to tame inflation. Under voluntary wage and price controls, the Carter administration still "jaw-boned" businesses and labor when they exceeded administration targets for price and wage increases. Also, implied coercion existed, because many economic actors thought that if they did not comply, Carter would eventually convert the voluntary controls to mandatory ones. Sure enough, in phase two of his anti-inflation program, some government actions were taken if wage and price standards were exceeded. Business leaders criticized Carter for dealing superficially with the problem and for not rectifying the underlying causes of inflation, which were expansion of the money supply and a growing budget deficit. Because overt wage and price controls were a disaster under the Nixon administration, Carter was trying a subtler approach—but this policy still failed to stem inflation. Carter was laudably trying to rein in the money supply and federal spending.

In general, Carter at first tried too hard to coordinate with friendly industrial nations—really lead them in multilateral disguise—on energy and economic policies to spur economic growth, but he later correctly realized that fighting inflation through fiscal and monetary austerity at home should take priority. In 1978, although Carter coordinated with the German Bundesbank to stabilize the plummeting dollar, he commendably resisted efforts to go back to a system of fixed exchange rates.

Prosperity in the 1980s and 1990s

Carter inherited stagflation from Nixon and Ford. Knowing that he would try to get elected on his own in 1976, Ford had switched in 1975 from whipping inflation—he had not—to stimulating economic growth. Thus, in 1976, the US economy grew by more than 5 percent. Keynesian economists were flummoxed by such stimulus initiatives in the mid-1970s because they spiked inflation without reducing unemployment.[50]

At first, Carter made economic mistakes, including making sporadic efforts to stimulate the domestic economy and selecting a first Federal Reserve chairman who expanded the money supply too generously. Carter took such actions because by the time he took office, inflation, in double digits in 1974–1975, had dropped to 5.2 percent. Carter thus initially prioritized economic growth over price stability, and the Federal Reserve had an easy money policy. Thus, the economy grew rapidly during 1977 and 1978 and inflation then rebounded. Then Carter dropped his international Keynesianism of multilateral economic policy coordination of 1977 and 1978 and adopted policies of fiscal frugality and monetary restraint at home. To fight inflation, Carter wisely curbed federal spending and adopted deregulation, but he unfortunately also pled with business and labor to adopt the previously mentioned "voluntary" wage and price guidelines.[51]

In one of the best decisions of his one-term presidential tenure, Carter eventually nominated a monetary hawk to be chairman of the Federal Reserve Board—Paul Volcker, formerly undersecretary of the treasury for international monetary affairs under Republican Richard Nixon—and gave him mostly free rein. Although almost all of his advisers warned Carter that appointing Volcker might endanger his chances of reelection, Carter courageously did so anyway, knowing full well what the consequences might be. Stuart Eizenstat, Carter's leading White House domestic policy adviser, noted that Carter had told his staff that he had tried budgetary restraint, two anti-inflation czars, and voluntary wage and price controls to curb raging inflation and all had had little effect. Carter said he would rather lose the election in 1980 because of Volcker's tight monetary policies than transmit entrenched inflation to the next generation.[52]

Volcker turned out to be one of the best Fed chairmen ever appointed. Volcker put on the monetary brakes, subjecting the United States to the first monetary discipline since Nixon went off what was left of the gold standard in 1971. Volcker's tight money policy led to plummeting inflation and a stronger dollar.

Even then, Carter's economic policies were not perfect. Before appointing Volcker as Federal Reserve Board chairman, Carter had mistakenly appointed

G. William Miller, an advocate of expansionary monetary policy. Then, for the only time in the entire history of the Fed, a presidential administration pressured the Fed to tighten, rather than loosen, the money supply. When Miller proved unresponsive, Carter yanked him as chairman for the more tight-fisted Volcker. Carter even appointed another member of the Fed's board who was more of a monetary hawk than Volcker.[53]

Carter became so zealous in trying to tame inflation that he went too far and unwisely established controls on consumer credit, which contributed to a brief, but steep, economic slowdown in 1980, which was a key factor in Carter losing the election to Ronald Reagan. In an election year, Carter had the lowest presidential approval rating ever, including that of Richard Nixon during Watergate. Yet Carter earned this low approval rating for bravely imposing much more conservative fiscal and monetary policies in his last two years as president than had the more economically progressive Nixon, who earned his low rating for corruption in the Watergate scandal and for the Vietnam War quagmire.

As his term wore on, Carter initially resisted the advice of his key advisers to raise spending and cut taxes to goose the economy to improve his chances in the 1980 election, thus sticking with his principled pledge to balance the budget for fiscal year 1981 in order to fight inflation. Unfortunately, just before the election, Carter was persuaded to publicly encourage Volcker to loosen the money supply a bit (it is unclear whether Volcker did so) and to endorse bolstering government spending.[54] He also had his administration offer a modest business tax cut to encourage investment. Ronald Reagan, his successor, continued these capital gains tax cuts and also Carter's deregulation program. He also took Carter's slippage up a notch—continuing spending, promulgating massive essentially fraudulent tax cuts, and failing to tell the American people that somehow that spending had to be paid for one way or another.[55]

During the first years of Reagan's first term, Volcker's continuing tight monetary policy led to a steep recession. The recession finally wrung the inflation of the 1970s out of the economy, to which it has never returned even decades later. Thus, the prosperity for the rest of the Reagan years and the Clinton years can be attributed to tight money policies first pioneered by a

Carter appointee. Unfortunately for Carter, he was penalized politically in the 1980 election for beginning the tight money policies that would initially lead to a recession during that year and would not lead to prosperity until the longer term in the mid-1980s and 1990s. Even before Volcker took office, however, the Carter administration had begun tightening credit to fight inflation, despite the risk of starting a recession—to which it did contribute.

Budget Wars

In addition to economic deregulation, a restrictive fiscal policy can fight inflation. Carter chose to restrain spending and attempt to balance the budget, even at the expense of higher unemployment. Traditional Democrats did not like this prioritization. Carter did work in a tax cut, but concerned about the budget deficit, he nixed the huge 30 percent, across-the-board income tax cuts pushed by Congressmen Jack Kemp and William Roth.[56] (However, even before Reagan took office, the Carter White House and a committee run by Democrats in the Senate touted supply-side economics—tax cuts that stimulated economic growth by spurring investment rather than hiking consumption.[57]) A version of the Kemp-Roth policy later became Ronald Reagan's domestic centerpiece, which blew a hole in the budget because Reagan, over the course of his administration, increased federal spending as a proportion of GDP.

In contrast, Carter was a more traditional and rare type of conservative, worrying about the budget deficit and thus elevating the priority of cutting spending over cutting taxes. Carter once reflected, "The Great Society days are over, the problems of the nation can't be solved with massive spending programs, public works, et cetera."[58] Carter did slightly increase federal spending as a percentage of GDP, but such growth was fairly restrained (he was the fourth best president since Truman in exhibiting such restraint), and Carter slashed the budget deficit as a percentage of GDP (second best next to Clinton during the same time frame) and thus reduced debt accumulation as a portion of GDP (third best in this category). Carter also restrained welfare and social spending. As a result of such restrained federal spending and deficit and debt reduction, Carter was third among post-Truman presidents in increasing income and wealth and fourth best in growth in real GDP per capita. Carter also had the fourth best record in cutting civilian federal executive branch personnel as a percentage of the population (Reagan was the second worst in increasing it).[59]

Examples of Carter's attempts at fiscal restraint abound. Carter advocated reforming welfare, without increasing the budget for such programs, many years before Bill Clinton did it and then Barack Obama undid it. Carter's conservative initiatives to reform welfare and the tax code went nowhere because Thomas P. "Tip" O'Neill, the liberal Democratic speaker of the House, opposed them.[60]

Similarly, in trying to fulfill his commitment to achieving a balanced budget by 1981, Carter attempted to reduce the minimum prices farmers received for crops—that is, farm subsidies. But because Congress passed higher target prices than existing ones with veto proof margins, it made no sense for Carter to veto the bill. His original proposal to cut farm price supports would have cost $1.4 billion per year from 1978 to 1981; in contrast, Congress's lavish spending on such subsidies cost $6.2 billion per annum.[61] Although also under severe pressure from urban constituencies, the support of which he needed to win reelection, Carter courageously tried to restrain increases in funding for cities. He refused to include any new federal urban initiatives in the 1979 budget. His urban policy emphasized the role of neighborhood and volunteer groups and state and local governments, not just slathering cities with more federal largesse.

In addition, Big Labor remained angry at his support of restraint on minimum wage increases, his fighting inflation at the expense of stimulating the economy, and his use of a Taft-Hartley injunction to force coalminers back to work during the coal strike of 1978. Much to the chagrin of primarily Democratic steel workers (and the steel companies), Carter refused to protect the declining US steel industry from foreign competition.[62] This free market policy made Carter look better than the later Reagan administration, which claimed to have a "free market" orientation but, in reality, pursued some protectionist policies. As previously discussed, Carter did many brave things politically that sabotaged his reelection chances (it was surprising that the election ended up so close anyway).

Another one of these unpopular measures was welcoming with open arms all the Cubans—125,000 to be exact—that Castro wanted to get rid of during the Mariel boatlift. Most of these refugees went to the key election state of Florida, which was none too happy with the influx.[63] Furthermore, Carter opposed federal funding for abortions, a favorite issue with Democrats. Finally, even before the Soviet invasion of Afghanistan, Carter had promised NATO allies to increase US inflation-adjusted defense spending by 3 percent per year. However, he had also pledged to hold the deficit in fiscal year 1980 to $30 billion or less, so most of the budget cuts had to come from domestic programs.[64] Carter's fiscal belt-tightening and Volcker's interest rate hikes led to a brief, but severe, election year recession in 1980 that helped cost Carter a second term.[65] None of the above measures would make Democratic constituencies happy.

At election time, Carter would suffer the loss of Democratic progressives because he challenged their ideas about an interventionist federal government.[66] Also alienating key voting constituencies in his party, Carter, remaining a true outsider during his presidency, disdained the interest group politics of pork and often refused to offer pork in exchange for legislation he wanted. In fact, he tried to cut dam and water projects and was successful in reducing the budget for them. Thus, like many of the better presidents in American history, he made enough enemies that he was only permitted by voters to serve one term.

To keep the budget in check and fight inflation, Carter rejected Edward Kennedy's budget-busting National Health Insurance proposal that would have provided mandatory healthcare to people from a payroll tax and general tax revenues.[67] By rejecting Kennedy's proposal, Carter insured himself a rare primary challenge to a sitting president in 1980, thus ensuring a party split that usually dooms the party to electoral defeat in the fall; it did.

Limited Frugality

Carter was not always so frugal. Carter and Congress established, much to conservatives' chagrin, standalone departments for education and energy; these functions already existed in the federal government before Carter did so but are ideally better located at the state and local level. For example, to create the new Department of Education, Carter ripped the education function from the Department of Health, Education, and Welfare. He also increased college tuition grants for teenagers from low-income households.

As part of his energy plan, Carter established the Energy Security Corporation to fund the development of synthetic fuels. Chasing the bipartisan canard of the desirability of independence from foreign oil or energy imports, those fuels were expensive to make and a total waste of taxpayer dollars.

Carter and Congress provided federal loan guarantees to then bankrupt New York, so that the city could reenter credit markets. Carter also bailed out the Chrysler Corporation, which should have been allowed to go out of business and had to be bailed out again later by George W. Bush and Barack Obama.

One more complication was the Social Security program. Inflation was causing benefits to increase, but revenues were declining, leading to red ink. To keep the program solvent, Carter proposed a modest increase in the payroll tax, which would be offset by a cut income tax as a part of his tax reform proposal.[68]

Although in contrast to most forms of federal regulation, which are designed to help special interests, one could make the case that some environmental regulation is done for the "general welfare," a requirement stipulated in the Constitution for federal involvement. For example, Carter reauthorized the Clean Air and Clean Water acts and protected the offshore outer continental shelf. However, most environmental regulation, if done at all, should be done in the most efficient method possible and is probably best carried out at the state level. Yet, no explicit delegation of authority to the federal government over natural resources is given in the Constitution; it is a stretch to allow such regulation under Congress's authority to regulate interstate commerce. For example, Carter's Alaska National Interest Lands Conservation Act, which provided federal protection for rivers and lands in Alaska and greatly expanded national parks and wilderness areas there, instead should have been done by that state. Similarly, Carter signed a law providing federal funds to clean up toxic wastes (Superfund) and approved surface mining control legislation, both of which also probably would have been better done at the state level.

Miscellaneous Policies

In reaction to Watergate, Carter advocated for and passed the Ethics in Government Act, which attempted to use transparency to keep government officials away from corruption—for example, the president and others would have to publically disclose income and gifts. Also, the act authorized a three-judge panel to appoint an independent counsel, at the attorney general's request, to investigate government wrongdoing. The Supreme Court ruled this provision constitutional, because the judiciary may appoint "inferior officers." However, the provision ran into controversy, with some saying the independent counsel investigations were too many, too long, and too costly, thus motivating President Clinton and Congress to let the independent counsel law expire. Less beneficial were the law's restrictions on lobbying and the creation of the Office of Government Ethics to investigate, in conjunction with the attorney general, government corruption.[69] Although well-meaning, the real way to have less government corruption, which stems from poor incentives on the part of public officials, is to have less government.

Carter endorsed extending the seven-year period for ratifying the Equal Rights Amendment (ERA) when enough states could not get it passed by the cutoff date. (The proposed amendment never got enough state ratifications to be enacted.)

The Carter administration filed a brief for the Supreme Court's deliberations in the case of Bakke, who charged that the University of California, Davis's setting aside a 16-percent quota for minority students in its medical school violated the Equal Protection clause of the Fourteenth Amendment and the Civil Rights Act of 1964. The administration defended affirmative action programs that used race as a factor for admission but opposed quotas. And that is how the Supreme Court ruled in the case.[70]

Precedent-Setting Policies

Although today's conservatives would be apoplectic at this reality, Jimmy Carter set many precedents, for better or worse, for "conservative" Reagan's policies. Historian Daniel J. Sargent best sums up the continuity in tack and bears quoting at length:

> Carter's strategic evaluation entailed policy departures that would become identified with his successor, Ronald Reagan. The continuities between Carter and Reagan would be clear in economic policy, where the dollar-rescue package of 1978 and the Volcker shift of 1979

prefigured the dogged pursuit in the early 1980s of price stability at the expense of other goals. Continuities would also be apparent in defense policy, where Carter initiated an increase in military spending that reversed Nixon's efforts to tame the Cold War's costs.

The White House in the winter of 1979–1980 pushed Congress to increase defense appropriations, and it elaborated a five-year plan for modernizing America's nuclear and conventional forces. Supplemental appropriations would increase military spending for 1981 beyond the levels that Carter proposed, but it was Carter who initiated the return to elevated levels of defense spending, marking the end of détente's fiscal dividend. . . . Besides increasing expenditures, the Carter administration elaborated military doctrines that anticipated its successor's new Cold War posture. In July 1980, Carter signed PD-59, directing the elaboration of specific plans for waging and winning a limited nuclear war. While the directive was less radical than its critics presumed, public disclosure of the PD-59 exercise confirmed the remilitarization of the Cold War, stirring fear and debate. Jimmy Carter's early hopes that he and Brezhnev would negotiate unprecedented cuts in the size of their nuclear arsenals and roll back a thirty-year-old strategic arms race now seemed distant.

Afghanistan became the cockpit of the resurgent Cold War. US aid to the mujahideen in fact antedated the Red Army's invasion, but Carter escalated US involvement in December 1979, channeling military assistance to the anti-Soviet guerillas. The consequences of the new Cold War reverberated elsewhere in the Third World, including Central America. Having indulged a leftist regime in Nicaragua, the Carter administration threw its support behind the right-wing junta that seized power in neighboring El Salvador in October 1979. This was a turning point in Carter's Latin American policy, away from human rights toward anti-Communism.[71]

Writing mainly about foreign policy, Sargent does not mention that Reagan continued Carter's deregulation of the economy and may not have done as good a job of it. As for monetary tightening to fight inflation, Carter had appointed Paul Volcker and given him mostly free rein, but then Reagan supported him for a while and then fired him in favor of the inconsistent Alan Greenspan. Thus, Carter was the first conservative president since Warren Harding and Calvin Coolidge, not Reagan; in some cases Carter was more conservative than Reagan, who was mostly image.

In defense and nuclear matters, Carter baited and then overreacted to the Soviet invasion of Afghanistan. Reagan jacked up Carter's aid to the Afghan mujahideen and also lavished unneeded largesse on the already bloated Defense Department, thus contributing significantly to the ballooning budget deficits of the 1980s. Carter's PD-59 plan to fight a limited nuclear war was downright dangerous, and Reagan continued Carter's overheated rhetoric toward the Soviet Union and thus almost caused a nuclear war in 1983. Reagan was even more reckless than was Carter in needlessly supporting thuggish forces in small, insignificant Central American countries in order to fight Communism. As noted previously, Reagan is given credit (or blame) for increasing defense spending, but Carter had started the military buildup and is tied for fourth among post-Truman presidents in Mike Kimel and Michael E. Kanell's *Presimetrics* index on military affairs (averaging presidents' ranks on the size of the US military as a percentage of the American population and defense expenditures as a portion of federal expenditures); Reagan was tied for first in the index with George W. Bush.[72]

Conclusion

An effective president is one who is effective in getting his policies—good or bad—instituted any way possible. A successful president is one who enacts good policies—by the standards of our discussion, those limiting government—instituted by constitutional means. The conventional wisdom would be that even if you agreed with most of Jimmy Carter's policies—I do—that he was ineffective in getting what he wanted. Yet the conventional script ignores the fact that most of Carter's initiatives were realized.

Carter is seen as a failure, largely because he did not get reelected to a second term. Yet this election loss is generally attributed to (1) Carter appointee Paul Volcker's much-needed tightening of the money supply to lower inflation, which caused a recession in an election year, and (2) the failed hostage rescue mission in Iran.

Carter just had bad luck to serve as president at a time of stagflation (high inflation and growing unemployment), caused by the Vietnam War, prior expansive monetary policy so that Richard Nixon could get reelected in 1972, and to a much lesser extent by a severe oil shock caused by the Iranian revolution. The last "crisis" masked economic growth at a healthy rate during most of Carter's years.[73]

The hostage rescue mission failure, blamed by Republicans on a "hollowing out of the military" under Carter, exempts the military from appropriate blame. Moreover, if the military was hollowed out, it was a result of the Vietnam War, and as noted, Carter was increasing defense spending even before Reagan took office.

In fact, many of the best presidents in US history served only one term, because they did unpopular things that needed to be done (or undone)—some even against the wishes of their own party. Carter was one of those presidents. In contrast to Reagan's pretending to be an outsider (he hired Washington insiders as staffers after he got elected), Carter remained an outsider by often going against the advice of his aides and the demands of key constituencies in his party whose support he needed to get reelected. For example, he made progressives, labor unions, and African-Americans mad by cutting domestic programs and emphasizing the fight against inflation rather than against unemployment. His more neutral stance in the Middle East allowed him to broker the Camp David peace accords between Israel and the Arabs but cost him among American Jews, who felt he had a pro-Arab tilt in his foreign policy. The uproar over this perceived tilt was a factor in Carter's loss in the New York Democratic primary to Senator Edward Kennedy and also may have figured into his loss of the Michigan, California, Pennsylvania, and New Jersey primaries, thus weakening his candidacy in the general election against Reagan.[74] So rather than stagflation or his inability to get the hostages quickly released, when a US military attack on Iran would have gotten them killed, Carter likely was not reelected mostly because he gored vested interests in his own party. An intra-party challenge to a sitting president is the kiss of death for reelection. Yet Carter invited this outcome from liberal Democrats because he had rejected Senator Kennedy's costly universal healthcare proposal. Had Carter had a solid party of Democrats behind him, he probably could have weathered stagflation and the hostage crisis.

Finally, Carter—not Reagan—was the first conservative president in the almost fifty years since Calvin Coolidge left office in 1929. Carter set many of the precedents for limiting government and deregulating the economy that Reagan unjustly was given all the credit for because of his "small government" rhetoric and Republican label.

7

Busting the Myths

MUCH OF THE mythology that Ronald Reagan won the Cold War and was a small government conservative has nothing to do with his policy record while president and everything to do with his legacy being used as a weapon by conservatives against a subsequent Democratic president. Reagan's rise as a conservative idol did not occur in the 1980s when he was president (from 1981 to 1989), but during the 1990s, when conservative activists needed a hero to use against the Clinton administration.

Conservatives did not have too many choices as chief executive to revere, because the last Republican presidents who were really for small government were Warren Harding and Calvin Coolidge, who served in the 1920s. Yet even conservative author Brion McClanahan compares Reagan unfavorably to Coolidge:

> Even Reagan, so often lauded by conservatives for his principled stand against Leftist innovation could not match Coolidge's record in relation to defending his oath of office. . . .
>
> Coolidge was more of a common man than Truman, more of a conservative than Reagan, and certainly the last man to occupy the executive office who truly believed in the Constitution as ratified. His vision was short-lived, and it returned only briefly as a shadow of its former self in the 1980s [when Reagan was president]. If Americans were to somehow regain their reverence for the executive restraint so lauded by the founding generation, Coolidge would be the only twentieth-century example to emulate.[1]

Although many conservatives during the Reagan administration and shortly thereafter were unhappy with Reagan's policy record, they did not have many icons to use against Bill Clinton; Reagan was charismatic, talked the talk of small government, and had the image of being a fairly successful president. Rhetoric is what people believe and remember because they have only limited means to assess a politician's actual policy record, and as memories of the Reagan years faded, conservative criticism of Reagan's policies morphed into praise for his anti-Communist and small government oratory. Subsequent to his leaving office, conservatives made an arduous effort to sanitize Reagan's record, thus burnishing his image as having done conservative things.[2]

Ironically, the man the new conservative Reagan superman was created to compete against—Bill Clinton—turned out to be more conservative on some issues than the Gipper, but he was a Democrat. As the entire discussion does for other supposedly "small government" presidents, this particular discussion attempts to destroy the Reagan myths and paint a more realistic picture of his real-world policy record.

Despite a long history of duplicitous politicians in America, many citizens still accept presidents' rhetoric at face value rather than researching their actual policy record to see if those match. In the case of Ronald Reagan, an actor whose administration revolutionized presidential image-making in the media, the rhetoric-policy gap is unusually large, especially with the image that Reagan "won the Cold War."

In fact, one deputy presidential press secretary, Leslie Janka, who resigned because reporters were banned from coverage of the US invasion of Grenada in 1983, said the public relations spin of the administration got out of hand and drove everything. "This is a PR outfit that became President and took over the country. And to the degree then to which the Constitution forced them to do things like make a budget, run foreign policy and all that, they sort of did. But their first, last, and overarching activity was public relations."[3] Even Mike Deaver, Reagan's chief image-maker, admitted, "We kept apple pie and the flag going the whole time."[4] Historian Lewis L. Gould concluded that Reagan was second only to Reagan's idol, Franklin D. Roosevelt, among modern presidents in his ability to use the media to communicate.[5]

Lou Cannon, a journalist who covered Reagan both as governor of California and as president, summed up Reagan's skills by saying, "He was better suited to leading the nation than commanding its government."[6] Similarly, Michael K. Bohn, the director of Reagan's Situation Room at the White House, noted that Reagan avoided reconciling his battling advisers, and this avoidance of conflict resulted in watered-down actions and policies.[7]

Ironically, Jimmy Carter, Reagan's predecessor and the first conservative president in the post–Great Depression era, had some policies that were more conservative than Reagan (for example, in deregulation of American industries), yet is not so credited because he was a Democrat and because he was lousy at public relations. Carter highlighted the nation's malaise, which he did not cause, in contrast to Reagan's sunny optimism. Yet underneath it all, at the policy level, Carter laid the groundwork for Reagan's policies (and even then, Reagan left a lot to be desired from a small government conservative perspective). For example, conservatives argue that the Reagan military buildup, his aid to mujahideen rebels against the Soviet invasion of Afghanistan, and a fleshed-out entente with China to counter Soviet power "won" the Cold War for America. Yet even if this dubious proposition were true, Jimmy Carter initiated all three policies, and Reagan merely followed up on them.

The Reagan administration PR machine also helped create many great speeches, images, and memories for latter-day publicists in the 1990s and beyond to dust off and spruce up Reagan's conservative credentials. At the time, however, Reagan's presidency arrested the long-term trend, beginning in the 1960s, toward more Americans identifying themselves as conservatives and shunning the "liberal" label. During Reagan's two terms, both the number of people claiming to be liberals rose and the number wanting greater government expenditure increased, while the number identifying themselves as conservatives declined. The long-term conservative identification trend then resumed after Reagan left office.[8]

James T. Patterson sums up the disconnect between Reagan's conservative rhetoric and his much more moderate policies:

> Like Coolidge, Reagan stood for fiscal restraint, tax reduction, and small government, yet as president he ran up record budget deficits. He was ideological in his rhetoric yet often chose to act the pragmatist: He denounced the Soviet Union as an "evil empire," for example, then did more to moderate the Cold War than any other president.[9]

In fact, Ronald Reagan had been a liberal Democrat for most of his life and converted to being a Republican only in 1962. Even then, Reagan was a moderate as Republican governor of California from 1967 to 1975. Although he confronted protesters at the University of California at Berkeley with the National Guard using tear gas, he also raised taxes and signed a law liberalizing abortion in California before the Supreme Court's *Roe v. Wade* decision did so nationally in 1973.[10]

Much of that moderation would carry over to what he did in the presidency, but times had changed and pragmatic policies had to be cloaked in conservative rhetoric. Fortunately for Reagan and his legacy, the world remembered only the rhetoric and forgot the policies.

Myth 1: Winning the Cold War

Like Jimmy Carter, his predecessor, Reagan believed that Communism was an unnatural, immoral system that repressed human liberty and would eventually implode. Curiously, however, in his presidential campaigns in 1976 and 1980, Reagan argued that the United States had fallen behind the Soviet Union in military power.[11] Although the Soviets had achieved rough parity in nuclear weapons in the early 1970s, overall this belief was nonsense, because US military technology, training, and logistics were vastly superior to that of the Soviet Union. After the USSR collapsed, the release of Soviet documents showed the Soviet military to be far less capable than purported by US defense and security agencies eager to get more funding for themselves.

Inflammatory Rhetoric Toward the USSR

The reason Reagan gets credit for defeating the USSR in the Cold War has a great deal to do with his strident anti-Soviet rhetoric. Reagan's foreign policy, at least rhetorically, was like that of the neoconservatives—many of whom, like Reagan, were former liberal Democrats. One of the reasons Reagan's rhetoric caught on with the public was because in the late 1970s, the Soviet Union was making territorial gains in poor Africa and Central America, despite their dubious strategic value to the United States.

Reagan did not say anything more severe about Communism than past presidents of both parties. Harry Truman had urged people to repudiate the "false philosophy" of Communism; Dwight Eisenhower had drawn a stark distinction between "freedom . . . against slavery, lightness against the dark"; and John F. Kennedy had pledged to "bear any burden" to assure the survival of liberty.[12] Reagan nevertheless repeated his verbal fusillades more often. In a 1983 speech before Christian evangelicals, he called the Soviet Union the "evil empire."

Thus, Reagan was not the first president to fling taunts at the Soviet Union. In June 1987, Reagan went to Berlin's Brandenburg Gate and, echoing JFK in the same city in 1963, demanded, "Mr. Gorbachev, tear down this wall." (The next year, singer Bruce Springsteen did the same when he got a bigger audience on the East German side of the wall.) Yet the circumstances surrounding these Reagan speeches have been long forgotten.

The 1983 speech was made to stop the inroads the nuclear freeze movement was making into key Catholic "Reagan Democrats"—the support of whom the Gipper needed to win reelection—after American Catholic bishops had endorsed the freeze. Reagan believed that a freeze in the production of nuclear weapons would lock in a US disadvantage vis-à-vis the Soviet Union. Unnoticed in the "evil empire" speech was Reagan's stated desire, at some future date, to eliminate nuclear weapons through negotiation. In addition, just weeks after the speech, he expressed regret for the "evil empire" comment. In 1988, in a speech just before leaving office, Reagan actually retracted the comment.[13]

The 1987 Berlin speech really did not change the longstanding stated US policy toward the Berlin Wall (other US presidents had called for its removal), and Condoleezza Rice, a Reagan National Security Council official and future secretary of state, admitted that the speech was overrated and that no policy follow-up occurred. The Berlin speech was designed as a rhetorical device to assuage conservatives—who had been virulent in their opposition to the impending Intermediate-Range Nuclear Forces (INF) Treaty with the Soviets and also US negotiations with the USSR over a journalist held hostage—and to change the subject from the ongoing Iran-Contra affair.[14] More important, just because the wall fell two and a half years after Reagan's demand to Mikhail

Gorbachev did not mean that his plea caused the iconic barrier to come down. Interestingly, Reagan's successor, George H. W. Bush, also went to Berlin and demanded that the wall come down, much closer to the time it actually fell, but gets no credit at all for this outcome from most analysts and journalists.

In fact, the Berlin Wall fell because of a mistake on the part of an official of the embattled East German government, who erroneously told the press that access routes were open between East and West Berlin. The illegitimate government of East Germany was embattled because Gorbachev had decided to no longer prop up Eastern European governments with subsidies and the Soviet Red Army, a decision over which Reagan had little influence.

Two Major Threats of the Cold War

Although all of the hype surrounding the Reagan presidency does not reflect it, the Cold War did not end during his two terms as chief executive. The Berlin Wall did not fall until November 1989, and the Soviet Union did not collapse until the end of 1991—both major milestones occurring during George H. W. Bush's tenure. It can be argued that the single most important event during the end of the Cold War occurred in mid-1989, when Soviet leader Gorbachev demonstrated that he would no longer prop up unpopular East European communist governments by using force—an event that happened well after Reagan had left office in January 1989.

However, conservatives have never regarded George H. W. Bush as really one of their own (he broke his "read my lips, no new taxes" pledge, even though Reagan somehow gets off the hook for raising taxes every year but two during his eight-year tenure). Neither did they so regard Harry Truman, the man who kicked off the Cold War by "scaring the hell out of the American people" in exaggerating the Soviet threat and launching, in the late 1940s, the worldwide crusade to contain it. If the United States won the Cold War—versus the more likely scenario of the Soviet bloc falling because the nonviable communist economic system finally collapsed—shouldn't all American presidents from Truman through George H. W. Bush be equally celebrated for successfully carrying out Truman's original containment policy?

Journalist Victor Sebestyen notes:

The classic narrative is that the toughness of Ronald Reagan brought down the evil empire of the Soviet Union. But Reagan was misunderstood. It was forty years of Western 'containment' that weakened the Soviet Union, and Reagan made no progress whatsoever in his first four years. It was only after Gorbachev emerged and Reagan tried a new, more conciliatory approach that a process began which ended the Cold War.[15]

Even this passage may exaggerate Reagan's role in ending the Cold War. The two main threats that emanated from the Soviet Union during the Cold War were the possibility of (1) global thermonuclear war or (2) a Soviet invasion of Western Europe, a region of high gross domestic product (GDP) and technology. Reagan did little to alleviate either threat.

As for the first threat, Reagan at first actually increased the possibility of nuclear war by scaring the Soviet Union into a heightened state of nuclear alert. Also, he refused a deal with Gorbachev to make deep cuts in the most threatening Soviet weapons to the United States, long-range strategic nuclear weapons, because of a refusal to bargain away his strategic missile defense fantasy (Star Wars). Reagan had to settle for a lesser deal to eliminate intermediate-range nuclear missiles from Europe, and many defense experts of the day saw this agreement as altering the East-West military balance to the United States' disadvantage. Reagan left to his successor, George H. W. Bush, to sign two START treaties with the Soviets making those deep cuts in long-range nuclear weapons, thereby reducing significantly the chance of general nuclear war.

On the second threat, in 1988, the last full year of Reagan's second term, the Soviets were pushing to reach a deal to withdraw conventional forces from Europe. Because Reagan stonewalled him on this issue, Gorbachev grew impatient and unilaterally announced at the United Nations in December 1988, one month before Reagan left office, the withdrawal of a half million Soviet troops from Europe over the next two years (including six tank divisions). This new policy was a dramatic reduction of the overall size of the Soviet military, and its conversion from an offensive to defensive posture. Gorbachev's acts removed the primary justification for the containment policy of the American-led NATO alliance for the duration of the Cold War. Later, in 1990, Gorbachev signed a formal treaty on conventional forces in Europe with Bush, removing 370,000 Soviet troops from central Europe but only withdrawing 60,000 US forces—a clearly one-sided agreement favoring the United States.

Also, in that UN speech, Gorbachev spoke of nations' "freedom of choice" in adopting social systems, and then demonstrated, in mid-1989 after Reagan had left office, that he would no longer use Soviet troops to put down revolts in satellite Eastern European countries, thus ultimately leading to the fall of the Berlin Wall in November of 1989.[16] As noted previously, Gorbachev's clear indication that in practice he would no longer prop up illegitimate Eastern European communist governments using Soviet military power was the key development in ending the Cold War—and it happened during the George H. W. Bush administration, not that of Reagan. In sum, Gorbachev, not Reagan, was the driving force to drastically reduce or end, respectively, the two major threats of the Cold War.

No Master Plan to Topple the Eastern Bloc

In September 1984, in a personal meeting in the Oval Office, Reagan told Soviet Foreign Minister Andre Gromyko that he did not want to change the Soviet system. The argument that Reagan had a hardline master plan to topple the Soviet Union is also undermined by the fact that Reagan improvised US foreign policy during his first year and did not have a coherent policy toward the USSR until January 1983, with the promulgation of National Security Decision Directive 75 (the Reagan Doctrine). Even then, as one of its goals, this policy spoke of US limitations and gradual change in the Soviet Union: "To promote, within the narrow limits available to us, the process of change in the Soviet Union toward a more pluralistic political and economic system in which the power of the privileged ruling elite is gradually reduced." The doctrine also stated that "the policy outlined above is for the long haul. It is unlikely to yield a rapid breakthrough in bilateral relations with the Soviet Union." Finally, the document predicted that "the prospect of major systemic change in the next few years is relatively low."[17] Even Richard Pipes, an anti-Soviet hardliner working for Reagan's National Security Council, admitted, "Now no responsible persons can have any illusions that it is in the power of the West to alter the Soviet system or to 'bring the Soviet economy to its knees.'"[18]

Furthermore, NSDD 75, promulgated in January 1983, would not have had time to work before Reagan began to back away from it in fright in late 1983 after the Soviet nuclear alert—triggered by Reagan's hostile anti-Soviet rhetoric and actions and the NATO Able Archer 83 nuclear command and control exercise—and after the ABC television movie *The Day After* aired about the aftermath of an atomic war. In January of 1984, Reagan announced he was satisfied with his then brief military buildup. In addition, the Reagan Doctrine was in place only two years before Mikhail Gorbachev came to power in the Soviet Union in early 1985.

Moreover, high-level national security appointees in the Reagan administration have admitted that no grand strategy existed to bankrupt the Soviets using a defense buildup. Jeanne Kirkpatrick, Reagan's hardline ambassador to the United Nations, later admitted that the administration had never articulated such a policy and that no one in the administration ever talked about it, but she nevertheless argued that a small group of hardliners—Reagan, herself, CIA Director William Casey, National Security Advisor William Clark, and Secretary of Defense Caspar Weinberger—understood that that was the goal. Jack Matlock, a Soviet expert on Reagan's National Security Council staff, recalled that "nobody argued that the United States should try to bring the Soviet Union down." Similarly, Frank Carlucci, Reagan's second-term national security advisor and secretary of defense, and Helmut Kohl, the chancellor of Germany, did not think Reagan's goal was to bankrupt or topple the Soviet system. Even the administration's most strident hawk, Weinberger, admitted in 2002, "There were some people who said that the whole thing was just an attempt to run the Soviet Union into bankruptcy. Actually, it was not, in my view." In fact, many of the anti-Soviet hardliners left early in the administration.[19]

In fact, Reagan wanted to increase the US defense budget largely because he felt the US military had gone to seed after the Vietnam War. Weinberger, in 2002, best summarized the reason for the Reagan military buildup: "What [Reagan] needed, what we needed and were in full agreement on, was to restore our military deterrent capability—to get a capability that would make it quite clear to the Soviets that they couldn't win a war against us."[20] However, although militaries always need replenishment and repair after fighting a war (which is a great argument for not getting involved in long, nonstrategic brushfire conflicts, such as the war in Southeast Asia), this disarray was overstated. Jimmy Carter had already increased the defense budget in the last two years of his four-year term, and Reagan merely continued the trend. Reagan also honored the limits on nuclear weapons in Carter's Strategic Arms Limitation Treaty II (SALT II), even though it was not ratified by the Senate after the Soviet invasion of Afghanistan in 1979 sealed its fate. During his first term, much more hawkish than his second, Reagan essentially followed Carter's existing policy toward the Soviet Union, except he did away with one of Carter's anti-Soviet post-Afghan invasion measures: the grain embargo. Reagan terminated the embargo to curry favor with farmers, a powerful Republican political constituency, just when US-Soviet tensions were rising over the advent of Poland's Solidarity union.[21]

And, according to hardliner Richard Pipes, the author of Reagan's 1983 executive order NSDD 75—which some conservatives try to construe as a strategy to bankrupt the Soviet Union because of vague language stating that one strand of US policy was to put "internal pressure" on the Soviet regime—Reagan deleted provisions designed to block Soviet access to hard currency. The USSR used hard currency proceeds from oil and a few other energy and mineral exports to buy consumer goods produced abroad (Soviet-produced consumer goods were shoddy). Reducing the USSR's hard currency revenues would have required the Soviets to shift internal resources from defense production to the manufacture of consumer goods to make up for the lost imports. In addition, Pipes admitted that when Reagan signed this executive order, he emphasized the importance of compromise with the Soviet Union.[22]

Anti-Soviet Rhetoric More Severe than Policy

Reagan's anti-Communist rhetoric was harsh but his policies toward the Eastern Bloc did not always match—right from the beginning of his administration. In other words, sometimes he did not really try very hard to roll back Communism. In March 1981, two months after Reagan took office, as Polish independent union Solidarity geared up for a general strike in response to the Polish Communist Party's attempted repression of the movement, the pope and, according to some reports, the Reagan administration warned Solidarity that a general strike was too perilous. As Reaganophile Steven F. Hayward admits, "In hindsight, Solidarity may have missed its best chance to bring down Communist Party rule."[23]

In December 1981, only eleven months after Reagan took office, with too little time for any of his hawkish anti-Soviet pressure to have had a major effect, Polish strongman General Wojciech Jaruzelski begged the USSR to invade Poland to crush the Solidarity trade union. The Soviet leaders said no because they could not afford another Afghanistan-like bog and anticipated being targeted by more economic sanctions—added to the ones Jimmy Carter had slapped on their already fragile economy after their invasion of that country in late 1979 before Reagan took office. So Jaruzelski had to use his own riot police to impose martial law.[24] US intelligence had learned of the Polish regime's plan in advance but curiously did not publicly or privately protest or even warn Solidarity of the coming crackdown.[25]

To protest the Polish repression, Reagan imposed only light economic sanctions on Poland but embargoed exports that could be used to build the Soviet natural gas pipeline from Siberia to Western Europe. The pipeline sanctions caused a furor in Europe when he prohibited the use of US technology and parts in Western European components for the pipeline. The Europeans, including British Prime Minister Margaret Thatcher, cried hypocrisy, because the Reagan administration had lifted Jimmy Carter's grain embargo on the Soviet Union to assuage the Republican farm constituency.[26] Reagan's pipeline sanctions policy was a failure, and sanctions were lifted less than a year later, in November 1982. Thus, US grain and pipeline technology began to flow again to the USSR.[27] The entire pipeline sanctions episode was hypocritical, very divisive in the Western alliance, and ineffectual in punishing the Soviets.

Then, in September 1983, the Soviets accidentally shot down a South Korean civilian airliner—with 269 people, including 61 Americans, on board—that had strayed over their territory near a military base. However, Reagan, apparently having learned his lesson from the pipeline sanctions debacle, rejected suggested tougher sanctions and instead infuriated conservatives by taking only weak measures, such as slowing down cultural exchanges and extending limitations on US landings of Soviet airliners imposed during the Poland episode. He also continued arms control talks with the Soviets.[28] What

Reagan left unsaid in his rhetorical bombast against the attack was that a new Soviet law mandating violent measures against aircraft encroaching on Soviet air space was the result of two prior years of a dangerously aggressive Reagan-initiated program to intimidate the Soviet Union by conducting simulated attacks that would aggressively probe its air space and territorial waters. Later, the US ship *Vincennes*, secretly in Iranian territorial waters during the unde-clared "tanker war" in the Persian Gulf during the late 1980s, accidently shot down an Iranian civilian airliner, killing all 290 passengers; when the shoe was on the other foot, Reagan expressed only token regret and gave the crew of the ship combat awards.[29]

Marginal Effects of Policy

Reagan's strident anti-Communist rhetoric and peacetime military buildup may have had some effect at the margins in putting pressure on the Soviet Union, but revolutions of the nature and magnitude that ended the Cold War are usually caused by internal factors, not pressure from external sources. The real end of the Cold War came, not when the Reagan and Soviet leader Mikhail Gorbachev negotiated the Intermediate-Range Nuclear Forces (INF) Treaty in 1987 or when the USSR fell in 1991, but when Gorbachev concluded in mid-1989 that it was too expensive to use the Red Army and approximately $40 billion in annual subsidies (including subsidized oil, natural gas, and min-eral sales) to prop up and stabilize heavily indebted Communist regimes in Eastern Europe. Gorbachev repeatedly refused to carry out the Brezhnev Doc-trine of intervening militarily in the turmoil of Eastern European countries.

Soviet defense spending, after a delay, had begun to rise in reaction to Reagan's defense spending spree, but Gorbachev, after taking power in early 1985, slashed defense spending and Soviet military personnel unilaterally, began to make significant withdrawals of Soviet forces from the USSR's East-ern European empire, and began to make dramatic arms control proposals to avoid a future arms race. He said the use of force was not appropriate in foreign policy, took ideology out of relations between countries, and renounced Marx-ist international class struggle. Also, the Soviet Union could no longer afford to implicitly guarantee Western loans to prop up already nearly bankrupt

Communist Eastern European governments, as a substitute for the freeing up of their economies.

However, as a true Communist—who wanted to maintain central planning and believed that markets could exist without privatizing property—Gorbachev committed only to reform the Soviet system, not scrap it. He wanted to move from Communism to "democratic socialism." His perestroika (economic restructuring) and glasnost (political openness) reforms were only mild and merely turned a totalitarian state into an authoritarian one. Initially, Gorbachev had wanted economic reform without political reform (the Communist Chinese model), but then in early 1987, he needed to pressure reluctant Communist Party cadres to make economic changes and thus opened up a Pandora's box by using increased political openness to allow the Soviet public to turn up the heat on the recalcitrant party bosses. Also, Gorbachev naïvely believed that Eastern European Communist regimes, which ruled only because the Soviets had imposed them on other countries using military power, could also reform. Instead such regimes, with no legitimacy, collapsed in 1989. Moreover, Gorbachev's "reformed" Soviet Union lasted only a short while until it collapsed in 1991.[30]

The Soviet Union's economy was too weak to continue its prior imperial policies. Thus, Gorbachev wanted to have permanently better relations with the West, because he wanted to be able to cut the defense budget to institute limited domestic reforms to save Communism without taking the unpopular step of reducing consumption,[31] not because he was unnerved by Reagan's military buildup. The Soviets could no longer afford their empire, and Gorbachev therefore felt that relations with the West were more important than relations with Eastern European satellite nations.

In short, like many collapsing empires of yore, the Soviet Empire eventually went down because it became overextended, even before Reagan took office. The nonviable Soviet command economy began to weaken in the late 1960s and could no longer support the already high Soviet defense spending. According to historian Daniel J. Sargent, because the Soviet economy was too rigid to adapt to the globalization of the 1970s, as the American and other Western capitalist economies did, the Soviet economy by the 1980s had nearly deteriorated into Third World status. Flush with cash in the 1970s from the high price of oil, its principal external source of hard currency, the Soviet Union had little incentive to launch economic reforms. Thus the economy remained reliant on oil exports, heavy industry, and central planning, and it rattled forward until the oil price crash in the mid-1980s. Mikhail Gorbachev, in desperation, then tried to open the Soviet economy to globalization by making economic reforms, but these were unsuccessful and plunged the Soviet Union into crisis.[32]

At that point, the plummeting price of oil, one of the few Soviet exports the world wanted, probably sealed the USSR's fate. The Soviet Empire was perhaps a unique empire in history, one in which the imperial center was poorer than its satellite possessions.[33] Thus, it was likely doomed to inevitably fall—as Truman administration official George Kennan had predicted long ago.

The original US containment strategy, really masterminded by Kennan, envisioned politically containing the spread of Communism until the despotic Soviet Union collapsed economically from excessive military and imperial expenditure—which is what eventually happened. Although Reagan's military buildup might have put marginal pressure on the Soviet economy, the USSR was already spending a good portion of its GDP on the military before the Reagan era. By the final months of Brezhnev's reign (very early in the Reagan administration), defense spending made up about 40 percent of the USSR's budget, much more than even when the Soviet Union was preparing for World War II.[34]

At the time of Reagan's death, Gorbachev said that Reagan's military buildup during the 1980s had little effect on the Soviet Union.[35] This statement seems to square with the facts, because only a small hike in competitive Soviet defense spending occurred during that time, before Gorbachev put the brakes on even that.

Even Reagan's putting marginal pressure on the Soviet economy may be in doubt. David Stockman, Reagan's budget director, has written, "So the idea that the Reagan defense buildup somehow spent the Soviets into collapse is a legend of remarkable untruth. . . . The now open Soviet archives also prove there never was a Soviet defense-spending offensive. By the early 1980s Soviet military outlays were growing at only 1–2 percent per year. . . ."[36] Jeffrey W. Knopf of the Naval War College concluded that "[t]he Soviet Union never increased its military spending to match the Reagan buildup and hence avoid[ed] exacerbating the defense burden on the Soviet economy."[37] In fact, quite the opposite of consciously trying to bankrupt the USSR—as some conservatives now claim was Reagan's goal—Reagan's Secretary of State George Shultz suggested to Gorbachev that he integrate the Soviet economy into the international economy to reinvigorate the USSR, but after seventy years of dysfunctional Communism, this idea was simply not feasible.[38]

A more likely cause of the Soviet economic Waterloo was Saudi Arabia's driving down world oil prices, beginning in the mid-1980s. This development came after the oil boom of the 1970s, which mitigated somewhat the USSR's economic decline since the late 1960s. The Communist Soviet Union had little to sell that anyone else wanted to buy, except its oil production; the Soviets relied heavily on oil revenues to earn scarce foreign exchange. The collapse of world oil prices slashed Soviet foreign exchange earnings by half.

Some analysts have tried to give Reagan's pressure on the Saudis credit for their opening of the oil market's trap door in the mid-1980s, thus reducing Soviet hard currency revenues from oil sales. However, the Saudis would not likely have taken such an important step affecting their primary livelihood even to satisfy the leader of a superpower. The real reason for the plummeting oil prices in mid-decade was that the Saudis were tired of bearing the costs of cheating by other OPEC cartel members—which were secretly selling more oil than their production quotas allowed—and decided to teach them a lesson by drastically forcing oil prices down.

Star Wars and the Collapse of the Communist Bloc

Even more far-fetched is the argument that Reagan's Strategic Defense Initiative (SDI), or "Star Wars," led to the end of the Cold War. What this much-mocked fantasy ballistic missile defense system—few in Washington, let alone Moscow, took it seriously as technological possibility—directly had to do with Gorbachev's decision to abandon the military support of illegitimate Communist Eastern European regimes (the Brezhnev Doctrine) is very much in doubt. Reaganophiles' current efforts to make the case that Reagan's Star Wars ended the Cold War seem to have more to do with getting funding for missile defense at the present time rather than being aimed at forming a realistic interpretation of historical events.

According to George H. W. Bush's, White House Chief of Staff John Sununu, Soviet Defense Minister Dmitri Yazov told him at a dinner once that the Soviets were being pushed to reforms because they did not have the economic resources to compete with Star Wars, which they feared would give the United States permanent military superiority.[39] Such open admission of weakness from a hawkish hardliner in a notoriously secretive totalitarian nation should be suspicious on its face; Yazov could have been cleverly trying to spur the United States to waste even more money on the fanciful system. In contrast, Aleksandr Yakovlev, a close Gorbachev adviser and intellectual father of his glasnost and perestroika reforms, said that Kremlin hawks used Star Wars to try to impede Gorbachev's reforms. The latter argument seems more logical because Gorbachev was trying to reduce Soviet defense spending to free up resources for reforms. Yazov and others in the Soviet security apparatus were arguing that more money needed to be spent on defense—and thus not on reforms—to counter Star Wars.

At any rate, no matter who in the Soviet Union was telling the straight story, American Star Wars probably had minimal effect either way, because budgets for strategic warfare systems (offensive nuclear-tipped missiles and missile defense), as opposed to much more expensive conventional battle-field systems (armies, navies, air forces, and all of their weapons, personnel, infrastructure, and logistics), are only a small part of any defense budget; furthermore missile defense was only a small part of the strategic section of the budget.

If anything, Reagan's softening in his second term and negotiation with Gorbachev eased Gorbachev's ability to achieve the reforms, according to Anatoly Dobrynin, the Soviet Union's longtime ambassador to the United States.[40]

However, perhaps Reagan's quest for strategic missile defenses achieved an indirect minor adverse impact on the Soviet economy by having a political rather than strategic effect. Rather than having any strategic fear of the pie-in-the-sky American Star Wars per se, Gorbachev opposed the program vehemently because of his apprehension that it would allow his own military to demand to counter it, which would consume more money that he wanted to use for reforms. Gorbachev's generals could have argued that Reagan's missile defenses eventually just might have nullified the Soviet nuclear deterrent, thus demanding more money for an offensive nuclear arms race. Yet Andrei

Sakharov—nuclear physicist, father of the Soviet H-bomb, and dissident—urged Gorbachev to ignore Star Wars as a technological impossibility and thus only a chimerical strategic problem. Eventually, Gorbachev did so and agreed to the Intermediate-Range Nuclear Forces (INF) Treaty with Reagan (and later Strategic Arms Reduction Treaties with George H. W. Bush) without limitations on Star Wars.

And the Soviets just might have undertaken a nuclear arms race caused by Star Wars at lower cost than would have accrued to the United States. For that reason, Gorbachev actually dismissed Star Wars, saying that even if the United States did succeed in building such futuristic missile defenses, which he doubted, they would be relatively expensive. Gorbachev argued that he could outbuild those defenses with much cheaper offensive nuclear missiles, including fooling the defense system with cheap, hard-to-distinguish decoys. Gorbachev claimed, probably with some truth, that these added missiles would cost only 10 percent of US expenses for Star Wars.[41] Western experts on strategic systems have long realized that such relative cost ineffectiveness of defense systems versus offensive missiles is a major problem with these defenses.

Thus, even if Reagan had formulated a master plan to bankrupt the Soviet Union, which top officials of his administration say he had not, the imbalance of costs here likely would have made this method a nonviable way to do so. Also, as noted earlier, any such indirect adverse budgetary, and thus economic, effect on the Soviet Union would have had to be marginal, because strategic portions of defense budgets are relatively cheap to buy compared to conventional military forces.

In fact, Star Wars had arisen because General John Vessey, the chairman of the Joint Chiefs of Staff (JCS), had misled Reagan about the feasibility of protecting the American population with missile defense. Neither JCS nor Pentagon experts thought that a more feasible "point defense" program to protect US intercontinental ballistic missile (ICBM) fields could be extended to protect the American population. According to Lou Cannon, a journalist who covered Reagan both as governor of California and as president, Reagan saw a nuclear holocaust as fulfilling the biblical prophecy of Armageddon between good and evil and believed that nuclear deterrence based on the mass killing of civilians (Mutual Assured Destruction) was immoral; he therefore embraced with great gusto Vessey's disingenuous and impractical idea of creating a missile defense to protect the entire American population and the equally idealistic goal of eliminating all nuclear weapons (a goal shared by Gorbachev).[42] (One wonders about Reagan's logic in trying to stop a nuclear Armageddon that would, by his own belief, fulfill an inevitable biblical prophecy.) Reagan, in opposition to most of his national security advisors, jumped at the chance to give a naïve speech that asserted that such strategic missile defenses could protect the American people and thus make nuclear weapons obsolete. Reagan's military commanders later backed off from this grandiose claim, but the president never did.

Soviet leader Yuri Andropov, one of Gorbachev's more militaristic predecessors, already suspicious from Reagan's overheated anti-Soviet rhetoric that the United States was going to launch a first strike nuclear attack, found Reagan's Star Wars speech frightening. Andropov, who had called Reagan's "evil empire" speech "lunatic," deemed the Star Wars speech shortly after that "insane."[43] Although seemingly defensive, Star Wars ballistic missile defenses (if ever they came to fruition), after any US first strike, could nullify a retaliatory strike from remaining Soviet nuclear forces—thus allowing the United States to win any nuclear war. That's why, in the nuclear balance, any ballistic missile defenses can be so destabilizing and why they were limited in the 1972 Anti-Ballistic Missile Treaty between the United States and the Soviet Union.

However, Reagan's advisers thought missile defense at least could take the zest out of the nuclear freeze movement, defend the vulnerable MX missiles (at least a more modest and technically possible "point defense" version of any such system), and provide the United States with a bargaining chip at arms control negotiations with the USSR. Reagan, to his discredit, later refused to trade off fantasy missile defense for deep cuts in strategic offensive nuclear warheads.[44]

The entire episode appears as an "emperor has no clothes" situation that has since wasted hundreds of billions of dollars. At this writing, after all the time passed since Reagan's Star Wars speech in 1983, the United States has deployed only a vastly scaled down strategic missile defense system that still does not work very well. In fact, Reagan's grandiose SDI research scheme set back progress on a more limited and realistic missile defense system, using off-the-shelf technology, which actually could have been deployed in a reasonable time period.

The Funding of Afghan Rebels

Some analysts have argued that Reagan's aid to the Islamist mujahideen fighting Soviet invaders in Afghanistan caused the Eastern Bloc's collapse. This argument is certainly more plausible than Star Wars having caused the demise but probably falls short. Again, because no grand Reagan plan existed to bankrupt the USSR into collapse, the real purpose of aiding the Afghan mujahideen was to mire the Soviet Cold War adversary in a quagmire (Reagan also tried using "covert" aid to proxies in places like Nicaragua and Angola to create problems for those Marxist governments). One problem with giving Reagan too much credit, however, is that, once again, it was the idea of Jimmy Carter and Zbigniew Brzezinski, his national security advisor, to begin aiding the mujahideen to "give the Soviets their own Vietnam"; Reagan continued and expanded the policy.

Also, it is commonly thought that Reagan's shipment of US Stinger hand-held anti-aircraft missiles, beginning at the end of 1986, won the Afghan war for the ragtag mujahideen. The Stingers did keep Soviet helicopters off the backs of the insurgents. Yet, even before Gorbachev took power in 1985, his predecessor Yuri Andropov had realized that the Soviet invasion had been a mistake and, as early as late 1983, began trying to get out of Afghanistan. After Gorbachev took office, he made the decision to get out in October 1985,[45] even before the United States introduced Stingers into the war. As the United States found out later in its own foolish invasions of Afghanistan and Iraq, such quagmires can take a long time to wind down, even after the decision has been made to get out; the last Soviet forces did not leave the country until early 1989.

Another problem with celebrating Carter and Reagan covert aid to the Afghan mujahideen is the unintended consequences of the policy, which were catastrophic. Although it seemed like a great idea at the time to tie down the Soviet Union in a backwater conflict, the US "covert" action inadvertently spawned the only foreign threat to the US mainland since the War of 1812: al Qaeda. The first duty of governments is to defend their land and people. Yet the blowback from Afghanistan on 9/11 showed that the US imperial foray there during the Carter and Reagan administrations got in the way of providing for the common defense, the only military action actually allowed by the US Constitution. Thus, having an unconstitutional overseas empire does not equal generating security at home and often may be counterproductive to achieving it.

Strategies for Defeating Communism

Costs, both direct and unintended, of the forty-plus-year US containment policy should have led to questions about whether an alternative strategy might have been more cost-effective for the United States to get to the same end state—eventual Eastern Bloc collapse. For my book, *The Empire Has No Clothes: US Foreign Policy Exposed*, I reviewed the academic literature on empires, which notes that many empires fall because they can no longer afford all of their military commitments (that is, imperial overstretch). For example, the British and French empires fell apart even though—really because—these countries ended up on the winning side of two huge world wars. The high costs of winning such wars eventually caught up with them. The classical economists of the late eighteenth and nineteenth centuries demonstrated that empire (trade limited to that between the imperial center and its colonies and enforced with costly military power) is not cost-effective compared to a system of free trade—that is, it is cheaper to buy products than to create the military forces to essentially steal them at gunpoint. Given these facts, perhaps instead of trying to contain Communism everywhere around the globe—Reagan's rhetoric of rolling back Communism was even more grandiose, but his military buildup and foreign policy were only incrementally more ambitious than all the other presidents from Truman on who practiced the containment policy—a less costly alternative would have been more appropriate.

US security policy always assumed that the Soviet Union would use any Communist inroads in other countries to turn the resources and industry captured toward the United States or its allies in a snowballing fashion (the domino effect). Yet most of the societies susceptible to Communist takeover were economic basket cases in the developing world—Korea in 1950, Cuba, Vietnam, Laos, Cambodia, Angola, Afghanistan, Nicaragua, El Salvador, and so on. Thus, instead of being an interventionist military superpower during the Cold War, a better US strategy might have been to use the already proven concept the United States had used in the two World Wars—being a balancer-of-last-resort to help defend temporary major allies from an aggressive potential hegemon in regions of advanced economic and technological power. In contrast, in the developing world, the United States should have allowed the Soviets to have all the economic basket cases they could grab, the theory being that all of the costs of aid and administration to prop up Communist regimes in these places would have also caused eventual Soviet systemic collapse. Thus, the United States could have kept its powder dry and avoided massive quagmires, such as those in the then backwaters of Korea and Vietnam, while keeping its defense budget lower because it remained a second line of defense, even in the economically advanced regions of Europe and East Asia.

Late in the Cold War, even the hawkish Daniel Patrick Moynihan ended up opposing Reagan's aggressive anti-Communist policies in Grenada and Nicaragua, because he felt the Soviet Union and Marxism were in decline. He thought that "our grand strategy should be to wait out the Soviet Union; its time is passing."[46] Unfortunately, Moynihan adopted this view late in the Cold War. Furthermore, all presidents during the Cold War, including Reagan, never had the confidence in Western capitalism and democracy to believe that these systems would triumph over Communism without the United States resorting to the heavy military expenditure that has undermined the republic over time. As previously discussed, Jimmy Carter had such confidence early in his term but panicked unnecessarily after the Soviets invaded Afghanistan, hiking the defense budget and establishing the Carter Doctrine, which pledged for the first time to directly defend Persian Gulf oil with US forces.

The United States provided other countries' defense and used the exaggerated Soviet threat to justify its own hegemonic global empire. In fact, to bribe Japan and the Western European allies into letting the United States provide their defenses, the United States had to open its markets to these countries' goods without reciprocal free markets in those nations. The taxpayer received no bargain here in satisfying the US foreign policy elite's grandiose visions of an informal world empire. So Reagan's hyped anti-Communist rhetoric and incremental intensification of containment actually took US policy the wrong way, helped increase government spending as a portion of GDP, and racked up then record government budget deficits and debt at home.

Arms Control Implications

If Reagan deserves any credit for ending the Cold War, it comes not from his largely overstated toughness, but instead from his emotional willingness to believe Gorbachev was a new-style Soviet leader and negotiate with him, much to the chagrin of today's hawkish neoconservatives. (Reagan's successor, George H. W. Bush, was a hard-nosed realist and was more suspicious that Gorbachev was a phony.) Reagan gave up his long-held view that the United States should have strategic nuclear superiority over the Soviet Union, accepting nuclear parity as a basis for arms control negotiations, which the Soviets had always desired. Yet Gorbachev had to sustain the pressure with repeated bold arms control proposals to get Reagan to deal on nuclear weapons—and did so even when Reagan had threated to back away from informally observing the existing limits on strategic (long-range) nuclear weapons in the unratified SALT II Treaty.

However, although Reagan eventually reached an arms control agreement with the Soviet Union on intermediate-range nuclear weapons, its significance has been overstated, and his earlier turbocharged anti-Communist rhetoric almost led to nuclear war. Although the narrative of Reaganophiles is that Reagan's early hardline policies toward the Soviets eventually drove them to the arms control bargaining table, Jimmy Carter had made the original decision to install intermediate-range Pershing II and Ground Launched Cruise Missiles (GLCMs) in Western Europe in response to Soviet deployment of SS-20 intermediate-range missiles in Eastern Europe. Reagan merely implemented the installation. In addition, Reagan's own ardor for arms control increased in his second term in an attempt to divert attention from the Iran-Contra scandal.

Although ultimately a favorable, if exaggerated, accomplishment, the Intermediate-Range Nuclear Forces (INF) Treaty, which removed all such nuclear weapons from Europe, was scorned by conservatives and nuclear policy wonks at the time Reagan and Gorbachev signed it in 1987. The thinking among this crowd was that the treaty removed a link in the nuclear escalation chain from conventional defense of Western Europe to the use of tactical battlefield nuclear weapons to the employment of intermediate-range nuclear forces to the unleashing of US long-range nuclear weapons—intercontinental ballistic missiles (ICBMs) and submarine-launched ballistic missiles (SLBMs).

Removing the link, the reasoning went, thus contributed to decoupling the United States from defense of its European allies. US nuclear weapons were supposed to counter alleged Soviet conventional superiority; eliminating a key link in nuclear escalation thus favored the Soviets, according to most conservatives, the Republican national security policy establishment (for example, Richard Nixon and Henry Kissinger), and Republican presidential candidates. On the other hand, most Democrats, especially progressive advocates of arms control, were ecstatic over the treaty.[47]

Although Reagan refused to help Gorbachev exit Soviet forces from Afghanistan right up until the end of his term, his INF agreement undermines the argument that he had a master plan to bankrupt the Soviet Union via an arms race. The INF Treaty was the first treaty to reduce, rather than just limit, nuclear arms and eliminated an entire class of nuclear weapons; but this category was only about 4 percent of the nuclear arsenals of both sides. Slightly reducing the number of nuclear warheads, getting the Soviets to accept rigorous verification inspections, and decoupling the sacrifice of US cities from being used to defend allies, who were wealthy enough to defend themselves, were good things. However, with tens of thousands of warheads left with vast destructive power even after the INF Treaty was implemented, the accomplishment needs to be put in perspective. And to the extent that the US strategic submarine force was used in a theater role to replace the Pershing and cruise missiles, it is doubtful whether the nuclear escalation chain was broken all that much.

In fact, Reagan should be faulted for failing to use his Star Wars fantasy, the expensive quest for strategic defenses against nuclear missile attacks, as a bargaining chip to get Soviet agreement to make deep reductions in the far more dangerous (than INF) strategic long-range nuclear weapons (missiles that could actually hit the United States)—a deal Mikhail Gorbachev had offered him. Reagan, naïve on nuclear weapons to the point of being scary, cared about futuristic and implausible strategic missile defenses more than about reducing the huge US and Soviet arsenals of long-range strategic weapons, as evidenced by his desire to unilaterally abandon the voluntary limits on the unratified SALT II Treaty, which had been informally observed by both countries since 1979. US allies protested this possibility, Reagan backed off on it, and Congress voted to keep the limits.

Although Reagan was instinctively and secretly anti-nuclear and naïvely believed that strategic defenses could make nuclear weapons obsolete, his hawkish advisers, US allies, and the Soviets correctly saw that any effective US defenses might allow the United States an unanswered nuclear first strike against the USSR. This reality likely would have upset the balance of mutual nuclear deterrence, making nuclear war winnable. Thus, the Soviets then might have had a great incentive to cheaply build up their offensive missiles to offset the expensive US defenses, thereby accelerating the arms race.

Possibility of a Nuclear War

Given the already vast destructive power in the immense nuclear arsenals of Soviet Union and the United States, more important to avoiding nuclear war than even reducing numbers of strategic warheads was the general climate of relations between the two countries. The Russian expert Condoleezza Rice remembers thinking that Reagan's overheated rhetoric—for example, calling the Soviet Union an "evil empire" and "focus of evil in the modern world"— could lead to war.[48] She was very perceptive.

Reagan's sustained use of inflammatory anti-Communist rhetoric, defense spending spree, planned US missile deployments in Europe, SDI speech, early prohibition of high-level contacts with the Soviet leadership, and invasion of communist Grenada led to the second-closest brush the planet has had with possible nuclear Armageddon next to the Cuban Missile Crisis.[49] Reagan's early incendiary rhetoric, including his "evil empire" speech in March 1983, helped lead then Soviet leader Yuri Andropov to believe that the United States was planning to launch a surprise nuclear strike against the Soviet Union. Andropov commissioned the KGB to create a special surveillance program to look for indications of such a strike. In particular, the Soviets were worried that this surprise attack would come under the guise of NATO's Able Archer 83 nuclear command and control exercise in the fall of 1983. During the unprecedented exercise, NATO, simulating the start of an atomic war with the USSR, put its nuclear forces on the highest state of alert. In response, Andropov put Soviet nuclear forces on the highest level of alert and, for the first time since the Cuban Missile Crisis, deployed Soviet nuclear submarines along the US coastline. The Soviets transported nuclear weapons to launchers and chose priority targets. Even Reaganophile Steven F. Hayward admits that evidence suggests that the Soviets, fearing a US nuclear first strike, may have even contemplated preempting that with a first strike of their own.[50] Reagan had made worse the only existential threat to the American way of life in its history.

Fortunately, the near-nuclear war shocked the emotionally anti-nuclear Reagan into seeing that Soviet fears of US nuclear intentions were real and that his hawkish rhetoric toward the USSR was eliciting a counterproductive, aggressive response. According to a recently declassified report from the president's Foreign Intelligence Advisory Board written in 1990, Reagan in June 1984, after reading a CIA report cataloging all of the Soviet martial responses to the Able Archer 83 exercise, exclaimed, "Really scary."[51]

After the Able Archer 83 incident, less than three years into his eight-year tenure, Reagan, much to the consternation of the hawkish wing of his advisers, disavowed his early characterization of the USSR as the "evil empire," changed direction, and became much more willing to negotiate with the USSR on reducing or even eliminating nuclear missiles and weapons, including the signing of the aforementioned Intermediate-Range Nuclear Forces (INF) Treaty.[52]

Also, in the fall of 1983, in response to public angst about Reagan's severe anti-Soviet rhetoric, his increase in defense spending, and the resulting nuclear freeze movement, ABC television network in the United States broadcast the movie *The Day After* about the fictional aftermath of a nuclear war between the superpowers. Reagan, a veteran of the movie business, reported that the film had a great effect on him, helping to motivate him to attempt to intensify his efforts to negotiate arms control with the USSR. If anything, Reagan, with a little help from Hollywood, scared himself into negotiating on nuclear weapons with the Soviets. After the accidental radioactive disaster at the Chernobyl nuclear power plant in April 1986, Gorbachev accelerated his efforts to negotiate with the United States for reductions in nuclear arms.

In addition to the INF Treaty, Reagan and Gorbachev reached a useful treaty whereby the United States and the Soviet Union would warn each other of missile launch tests. Again, reality undermines the narrative that Reagan, for most of his administration, had an active plan to bankrupt or scare the Soviets and parlay such Soviet weakness into US gains or even victory in the Cold War.

Thus, despite the much touted arms control agreement of limited scope, Reagan gets an overall negative score in the all-important category of nuclear policy for not trading away Star Wars to get significant bilateral cuts in long-range strategic warheads and for scaring the Soviets into a dangerous nuclear crisis.

Summary

In sum, Reagan probably did frighten the Soviets in certain respects, and his military buildup may have put some marginal pressure on their economy. However, the Reagan administration had no plan to attempt to bankrupt the USSR using that buildup, according to former administration officials. In fact, the unviable Soviet economy had already started to decline during the late 1960s, years before Reagan ever took office, and the bottoming out of oil prices in the mid-1980s may have been the crowning blow for it. Such critical internal factors, not Reagan's incremental hardening of longstanding US containment policy, likely motivated Gorbachev to give up supporting East European Communist dictatorships with the Soviet Red Army, thus ending the forty-plus-year-old Cold War.

James Mann, a former foreign correspondent for the *Los Angeles Times* and author of the book *The Rebellion of Ronald Reagan: A History of the End of the Cold War*, best summed it up: "There is little evidence that the American actions brought down the Soviet regime." He continued:

> The Soviet economy was foundering because of deep-seated and chronic problems that had little or nothing to do with the Reagan administra-tion's policies. Although the Soviet system was in decline, it was not headed toward a collapse, and Reagan's first-term policies, including the defense buildup and the covert-action programs, did not cause the collapse. "Even though Soviet socialism had clearly lost the competition with the West, it was lethargically stable, and could have continued muddling on for quite some time," observed one scholar who studied the Soviet economy for this era.
>
> The Soviet leadership was overextended and would have had to retrench in one way or another, but it could have survived. Confronted

by the new challenges from the United States, the Soviet Union might have sought to cut defense spending in the short term while slowly regaining strength over the long-run, meanwhile maintaining the existing, repressive political order. . . .

Instead, the proximate cause of the Soviet collapse was Gorbachev. It was Gorbachev who made the historic decision not to intervene with force in Eastern Europe in 1989 [after Reagan had left office]. It was Gorbachev who elected to reform the Soviet system in a way that left it partially opened and partially closed, partially democratized but with the Communist Party and the KGB still the country's most powerful institutions. This was the peculiar, unworkable hybrid arrangement that led eventually to the Soviet implosion.[53]

Will Bunch, author of *Tear Down This Myth: How the Reagan Legacy Has Distorted Our Politics and Haunts Our Future*, notes that historians are coming to a similar conclusion about Reagan's contributions to the end of the Cold War:

The growing consensus among historians is that Reagan's contributions, while positive, weren't the definitive factor that America-centric commentators make them out to be.[54]

Myth 2: Image and Interventionism

Some Reaganophiles claim that Reagan's assertive rhetoric in foreign policy allowed him to use direct military intervention sparingly and that he instead relied on covert action to attempt to overthrow unfriendly governments (the Reagan Doctrine)—for example, aiding the Contras in Sandinista Nicaragua, rebels in Marxist Angola, and the mujahideen against the Soviets and their Communist puppet government in Afghanistan. Yet when saying that Reagan did not use military power all that much, it depends on what his record is compared to. Coming after the years of military restraint caused by the "Vietnam Syndrome" during the Ford and Carter administrations, Reagan began the ramp-up back toward direct US interventionism. Gerald Ford had only the minor *Mayaquez* incident and Jimmy Carter had only the failed helicopter rescue attempt of the hostages in Iran. In contrast, Reagan's three major direct interventions—in Libya, Lebanon, and Grenada—were unprovoked, aggressive, unnecessary, and against small, feeble countries. As when then Secretary of State Al Haig told Reagan that, in aiding the government in El Salvador against Communist rebels, "Mr. President, this is one you can win,"[55] Reagan seemed to choose nonstrategic weak countries to beat up on to show that, under his leadership, the Vietnam Syndrome was in the past. The US invasion of the small island of Grenada in 1983 was the first major offensive use of American ground forces since the Vietnam War ended in 1973. However, Reagan first picked a smaller fight with another weak country.

Dust-Ups with Libya

In 1981, shortly after Reagan took office, he began intentionally provoking Libya's dictator Muammar Gaddafi,[56] the purpose of which some alleged was to help justify his peacetime defense buildup. Reagan regarded Gaddafi as a terrorist and stooge of the Soviets, who his administration believed, contrary to the evidence, were behind almost all of the drastically disparate terrorist groups worldwide.[57]

After the killing of a Libyan opposition figure in Chicago had questionably been attributed to a Gaddafi hit squad (the doubtful claim was made by Manucher Ghorbanifar, an Iranian arms dealer and chronic liar, who was later implicated in the Iran-Contra scandal), Reagan launched a large naval force, centered around two aircraft carriers, into the Gulf of Sidra. The gulf is surrounded on three sides by Libya and was claimed by Gaddafi as Libyan waters. A good case in international law can be made that such enclosed bodies of water, even beyond the internationally recognized twelve-mile limit for territorial waters, are part of a nation's waters, although only a few other nations honored Libya's claim.[58] At any rate, Reagan's was an unnecessary provocation of a country halfway across the world that posed little threat to US security.

A US S-3 Viking pilot later wrote that he was ordered to fly his aircraft in a racetrack orbit inside Gaddafi's claimed zone in the Gulf, but outside the twelve-mile territorial water limit, to be the bait to provoke a reaction from Gaddafi. In March 1981 and again in August 1981, the US Navy launched aggressive maneuvers off the coast of Libya in the Gulf. In the second episode, two Su-22 Libyan aircraft took that bait and one fired a missile at two US Navy F-14 Tomcat fighters. The vastly superior Tomcats then shot down the Libyan fighters. Yet despite all this US provocation, Gaddafi's support for terrorism remained focused on non-US targets.[59]

More US military skirmishing occurred with Libya later in the 1980s. Reagan again began launching aggressive naval maneuvers off Libya's coast in March 1986, hoping again to pick a fight with Gaddafi. This time, Gaddafi responded directly by unsuccessfully firing surface-to-air missiles at US aircraft over the Gulf. In response, US carrier-based aircraft destroyed the Libyan SAM sites and two patrol boats.

Gaddafi also responded indirectly by bombing the La Belle nightclub in Berlin, killing three off-duty American soldiers. According to Reagan's director of the White House Situation room at the time of the Libyan altercations,

> [t]he Reagan administration was partially responsible for the La Belle bombing and a flurry of simultaneous Libyan-based terrorist incidents. The bombing was a Libyan move in a series of tit-for-tats with the United States that began in 1981.[60]

Despite this official's general candor, by using the passive voice in the last sentence, he still understated Reagan's culpability in starting the bilateral back-and-forth violence with Gaddafi.

In retaliation for the La Belle bombing, Reagan launched a large US air attack on Tripoli in April 1986, designed to avoid the executive order banning US assassinations by designating Gaddafi's headquarters as a legitimate military target. This air raid killed forty-one civilians, including Gaddafi's adopted daughter, but not Gaddafi. Shortly thereafter, three US hostages in Beirut were found dead. In 2008, the United States later acknowledged its role in the cycle of retribution by paying damages to the families of innocent Libyan victims—much as Gaddafi paid damages for the later retaliatory Pan Am 103 bombing over Lockerbie, Scotland, in 1988, which killed all 259 on board.[61]

The common wisdom is that Reagan's aggressive approach "put Gaddafi back in his box" and made him give up terrorism. In reality, Gaddafi just went underground and accelerated his terrorism, some of it carried out by proxy groups to hide its origin. Prior to Reagan's provocations, Gaddafi had focused his terrorism on non-US targets, but he subsequently began redirecting it toward American targets, culminating in the dramatic bomb attack on US-bound flight Pan Am 103.[62]

Thus, Reagan's provocations had created a new US enemy. His actions showed that the informal American empire has nothing to do with the security of its citizens—quite the contrary.

Withdrawal Under Fire from Lebanon Emboldens Bin Laden

In August 1982, the US military intervention in Lebanon's civil war to provide "peacekeeping" forces was really to help American ally Israel stabilize this neighboring country after its invasion and bombing of that nation. Even though Israel had originally deceived the United States about the ambitious goal of its invasion of Lebanon—to kick out the Palestinian Liberation Organization (PLO)—and had launched brutally destructive attacks on the country that had soured world opinion (and would eventually alienate Israeli public opinion), the United States rewarded Israel for such bad behavior. It did so by negotiating an evacuation of the PLO by ship to Tunisia in North Africa and by providing peacekeeping forces for Lebanon. Furthermore, shortly after US peacekeepers arrived as part of a multilateral force, the Israeli Defense Forces allowed Christian militias to conduct massacres and atrocities at two Palestinian refugee camps in the country.

The United States shelled from the sea and conducted airstrikes on Muslim positions (operations not often seen coming from "peacekeeping" forces), and US Marines began patrolling with and supporting one side in the civil war: the minority pro-Israeli Christian Lebanese government. Naturally, the government's Shi'i Muslim opponents did not perceive the vulnerable US Marines as providing neutral peacekeepers. Thus, the marines were now taking fire from Shia militias operating from the Israeli-abandoned high ground after their withdrawal. Furthermore, the marines were even more vulnerable because Reagan, in trying to flout the timetables for troop withdrawal in the 1973 War Powers Resolution, ordered the marines to follow peacetime rules of engagement. Yet Congress was complicit in allowing Reagan to get away with this violation, as Democratic Speaker Tip O'Neill, despite his aversion to another Vietnam, refused to invoke the resolution's timetable for withdrawal and even helped Reagan pass a resolution that allowed US Marines to remain in Lebanon for another eighteen months.[63] That complicity would become a tragic mistake.

In deploying the marines in the first place, Reagan had ignored protests from the military leadership, including the chairman of the Joint Chiefs of Staff. The US embassy had been bombed in April 1983. With US intelligence warning that the marines might be the target of terrorist attacks, Secretary of Defense Caspar Weinberger made the case for withdrawing them, but Reagan declined to do so.[64] And he did not even make their position more secure. On October 23, 1983, the Shi'i fighters bombed the Marine barracks, killing 241 US service personnel. The debacle of the barracks bombing eventually caused Reagan to shamefully withdraw US forces from Lebanon under fire.

Reagan had previously said, "If we cut and run, we'll be sending one signal to terrorists everywhere." Yet he withdrew US forces, and the message was duly sent. Osama bin Laden later said that the barracks bombing in Lebanon had first convinced him that terror attacks could be effective in removing US military forces from Islamic countries. The Taliban in Afghanistan and Iraqi insurgents also later took advantage of this lesson. Will Bunch, a writer for the *Philadelphia News*, observed that Reagan's legacy-builders give him credit for winning the Cold War, even though it ended after he left office, but avoid blaming him for burgeoning anti-US Islamist terrorism as a result of his debacle in Lebanon.

After the Marine barracks bombing, one of the biggest disasters of Reagan's presidency, he offered merely an unenthusiastic, skimpy bombing raid to respond to the Syrians firing a shoulder-fired anti-aircraft missile at US aircraft over Lebanon. One airman was killed and one captured, only to be released in the care of Jessie Jackson, which embarrassed the Reagan administration. Reagan had earlier ordered larger-scale retaliation, but in a startling act of insubordination, Secretary of Defense Weinberger refused to carry it out. Instead of firing Weinberger on the spot, Reagan remained befuddled about why the retaliation had not occurred.[65]

More generally, creating future foreign policy problems was Reagan's specialty—helping to create bin Laden's al Qaeda and the Taliban, which harbored the group in Afghanistan before and after the 9/11 attacks, by building up the radical Islamist mujahideen in that country. Also in the 1980s,

Reagan aided Saddam Hussein's Iraq in its war with Iran, including providing it with precursors to make chemical weapons used against the Iranians and Iraqi Kurds. Thus, Reagan helped make the victorious and more aggressive Iraq dominant in the region and a future threat therein.

Invasion of Grenada

Instead of retaliating in Lebanon for the barracks attack, two days after the bombing (October 25, 1983) Reagan invaded the small, strategically insignificant island of Grenada in the southern Caribbean, which had the effect of diverting attention from the fiasco in Lebanon. Foreshadowing the later style of George W. Bush, who falsely conflated Saddam Hussein with the 9/11 attacks and al Qaeda to justify his invasion of Iraq, Reagan gave a disingenuous speech, using anti-Communist rhetoric, to conflate the US intervention in Lebanon with the unconnected invasion of Grenada; the problem was that the United States was not fighting Communists in Lebanon.[66] From the Oval Office, Reagan told the nation that "events in Lebanon and Grenada, though oceans apart, are closely related" and that the USSR backed "the violence in both countries . . . through a network of surrogates and terrorists."[67]

Michael Deaver, Reagan's chief public relations aide, later acknowledged that he backed the US invasion of Grenada because "it was a good story." He added that "I think this country was so hungry for a victory, I don't care what the size of it was, we were going to beat the shit out of it."[68] The October 1983 military "success" in Grenada caused an uptick in Reagan's approval ratings on the eve of his reelection year in 1984.[69] Although many American voters always seem to like "kicking ass" in small developing countries, Margaret Thatcher, the prime minister of Great Britain, the former colonial master of the island, was apoplectic about the US operation in Grenada, because Reagan did not tell her in advance that he was going to conduct this invasion of a British Commonwealth country. In fact, in March 1983, Reagan had publicly promised that US troops would not be sent into combat in Grenada.

It was alleged that US medical students in Grenada were in danger, yet the medical students appeared to be in no acute peril. Also, Cubans were helping to build a long runway at the airport. It was alleged that this runway could be used by Soviet aircraft in any war. Yet in any conflict, the airfield could be taken out fairly quickly. One also wonders why the United States did not instead take out airfields in more important Nicaragua. CIA Director William Casey told reporter Bob Woodward that one of the benefits from invading Grenada was the intimidation of the Soviet Union and Cuba by making them think that the United States might next strike Marxist Nicaragua.

At any rate, subduing a small island nation, possessing negligible military forces and only sparsely defended by Cubans, should not have been that difficult for the world's premier superpower. Although eventually successful, the US military operation was shaky, despite almost three years of Reagan's huge funding increases for the Department of Defense. US interservice communications were so bad that one soldier, to communicate with another service, had to use a pay phone on the island to call back to the Pentagon. Nineteen US service personnel needlessly died and a civilian mental hospital was bombed, killing twelve civilians. Besides, how could the United States criticize Soviet activities in its sphere of influence near its borders in Afghanistan when the United States was invading Grenada under the Monroe Doctrine and in flagrant violation of international law?

Covert Actions

Like the direct invasion of Grenada, even Reagan's covert actions had major implications. The selling of weapons to terrorism-sponsoring Iran in an attempt to free US hostages in Lebanon, and using the inflated proceeds from the sales to covertly fund the Nicaraguan Contras, resulted in the worst constitutional scandal in US history. Portending Reagan's soft spot for negotiating with terrorists for the potential release of such hostages was his dealings with Iranian-sponsored Hezbollah over the hijacking of TWA flight 847 in June 1985. The hijackers made reference to the earlier US military intervention in Lebanon, which is Hezbollah's main area of operation. In that intervention, the US battleship *New Jersey* shelled Lebanon, killing many civilians. The hijackers also mentioned the US massacre of eighty civilians in 1985 in Beirut's Bir al-Abed, when US bombing failed to kill a Hezbollah leader there.

A surprisingly candid assessment of this hijacking was made by Reagan's former director of the White House situation room. The director, presidential spokesman Larry Speakes, reiterated administration policy:

"We do not make concessions. We do not give into demands. We do not encourage other nations to do so." Yet over the next thirteen days, that's essentially what Reagan did, although with a bit of saber rattling.[70]

Reagan and his administration were always good at macho posturing (during his presidential campaign, he had criticized then President Carter for negotiating with Iran for the release of US embassy hostages and said he would have instead used threats and ultimatums), but oftentimes was a lot less courageous in practice. If you want to be hardline, doing so when dealing with hostage-taking is the time to do so. (Although to get the embassy hostages released, Carter only unfroze Iranian assets in the United States that he had frozen after Iranians had taken over the embassy.) As Reagan later found out in the Iran part of the Iran-Contra affair, giving into terrorists to win release of hostages may be a "win" in the short term but can backfire when the terrorists take additional hostages to trade for more ransom or prisoners held by their enemies in the future.

In the TWA case, Reagan blustered and pretended not to negotiate but achieved the release of the TWA passengers by pressuring Israel to release Lebanese prisoners in exchange and promising Syrian President Hafez al-Assad, Hezbollah's patron and mediator during the crisis, not to retaliate against Hezbollah targets in Lebanon.[71] The terrorists were allowed to get away scot-free.

Also, in addition to inspiring Osama bin Laden with his ignominious retreat from Lebanon (Reagan never should have sent US forces there in the first place to get in the middle of a local civil war insignificant to US security), Reagan ended up helping bin Laden to create al Qaeda by providing weapons and training to radical Islamists fighting against the Soviet invasion of Afghanistan. Although Jimmy Carter started assisting the Afghan mujahideen to bog down the Soviets in their own Vietnam-like conflict, Reagan vastly expanded the military aid program to try to actually win the war and kick the Soviets out. Although it seemed like a good idea during the Cold War to take on the Soviets in every backwater region, the Afghan war hardly single-handedly brought down the USSR and inadvertently created the most severe foreign threat to the usually secure US continental homeland since the War of 1812. According to one defense analyst,

[i]n Afghanistan, we made a deliberate choice. . . . [W]hat we [had] to do is to throw the worst crazies against them that we can find, and there was a lot of collateral damage. We knew exactly who these people were, and what their organizations were like. . . . Then, we allowed them to get rid of, just kill all the moderate leaders.[72]

Two lessons arise from this episode: (1) again, the interests of the US Empire often run counter to the ultimate security of American citizens; and (2) the US government should be careful when and where it intervenes overseas, because the often unintended consequences can be severe. Sometimes those unintended consequences undermine the very republic that such "security" measures are supposed to protect.

In his overzealous fight against Communism, which he justifiably hated with a passion, Reagan cozied up to some very brutal dictatorships in nonstrategic backwater places, including Chun Doo Hwan in South Korea, Ferdinand Marcos in the Philippines, the racist government in apartheid-era South Africa, and the right-wing regime in El Salvador, which sponsored death squads and had a much poorer human rights record than the Communist rebels it was fighting. The Commission on Truth for El Salvador documented accounts of 22,000 atrocities, with El Salvadorans attributing almost 85 percent of them to the security forces and only 5 percent to the Communist rebels.[73] In all of these countries, Reagan followed the advice of Jeanne Kirkpatrick, his hawkish neoconservative Democratic ambassador to the United Nations.

Reagan also got involved on both sides of the long, bloody Iran-Iraq War that lasted most of the 1980s. Although Saddam Hussein, in a portent of things to come, had invaded neighboring Iran in 1980, the United States feared the new fundamentalist Shi'i regime of Iran's Ayatollah Ruhollah Khomeini more than the brutal, secular Iraqi dictator. Thus, although the United States was ostensibly neutral in the war and imposed an arms embargo on both nations, it favored Iraq by shipping "non-lethal" military items, provided valuable intelligence and military planning capabilities, and encouraged other nations to ship arms to Iraq. The Reagan administration even continued to support the brutal Saddam after he used chemical weapons against his own Kurdish minority, whom he believed were supporting Iran in the war. As part of support for Iraq, the United States reflagged the oil tankers of Kuwait, a Saddam ally at that point, to protect them against Iranian attacks. The US Navy was thereby dragged into a shooting war with the Iranian Navy.

However, important exceptions to this pro-Iraq policy occurred. In 1981, Reagan secretly authorized Israel to sell US weapons to Iran and, later on, in what was to be part of the Iran-Contra scandal, the United States sold antitank and antiaircraft missiles to the Iranians in an attempt to get the Iranian-supported Hezbollah group to release US hostages held in Lebanon. Those hostages had been taken in the first place in retaliation for Reagan's aforementioned military intervention in Lebanon in the early 1980s in support of Israel. As this US military intervention receded into history, Hezbollah's attacks on the United States gradually dissipated—an unheeded lesson for later presidents, who also attacked and occupied faraway countries to allegedly make inroads in fighting "terrorism," but merely caused more of it.

More generally, in the Middle East, Reagan created the tools used for a future ramp-up of US military intervention in the region. To compensate for the British withdrawal from the region and the loss of Iran as a major US ally, Jimmy Carter had promulgated the Carter Doctrine, which pledged US defense of the oil-soaked Persian Gulf and created a Rapid Deployment Force (RDF) to do so. Yet the RDF had very little military capability to actually carry out Carter's new policy. Reagan created a new bureaucratic organization, called the Central Command, to flesh out Carter's ill-advised doctrine with actual military forces. As a result, the United States spends more money per year on such forces than it pays for imports of oil from the region. In the book, *No War for Oil: U.S. Dependency and the Middle East*, I explain why oil is not strategic and why the market instead should be allowed to provide the United States with oil at the cheapest prices possible.[74] (This analysis is even more applicable, as the United States has again become the world's largest oil producer because of the advent of oil fracking technology.)

Finally, in 1983, Reagan created the National Endowment for Democracy, which intervened in the internal affairs of other countries to support US-friendly societal forces, including Poland's Solidarity movement.

In conclusion, Reagan pioneered the ramp-up of US military intervention from the more restrained immediate post–Vietnam War era of Gerald Ford and Jimmy Carter. On the other hand, Reagan's successors, the two

Bushes and Clinton, were much more ambitious in their foreign meddling than Reagan. For example, even after Manuel Noriega, Panama's strongman, was indicted for drug offenses, Reagan handled the matter using diplomacy. George H. W. Bush launched an invasion of Panama, overthrew Noriega, and threw him in jail. The Bushes and Clinton no longer had a strong rival superpower, the Soviet Union, to constrain US military interventions around the world.

Myth 3: The Administration's Scandals Were Not Severe

Ronald Reagan was a delegator of authority, which can be good, but which can also lead to trouble if the right people are not chosen for subordinate offices. In addition to the worst constitutional scandal in US history—Iran-Contra—Reagan also had a fair amount of less severe alleged and confirmed venality during his administration, as discussed in this section.

Iran-Contra Scandal Was Worse than Watergate

When the worst scandals of American history are assembled, most of them happened during Republican administrations, with the exception of the Monica Lewinsky sex/perjury scandal under Bill Clinton. The other major Republican scandals included corruption under the Ulysses S. Grant and Warren Harding administrations, Watergate under Richard Nixon, and Iran-Contra under Ronald Reagan.

The graft scandals under Grant and Harding involved people deriving personal financial gain from their government service (Republicans do have a point that the similar substantial corruption during the Truman administration is rarely mentioned by fawning historians), but they did not compare to the abuse of the Constitution during Watergate and Iran-Contra.

In the Watergate scandal, the Nixon administration tried to use US security agencies in government to cover up its petty campaign dirty tricks. However, the Reagan administration violated a criminal law and its own international arms embargo by selling heavy weapons at elevated prices to a terrorist-sponsoring nation, Iran, to attempt to ransom hostages held in Lebanon by the Iranian-backed Hezbollah group. This action was an unbelievably bad policy choice, because it merely led to the kidnapping of more hostages by the group. The policy also violated Reagan's loud macho rhetoric toward unfriendly Iran and his claims that he did not negotiate with terrorists. Reagan had earlier characterized Iran as an "outlaw state, run by the strangest collection of misfits, looney tunes and squalid criminals since the advent of the Third Reich."[75] Yet, in a December 1985 meeting, Reagan said, "I don't care if I have to go to Leavenworth; I want the hostages out."[76] The hostages that Reagan always had a soft spot for, however, were taken in retaliation for his intervention in Lebanon on behalf of Israel.[77] (Reagan, a secret bleeding-heart, also contravened this official hardline policy when he got Syria to push Hezbollah for the successful release of passengers on hijacked TWA flight 847 in exchange for Israel's release of Arab Shi'i prisoners.)

The administration then used the inflated proceeds from arms sales to Iran to violate an explicit congressional ban on providing assistance to the Contra rebels (the second Boland Amendment), who were trying to destabilize and overthrow the Sandinista government in Nicaragua. The Contras, by themselves, never had any chance to overthrow the Sandinistas. Reagan was trying to disrupt the Sandinista government because it was providing aid to a Marxist insurgency against the brutal government of El Salvador, which Reagan was supporting by sending advisers and military aid. This US support was given even though the El Salvadorian government's death squads had a worse human rights record than the Communist guerrillas.

Funding a secret war in violation of an explicit congressional ban thereon cuts to the heart of the American constitutional system of checks and balances, eroding Congress's most important remaining power that had not already been usurped by the chief executive: the power to direct where federal monies are spent. Congress's ban on US government funding of the Nicaraguan Contra rebels in the second Boland Amendment began after conservative Barry Goldwater was shocked to discover in mid-1984 that in late 1983, Reagan had secretly ordered the mining of Nicaraguan harbors—an act of war—to damage international shipping to undermine the Sandinista government's foreign trade. Nicaragua won a judgment in the International Court stating that such paramilitary activities violated international law and that the United States should desist.[78] (In addition, such an act of war should have had congressional approval.)

So one could argue that Iran-Contra was a more severe breach constitutionally than Watergate. Nixon's personal involvement in the Watergate
cover-up eventually became obvious, but Reagan clearly knew that the arms
shipments to Iran violated the Arms Export Control Act, a criminal statute,
because his secretaries of defense and state had told him that was likely;
Reagan even joked about him and his advisers going to jail because of the
sales. Lt. Col. Oliver North, the National Security Council aide who was at
the center of the Iran-Contra scandal, later confirmed that Reagan knew all
about the illegal arms-for-hostages trade and approved of it. If nothing else,
Reagan was guilty of violating the National Security Act, which required
the president to notify a small number of members of Congress "in a timely
manner" about covert action; Reagan had not informed Congress about the
mining of Nicaraguan harbors nor of the arms sales to Iran during the year
prior to its "outing" in November 1986. Also, North admitted to conducting
covert operations without the proper legal authorization.[79]

Although it is less clear whether Reagan personally knew about the diversion of arms sale profits to the Contras, he was keenly interested in the welfare
and progress of the Contras and his staff gave him regular briefings on the
issue. John Ehrman maintains that Reagan's personal correspondence indicates that the president knew nothing of North's diversion of Iranian profits to
finance the Contras.[80] However, whether Reagan would admit to something
ultra-secret that was clearly illegal and unconstitutional in his personal correspondence is doubtful. While Reagan admitted that he knew and approved
of the Contras receiving money from private sources and third countries,
he denied knowing about the diversion of arms sale profits to the Contras.
National Security Advisor John Poindexter testified at congressional hearings
that he had not told Reagan about the diversion, but Poindexter could have
been falling on his sword for the boss. The extensive obstruction of justice
by North and Poindexter, by destroying documents and creating false ones,
may have been to cover up Reagan's knowledge of both parts of the scandal.

Yet all this attention about whether Reagan knew about the diversion
of funds is misplaced, because in May 1987, he admitted about the effort to
illegally circumvent the congressionally passed Boland Amendment, which
banned funding of the Contras, "It was my idea to begin with."[81]

Even with this admission by Reagan, some have tried to argue that Reagan could not have known of such unconstitutional and illegal behavior because of his inattention to detail or even because his Alzheimer's affliction was already affecting him in November 1986 during the Iran-Contra crisis.[82] Even if Reagan was diminished by such issues, the aforementioned discussion indicates that he was quite aware of many things about policies that led to the scandal. And inattention to detail is no excuse: Presidents Warren Harding and Ulysses S. Grant certainly have not been excused by history for their subordinates running amok and doing illegal things without their knowledge. Any president is ultimately responsible for selecting honest and capable subordinates and ensuring their legal and constitutional conduct.

Finally, Reagan's documented role in soliciting funds from other countries and private donors illegally violated the Boland Amendment. At bare minimum, Reagan had earlier instructed Robert McFarlane, his national security advisor, to keep the Contras together "body and soul." To achieve this goal, McFarlane, with Reagan's knowledge and participation, had secretly arranged outside funding for the Contras from Saudi Arabia. North also got financing from private donors and governments of Taiwan and Brunei and arms from other countries for the Contras, with Reagan actually meeting with the private donors. Not knowing they had finagled such financing, Secretary of State George Shultz had deemed brokering funds from private donors or other countries "very likely illegal," and White House Chief of Staff James Baker had thought it would be "an impeachable offense."[83] Shultz had agreed. Even Reagan himself said that "if such a story gets out, we'll all be hanging by our thumbs in front of the White House until we find out who did it." (Reagan self-servingly later claimed that he was referring to leaking, not the creative financing.)

At that same meeting, Vice President George H. W. Bush opined that the only problem with soliciting third-party funding for the Contras was if the United States, in return, did favors for the third parties. Years later, in the legal case against North, the US government would list many such favors by the Reagan administration dispensed to Saudi Arabia, Brunei, Honduras, Israel, and others in return for their aid to the Contras. During the time of the restrictive second Boland Amendment banning aid to the Contras, Reagan himself signed a directive to send military and economic aid and CIA support to the government of Honduras so that it would continue its support for the Contras, and he personally called the Honduran president to get arms to the Contras flowing again after Honduras suspended them. Bush, despite his earlier analysis of the legal problems with American quid pro quo actions to benefit nations helping the Contras, met with the Honduran president to grease the skids for the deal.

In addition, appallingly, despite the Reagan administration's "War on Drugs," North also appeared to be using his White House–run covert operation's aircraft to move cocaine into the United States to help the Contras get money, as evidenced by references to such illegal activities in his notebooks. North also appropriated funds from the covert operation for his own personal use.[84]

In fact, the second, more restrictive Boland Amendment for fiscal year 1985 specified, "During fiscal year 1985, no funds available to the Central Intelligence Agency, the Department of Defense, or any other agency or entity of the United States involved in intelligence activities may be obligated or expended for the purpose or which would have the effect of supporting, directly or indirectly, military or paramilitary operations in Nicaragua by any nation, group, organization, movement or individual."[85] Because the White House was clearly involved in intelligence activities and was even freelancing on covert operations as well, and since the salaries of Reagan, Bush, McFarlane, and National Security Council aide Oliver North were being paid for them to indirectly aid the Contras, the Boland Amendment was clearly violated.

The diversion of funds to the Contras from arms sales to Iran aside, by brokering any outside funds for the Contras from third parties, Reagan was clearly circumventing one of Congress's main powers under the Constitution: the power of the purse. Yet Bud McFarlane, Reagan's national security advisor, lied to Congress, claiming that the administration had not solicited funds from third-party donors for the Contras, facilitated such contributions, or organized the efforts of the Nicaraguan guerrillas.

General Richard Secord (Ret.), heavily involved in the Iran-Contra caper, and Oliver North later said that they believed Reagan knew everything about the Iran-Contra scandal. According to an irate Secord in 1990,

I think former President Reagan has been hiding out. I think it's cowardly. I believed earlier and I still believe that he was well aware of the general outlines of the so-called Iran-Contra affair.

Similarly, North wrote in his memoir, *Under Fire*: "President Reagan knew everything"—that is, about the Iranian arms sales, the illegal Contra supply operation, and the diversion of profits from the first to the second.[86]

Caspar Weinberger, Reagan's secretary of defense, was indicted and then later unconstitutionally pardoned (along with five others in Iran-Contra) in a likely cover-up by President George H. W. Bush of his own activities during Iran-Contra. George Shultz, Reagan's secretary of state, was accused by the Iran-Contra special counsel, without indictment or conviction, of perjury, but only one minor figure in the entire caper was ever jailed. The convictions of Reagan National Security Advisor John Poindexter and National Security Council employee Oliver North were overturned on appeal because of contamination of the cases against them by grants of immunity during simultaneous congressional investigations of Iran-Contra.

The illegal and unconstitutional activities during the Iran-Contra affair, perpetrated to fund a secret and prohibited war, probably exceeded the severity of violations of the Constitution during Watergate, despite a somewhat more elevated purpose than merely covering up nefarious campaign activities. Iran-Contra was also more serious because, unlike Nixon, Reagan escaped the impeachment process—principally because post-Watergate politicians and the public did not want to bring down another president—thus likely undermining the respect future presidents will have for the Constitution.[87] Other developments that saved Reagan were his appointment of the respected former Senator Howard Baker of Watergate fame as White House chief of staff, thus improving relations with Congress, and a Tower Commission report that changed the paradigm from presidential illegalities to that of a slumbering executive being taken down the river by out-of-control subordinates. Yet Reagan had knowingly violated laws: the Arms Export Control Act and the National Security Act of 1947. And as noted previously, in a fit of frustration in May 1987, Reagan admitted of the effort to get around the Boland Amendment, "It was my idea to begin with."[88]

The Iran-Contra scandal—when combined with a Democratic majority in the Senate after the 1986 election to go along with that in the House since the beginning of the administration[89]—did reduce Reagan's presidency to almost a caretaker status for his last two years in office, much to the ire of conservatives.

Only tangentially related to Watergate, Nixon had run an even larger secret war, using US ground forces in Cambodia briefly in 1970. However, this side conflict was part of a wider war in Southeast Asia, on which Congress, in the vague Gulf of Tonkin Resolution passed in the mid-1960s, unfortunately had given a virtual blank check authorization for presidential actions. Although the president running a clandestine war without Congress's and the American people's knowledge is never good in a republic, Nixon could argue that Congress had nevertheless earlier authorized such presidential efforts and that he had violated no specific congressional ban on getting involved in Cambodia. Thus, unlike in the Iran-Contra affair, the president was not completely at fault here, and Congress, trying to look the other way, must also bear part of the blame. The secret war in Cambodia was originally included in the articles of impeachment against Nixon but was then removed.

Like Richard Nixon and other post–World War II presidents, Reagan wasted much time during his administration excessively worrying about Communist penetration of small, poor nations in the developing world that had little strategic value to the United States, and thus presented little threat to it. Yet Reagan was the only president that almost had his administration brought down by illegalities committed in the process of intervening in such places.

Lewis L. Gould, in his history of the Republican Party, best presents a concise summary of the implications of the Iran-Contra scandal when he concludes that it:

> suggested that a separate foreign policy apparatus had been established outside the restraints of Congress. Republican officials had regarded the Constitution not as a check on their power in conducting foreign policy but rather as a troublesome obstacle to be circumvented by any means necessary to achieve their ends. In that sense, Reagan's conservative administration displayed quite radical tendencies toward the traditional procedures of the American government.[90]

And why did Reagan risk so much in the Iran-Contra affair to get so little? The hostages in Lebanon, even if they had been released, would not have been a major foreign policy victory. Similarly, the Nicaraguan rebels were unlikely to be successful, and even if they were, Nicaragua was not a country of major significance. As Doug Rossinow noted:

> Haig called the land bridge between continents a "strategic choke point" where Soviet influence was impermissible, but had difficulty explaining what of importance would be choked off there.[91]

The Panama Canal was near Nicaragua, but even its strategic value had diminished significantly because US aircraft carriers had grown too big to transit the waterway. To convince a skeptical public that the Central American region was important, Reagan claimed that in any future world war, a rival with a military presence in the region could interdict US oil supplies. Yet most analysts were skeptical of this argument.[92] Most US imports could take other routes to America. The real reason the Reagan administration did not want any Soviet influence in even a small, insignificant Latin American country was likely just enforcement of the Monroe Doctrine. The doctrine, promulgated in 1823, had always bristled against the influence—no matter how limited—of any outside power in the Western Hemisphere.

Accompanying Reagan's interventions in Central America was the violation of civil liberties of the people in the United States who opposed them. The FBI targeted groups such as the Committee in Solidarity with the People of El Salvador, compiling lists of members, harassing them, and recruiting conservative university students to spy on them.[93]

Corruption Continues

The following is a brief list of corruption during Reagan's tenure:

- Richard Allen, Reagan's first national security advisor, resigned over fuzzy connections to Japanese politicians and business interests. He took small gifts from foreign interests.[94]

- After leaving the White House, Michael Deaver, Reagan's chief publicist and the man who revolutionized presidential public relations, got in trouble with the Ethics in Government Act of 1978 when he tried to cash in on his White House years by peddling his connections with the administration to rich clients. The law restricts lobbying by former government officials. Deaver was convicted of three counts of perjury.

- Lyn Nofziger, a close personal friend of Reagan and White House political director early in the Reagan presidency, was convicted for illegal lobbying for Wedtech, a military contractor, but eventually got his conviction overturned.

- To get personal financial assistance, Ed Meese, a longtime Reagan associate and counselor to the president, gave out jobs in the Reagan administration to financial benefactors. Unwisely, Meese had not kept away from friends seeking influence. Also, Meese took money improperly from Reagan's 1980–1981 transition funds. Yet, in 1985, despite this apparent corruption, Reagan appointed Meese as US attorney general, the top law enforcement job in the federal government, and a friendly Republican Senate confirmed him. As attorney general, Meese was also involved in the Wedtech scandal and failed to pay his taxes. A second independent prosecutor found that Meese's conduct probably violated criminal law, but that no prosecution was warranted. He was the highest-level example of crony capitalism in an administration troubled by it.

- The largest military procurement scandal in US history was predictable when so much money was being thrown at the Department of Defense (DoD) in so little time to fulfill Reagan's campaign promise and burnish his macho image. Even in more normal times, DoD, in contrast to the image of military efficiency, is chronically the worst-run department in the federal government because excessive secrecy shields it from adequate public scrutiny; the department is the only one that has not, and cannot to this day, pass an audit to show where all the trillions of dollars end up. When the department benefits from largesse on the scale provided by Reagan, fraud, waste, and abuse are even more likely.

- Because of poor supervision, several Department of Housing and Urban Development (HUD) officials were jailed for accepting payoffs and bribes and overlooking massive fraud. Reagan's officials were channeling government funds from low-income housing to Republican cronies. This scandal occurred because of the lax management of Reagan's secretary for housing and urban development, Samuel Pierce.

- Secretary of Labor Ray Donovan was investigated for alleged links to organized crime.
- Rita Lavelle, the chief of the Environmental Protection Agency's effort to clean up toxic wastes (called Superfund), was convicted of perjury and obstructing a congressional investigation.[95] In trying to protect her old employer, which was a corporate polluter, she was another example of crony capitalism. Ann Gorsuch Burford, another EPA official, was cited by Congress for contempt for not turning over documents on the Superfund program. In disgrace, these two officials led a mass resignation from EPA of over twenty officials.[96]

It is interesting that the fawning historians ignore the volume of such petty corruption during Reagan's two terms but let it define the presidencies of fellow Republicans Warren G. Harding and Ulysses S. Grant, who were otherwise better chief executives than commonly believed, and certainly better than Reagan.

Myth 4: A Smaller Federal Government?

According to conservative Reaganophile Steven F. Hayward, during the 1980 campaign, three of four parts of Reagan's economic agenda were not very different from Carter's program: regulatory relief, federal budget reductions, and restraint of the money supply. Only the fourth part—cutting income tax rates substantially—was novel; it had not yet entered Republican orthodoxy.[97] (Jimmy Carter had pioneered the supply-side tax cut, cutting the capital gains rate to encourage investment, but had nixed the huge Kemp-Roth income tax rate cuts because he feared blowing a hole in the budget.) So Reagan, in effect, was to pioneer massive, irresponsibly fraudulent tax cuts—tax reduction without concomitant budget cuts—for Republicans, such as George W. Bush, to use in the future to win elections. This legacy was a primary one for Reagan, but not a commendable one.

Budget Deficit Balloons

In reality, when Reagan came into office, his three conflicting goals were to cut taxes, increase defense spending, and balance the budget (the budget had been running a small deficit under Jimmy Carter). He achieved the first two goals, but at the expense of the last one. Reagan can be blamed for putting the emphasis in his administration on the first two objectives and not being that concerned with more important spending reductions to achieve the third one or go beyond it. Reagan said, "If it comes down to balancing the budget or defense, the balanced budget will have to give way."[98] Spoken like a true big-government conservative. So during his first year in office in 1981, when his political capital was the highest, although he offered and achieved some cuts in nonentitlement domestic spending, he used his political capital instead to emphasize passing tax cuts and needlessly ballooning defense spending. As his political capital waned with the recession beginning in 1982, and even as the federal budget deficit opened wider because of that downturn and his spend-but-don't-tax policies, he shifted away from unpopular spending cuts to surreptitious tax increases.[99] (The priorities of social conservatives were never high on Reagan's list. In 1982, Reagan admitted to a journalist that those priorities—for example, legally nixing abortion and instituting prayer in the public schools—were not central to his philosophy and were mere adornments.[100])

Although Reagan had been rhetorically railing against federal budget deficits for decades, beginning in 1981 when he assumed the presidency, Reagan ballooned the deficit by slashing income tax rates dramatically each year for three years (he later cut income tax rates again in 1986), indexing tax brackets to inflation to hold down taxpayers' bills, cutting taxes on capital gains and on investment income, raising the dollar threshold when estate and gift taxes kick in to allow greater wealth to be passed to heirs, and increasing defense spending. Marginal tax rates at all levels had to be cut to sell the real goal of supply-side economics—to reduce the top marginal rate from 70 percent to 50 percent on rich investors to stimulate the economy[101] (and, perhaps as important politically, to throw a bone to that powerful Republican constituency). The assassination attempt on Reagan at the end of March 1981 caused Reagan's popularity to soar and revived his chance to pass his economic program.

David Stockman, Reagan's budget director, later admitted that the tax cuts were designed to lower taxes on high incomes—the class most likely to save and invest the extra money—and studies on rising income inequality showed that they did just that. To pass his multi-year program of "supply-side" income tax rate cuts and Keynesian defense spending hikes, while simultaneously balancing the budget, he would have had to make deep cuts in nondefense spending. Instead, to get his program through Congress, he had to increase nondefense spending even more than defense spending (also all very Keynesian). (Also, to pass his income tax rate cuts for individuals, Reagan had to hand out tax subsidies and loopholes to special interests.) Thus, over the Reagan years, despite a huge and unnecessary military buildup, federal spending on social programs increased in real terms and as a percentage of the federal budget.[102]

Even in the first fiscal year of Reagan's program, the high water mark of his budget cutting, when he did manage to get some restraint on real nondefense discretionary spending (reductions of only a paltry $16 billion in fiscal year 1982), increases in entitlement programs more than offset this cut to result in a net $53 billion increase in social programs from 1980 levels.[103]

In addition, the deficit began ballooning because of an error by Reagan's White House Office of Management and Budget (OMB). Reagan wanted a 7 percent real increase in defense spending for the first few years, but the outgoing budget for FY 1982 inherited from Carter had already increased defense spending substantially by 4.5 percent. Budget director Stockman simply added the 7 percent growth per year to the already elevated number.[104] The growth of the defense budget was accidentally double even the substantial increase that Reagan proposed during his 1980 campaign.[105]

So the Department of Defense (DoD) was slathered in peacetime with more funds than it could realistically spend efficiently. According to Stockman, "[n]o fresh start or strategically coherent defense plan was ever developed by the Reagan administration. This immense, content-free 'top line' [total defense spending] was simply backfilled by the greatest stampede of Pentagon log-rolling and budget aggrandizement by the military-industrial complex ever recorded."[106] Reagan's defense budget bought systems that were technologically infeasible, were unneeded, were white elephants, or had no viable strategic rationale—for example, the Star Wars missile defense fantasy, the vulnerable MX intercontinental ballistic missile (ICBM), the B-1 bomber, and the six-hundred-ship navy to be used for the herculean and dangerous mission of attacking Soviet ports, respectively. It is not clear that the massive injection of cash was spent prudently.[107] Obviously, in Reagan's alleged quest for smaller government, the DoD was exempted.

Moreover, Reagan's more macho foreign policy and defense largesse took place at a time when the United States went from being a creditor nation (since World War I) to a debtor nation in the mid-1980s and beyond. Essentially, the United States began borrowing from rich, friendly countries to pay for increased defense budgets to protect these nations and also to expand its overseas empire. The Reagan administration set up the new Central Command of substantial US military forces to secure Middle Eastern oil, which the two Bushes and subsequent presidents have used to conduct many unneeded direct military interventions in the Middle East. Thus, Reagan's imperial overextension continues to this day.

Another reason that the deficit significantly widened during Reagan's first year in office was that Reagan's tax cut was three to four times his spending restraint.[108] If given the choice to make popular tax cuts or unpopular spending reductions, Reagan emphasized the tax cuts, and domestic discretionary spending cuts only lasted one year. Worse, Reagan's tax cuts ballooned in size during the give and take of the legislative process. Reagan knew of projections of burgeoning budget deficits before he signed the tax cut in 1981, and Stockman knew of the problem even earlier but jiggered the administration's economic models to hide the future red ink.[109] Also, projections did not include the recession triggered by Fed Chairman Paul Volcker's slamming on the monetary brakes. Thus, contrary to the ex post facto "starve the beast" rationale, the deficits and mounting debt came about because of accidental incompetence and an attempt to garner political advantage and were not a purposeful strategy to reduce the size of government. Thus, the size of government during the Reagan years increased, both in absolute terms and as a percentage of GDP.

In later years, the deficits just kept swelling to then record levels, because nondefense discretionary spending began burgeoning—more than offsetting the cuts of the first year—and was combined with continued huge hikes in defense expenditures and restrained revenues arising from the multi-year tax cuts. So domestic discretionary spending experienced one year of budget cuts in 1982, followed by rapid budget increases. Also, Reagan did not significantly restrain spending on domestic entitlement programs; entitlement spending continued to increase from 1980 to 1987, with the three largest programs—Social Security, Medicare, and other healthcare spending—increasing 84 percent. Yet because Reagan did not end up reducing taxes that much overall—he subsequently increased taxes in six of eight years of his presidency—most of his large budget deficits came from increases in spending.[110]

In September 1985, Reagan's budget deficit had gotten so bad that Republican senators Phil Gramm and Warren Rudman, with the bipartisan approval of their Senate colleagues (the chamber was then controlled by Republicans) and support from the Democratic leadership of the House of Representatives, got the severe Gramm-Rudman-Hollings law (The Balanced Budget and Emergency Deficit Control Act of 1985) enacted. If the Congress did not reduce the yawning deficit through normal budgetary procedures, the law would make automatic across-the-board budget cuts to reduce the deficit to zero by 1991. (This law was a model for Barack Obama's across-the-board "sequestration," which actually took effect because of budget gridlock between Obama and a Republican Congress.) In general, although some gaming of the numbers occurred, the Gramm-Rudman-Hollings law helped improve the nation's fiscal picture, especially when the Democrats gained control of both houses of Congress during 1987 and 1988 and helped Reagan start to reduce his massive self-generated deficit.[111] In at least one instance running counter to this general narrative, however, Reagan did try to veto a highway bill in 1987 but was overridden by Congress.[112]

Despite his small government rhetoric, Reagan seemed to have little sustained desire to cut nondefense spending, actually added a cabinet department (the Department of Veterans Affairs), and increased the number of federal employees from 2.8 million to 3 million (whereas his successors, George H. W. Bush and especially Bill Clinton, cut back the federal workforce to 2.68 million).[113] Thus, Reagan added annually on average more civilian (nonmilitary) federal government personnel as a percentage of the US population than any other post-Truman president, except during the eight years of the John F. Kennedy/Lyndon B. Johnson terms.[114]

Net Tax Cuts Were Relatively Small and Fraudulent

Many conservatives, who in earlier eras were adamantly and correctly opposed to deficit spending, retroactively asserted that Reagan was cutting taxes and running deficits to "starve the government beast"—that is, he was running deficits to compel budget cuts. Yet Reagan seemed to contradict this line of thought by rhetorically buying into a bastardization of supply-side economic theory: that lowering income tax rates would actually increase government tax revenues.[115]

Republicans before Reagan had been accused of favoring "root canal" economics, which meant cutting federal deficits and balancing budgets by cutting government spending. Politically, this rhetorical position had made them a minority party for decades, losing out to Keynesianism—economic growth through tax cuts and increased government spending, with budget deficits being acceptable. However, to deal with this problem and compete with Keynesianism, some Republicans, including Reagan, bought into the extremities of supply side theory, which focused on the popular idea of cutting taxes to stimulate the economy.[116] However, the Reaganites were much less enthusiastic about cutting the equally popular, but massive, entitlement spending programs, such as Social Security and Medicare. That is, Republicans would criticize unpopular welfare for the poor, as Reagan did, but not mess with middle-class entitlements.[117] Tax cuts without spending cuts are fraudulent because taxes either need to be raised at a later date to close the budget deficit, interest has to be paid on money the government borrows to finance the deficit, or money has to be printed (the worst option). So although Reagan always derided those who sought a "free lunch," Reagan himself did so by cutting taxes while increasing federal spending as a portion of GDP, leaving a deficit mess for George H. W. Bush and Bill Clinton to clean up, which they did. As Alan Greenspan—the chairman of the Federal Reserve who had been appointed by Reagan and also served under George H. W. Bush, Bill Clinton, and George W. Bush—noted, "The hard truth was that Reagan had borrowed from Clinton, and Clinton was having to pay it back."[118]

Thus, Republicans under Reagan implicitly confirmed the New Deal as untouchable. In addition, Reagan and other Republican presidents have reaffirmed the more basic belief, only accepted since the presidency of Herbert Hoover, that it was the government's responsibility to foster economic growth and keep people employed, which the Keynesians also have heartily endorsed. The main difference between supply-side Republicans and liberal Keynesianism is whether tax cuts should be given to savers and investors (the supply side) or consumers (the Keynesian demand side).

Average annual growth in national debt as a portion of GDP actually has been much worse under supply side presidents, such as Reagan and imitator George W. Bush, than it has been under Democratic presidents—annualized debt as a percentage of GDP actually went down under these presidents. A major reason is that since the Truman presidency, contravening conventional wisdom, Democratic presidents, on average, have restrained increases in federal spending as a percentage of GDP more than Republican ones.[119]

Although supply siders are correct that increased economic activity from income tax rate cuts will provide some added tax revenue to help offset some of the revenue lost from rate reductions, tax cuts hardly pay for themselves, as Reagan rhetorically maintained in February 1981, shortly after his inauguration:

> There's still that belief on the part of many people that a cut in tax rates automatically means a cut in revenues. And if they'll only look at history, it doesn't. A cut in tax rates can very often be reflected in an increase in government revenues because of the broadening of the base of the economy.[120]

George H. W. Bush, when running against Reagan in 1980 before becoming his vice presidential running mate, correctly dubbed this concept "voodoo economic policy."

Even if income tax rate cuts had the miraculous effect Reagan said they did, would not supply siders then just be "tax collectors for the welfare state"? Instead of supporting fraudulent tax cuts, politicians, especially popular ones like Reagan, should put all of their political capital behind support for difficult spending cuts, which are required to shrink the size of government. Unfortunately, that stance is not a political winner, as has been demonstrated by subsequent Republicans. Those politicians included George W. Bush and Dick Cheney, who promulgated even larger tax cuts, bigger spending increases, and wider budget deficits as a portion of GDP than did Reagan and proclaimed that Reagan showed the nation that deficits did not matter.

The other problem with the "starving the beast" argument is that as deficits mushroomed, instead of pressing hard for spending cuts, Reagan slyly began raising taxes in parts of the tax code that were less visible than the well-publicized income tax rates—for example, increasing "user fees," reducing various tax breaks, and calling tax increases "revenue enhancements." When taken together, his tax hikes in 1982 and 1984 then constituted the biggest tax increase ever in peacetime.[121] In fact, Reagan had major tax increases in 1982 (including hikes in business taxes and fees and gas and excise tax increases), 1983 (an increase in payroll taxes to save Social Security), 1984 (closing tax "loopholes"), and 1986 (tax reform). In all, Reagan raised taxes every year of his presidency, except in his first year (in 1981) and in his last (in 1988, so that his vice president could get elected president)—thirteen tax hikes in all from 1982 to 1987.[122] These tax hikes were regressive, because they disproportionately affected the poor, thereby worsening economic inequality in the United States.[123]

Despite Reagan's rhetoric, and thus reputation as a tax cutter, a summary accounting, including the three-year income tax rate cut in 1981 and the aforementioned tax increases, gives Reagan only a slight net annualized tax reduction as a percentage of GDP over his eight years in office—the worst of any post–World War II Republican president.[124]

The Tax Reform Act of 1986—perhaps the greatest accomplishment during Reagan's time in office and a much more important policy change than his celebrated income tax rate cuts of 1981—came from Democrats in the House and Senate. The act reduced income tax rates for the wealthy, even below the levels of the 1981 law, in exchange for closing tax loopholes, some of which had been adopted in Reagan's 1981 statute, and increasing the earned income tax credit. The latter effectively reduced the tax burden on the working poor. Also, the law simplified the tax code by drastically reducing the number of tax brackets.

Although the 1986 tax reform did not live up to expectations, economic studies showed that it did increase business investment in technology, broaden the tax base, and improve tax system fairness and economic efficiency by closing loopholes, but it did not increase savings or the labor supply; the American tax system remained complex.[125] William Niskanen, a former Reagan economic adviser but not always celebratory of the Reagan administration, concluded, "For the most part the structure of the federal tax code is now simpler, fairer, and of lower cost to the economy than in 1981."[126]

Overall, the 1986 tax reform statute was progressive in effect. Unfortunately, however, the law transferred some of the tax burden from individuals to corporations, with the largest increase ever in corporate taxes. Since corporate taxation is double taxation (profits are taxed both at the corporate and individual level), this policy change was the wrong action to take. Although Reagan supported the Tax Reform Act, Bob Packwood, the Republican chairman of the Senate Finance Committee, had a prominent role in designing it and guiding it through Congress when the possibility of tax reform seemed dire.[127]

Evaluating his entire administration, Reagan patented the irresponsible fraudulent tax cut—scoring political points by lowering taxes while avoiding the political firestorm of cutting popular spending programs—which subsequent presidents, such as George W. Bush, unfortunately imitated, once again producing huge budget deficits. In fact, during the George W. Bush administration, his vice president, Dick Cheney, told the American people that Reagan had taught us that deficits did not matter.

Essentially, Reagan converted the Republican Party, formerly worried more about cutting spending and balancing budgets, into a more statist political organization, which argued that government cuts in income tax rates are constantly needed to stimulate the private economy and to recoup revenues for the federal government.[128] Economically, as previously noted, if politicians cut taxes and do not cut spending, they either will need to raise taxes in the future (which Reagan did multiple times), borrow money (which must be paid back with interest), or print money (which is the worst option, because it usually causes inflation). Public borrowing to finance government deficits "crowds out" needed private borrowing, thereby raising interest rates and slowing economic growth. Concerns about the huge Reagan deficits had been one cause of the stock market crash in 1987, according to economists.[129]

Thus, tax cuts are certainly laudable, but only when they are real—when the much harder political job of cutting spending is done before or simultaneously with the tax cuts, so that budget deficits do not occur. Tax cuts without spending reduction usually are not tax cuts for future generations, which must pay back the borrowed money plus interest costs. Reagan helped pioneer the fraudulent tax cut—that is, sticking politically powerless future generations, who are not old enough to vote or are not even born yet, with the bill for government services that the current generation receives and does not want to cut but does not want to pay for either. Regrettably, George W. Bush and Barack Obama later learned the same lesson as Dick Cheney did from the Reagan administration: deficits do not matter—but only politically; in fact, current voters may actually like them, because they do not have to pay for some of the government services they enjoy. Unfortunately, yearly deficits, and the accumulated debt they create, matter greatly economically because they contribute to a drag on future economic growth—therefore harming future generations.

A New Record for Deficits and Debt

As noted earlier, instead of starving the beast, Reagan traded increases in defense spending for even larger increases in nondefense spending. Conservatives, including Reagan, did not seem to consider defense expenditure hikes as government spending increases, which they clearly were. Finally, Reagan's own budget director, David Stockman, pooh-poohed the idea that a plan existed to starve the government beast.[130] Even if there were, as Cato Institute analyst John Samples concluded, denying revenue to the federal government did not appear to work in constraining spending.[131] Samples points to an empirical study to show evidence for this failure.[132]

Also, any master plan to "starve the beast" by purposefully running deficits contradicted the reality of red ink that resulted from bad data, erroneous economic assumptions (reduced GDP growth and lower inflation, both from the recession of 1981–1982, which shrunk tax revenues), wishful thinking, crass dishonest manipulation by Reagan's OMB, and inaccurate administration projections, based on supply side logic, that tax cuts would spur economic growth, thus turning the estimated $55 billion deficit in 1981 into a surplus in 1984 and after. Also, such a master plan would have required more ardor to cut spending, which really was not there—as evidenced by the "magic asterisk" of cuts to be determined later in Stockman's budget and Reagan's failure to pressure cabinet secretaries, including the secretary of defense, to make budget reductions.[133]

As Steven F. Hayward noted, the asterisk was Stockman's euphemism for cutting Social Security, which Reagan had ruled out in a speech, but which had bipartisan support—at least for making some funding reductions. More generally, Hayward said the administration knew that the window to make substantial budget cuts would close rapidly but still did not propose any cuts in the big entitlement programs making up 40 percent of the budget, such as Social Security, Medicare, and veterans' benefits. In fact, the administration touted not making any cuts in the "social safety net."[134] During the Reagan administration, the domestic welfare state remained at about 15.5 percent of GDP, roughly where it had been during the Carter administration.[135]

At any rate, during Reagan's first term, the yearly federal budget deficit grew from 2.7 percent to a then record of 6.3 percent of GDP. By 1989, at the end of his second term, the national debt stood at $2 trillion, making him one of the worst peacetime spendthrifts in US presidential history.[136] Of any president since Truman, Reagan grew average annual federal debt as a portion of GDP more than any other chief executive.[137] The federal debt increased from 26.2 percent of GDP at the end of 1980 to 42.8 percent at the end of 1990.[138] At the beginning of the subsequent Bush administration, budget director Richard Darman outlined the dire state of federal fiscal affairs that the outgoing Reagan administration had left, leading John Sununu, White House chief of staff, to remember: "The reality of the budget irresponsibility he outlined didn't surprise me, but the complete loss of fiscal control in Washington was a disappointment to the patriot in me."[139]

In his campaign for president, Reagan never promised to roll back government by cutting government spending. He cagily promised only to reduce the growth of such spending to less than the percentage increase in the size of the economy—that is, he had the much more modest goal of bringing federal spending down as a portion of GDP. As John Samples of the Cato Institute notes, "Ronald Reagan sought to reduce the scope of government, largely as a means to promote prosperity and thereby win elections. . . . Reagan from the start was primarily a reformer of the old regime."[140] In other words, contrary to the later-generated myth, he was not a revolutionary.

Reagan failed to attain even his modest goal. He not only increased federal spending (most presidents have done that), he hiked average annual federal spending as a percentage of GDP in a prospering economy.[141] (In contrast, Bill Clinton and Dwight Eisenhower, the two budget hawks of recent presidents, decreased this ratio.) Federal spending during the Reagan years was an average of 22.4 percent of GDP, compared to the much lower 20.8 percent average during the preceding Carter administration and the similar forty-year average of 20.7 percent.[142] Although a rhetorical advocate of small government, Reagan actually increased federal spending per capita in constant dollars by 11 percent during his tenure.[143] (Clinton, the champion budget cutter of the post-Truman world, was the only president since Truman to reduce such per capita federal spending.) With his harsh anti-Soviet rhetoric, emphasis on an unneeded and extravagant peacetime military buildup, and acquiescence to a huge and expanding federal government, Reagan was more in the neoconservative rather than the libertarian camp.

Reagan's increased spending and mildly reduced taxation added huge amounts to the national debt—forfeiting the country's status as a "creditor" nation, held since 1914, and reverting it to the greatest debtor nation. In all, with all of his accumulating budget deficits, Reagan tripled the national debt.[144]

Even worse, the government's irresponsible fiscal behavior signaled citizens that it was all right to do the same—personal savings continued to fall during the 1980s and consumer debt ballooned during the decade. Even a prominent former member of Reagan's Council of Economic Advisors, William A. Niskanen, criticized Reagan's spending record in 1987: "The major failure of the Reagan Administration was the failure to discipline spending. We have a bigger government, with higher spending. We've slowed regulation down, but we haven't reversed it. In other words, there was no Reagan revolution."[145]

Deregulation of the Economy?

Most experts on regulation agree that Reagan's record on deregulation was not even as good as that of Democrats Jimmy Carter or Bill Clinton.[146] Although Reagan occasionally finished Carter's decontrol (for example, of oil prices), Reagan in general only skimped on enforcement of existing regulations rather than committing to true deregulation. If regulations are still on the books, future administrations can merely reinvigorate enforcement. Conservative Steven F. Hayward summed it up best: "Unable to achieve wide-scale regulatory reform, the Reagan administration settled for regulatory relief, which, while effective, proved transient."[147] Expanding on this point, regulatory scholar Kip Viscusi said:

> Short-term efforts to alter regulatory policies by slowing the pace of regulation or altering the enforcement effort will not yield long-run changes in the regulatory approach. Ultimately, the agency's enabling legislation will determine the shape of these policies. A major failure of the Reagan regulatory reform effort is not just that such reforms were never achieved but that they were never even attempted.[148]

The administration did expand requirements for federal agencies to do cost-benefit analyses on new regulations and created a new section in the Office of Management and Budget—the Office of Information and Regulatory Affairs—to review such agency analyses. Yet OIRA rejected less than 3 percent of all new regulations on this basis.[149] Given that abysmal record, one might wonder if Reagan did not just add more government bureaucracy and complexity to the regulatory process. Reagan did, however, continue Carter's relaxation of antitrust enforcement on business takeovers and mergers.

In one area, Reagan's policy of deregulation backfired—ultimately costing the taxpayers, under his successor, George H. W. Bush, hundreds of billions of dollars to bail out the savings and loan (S&L) industry. Deregulation of the industry was a good idea, but the half-hearted effort during the Reagan administration resulted in S&Ls being given bad incentives to gamble depositors' money on risky loan, investment, and real estate transactions.[150]

Previously, excessive regulations governing savings and loans had impeded their ability to compete with banks, so S&Ls were partially deregulated. Yet the government guarantee against downside risk for S&Ls was increased by hiking government insurance of depositors' losses tenfold from $10,000 to $100,000 through the Federal Savings and Loan Insurance Company (FSLIC).[151] If profit-making is deregulated but losses are taken care of by the government (that is, privatizing profits but socializing losses), incentives for more reckless investments with higher earning potential ensue. By early 1987, the FSLIC was insolvent because of payouts for all of the S&L failures. Of course, even then, George H. W. Bush was at fault for his subsequent bailout of the industry. The same bad incentive structure was later recreated during the George W. Bush administration, which led to reckless mortgage lending by big banks that knew they would be bailed out by taxpayers, leading eventually to the necessity of such bailouts and to a worldwide economic meltdown.

Finally, although Reagan initially tried to slash the Internal Revenue Service (IRS), when he later needed to increase tax revenues to battle self-created budget deficits, the number of IRS workers ballooned to a record level.[152]

Tight Money Led to Prosperity

But didn't the economy boom under Reagan, despite the increased federal spending as a portion of GDP and ballooning budget deficits? The GDP number was a creation of Keynesian economists in the 1930s and 1940s, with government spending and consumption as major components. In addition, federal transfer payments (for example, welfare payments) inflate the consumption portion of the GDP figure. Thus, the GDP number is not a good indicator of growth in the private economy. This piece of information is critically important when assessing Reagan's legacy. The Keynesian deficit boom in the American economy in the 1980s was artificial prosperity. During the twelve years of Reagan's two terms and the following one-term George H. W. Bush administration, the public debt tripled, and all these budget deficits amounted to nearly 70 percent of the GDP growth during that time. During the Reagan-Bush years, government spending and consumption galloped compared to their long-term averages. In contrast, real private investment and private sector productivity gains were anemic compared to their long-term averages.[153]

Was the Reagan prosperity really a result of his deficit-inducing famous three-year income tax rate cuts in 1981? Reaganophiles, being mostly Republican, even attribute the more robust prosperity during the Clinton years to Reagan's tax cuts. According to John Ehrman, chronicler of conservative politics and economics, "The fact remains that anyone looking in economic literature for an independent confirmation that supply-side policies caused the recovery and boom of the 1980s will find little to support that view."[154] Similarly, Reagan's Budget Director David Stockman concluded, "With history thus rewritten, it did not require much of a leap for the next generation of GOP politicians to anchor their new antitax orthodoxy in an even greater legend: namely, that the economic boom of the mid-1980s had arisen from the original Reagan tax cut bill. The evidence goes entirely in the opposite direction." In fact, economic growth in the 1980s was pretty much the same as that in the 1970s—the US economy grew 36.7 percent in the 1970s and 37.6 percent in the 1980s. Reagan's "supply-side" tax cuts were also supposed to increase saving and investing, but the national savings rate declined from 8.9 percent of GDP during the 1970s to 3.7 percent from 1981 to 1988.[155]

Furthermore, with all of the hidden tax increases after the initial income tax cuts, Reagan's net tax reduction was the smallest per capita of any Republican president during the post–World War era. In fact, during the Reagan years, tax collection as a percentage of the economy (18.2 percent) was in line with the forty-year average (18.1 percent).[156] Furthermore, consistent with the "crowding out" of private borrowing for business expansion by government debt, the US conversion to a debtor nation under the Reagan administration robbed the American economy of 2.5 to 3.5 percent of its growth potential by the early 1990s, reported the Federal Reserve Bank in 1992.[157] Thus, an alternative explanation for the prosperity is needed.

From the mid-1970s to early 1980s, the US economy was wracked by stagflation—high unemployment combined with surging inflation. Contrary to popular belief, this malady was not caused by the Arab oil embargo and price increases of 1973 or the oil price spikes because of the Iranian revolution in the late 1970s. Stagflation was caused by the Vietnam War and poor fiscal and monetary policies by Republican and Democratic governments during the 1970s. For example, to get reelected in 1972, when the United States was still involved in the war, Richard Nixon put pressure on Federal Reserve Chairman Arthur Burns to print money to juice the economy before the election. The resulting surge in inflation would appear only after Nixon had safely won a second term.

Initially, Jimmy Carter's monetary policy also left a lot to be desired, and inflation was consequently severe. However, in 1979, Carter appointed Paul Volcker as chairman of the Federal Reserve. A consensus had arisen in the 1970s in the economics profession that inflation was caused by too much money in the system. Volcker conducted a monetarist experiment by drastically putting the brakes on the money supply.

Reagan's Budget Director Stockman seems to give most credit for the economic expansion under Reagan to Paul Volcker, the Jimmy Carter–appointed chairman of the Federal Reserve: "One of the longest-sustained GDP expansion cycles on record began after the third quarter of 1982, when the Volcker cure [tight monetary policy] had finally crushed the inflationary fires."[158]

After taking office, to his credit, Reagan initially supported Volcker's policy. Volcker's constricted monetary policy caused a double dip recession—a smaller one in 1979 that did in Carter's presidency and a fairly deep recession during 1982 and 1983 (then the worst since the Great Depression, with unemployment reaching 10 percent)—but bled most of the inflation out the economy, thus ensuring prosperity for the long-term. The Reagan administration stuck with Volcker for a time and sometimes supported his tight money policy; but the administration did successfully intimidate him—by threating to curtail Fed independence—into easing the money supply before the 1982 election, which occurred in the midst of the recession. Also, when an administration runs huge budget deficits with small net tax cuts and massive spending increases, as the Reagan administration did, pressure builds to monetize the ballooning federal deficits and debt—that is, to have the Fed print money so that investors can buy federal debt securities to cover the red ink. Thus, Reagan then appointed people to the Fed's Board of Governors who eventually overruled Volcker in favor of easier money, and finally Reagan replaced him with the more cooperative Alan Greenspan in 1987.[159]

The Reagan administration pressured Greenspan, and Greenspan largely granted the administration's monetary wishes.[160] During his long tenure as Fed chairman (nineteen years), Greenspan initially held the money supply in check but later let it surge, leading to the dot-com boom and bust at the turn of the millennium and the housing boom and bust and subsequent worldwide recession of 2008. Thus, the Reagan-appointed and supposedly libertarian Greenspan promoted statism through an activist monetary policy.

Some Reagan fans say that Reagan slowed the trajectory of increasing federal spending and won the Cold War, thereby allowing Bill Clinton to cut such spending during his two terms. This claim exaggerates Reagan's accomplishment and diminishes Clinton's claim to be the post-Truman champion presidential budget cutter. First of all, even if Reagan did slow the trajectory of federal spending, he still not only increased real federal spending (an average of 2.5 percent per year[161]) but hiked federal spending per capita and as a percentage of GDP. As noted previously, contradicting his goal of reducing federal spending as a portion of GDP, he increased this average annual percentage above what it was during the Carter administration.

In contrast, during the twentieth century, Warren Harding, Calvin Coolidge, Dwight Eisenhower, and Bill Clinton all actually reduced federal spending as a percentage of GDP. Congress always has a role in spending decisions, but even during the Clinton administration, Clinton cut the budget more in his first two years, when he had Democratic majorities in Congress, than he did in his last six years, when Republican Newt Gingrich was his congressional adversary. Gingrich, however, unlike Reagan, made a serious effort to cut the budget and deserves credit for helping Clinton do so.

Also, as noted above, Reagan hardly single-handedly won the Cold War. Even if US containment strategy partially succeeded in toppling the Soviet bloc, the inventor of it, Harry Truman, and all subsequent presidents through George H. W. Bush should get at least some credit for it. As noted earlier, however, they may have all just wasted a lot of money when cheaper methods of exhausting the Soviet Union could have been used.

Harding, Eisenhower, and Clinton did have the advantage of being presidents serving right after a war or Cold War had ended, which allowed them more freedom to cut spending. However, they could have just redirected military spending to domestic government initiatives but did not. In fact, Harding cut domestic spending too. Reagan hardly should be given much credit for Clinton's spending cuts. Clinton had to clean up Reagan's huge politically driven budget deficits, but as noted earlier, Reagan had no plan to "starve the beast."

Thus, with Reagan's defense-spending binge, his domestic spending spree needed as a trade to get the former, his invention of fraudulent tax cuts (reducing taxes significantly while increasing federal spending as a portion of GDP) bequeathed to his Republican successors (and designed primarily to win votes), and his resultant vast accumulation of government debt, Reagan's reputation as a small government Republican is a myth. His original proposal to enact a constitutional amendment requiring a balanced budget was traded in for an actual policy record of then record peacetime budget deficits and of entrenching the United States as a debtor nation.

John Sununu, chief of staff for Reagan's Republican successor, George H. W. Bush, blamed Reagan's busting of the federal budget for an economic slowdown as Bush took office. He alleged that "Reagan's defense buildup had overstressed the budget, and the economy was paying the price. There were signs of a real slowdown." He continued:

> The economic data that George Bush and our team were looking at indicated that 1989 would not be a very good year for the country. The rate of growth had slowed significantly, and the budget deficit loomed large. President Reagan's tax cuts had boosted government revenues for a while, but his spending to rebuild America's military strength had offset that boost, and required him to increase taxes. As a result, the economy was limping along and the deficit continued to expand."[162]

Some other examples of Reagan wielding the power of big government should also be noted.

Social Security, Taxes, and Benefit Cuts

Despite Reagan's campaign rhetoric of turning the Social Security old-age pension system into a voluntary system, one of the many "revenue enhancements" that Reagan coyly perpetrated was his tax hike to make Social Security temporarily solvent into the future—essentially "saving" the system in its current unstable form for a couple of generations. Social Security is an unfair system that has a regressive tax tethered to a mildly progressive benefit system. However, the question of why middle-class and rich people get any Social Security at all should be asked. Also, because the system does not allow people to save for their own future retirement—but instead uses payroll taxes from current workers to pay current retirees—the system is vulnerable to unfair intergenerational demographic time bombs. The country is just now beginning to see this time bomb explode as the ratio of workers paying into the system to retirees getting benefits shrinks as the huge post–World War II "baby boom" generation begins to retire. Yet, the Social Security System's future time bomb was well known at the time Reagan was president. Finally, Social Security penalizes minorities, who less frequently attend college, begin work earlier, and thus start paying into the system sooner, yet die earlier too, thus reaping fewer retirement benefits during their lifespan for what they have contributed into the system.

One would think that any president known for his "small government" orientation would have made his top priority putting Social Security—the largest government program and one that was spinning out of control—in his crosshairs for a major reform. However, instead of trying to abolish the system or privatize it, Reagan, in 1981, advocated restoring the program's minimum benefit, which had been abused by middle-class pension "double-dippers" and which his own budget director, David Stockman, had convinced Congress to eliminate a few months before.[163] Also, despite being a very popular president, he quickly backed off using this political capital to support a laudable proposal by Stockman to cut some benefits for early retirees.[164]

Reagan merely increased taxes to shore up Social Security temporarily, thereby passing the problem on to future presidents. In 1983, he signed Social Security "reform" legislation that sped up an increase in the payroll tax rate, required some people to pay income tax on part of their benefits, and made self-employed individuals pay the full payroll tax rate rather than just the part paid by employees. In this package, the retirement age was raised, at a glacial pace, from sixty-five to sixty-seven by the year 2027. In 1985, Reagan, no longer needing to stand for reelection, sawed the limb out from under congressional Republicans, many of whom were up for reelection, by again first supporting and then backing off from a one-year freeze in Social Security cost-of-living benefit increases. Reagan, a political animal to the core who feared the off-year electoral effects of cutting people's government goodies, also shied away from cutting other entitlement programs and government spending in general.

All in all, it's little wonder that with Reagan's tax policy—cutting marginal rates for the income tax (a progressive tax) and raising payroll taxes (a regressive tax) to shore up a faltering Social Security System for only a couple of generations—the wealth distribution in the country became more skewed toward the wealthy.

Expansion of Medicare

Reagan's weakness after the Iran-Contra scandal made him even more "pragmatic" in his policies. One effect was the expansion of Medicare to provide catastrophic health insurance for seniors, the wealthiest cohort of American society. According to conservative Steven F. Hayward, even though cabinet members and his Council of Economic Advisers warned him about the adverse consequences of expanding Medicare, Reagan approved it in late 1986 after he saw polling data showing that it was a popular idea that could help him bounce back from the Iran-Contra debacle. Conservatives were outraged, but progressive Ted Kennedy heartily endorsed the new law. Congress added some additional bells and whistles, as opponents had predicted[165] (this phenomenon happens when any new government initiative goes through Washington). However, Congress repealed the law in 1989 when the powerful senior citizens' lobby vigorously protested that seniors were required to pay something toward their new, subsidized insurance coverage.

Also, Reagan gave up his campaign promise to introduce market reforms into the Medicare program—that is, vouchers—in favor of imposing price controls on what doctors and hospitals could charge.[166] Price controls could restrain prices in the short term but did not deal with the pent-up underlying factors driving up healthcare costs in the long term.

Conservative Policies?

The saying that the present shapes perspectives on the past is an old adage but is nevertheless true. At the time Reagan served as president, conservatives were livid about many of his policies, which were not very conservative. Reagan moderated his policies even more during the last two years of his presidency, when he was under political attack over the illegal and unconstitutional Iran-Contra affair. However, in the 1990s, to compete with the very popular and charismatic Democratic President Bill Clinton, conservative activists, needing their own icon, resurrected Reagan and whitewashed his image by highlighting his conservative rhetoric rather than his pragmatic policies. However, his real-life pragmatism should have surprised no one, given his previous moderate record as governor of California. Lou Cannon, a journalist who covered Reagan both in California and in Washington, said that he was, above all, a pragmatic compromiser, not the uncompromising conservative icon celebrated at the Reagan Library.[167]

As noted above, the Reagan Revolution that brought in an era of small government and won the Cold War never really happened. For example, at the end of Reagan's presidency, conservative Midge Decter wrote in *Commentary* that "there was no Reagan Revolution, not even a skeleton of one to hang in George Bush's closet." *Time* magazine said, "For all its radicalism, Reagan's plan calls for something much less than a repeal of Lyndon Johnson's Great Society, let alone Franklin Delano Roosevelt's New Deal. Among the spending programs that Reagan picked as targets, only a few would be axed completely; most of the others would not only continue but would grow, albeit more slowly." Reagan acolyte Steven F. Hayward opined that "this was hardly the stuff of a revolution." One reason no revolution happened was that Reagan favored more seasoned pragmatists in the appointment process over movement conservatives with little or no government experience; also, pragmatists were more skilled at political maneuvering than appointed conservatives and frequently bested them in policy fights.[168]

The only revolutionary aspect to Reagan's presidency was converting the office into the nation's Pitchman-in-Chief, which subsequent presidents, such as Clinton, George W. Bush, and Barack Obama, have imitated. Reagan's chief image-polishers—Michael Deaver and David Gergen—used memorable made-for-television backdrops and high-flying patriotic and conservative rhetoric to build Reagan's public image.[169] Later, Clinton even hired Gergen to work for him. So the revolution was one of public relations, not policy. And because most people pay attention to what politicians say, instead of undertaking the hard work to find out what they really do, Reagan's conservative rhetoric came in handy when the conservative activists revamped his image in the 1990s.

Some Reagan policies that were unpopular with conservative contemporaries already have been discussed: multiple tax hikes, increases in federal spending as a portion of GDP, and Reagan's negotiations with Gorbachev on arms control, which toyed with the idea of eliminating nuclear weapons and eventually reached an INF Treaty that did away with the entire class of intermediate-range nuclear forces.

Social Issues

If they had ever heard about it, many of today's conservatives would cringe at Reagan's signing of the Immigration Reform and Control Act of 1986, which legalized almost three million undocumented aliens.[170] Also, according to John Sununu, the White House chief of staff for the subsequent Republican George H. W. Bush administration, the law did not provide enough funds to stop border crossings and penalize employers for hiring illegals.[171] However, conservative activists have swept under the rug this laudable immigration law, which provided the largest amnesty on record for hardworking immigrants who spur economic growth and work to support increasing numbers of retirees.

In some areas, Reagan expanded government. He launched a vigorous effort against pornography and obscenity. Also, Reagan widened Nixon's "War on Drugs," including Nancy Reagan's effort to get teenagers to "just say no" to drugs. However, he placed less emphasis on treatment of users than Nixon did and more on law enforcement's expensive and futile attempts to interdict incoming drugs designed to satisfy a brisk and continuing demand. Despite increased arrests of drug smugglers, cocaine imports and consumption increased, as the smugglers merely shifted their trafficking routes.

Mrs. Reagan's "Just Say No" program became the butt of late-night comedy jokes. Some teens would have never thought about doing drugs if Mrs. Reagan, an elderly woman not known for either her warm image or her rapport with teens, had not indicated that the establishment demanded that young people stay away from them. Another new federal program of questionable effectiveness was the Drug Abuse Resistance Education (DARE) program, in which police visited schools to teach a "zero-tolerance" message for drug abuse.[172] Like the "Just Say No" program, the DARE effort may have just educated kids that drugs were available and that they could stick it to "the man"—that is, authority figures—by experimenting with them.

In expanding the War on Drugs, Reagan failed to apply his small government rhetoric to law-and-order issues and agencies. Reagan, to burnish his "get tough" image, signed laws that jailed many nonviolent offenders with mandatory minimum sentences for drug offenses[173]—vastly expanding the federal prison population and contributing to the era of mass incarceration, which by the second decade of the new millennium even many Republicans were repudiating as a failure. During the Reagan administration, the Bail Reform Act of 1984, the US Sentencing Reform Act of 1984, and the Anti-Drug Abuse Act of 1986 set mandatory minimum sentences for drug possession and distribution. Previously, indeterminate sentencing allowed judges discretion on how they punished people, which could be based on the specifics of each case and extenuating circumstances. The new legal regime led to more people going to jail and longer sentences served.[174] Prisons were factories for growing even worse criminals by converting some nonviolent drug offenders into violent marauders. Also, the government's tough enforcement of laws on illegal drugs merely drove the price up, leading to more violent crime to obtain either the drugs or the money to buy them—thus further increasing the number of people in prison.

In addition, the War on Drugs led to the militarization of the police, including the use of excess military equipment for ordinary policing.[175] Finally, in order to use the Navy and Coast Guard to interdict cocaine coming from Latin America, Reagan had to suspend the posse comitatus law, which had wisely kept the military out of domestic law enforcement. Slowly, society is rejecting Nixon and Reagan's big government approach to drug abuse by decriminalizing or even legalizing some drug use, with the implicit conclusion that the government has no right to tell adults what to put in their own bodies, even if it is unhealthy.

The Supreme Court and Other Legal Issues

Of Reagan's four picks to the Supreme Court, Robert Bork (rejected by the Senate) and Antonin Scalia were "conservative"; the other two were moderates, Anthony Kennedy and Sandra Day O'Connor. Reagan knew O'Connor was pro-choice and pro–Equal Rights Amendment for women when he nominated her. She and Kennedy allowed the states more flexibility in restricting abortion but would not overturn the court's earlier *Roe v. Wade* decision, which guaranteed the legality of abortion. For decades, Kennedy arguably would be the most important justice, because he was the swing vote on a court divided between progressives and conservatives.

Both Bork and Scalia claimed to favor a judicial philosophy of original intent that was narrowly textual—that is, they allegedly tried to deduce what the Constitution's framers intended by attempting to determine the original meaning of the text of the document at the time it was written. Yet theirs is almost textualism from a parallel *Star Trek* anti-universe. For example, Bork believed that if an individual right or proscription of government power is not in the text of the Constitution, the courts have no basis for overruling legislative action on these matters. Thus, he believed the Ninth Amendment—which states, "The enumeration in the Constitution, of certain rights, shall not be construed to deny or disparage others retained by the people"—essentially had no meaning. Conservative Steven F. Hayward concluded that the root of Bork's disparagement of the Ninth Amendment was its use to identify a right to privacy in *Griswold v. Connecticut* in 1965, which was the critical precursor to *Roe v. Wade*, guaranteeing a woman's right to choose whether or not to have an abortion. Hayward then correctly pointed out that "Bork's position would imply that a passage of the Constitution [the Ninth Amendment] is practically meaningless, that there are rights judges are powerless to protect, and that the Founders were bad draftsmen."

Hayward also cogently noted that Bork's position came close to the position that the only rights people had are those enumerated in the Constitution or passed by the legislative branch. Hayward noted that many conservative legal scholars parted ways with Bork, because his view smacked of the tyranny of the majority, which the framers thought was the primary hazard of popular government. In other words, Bork deviated from the founders' original intent in favor of judicial restraint.[176]

It is very clear that the Ninth Amendment and the Tenth Amendment ("The powers not delegated to the United States by the Constitution, nor prohibited by it to the States, are reserved to the States respectively, or to the people.") were put in the Constitution to dramatically restrict the purview of the federal government. Yet Bork's view that if an individual right or prohibition of government power is not in the Constitution, the government can fill the void and expand its power, turns the text of the Constitution and the framers' intent on its head. Bork's view was statist and therefore dangerous. Thus, if you define "conservative" by being an advocate of small government, Bork was no conservative. For the most part, the same criticism could be made of Antonin Scalia's similar "textualist" views. In one prominent exception, however, Scalia seemed to deviate from the text of the Constitution in favor of smaller government when defending a personal right to self-defense with a gun under the Second Amendment.

In contrast to Bork and Scalia, O'Connor's swing vote helped secure abortion rights for women for an entire generation. Moreover, although talking the talk of religious conservatives, including opposing abortion, Reagan never really put much effort into realizing their agenda. He never really pushed too hard for constitutional amendments permitting prayer in schools and banning abortion. Lewis L. Gould, in his history of the Republican Party, best sums up Reagan's swindle of religious conservatives:

> Another characteristic of the changed Republican Party was the new president's attraction among religious conservatives. Despite his own lack of churchgoing and strong public piety, Reagan knew what the religious right wanted to hear. He stood against abortion, supported voluntary prayer in public schools, and questioned whether evolution was a valid scientific theory. Careful not to push the agenda of the Moral Majority into substantive legislation, Reagan gave these groups and their leaders enough rhetorical endorsement to keep them reasonably contented throughout his administration.[177]

However, conservatives did blanch at the activism of the Reagan Justice Department's Civil Rights division. The division's enforcement actions in Reagan's first term bested the four years of the Carter administration in civil rights prosecutions, voting rights cases, employment discrimination suits, and objections to discriminatory redistricting plans.[178] (In housing discrimination suits, however, Carter bested Reagan.) Also, conservatives were disappointed that Reagan never took on affirmative action preferences for minorities through legislation or executive orders. Throwing away the states' rights doctrine, Reagan embraced enforcement of the Constitution's Fifteenth Amendment and thus signed a twenty-five-year extension of the Voting Rights Act of 1965, which allowed the Justice Department to continue to monitor elections in the South. And despite his initial instinct to give way when Bob Jones University, which banned interracial marriage, sued to preserve its tax-exempt status, Reagan later abandoned his support for the university in the wake of a firestorm of protest. Finally, Reagan changed his mind, ended his opposition to, and signed rather than vetoed a national holiday for Dr. Martin Luther King Jr.[179]

Reagan also signed an extension of the independent counsel law. The Constitution provides for only three branches of the federal government; like regulatory agencies that are independent of the other branches, independent counsels appear to create added unconstitutional governmental branches. Independent counsels are independent from the Justice Department (Executive Branch), the Congress, and the federal courts.

Economic Issues

Although Reagan did veto some protectionist trade bills, he was more of a trade protectionist than either George H. W. Bush, his vice president and successor, or Bill Clinton. Despite his free-trade image and campaigning, Reagan when in office supported protecting the inefficient American auto and steel industries, making them even more sluggish. "Voluntary" restraints, which cut Japanese auto imports by 50 percent, cost American consumers more than $5 billion, about $160,000 for every American job saved. Even pro-Reagan Steven F. Hayward admits that such auto import restriction "was not one of the Reaganites' finest free market moments."[180]

Despite such protectionist moves, the US balance of trade went from a slight surplus in 1981 to a substantial deficit by 1986. Free market economics would say that this was nothing to worry about and that it was caused by increased imports as the American economy boomed.

Usually, in times of trade deficit the dollar is weak, but from 1981 to 1985, it strengthened. In 1985, to push the dollar lower—so US exports would increase, imports would decline, and the politically monitored trade deficit would be lowered—the Reagan administration convened the governments of the biggest economies in the world at the Plaza Hotel in New York to lower the value of the dollar by a coordinated intervention into the international currency markets. Central banks dumped dollars onto the market, lowering the dollar by 50 percent, thus increasing US exports by 38 percent.

However, by early 1987, the dollar's value was now deemed to be falling too fast. The same currency-manipulating governments met at the Louvre in Paris to prop up the dollar and sent interest rates soaring. Add to the fact that the Reagan-appointed head of the Securities and Exchange Commission publicly ruminated over closing the New York Stock Exchange because of market instability. In the ensuing market crash in October 1987, the Dow Jones Industrial Index lost one-third of its value (the epic crash of 1929 had seen only a decline of 13 percent); the panic spread worldwide and caused foreign markets to plummet. Unlike the Great Depression after the 1929 crash, however, both the market and the economy rebounded. Some have blamed the budget and trade deficits for the crash and some have blamed the possibility that Reagan's economic policies would be reversed.[181] It is hard to believe, however, that Reagan administration policy switches while manipulating the international currency markets did not have some ill effect on international stock markets.

More Big Government

The federal role in education did not diminish under Reagan compared to that in prior presidential administrations.[182] Instead of fulfilling his admirable pledge to eliminate the Energy and Education departments, Reagan instead added a new federal department—that of Veterans Affairs.

Moreover, experts said that Reagan's New Federalism program, which attempted to devolve more authority to the states from the federal government, was a failure. No significant devolution was achieved.[183]

However, much to conservatives' delight, Reagan laudably fired the federal air traffic controllers, who as government employees were conducing illegal collective bargaining for pay increases and running an unlawful strike. Despite the illegal collective bargaining, Reagan first quietly offered the controllers more money. When they did not take it and went on strike, he fired them and hired new ones as federal employees.[184] However, Reagan chose this approach rather than privatizing the air traffic control system—a more conservative and efficient solution.

Conclusion

Those who put Ronald Reagan on a pedestal as a champion of small government should be disillusioned by reading this chapter. Reagan failed to use the political capital generated from both of his landslide election victories to make reducing the size of government a high priority. On several important measures, the federal government grew substantially under Reagan's watch. Among post–World War II Republicans, only Dwight Eisenhower actually cut federal spending as a percentage of GDP. Of course, the overall budget-cutting champion in the post-Truman era was a Democrat, Bill Clinton, who not only cut federal spending as a portion of GDP but also reduced per capita federal expenditure.

Reagan made flashy cuts on individual income tax rates, but these turned out to be largely fraudulent, because as federal spending as a portion of GDP increased and budget deficits ballooned, he quietly raised other taxes in the tax code. Thus, his net tax reduction was actually the smallest of any post–World War II Republican. Reagan also saved Social Security, a costly and grossly unfair system, by raising the payroll tax. However, he did laudably—not in the minds of conservatives, however—give amnesty to almost three million illegal immigrants.

The Iran-Contra affair was the worst constitutional scandal in American history. Reagan undermined restraints on executive power enshrined in separation of powers of the US Constitution by usurping Congress's power of the purse in order to continue a secret war, even after that supreme legislative body explicitly had told him to end it. Finally, Reagan's over-the-top hawkish rhetoric and unneeded expansion of government in national defense so alarmed the Soviet Union that his administration's policies almost caused a nuclear war. In addition, he was so enamored with his pie-in-the-sky Star Wars fantasy that he blew a chance to trade the system away for steep cuts in dangerous offensive nuclear weapons.

Lovers of small government should remember wars and the threat of them are the most important cause of big government in both human and American history. Thus, the Warren Harding/Calvin Coolidge model of a more restrained foreign policy and actual cuts in spending is a much better one than the Reagan model of a chest-thumping expansion of US government (military) power overseas, combined with increased federal spending as a portion of GDP at home, fraudulent tax cuts, and the rapid accumulation of national debt.

8

Hawkish Tendencies

GEORGE H. W. BUSH (president from 1989 to 1993), despite his public image as a "wimp," launched a full-scale war on Saddam Hussein's Iraq and invaded Panama,[1] whereas Reagan invaded the tiny island of Grenada and launched pinprick airstrikes against Muammar Gaddafi in Libya. Bush was also more suspicious of Soviet leader Mikhail Gorbachev's intentions than was Reagan.

With the end of the Cold War, the United States reached the height of its relative power under the presidency of George H. W. Bush. Bush took advantage of the fall of the Soviet superpower to implant an unnecessary permanent US military presence on the ground in the Persian Gulf, which had not been needed to protect oil even during the Cold War. As a result, Osama bin Laden, incensed, as most Islamist radicals are, with non-Muslim forces on Muslim lands—especially in Saudi Arabia, the land of the holiest sites in Islam—decided to mount a terrorist campaign against the United States. The elder Bush's unneeded intervention in the first Gulf War and subsequent establishment of a lasting US military footprint in Saudi Arabia set the stage for the rise of al Qaeda, the 9/11 attacks, his son's even more ill-advised invasion of and ensuing quagmire in Iraq, the rise of radical Islamists worldwide and specifically al Qaeda in Iraq, its morphing into the brutal Islamic State group and takeover of Sunni portions of a destabilized Iraq, and finally the American reentry into Iraq, and also entry into Syria, with military force.

No end in sight exists to this downward spiraling chain of events that the elder Bush began. Then Secretary of State Colin Powell cautioned the younger Bush before he invaded Iraq, saying, "You break it. You own it."[2] Unfortunately, this warning was too late. Powell, earlier chairman of the Joint Chiefs of Staff for the elder Bush, had been reluctant to launch the first Gulf War. That's when Powell's warning should have been given and heeded.

The Long Fiasco in Iraq

Although April Glaspie, US ambassador to Iraq, was blamed for giving Saddam Hussein an implicit green light to invade Kuwait in 1990, the George H. W. Bush administration policy of staying out of territorial disputes among Arab nations, which she merely reiterated to Saddam, had been enunciated publicly by other administration officials at the time. Also, Bush apparently did nothing stronger to deter Saddam when US intelligence, in the last week before the Iraqi invasion, reported that Iraq's dictator had amassed 120,000 troops on his border with Kuwait.[3]

The Bush administration made the same mistake as the Truman administration did with South Korea, when it declared that the country was not inside the US defense perimeter. In both cases, these similar statements encouraged aggressors to think the United States would not respond to an invasion. And in both cases, after the invasion occurred, the administrations panicked and sent US troops to defend countries that were not really strategic to American vital interests. Historians always give presidents credit for winning wars but never ask if the conflicts could have been avoided. War is a failure of diplomacy and deterrence, and the elder Bush's diplomacy and deterrence had failed, but he is never criticized for this neglect. Also, few analysts ever ask whether, even if deterrence had failed, a US war to liberate Kuwait was necessary and whether the aforementioned long line of horrible unintended consequences—war always produces such severe unintended outcomes—was worth the mesmerizing short-term military triumph.

The First Gulf War

Many analysts thought that defending oil in neighboring Saudi Arabia was the strategic US interest secured in the case of George H. W. Bush's Gulf War. Yet, David Henderson, a former Reagan administration economist, calculated—after Saddam had invaded Kuwait but before the United States attacked Iraqi targets in occupied Kuwait and Iraq—that even if Saddam had planned to further invade and conquer Saudi Arabia and the United Arab Emirates (little evidence exists of that intent because he could have done so but did not before US forces arrived to defend Saudi Arabia), the effect of Saddam's consolidation of the world market shares of four oil-producing nations would have been only marginally higher oil prices that would have been less than 0.5 percent of American gross domestic product (GDP).[4] In other words, no need existed for the United States to "defend" American oil supplies by using force to oust Saddam from Kuwait. In fact, the amount of oil removed from the world market by a global ban on the purchase of Iraqi oil and by Saddam's destruction of Kuwaiti oil wells, as the United States attacked him in Kuwait, exceeded Henderson's estimate of the amount of oil that Saddam would have held off the market—after grabbing Kuwait, Saudi Arabia, and the UAE—just to increase his oil revenues. Thus, if Bush fought in Kuwait for oil (or as James Baker put it more euphemistically, for "jobs, jobs, jobs"), economic sanctions and war were counterproductive to the objective.

Moreover, even after Saddam's invasion and occupation of neighboring Kuwait, Bush essentially had to beg the Saudi royal family to accept US military forces on its territory to defend Saudi Arabia from the alleged new menace on its border. According to John Sununu, Bush's White House chief of staff, the Saudis claimed that the United States had a reputation in the region of being an unreliable partner, citing Ronald Reagan's withdrawal under fire from Lebanon in the early 1980s after the bombing of the Marine barracks there.[5] (This incident, according to Osama bin Laden, taught him that the United States could be pushed out of the Middle East through terrorist acts.) Also, the Saudis were worried more about the possibility of internal turmoil or revolution triggered by the presence of a non-Muslim army in the Islamic holy land than they were of Saddam's troops right across the border in Kuwait. Bush said in his diary that he was worried about a Saudi or Kuwaiti payoff to Saddam to withdraw his forces from Kuwait.[6] Yet even if this scenario occurred, that outcome would have been better than the extensive destruction of war and long chain of previously noted unintended adverse events arising from the United States' first attack on Saddam. In any case, the massive US military response to Saddam's invasion was just one of the many instances in which the superpower was more worried about developments in a region of the world than the countries living there.

Once massive US forces were placed in Saudi Arabia, the march to war took on a life of its own. Before the war, instead of quick military action to expel Saddam's forces from Kuwait, General Colin Powell, the chairman of the Joint Chiefs of Staff, advocated continuing economic sanctions against Saddam Hussein's Iraq for a longer period. Showing that domestic political concerns were a factor in the war, Bush replied to Powell that that policy tack was not politically feasible.[7]

In addition, Bush admitted in his diary that he had "personalized" Saddam's invasion of Kuwait, seeing Saddam as "the epitome of evil."[8] Both of these factors led Bush to choose the military option before most of his advisers. As he and his son both demonstrated, the Bush clan was ever eager to demonize Saddam and pull the trigger on him. Bush the Elder also believed in the imperial argument that the United States needed to eject Saddam from Kuwait using force, thus reaffirming US strength as a world leader—a particularly ridiculous notion given that the United States was clearly emerging as the victor in the Cold War.

Although Bush believed he was extending a courtesy to Congress to let it authorize military action that he thought he had a constitutional right to undertake unilaterally as commander-in-chief (the nation's founders would have passed out, having established a firm requirement that the people's houses of Congress needed to authorize war), he had already created a fait accompli for the legislative body. Without congressional authorization, in October 1990, he had dispatched 200,000 US troops to supposedly defend Saudi Arabia from attack (that is, into potential hostilities) and then doubled that number the next month. The very presence of a large military force-in-being provided the impetus for war. It was argued that the costly presence could not endure in the desert conditions for long and that the weather would worsen, making success in any delayed attack less likely.[9] Another early unauthorized act of war was a naval blockade—to enforce the UN resolution imposing comprehensive economic sanctions on Iraq—which was not authorized by the resolution itself. The Bush administration, as did John F. Kennedy during the Cuban Missile Crisis, chose to call the provocative blockade by the euphemism "quarantine."[10]

The war did not end up costing the United States much in monetary terms, because the Bush administration went hat in hand to Saudi Arabia and other rich allies—for example, the oil-consuming nations of Japan and Germany—

to get them to pay for the conflict. Concentrating on the overwhelming military victory, few in the United States focused on the unseemly fact that this arrangement made the United States the mercenary for the world against Iraq.

War and Long-Term Strategies

The war was a tactical and operational triumph, as the Bush administration redirected an unenthusiastic US defense establishment from a frontal attack to a smarter flanking maneuver—as well as an achievement in international coalition-building. (Bush did stop the ground war rather arbitrarily after one hundred hours, even though some key Iraqi forces escaped.)[11] However, as is the case with many wars, the unintended long-term strategic effects were disastrous. One was bin Laden's retaliation by the 9/11 and other terrorist attacks for the long-term and unneeded US military presence in the Persian Gulf, especially the holy land of Saudi Arabia. Second, although George H. W. Bush wisely stayed within the governing UN resolution and merely expelled Saddam from Kuwait (he did not want to make Saddam into a hero in the Arab world by invading Iraq), a second war on Iraq by his son, George W. Bush, finally ousted Saddam. The second war brought about a drawn-out American occupation, chaos, civil war, and eventual violent partition of the country, which led to a group worse than al Qaeda—the Islamic State—controlling a third of its territory. Although criticized for not going on to Baghdad and ousting Saddam, George H. W. Bush had feared what his son later became immersed in: a protracted and destabilizing urban war against guerrillas in Iraq.

The Gulf War victory was George H. W. Bush's biggest triumph in the short term (Bush's approval rating reached an astounding high of 91 percent, highest in the history of Gallup presidential approval ratings[12]) and most calamitous legacy in the long term. However, in the American "here-and-now" culture, reinforced by 24/7/365 cable news, history is quickly forgotten, especially with regard to US foreign policy. Even at the time, Americans and their media tended to focus on the dazzling technological military "victory" backed by adept diplomacy and coalition-building, which were undertaken to achieve often less exciting political ends—throwing Saddam out of Kuwait.

Yet the amazing camera footage of strikes by US precision weapons released by the American military to the media applied to only 7 percent of the munitions used. Also, the United States, in addition to targeting military, communication, electrical, transportation, and oil-related targets, purposefully and illegitimately targeted civilian vehicles, water treatment plants, irrigation water pumping stations, animal vaccination facilities, and food processing, storage, and distribution facilities. The latter group of illegitimate targets was questionable because they would inflict casualties and hardship long after the war among Iraqi civilians. One Air Force officer told a reporter that the US military was trying to apply pressure on Iraqi civilians to get them to over-throw Saddam.

The comprehensive economic embargo imposed before, during, and after the Gulf War—which banned importation of some medical items, pumps for water treatment plants, and farming items—was designed to do the same. The embargo contributed to the deaths of more than a half million Iraqi children from disease, malnutrition, and inadequate healthcare, according to an epidemiological study by the British medical journal *The Lancet*. (The deaths of those children were "worth it," to contain Saddam, according to later comments by Madeleine Albright, Bill Clinton's secretary of state.[13]) Yet when Osama bin Laden later used a similar rationale to strike American civilian targets on 9/11 to try to induce them to pressure their government to run a less interventionist policy in the Middle East, the US government labeled it "terrorism." A good objective working definition of "terrorism" is the targeting of civilians to achieve the political goal of getting them to pressure their government to change its policies. Strangely, this definition is usually generally applied only when small groups attack targets. Somewhat unnervingly, governments intentionally targeting civilians with war and economic sanctions for similar ends, but on a much more massive scale, seems to fit this definition too.

And bin Laden's main stated reasons for his jihad against the United States, leading to that tragic day in 2001, were the continued grinding economic embargo on Iraq and the permanent presence of non-Muslim US soldiers in the Islamic holy land of Saudi Arabia, the latter of which the United States had promised both the Saudi king and Mikhail Gorbachev would not happen. During the first Gulf crisis in 1990 and 1991, George H. W. Bush initiated both of these continuing policies, which later motivated bin Laden to launch the horrendous terrorist attack on 9/11 during the administration of George W. Bush.

However, now some vague awareness is dawning that George H. W. Bush's Gulf War may not have been the grand achievement in the long term that the crushing tactical military victory seemed to be at the time. The problem with war is that it often unleashes many unintended consequences, which can steal defeat even from the jaws of apparent victory. Unfortunately, that is the primary policy legacy of a personally humble and honorable man.

The Cold War Is History

Although the Cold War actually ended on the elder Bush's watch, Ronald Reagan is often given too much credit for this development because of his inflammatory anti-Soviet rhetoric and because conservatives regarded Reagan as one of them but did not think the same of Bush. Reagan's dangerous rhetoric almost caused an accidental nuclear war—as the Soviets went on nuclear alert out of fear of an imminent US nuclear first strike—yet he really did little to "win" the Cold War. In fact, rather than the United States winning the Cold War, the Soviets lost it, their creaky Communist command economy and society no longer able to bear the burdens of empire. The US policy of containing the Soviet Union until it fell from within from such "internal contradictions" actually worked (although it could have been done much more cheaply). Reagan was only one of a long string of presidents who practiced this containment policy, starting with Harry Truman.

Cold War Ends When?

The beginning of the end of the Cold War came only shortly before the fall of the Berlin Wall in November 1989. In mid-1989, well after Reagan had transferred the office of president to Bush, Soviet leader Mikhail Gorbachev decided that the USSR could no longer afford to prop up unpopular and financially destitute Communist governments in Eastern Europe using military power and subsidies. After that change in Soviet policy, the fall of Eastern Europe's Communist regimes was fairly preordained, with the only major question being whether the revolutions would be violent or peaceful. Fortunately, they were mostly peaceful.

Gorbachev later said that the Cold War ended at the summit between him and Bush in Malta in early December 1989, which was held a few weeks after the fall of the Berlin Wall and led to a more cooperative environment between the superpowers in which changes in Eastern Europe could take place.[14] Reagan always gets credit for his dramatic speech in June 1987, almost two and a half years before the fall of the Berlin Wall, demanding that Gorbachev tear down the barrier, but long forgotten is Bush's speech in Germany in May 1989 that also called for the fall of the wall only six months before it actually fell.[15] If either speech had anything to do with the wall falling—extremely unlikely—Bush's speech was closer in time to the event than Reagan's.

If Reagan had had any influence in ending the Cold War, it was because he got to know Mikhail Gorbachev personally and decided he was one Soviet leader he could work with—not because Reagan was a tough guy. In fact, although George H. W. Bush, a foreign policy realist, quieted Reagan's dangerous inflammatory anti-Soviet rhetoric, he was more skeptical of Gorbachev than was Reagan, even after Gorbachev's speech to the United Nations in December 1988 in which he announced a unilateral withdrawal of 40 percent of Soviet divisions from Eastern Europe, the end to the USSR's offensive strategy in Europe, and the value of self-determination, which hinted that the Soviets would no longer defend Eastern European Communist regimes using force.[16]

Yet to promote "stability," Bush actually tried to help Communist governments mitigate the effects of the revolutions in Eastern Europe—going so far as to orchestrate the run for reelection by Poland's Communist president General Wojciech Jaruzelski, who had much earlier imposed brutal martial law. Jaruzelski won that election.[17] In 1991, to promote stability in the Soviet Union and a few weeks before the failed coup there against Gorbachev, Bush went to Ukraine, which was then still part of the USSR, and tried to dampen Ukrainian efforts toward independence. Conservative William Safire called Bush's appearance the "Chicken Kiev" speech. Finally, Bush had a muted reaction when Gorbachev sent troops to repress the Baltic regions of the Soviet Union.[18]

However, Bush was able to close a deal with Gorbachev—which Reagan was not—on the first treaty in history to actually reduce strategic (long-range) nuclear weapons, rather than just limiting them. Bush and Gorbachev signed the Strategic Arms Reduction Treaty I (START I) in July 1991 and then achieved further weapons cuts in START II.[19] START I cut the Soviet long-range strategic nuclear arsenal by 35 percent and the US atomic arsenal by only 25 percent.[20] START II eliminated an entire class of Russian strategic missiles—the dangerous heavy SS-18s. Bush also reached the Conventional Forces Europe (CFE) Treaty, which limited NATO, Soviet, and former Warsaw Pact conventional forces in Europe, thus making Europe much safer from war.[21]

Thus, Bush has the record for signing the most major arms agreements in only one term as president. Given that the Soviet/Russian strategic nuclear force is the only existential threat the United States has ever faced in its history, this accomplishment should not be understated. In contrast, Reagan was so enamored with his pie-in-the-sky Star Wars defense system that he had refused a Soviet offer of deep cuts in long-range offensive nuclear forces if the United States stopped development of it. Instead, Reagan settled for an Intermediate-Range Nuclear Forces (INF) Treaty in 1987, which many defense experts and conservatives at the time thought undermined US security, because it removed such weapons from Europe, where those missiles would have helped the United States offset Soviet conventional ground forces then assumed to be superior to NATO forces.[22]

Expanding the NATO Alliance Eastward

Bush pushed the reunification of Germany on a reluctant Britain, France, and USSR. To get Gorbachev to accept a reunified Germany absorbed into NATO, Bush gave him a trade agreement that allowed the Soviet Union to sell its products in the United States.[23] The Germans provided generous financial assistance for the stricken Soviet economy. Also, as part of the deal to get Gorbachev to agree to reunite Germany, which occurred in October of 1990, Gorbachev claimed that Bush had promised not to expand the NATO alliance. However, Bush said privately of Gorbachev's demand, "To hell with that! We prevailed, they didn't. We can't let the Soviets clutch victory from the jaws of defeat."[24]

Yet Gorbachev may have reached this conclusion from a Bush promise to him, just after the Berlin Wall fell in November 1989, that the United States had "no intention of seeking unilateral advantage from the current process of change in [East Germany] and in other Warsaw Pact countries." Bush also drafted a NATO declaration to assuage Gorbachev's fear of a unified Germany in NATO, most of which was never fulfilled. The declaration included NATO shifting its emphasis from a military to a political alliance and outlining a new nuclear strategy that would eliminate a nuclear first strike as an option.

In seeming contrast to what Bush promised Gorbachev, Bush told the European allies that NATO had been created "to provide for precisely the extraordinary evolution which is occurring in Europe today. . . . The task before us is to *consolidate* the fruits of this peaceful revolution . . ." (emphasis added).[25]

Even if Gorbachev's claim about Bush's promise of no NATO expansion is discounted, the United States formally signed an agreement that NATO troops and weapons would not be placed in the eastern part of Germany after it was reunited and joined NATO. At least the spirit of this agreement has been repeatedly broken by the United States, expanding NATO territory right up to the Russian border, leading to a weak and nervous Russia attempting to salvage what it can from Moldova, Georgia, and the Ukraine. Also, the United States pledged not to permanently station NATO forces in the territories of new alliance members in Eastern Europe; this promise has been circumvented by regularly rotating alliance forces through those countries for military exercises.

Historically, Russia having been repeatedly invaded by the Mongols, Poles, Swedes, French, and Germans, possessing limited natural defense barriers, and having lost 25 million citizens in World War II, a buffer zone is extremely important to that nation. Such historical insecurity in the past has caused Russia to take aggressive action to obtain such a buffer zone—by taking over part of Poland, the Baltic countries, and Finland at the beginning of World War II and by establishing totalitarian Communist dictatorships in Eastern Europe after that war.

After the Cold War ended with the fall of the Warsaw Pact alliance and the Soviet Union, the West foolishly has taken this buffer zone away. Currently, Russia may be run by an autocrat, Vladimir Putin, who has a miserable media image in the West, but the country does have legitimate security interests, as do other great powers. Putin, who took power in 1999, used US triumphalism during and after the Cold War—first exhibited by Reagan and subsequent US presidents, including George H. W. Bush—to consolidate power by espousing anti-US nationalism. Even Putin's aggressive military activities in the Ukraine can be explained by trying to keep that country from joining a repeatedly expanding NATO alliance, which is right now on Russia's borders.

Just after the Cold War ended, given the vast reduction of the military threat to Europe, Bush should have fulfilled the NATO declaration meant to assuage Gorbachev and also declared NATO obsolete and dissolved it. At minimum, he should have pushed for eliminating the alliance's Article V collective military defense commitment, converted NATO into a political talk shop for Europe's problems, and invited all European nations, including Russia, to join. Bush had pledged to end the decades-long US policy of containment and to help reintegrate the Soviet Union into the world community of nations. This promise turned out to be empty rhetoric, as his aforementioned private comments on NATO expansion indicated. US policy essentially eschewed imitating the successful precedent of inclusion of a vanquished foe at the post-Napoleonic conflict Congress of Vienna of 1815, which led to almost a century of relative peace, and instead followed the unfortunate precedent of the post–World War I Versailles conference in 1919, which rubbed the nose of the war's loser into the dirt and led to an even more cataclysmic Second World War. Thus, the downward trajectory of Russia since George H. W. Bush's administration belies the claim that he responsibly managed the end of the Cold War. (It also indicts the repeated expansion of NATO by Bill Clinton, George W. Bush, and Barack Obama.)

Instead, the elder Bush pretended to commiserate with Gorbachev's situation but ensured that Gorbachev's and the USSR's defeat on key issues was complete. This tack undermined Gorbachev's position internally and more quickly led to the collapse of the Soviet Union in 1991. Bush's successful pushing of the reunification of Germany on the weakened USSR had been one of the factors leading to the failed coup in August 1991 by Soviet hardliners against the Gorbachev regime, which preceded the USSR's collapse. And Gorbachev's decision in mid-1989, during the Bush administration, not to prop up corrupt and illegitimate Soviet satellite governments in Eastern Europe using military force really ended the Cold War even before that and helped lead to the USSR's implosion. So why doesn't Bush get more credit for ending the Cold War? The answer is that Reagan carried a more macho image because of his repeatedly strident anti-Soviet rhetoric, which Bush had toned down.

That is not to say that Bush had a realistic appraisal of the greatly diminished threat to the United States in a post–Cold War world and a visionary plan to take advantage of it. He wrote in his diary,

> Who's the enemy? I keep getting asked that. It's apathy; it's the inability to predict accurately; it's dramatic change that can't be foreseen. . . . There's all kinds of events that we can't foresee that require a strong NATO, and there's all kinds of potential instability that requires a strong U.S. presence.[26]

In other words, the international environment had changed dramatically for the better, but Bush clung to the same old interventionist paradigm, which limited US independence by continuing Cold War alliances and ways of thinking about the world.

Tiananmen Square

A visit by the reforming Gorbachev to China set off peaceful democracy protests in Tiananmen Square in Beijing in mid-1989. When the Chinese government cracked down on the protesters, killing hundreds of them, Bush publicly protested the action. However, reflecting the increasing economic ties between China and the United States, Bush correctly avoided meddling in the internal affairs of this important nation, refused to withdraw the US ambassador to China or break relations with that country, and inflicted only a moderate penalty on the Chinese by suspending arms sales and US military visits. But then he made a mistake by secretly sending Brent Scowcroft, his national security advisor, and Lawrence Eagleburger, the number two man at the State Department, to China to assure the Chinese of continued good relations with the United States. The visit then became public and was seen as an apparent endorsement of the Chinese crackdown on dissent.[27]

Despite the largely sensible Bush policy vis-à-vis China, the US-China entente against the Soviet Union, which Nixon symbolically initiated in 1971 and Carter reinvigorated in the late 1970s from its moribund state really flourished only in the early 1980s. As the Soviet Union weakened in the late 1980s, China, in a classic case of textbook rebalancing among great powers, became less friendly to the United States and patched things up with the Soviet Union, and later its successor state Russia, to balance against the now unipolar US superpower.

Invasion of Panama

An example of the United States policing its traditional sphere of influence was Bush's needless invasion of Panama. Although many Latin American leaders at the time were connected to the drug trade, the Justice Department decided to indict Panama's President Manuel Noriega in 1988. Noriega was likely on the CIA payroll at one time. In addition, as vice president under Reagan, Bush had had a big role in US anti-drug policy and also had been accused of being a wimp. These factors may have been a factor in Bush's decision to give a green light to the invasion in December 1989, which led to the jailing of Noriega on drug charges. The official and historically familiar justification for the US invasion was to protect Americans and defend democracy in the wake of Noriega's crackdown on Panama's opposition. Yet incidents of violence against a few US military personnel were minor, and elections had been stolen before in Latin America with no draconian US response. If all such justifications seem weak, journalist Matthew Carr alleged that the real reason for the invasion was the imminent implementation of the Jimmy Carter–Omar Torrijos Panama Canal Treaty, signed in 1977, which was to restore sovereignty over the US-controlled Canal Zone to Panama by the end of the century. This analysis also seems weak, simply because 1999 was still ten years away. Maybe the lack of a good justification for violating international law was why some US military officers at the time jokingly said that the name of the operation should be changed from "Just Cause" to "Just Because."[28]

Even before Desert Storm, the invasion of Panama relied on American technological weapons and restrictive rules of engagement so as not to unnecessarily endanger civilians. Also, motivating this precision targeting was the fact that 40,000 Americans lived in Panama and that the US military therefore wanted to keep much of the infrastructure of the country intact. For the most part, the battle restrictions were observed, but some criticized the attack on the military headquarters of the Panamanian Defense Forces (PDF) in a residential neighborhood. Although the United States said that the PDF purposefully started fires that destroyed the neighborhood and made 15,000 people homeless, witnesses and one foreign journalist said that US artillery and tracer bullets set the neighborhood on fire.[29] Other than this destruction, virtually nothing changed in Panama as a result of the American invasion. Was even this death and destruction warranted for such an illegal invasion that served no discernable major national interest, other than perhaps to enforce the Monroe Doctrine of US domination in the Western Hemisphere? Or perhaps it was intended to battle Bush's own reputation as a wimp.

Interventionism

Unlike Bill Clinton, his successor, Bush stayed out of the post–Cold War civil war breaking up Yugoslavia, because he rightly realized that it was a regional problem that did not involve US vital interests. However, just before he left office, Bush sent 28,000 American forces to Somalia at the behest of the United Nations to open truck routes for humanitarian aid that rival warlords were blocking during the civil war there.[30] Bush, in his diary, wrote that he wanted the United States to be seen as helping black and Muslim countries, but getting your successor involved in a potential quagmire as you're leaving office might be seen as poor form. Clinton was criticized for "mission creep" in the conflict, as he disastrously began ordering American forces to fight the warlords. However, the US military mission had begun to deepen under Bush even before the change in administration.

Bush continued Reagan's meddling in Nicaragua but did so less harshly and with better results. Reagan unwisely had risked his presidency in the Iran-Contra affair by continuing his obsession with overthrowing the socialist government of a small, insignificant country in Central America—even when Congress had prohibited him from doing so. Commendably, however, Bush ended this tragic Nicaraguan folly—but with some intervention of his own.

Oscar Arias, elected president of Costa Rica in 1986, not only refused to allow his country to continue to be used as a staging ground for the US-sponsored Contra war against Nicaragua, but he actively got the Sandinista government and the rebel Contras together to negotiate toward a peace deal. Reagan had tried to intimidate Arias throughout and nix the peace deal. With peace in the air, Congress turned down Reagan's last attempt to get aid for the Contras in 1988.

When Bush took office, he faced a Congress with substantial Democratic majorities in both houses (and which continued throughout his four years in office).[31] To get any cooperation from the Democrats in either foreign or domestic affairs, he had to heal the festering wound of Reagan's military aid to the Nicaraguan Contras against the Sandinista government. As Reagan's vice president, Bush too had been embroiled in the Iran-Contra affair, arguably the worst political scandal in American history. Thus, out of necessity and also to take advantage of the opportunity provided by the winding down of the Cold War, Bush, with legislative agreement by Congress, laudably ended military support to the Contras and substituted humanitarian aid for both the Contras and the people of Nicaragua. He gave financial aid to both sides and offered incentives for the Contras to end the civil war and reintegrate into Nicaraguan society via a free election in 1990.[32]

In 1989, the Sandinistas and Contras had signed a peace agreement, and elections were to be held in 1990. The Sandinistas accepted the agreement and the election because they had lost aid from their then declining Soviet patron. In the election, the CIA, the National Endowment for Democracy, and the Republican Party spent exorbitant sums of money to get Violeta Chamorro—the leader of an opposition newspaper who had long benefited from US money— elected over Sandinista leader Daniel Ortega.[33]

Reagan and Gorbachev had agreed to end superpower support for warring factions in the Angolan civil war, and Cuba and South Africa had also agreed to quit meddling in that conflict. Yet the United States under Bush was the only outside power to continue to intervene there, doubling US aid to brutal Jonas Savimbi's UNITA movement.[34]

In another foreign intervention, Bush used US forces stationed in the Philippines, a former US colony, to help put down a right-wing coup against Corazon Aquino, who had taken office after the "people power" movement had overthrown the Reagan-supported corrupt Ferdinand Marcos dictatorship.

Although former President Nixon had suggested that Bush take a more even-handed approach to the Israeli-Palestinian conflict than had Ronald Reagan—regarded as the most pro-Israeli president in American history—Nixon also cautioned him that the region was a quagmire and that he should stay out of it. However, after Bush's one-sided victory in the first Gulf War, his prestige was high and he could not resist getting sucked into the vortex of making a run for a peace settlement. Bush correctly regarded Israel's expansion of settlements in the Israeli-occupied West Bank as the major impediment to peace, and Yitzhak Shamir, the Israeli prime minister, promised that he would freeze the settlement process but did not do so. Bush did get Gorbachev to cosponsor the Madrid Conference, attended by Israel and many of the key Arab states. Yet little was accomplished; Nixon was right after all.[35]

The one positive intervention that Bush undertook entailed being the first president to cut aid to ally Israel as an incentive to negotiate peace with the Palestinians.[36] He froze $10 billion in loan guarantees to Israel for the assimilation of Soviet Jews until Israel stopped its settlement activities on the West Bank. Subsequent presidents should have followed suit and slashed aid—but did not—because as a wealthy nation, Israel should be embarrassed to take billions of dollars in annual security aid. That assistance only makes the already relatively secure Israel more reluctant to reach a lasting peace with the Palestinians by giving them back land stolen using armed force in 1967.

Trade and Finance in the Americas

In December 1992, Bush laudably signed the historic North American Free Trade Agreement, dropping trade barriers between the United States, Mexico, and Canada, but Bill Clinton, whose Democratic base was unenthusiastic about the pact because the party drew support from organized labor, later courageously pushed it through Senate ratification.

The United States, under the Brady plan, reduced and restructured the commercial bank debt of every major debtor nation in Latin America. Nicholas Brady, the US treasury secretary, helped heavily indebted Latin American countries to convert defaulted or nearly defaulted debt into marketable bonds guaranteed by US and Western governments to help them be attractive to investors. Thus, commercial banks in these countries could get bad debt off their books by selling the bonds. Unfortunately, this bailout model was used during the 1990s and into the twenty-first century in other parts of the world.[37]

Providing additional ways for Latin American countries to get their loans forgiven, the Bush administration also launched the Enterprise for the Americas Initiative (EAI) to provide additional support and incentives (via the

Multilateral Investment Fund) for Latin American countries to reform their markets by allowing more imports and investment and modernizing their tax structures. Illustrating the absurd lengths that were taken to forgive debt, countries could have their debt to the US government forgiven if they set up protected nature preserves, which the United States essentially funded. Also, the United States contributed to the Inter-American Development bank for loans to countries that liberalized their economies.[38]

Both the Brady Plan and the EAI were a veiled subsidy to lending American banks and corporations by using taxpayer resources to shore up the debt structure of shaky Latin American nations in exchange for opening of their markets, which would benefit American firms. Yet, the rewarding of irresponsible foreign borrowing behavior cost the American taxpayer plenty and merely made it more likely that such countries, knowing that they likely could get future American bailouts, would continue their egregiously bad financial behavior.

Reducing the Massive Budget Deficit

Unlike Ronald Reagan and George W. Bush, however, George H. W. Bush did have positive accomplishments during his presidency. The elder Bush did not win reelection—most presidents do not who make the sacrifices needed to govern well—because of his perceived lack of a domestic agenda and his breaking of a "no new taxes" campaign pledge, which especially enraged his party's conservatives. Although many conservatives see taxes as the only issue and can be duped by sly, unobtrusive tax increases, government spending as a portion of GDP, which measures the government's drag on the private economy, is a more important issue. Conservatives regard Reagan as the tax-cutting king, but of all post–World War II Republican presidents, Reagan had the least annual net tax cuts as a percentage of GDP.[39] While publicizing his famous cuts in individual income tax rates, Reagan raised taxes in less conspicuous portions of the government revenue stream—with, for example, increases in "user fees" for government services and what he called "revenue enhancements" and "closing tax loopholes." In fact, Reagan had major tax increases in all but two years of an eight-year presidency.

Reagan produced a lot of conservative rhetoric—leading to a conservative reputation—and not much conservative policy action, whereas conservatives had always been suspicious of the elder Bush, regarding him as milquetoast. Thus, conservatives have erased Reagan's multiple tax increases from their memories but helped throw Bush out of office for his one tax increase.

And that tax increase paid at least some dividends. Because of Reagan's slight annual net tax decreases as a portion of GDP and enlargement of government spending as a percentage of GDP during his eight years, federal budget deficits ballooned to then record levels (only exceeded by the younger Bush and Barack Obama later). Under Reagan, such accumulating deficits tripled the national debt.[40] The effects of tax cuts are fraudulent if government spending is not cut to match; resulting deficits and debt drag the economy. As a result, the elder Bush had to clean up Reagan's mess of huge deficits.

Bush's overall record on federal spending as a proportion of GDP was not that good, adding an average annual increase of almost 2 percent during his four-year term.[41] However, in the budget agreement of 1990, the president traded an increase in taxes (individual income tax rates) for about three times the amount in defense and domestic discretionary spending cuts. The agreement was spurred by Fed Chairman Alan Greenspan's threat to maintain a tight monetary policy, which was slowing the economy, until a multi-year budget agreement was reached.

Unfortunately, an earlier, better version of the budget deal was nixed by Congress. Conservative Newt Gingrich, a fellow Republican and future speaker of the House, torpedoed the first negotiated agreement, which would have slowed entitlement growth; those entitlement provisions were stripped in the revised pact and the increase in income taxes was added.[42] The Democrats took advantage of the split in Republican ranks to trade off increases in the marginal income tax rates (28 to 31 percent) for lesser consumption tax (for example, on gasoline) hikes. Such increases in the very visible income tax rates—voters seem to pay more attention to this issue that to the overall rate of federal taxation—helped doom Bush's reelection chances in 1992.

Although Bush's 1992 campaign team actually got him to repudiate the deal, the 1990 budget agreement and its spending caps started the nation on the long path to budgetary balance. That balance was achieved by Bill

Clinton, the elder Bush's successor, who was one of only two postwar presidents to actually cut government expenditure as a portion of GDP during his term—the other being Dwight D. Eisenhower, who did not quite measure up to Clinton's budget cutting.[43] However, as the Cold War ended, Bush laudably reduced unneeded defense spending at a faster rate than Clinton later did.

In any case, the elder Bush reversed Reagan's fiscal profligacy and began to move the nation back toward fiscal responsibility with the spending and tax agreement he reached with a Democratic Congress, even though conservatives disdained it at the time. During his presidency, Bush used his veto forty-four times to defeat spending, tax, social, and regulatory measures passed by Congress.[44]

A mild recession occurred in 1990 and 1991, worsening the budget deficit, but Bush, against the advice of most of his economic advisers, courageously resisted artificially stimulating the economy; he did, however, provide for more jobless benefits.[45] Although helping people in the short term, these benefits discourage people from seeking long-term employment.

Yet, unlike FDR, Ronald Reagan, and Barack Obama, who all got reelected with even more severe economic downturns, Bush was unable to convince the American people that he at least had a coherent program for returning them to prosperity. This lack of public confidence sprang from a breaking of the "Read my lips, no new taxes" campaign pledge made during his speech at the Republican National Convention in 1988. The clearly disingenuous pledge was effective in winning votes during the 1988 campaign (evidence shows that Bush knew that he would eventually need to raise taxes), but proved too restrictive for Bush when governing. The broken pledge was disastrous during his reelection quest in 1992, even though the economy had begun to improve that year.

As noted, to reduce the budget deficits inherited from Ronald Reagan, Bush increased the highest marginal income tax rate, reducing projected increases in the gas tax to help mitigate this hike. Although Reagan raised taxes in every year except two during his eight-year administration, he was better at public relations than Bush and therefore more skilled at cultivating an image of being a conservative. Thus, voters forgave Reagan for raising taxes, whereas they did not Bush, a perceived moderate.[46] Bush also had never cut taxes as Reagan had and instead raised the marginal income tax rate on the highest earners, a powerful Republican constituency—whereas Reagan hiked taxes in obscure parts of the tax code on which the media did not focus. All in all, Bush cut more spending than he raised in taxes—$350 billion versus $140 billion over five years[47]—but that did not save him among the Republican base, which had grown accustomed to Reagan's fraudulent tax cuts (tax cuts coupled with spending increases as a portion of GDP, leading to huge budget deficits).

The Bush recession generally overlapped the first Gulf crisis of 1990 and 1991, and the economy did eventually recover before the 1992 election; however, it came too late for Bush to get reelected. After the smashing war "victory," Bush's sky-high approval ratings plummeted in the fall of 1991 by 20 percentage points, yet Bush remained complacent.[48]

The Record in Domestic Affairs

One of the main reasons that George H. W. Bush did not get reelected in 1992 (he got only 37.5 percent of the popular vote in a three-candidate race), less than two years after reaching a stratospheric 91-percent post–Gulf War approval rating, was his perceived lack of emphasis on domestic policy—that is, not having "the vision thing." Because most American elections are usually decided on domestic issues, this perception was a reelection obstacle that Bush could not overcome.

Despite substantial congressional majorities held by the opposition party, the actual policy record shows that Bush was fairly active domestically but that most of what he did was bad. But Bush was not without domestic accomplishment—for example, the Immigration Act of 1990 increased legal immigration into the United States by 40 percent to 700,000 entrants per year. The law had to deal with the failings of the 1986 Reagan-era immigration law. (Reagan had, however, given praiseworthy amnesty to almost three million illegal immigrants, who were able to emerge out of the shadows and become productive members of the economy.) Immigration—which brings new ideas, talent, different cultural practices, and younger workers into the country to support the aging population—is a no-brainer to achieve robust and sustained economic growth.

Bailouts

On the other side of the policy ledger, Bush "cleaned up" Reagan's careless deregulation of the savings and loan industry—which had led to these financial institutions risking depositors' money in dicey loan, real estate, and stock transactions—with a massive bailout funded by the taxpayers to the tune of hundreds of billions of dollars.[49] The basic problem was that during the Reagan administration, government insurance for savings and loan (S&L) depositors was raised significantly, a subtle government subsidy insulating the savings and loan industry from downside loss. This cushion then allowed the industry to make riskier loans and investments, using depositors' funds, which had a potentially higher rate of return.

Using the tired argument that the already sluggish general economy could be further endangered with the S&L failures, Bush made the taxpayers pay through the nose when he cleaned up the mess and provided government bailouts to resuscitate the industry. Bush created the Resolution Trust Corporation to manage the closing of insolvent S&Ls, paid depositors with government insurance, and tried to reduce the burden on taxpayers by selling off into the market what assets could be salvaged. However, the taxpayers' bill was increased because Bush did not personally fire the obstructing head of the Federal Deposit Insurance Corporation (FDIC) quickly enough, as the value of the assets being sold off by the government deteriorated. Thus, the bailout bill for taxpayers was still enormous—$130 billion, which at the time was real money. The S&L "crisis" and bailout helped cause a recession,[50] which contributed heavily to Bush being thrown out of office, despite his smashing "victory" in the first Persian Gulf War.

Although at least the premiums S&Ls paid for deposit insurance were raised, the S&L industry was reregulated, including the imposition of increased reserve requirements. Instead Bush should have completely deregulated the industry, including scrapping the industry crutch of deposit insurance that had caused the crisis in the first place.[51] (Bailouts for the Republican-leaning financial industry ran in the Bush family. A similar scenario of government subsidization of downside risk for financial institutions, leading to risky behavior, banks faltering, and taxpayer bailouts, occurred during George W. Bush's mortgage crisis of 2008, which precipitated a worldwide economic meltdown.)

Energy and Environment

Bush's Clean Air Act Amendments of 1990 (which also made possible the Canadian-American treaty on acid rain[52]) probably impaired economic growth with its added regulations. The act tightened air pollution standards (for example, on acid rain, ozone-depleting chemicals, and toxic substances) for the first time since 1977 but did allow companies to trade rights of emissions ("cap and trade"). Although this regulatory framework was more market-oriented and flexible than government command-style environmental regulations, if a decision had to be made for the government to intervene to reduce air contaminants, a pollution tax probably would have been even more efficient. Similarly, Bush had trouble controlling Bill Reilly, his director of the Environmental Protection Agency, who ran with Bush's campaign pledge to protect existing wetlands and overregulated private interests from developing certain lands.[53]

In December 1989, Bush signed the Renewable Energy and Energy Efficiency Technology Competitiveness Act, which subsidized such technologies. Because the government has a poor track record of deciding which technologies will do well in the market, many of the technologies it subsidizes are not yet ready for the market and may never be, thus wasting taxpayer dollars. Instead, the unfettered market is the best decider of which technologies are most promising and cost-effective.

Similarly, the Energy Policy Act of 1992, which implemented most of Bush's National Energy Strategy, was mostly bad, although it did avoid tightening mandatory auto fuel efficiency standards, eschewed major new taxes on fossil fuels, and introduced more competition into the utility industry. The new law prohibited drilling for petroleum products in the Arctic National Wildlife Reserve (ANWR) in Alaska, subsidized clean energy and renewable energy, and included incentives for energy conservation, including measures designed to reduce dependence on foreign oil. Although a goal widely acclaimed by both political parties and the American public, reducing dependence on foreign oil usually just results in higher energy prices.[54] That is, foreign oil is usually much cheaper to produce than domestic oil.

In 1992, the Bush administration, with more than 150 other countries, signed the UN Framework Convention on Climate Change (Rio Treaty). The convention set voluntary curbs on greenhouse gases.[55] So George H. W. Bush was a pioneer in international climate change policy.

Whether federal environmental regulation was constitutional was another issue. Most federal taxes, subsidies, regulations, and other interventions violate the Constitution's requirement that the national government provide for the "general welfare"—that is, not advantage or disadvantage a particular group or groups in society. Although the Constitution does not specify a federal role in regulating the environment, at least federal environmental regulation may be "less unconstitutional" because it could be argued that such regulation "provides for the general welfare." Perhaps a case also could be made for the federal government's regulation of interstate pollution under Congress's power to regulate interstate commerce. Of course, the federal government's agreement with other nations (it clearly has a role in foreign policy and the making of treaties) on environmental regulation would affect such interstate commerce.

Similar to his son, George W. Bush, Bush the Elder was criticized for his response to a hurricane—Andrew in this case. The elder Bush eventually sent troops to help with hurricane relief.

Social Issues

Bush continued Reagan's "War on Drugs" and the mass incarceration policies it required. He became involved in a bidding war with the Democrats to see who could militarize the police, build more prisons, and enact long mandatory prison sentences for drug offenses. He also got the military deeper into police work by increasing funding for military interdiction of drugs from Latin America.[56] Bush got Colombia, Peru, and Bolivia to participate in a futile $2.5 billion US-funded effort to eradicate drug crops, processing, trafficking, and profiteering. Bush, allegedly a Republican lover of small government, persuaded Congress to double the federal money allocated to fighting drug-related crimes, triple the amount of federal funds given for state and local law enforcement to do the same, and double the federal expenditures on drug treatment programs, as reported proudly by Bush's conservative Chief of Staff John Sununu.[57] Yet as of this writing, even some conservative Republicans have begun to agree that the era of mass incarceration was a mistake. The United States has the greatest incarceration rate in the world, but about two-thirds of the US prison population is there needlessly for committing nonviolent crimes, most of them drug-related.

Someday maybe politicians of both political parties will admit that the overall War on Drugs was a tragic mistake—leading to the waste of hundreds of billions of federal dollars, increased crime in the United States, the militarization of the police at all levels, and destabilization of developing nations. Many economists say that the attempted interdiction of illegal drug supplies by law enforcement is futile when a robust demand continues to exist for them. Making the consumption of drugs by adults illegal—a crime that hurts only willing users putting the toxins into their own bodies—merely hikes the price of them and therefore makes people inclined to commit crimes to grow, produce, transport, distribute, and get the money to consume such substances.

Thus, making drug use illegal for adults increases violent crime, and sending even nonviolent drug offenders to prison may create hardened violent offenders in the harsh prison environment. If there is any useful government role to combat drug use—the Constitution does not even mention a role for federal civilian agencies in law enforcement—it would be in conducting education campaigns to reduce the demand for drugs and in administering treatment programs, but even these roles are best left to the states. Finally, nowadays, more people die of abusing government-regulated prescription drugs, than from illegal drugs.

Although likely falling within the text of the Second Amendment and the government's power to regulate imports, Bush's ban on importation of most semiautomatic weapons may not have had much of an effect on violent crime. Most such crimes are not perpetrated using these weapons.

Bush appointed two Supreme Court Justices during his term—David Souter and Clarence Thomas. The first proved to be much more progressive than expected and the second has been probably more libertarian than Ronald Reagan's court nominees. Souter voted to uphold abortion rights, disappointing conservatives who were hopeful that he would have been the fifth of nine votes required to overturn the Supreme Court's earlier *Roe v. Wade* decision, which had permitted abortion. In fact, Souter provided the fifth vote in *Planned Parenthood v. Casey* in 1992 to save *Roe v. Wade*. (He also provided the fifth votes to uphold the constitutionality of race-based affirmative action programs and laudably to prohibit the Ten Commandments from being displayed in a courthouse in Kentucky.)[58] Although Bush had once supported Planned Parenthood, as president, he vetoed a bill that would have allowed public financing for abortions in the cases of rape and incest and also defended a ridiculous rule that prevented federally funded family planning clinics from discussing abortion with patients.[59] Bush may have done these things merely in a vain attempt to safeguard his political base for reelection, while likely secretly supporting Souter's defense of abortion rights.

Several Supreme Court cases had made it harder for civil rights plaintiffs to win their cases against employers. Bush vetoed a congressionally passed civil rights bill designed to ameliorate that difficulty, because he felt it established racial quotas that made it too easy for civil rights attorneys to win cases in which no discrimination existed and then get businesses to pay the court costs. When Congress tried again, Bush signed the Civil Rights Act of 1991.[60] The final law was less comprehensive than the one initially vetoed but did provide a trial by jury in civil rights cases; however, it limited the amount of damages that juries could award. The new law also allowed damages for emotional distress.

Bush's signing of the Americans with Disabilities Act of 1990, a major new area of unconstitutional federal concern, seemed compassionate but added extensive requirements for accommodating disabled persons that may have actually discouraged employers from hiring them.

Although Bush inherited a huge budget deficit and claimed to be resisting federal intrusion into education, traditionally a state and local responsibility, he increased funding for the Department of Education by 40 percent. In his first three years, he quadrupled spending for early literacy programs, more than doubled financing for the Head Start program, and hiked funding for science and math education by 70 percent. Bush also provided the miniscule and symbolic sum of $60 million to help support black colleges and universities. However, with federal funding always comes federal meddling, and

Bush did so by creating a new bureaucracy, the Presidential Advisory Board on Historically Black Colleges and Universities, to advise him on ways for the federal government to intervene in their affairs to make them better.[61]

Also increasing the encroachment of the federal government on state and local responsibility for education, Bush's "Education Summit with America's Governors" formulated the first set of national performance goals for K–12 students. Such standards later led to extensive testing and federal funding-based incentive systems for schools predicated on test results, promulgated in the No Child Left Behind legislation during his son's administration.

As for childcare, Congress passed a Bush-signed block grant so that states could provide it, but they would also need to set up standards and implement them. Congress included a tax credit for low-income people who paid for childcare and also the aforementioned expansion of Head Start for the entire workday all year long. In a blurring of the separation of church and state, it included religious organizations as providers of childcare but excluded public schools.[62]

Bush had made voluntary community service a priority item on his domestic agenda by talking about a "thousand points of light," which was deservedly mocked by comedians. The problem was that the volunteers were paid and that the federal government provided the seed money for their pay to serve in local communities and to establish a nonprofit "Thousand Points of Light Foundation" to coordinate and reward "volunteerism" all over the country. Also, a new bureaucracy, the White House Office of National Service, was created to support such nationwide volunteerism.[63] The program smacked of Herbert Hoover's encouragement of "associationalism" to substitute for direct government intervention—sort of a Republican version of intrusion-lite or state-driven voluntarism.

Running one of the dirtiest presidential campaigns in memory during the 1988 election, Bush had practiced demagoguery on the flag-burning issue by backing a constitutional amendment to ban flag desecration. He continued that demagoguery as president by signing a law, backed by the Democrats, which protected the flag—even after the Supreme Court had ruled in 1989 that the Constitution's First Amendment, which allows free speech, was more important than a Texas law prohibiting flag burning. Unsurprisingly, the Supreme Court overturned Bush's handiwork in another similar ruling in 1990.[64]

Bush tried to make farm price supports more "market-based" instead of doing what needed to be done: eliminating this welfare program for a non-poor, mainly Republican constituency. Bush replaced subsidies tied to planting quotas with a "market-based" approach that gave farmers flexibility in what to plant.[65] Farm income increased, but taxpayers were still footing a hefty bill.

Ronald Reagan had laudably avoided increasing the minimum wage, but Bush did so in 1990. Higher pay for wage workers seems compassionate, but when you raise the price of anything—including labor—demand for it goes down. When the government imposes or hikes a minimum wage, employers usually reduce workforces, forcing the lowest-paid, least-skilled workers out of jobs, which is not very benevolent after all.

Pardons of Iran-Contra Figures

Iran-Contra Independent Counsel Lawrence Walsh reindicted former Defense Secretary Caspar Weinberger for lying to Congress about the Reagan administration's Iran-Contra scandal. Walsh also verbally implicated then Vice President Bush in the scandal but did not indict him.[66] Court documents filed with Weinberger's indictment indicated that Bush had known about the illegal attempt to exchange hostages for arms to Iran, which Bush had always denied.[67] For example, Weinberger's notes from a January 1986 meeting on the illegal arms deal had said, "V.P. approved."

Rumors had always swirled that Bush was more involved in the scandal than was publicly acknowledged, but he had never been charged. Felix Rodriguez, a former CIA official who was recruited to help supply the Contras during the congressional ban on aid to them during the time frame of the second Boland Amendment, had ties to Donald Gregg, the then vice president's national security advisor. Rodriguez advertised his closeness to Bush, met with him often, and had one meeting with the vice president with an agenda title "Resupply of the Contras."

At the end of his presidential term, Bush, in a repeat of Ford's unconstitutional pardoning of Richard Nixon, pardoned Weinberger even though

Weinberger had not been yet convicted of any crime. Bush also pardoned five other Reagan administration and CIA officials. Had Weinberger gone to trial, Bush's vice presidential diary—and any contents related to Iran-Contra— would have been made public.[68] Any evidence therein of Bush's lying about his role in the Iran-Contra affair as vice president would have embarrassed the president publicly.[69] In the wake of the pardons, Independent Counsel Walsh accused Bush of continuing the "Iran-Contra cover-up."[70]

Bush's chief of staff, John Sununu, had to resign under a cloud. He had been accused of using government jets and limousines for personal trips.[71]

Conclusion

Although George H. W. Bush was branded a wimp, he was even more aggressive using the US military than Ronald Reagan. He not only invaded a small country—Panama—for no good reason; he ran an unneeded huge ground and air war against Iraq. The war was a smashing tactical success but led to many future unintended consequences: a permanent US military presence in the Persian Gulf; a retaliatory terrorist campaign by Osama bin Laden, including the 9/11 attacks; a second war in Iraq by Bush's son; the resulting creation of al Qaeda in Iraq, which morphed into the brutal Islamic State and took over a third of Iraq; and the reintroduction of US forces into Iraq for a third time (and also into Syria).

Although Bush gets some credit for managing the end of the Cold War, Reagan gets most of the credit for causing the fall of the Soviet bloc. Both notions are misplaced. Although Bush reached two important agreements to reduce the only existential threat in American history—long-range Soviet nuclear weapons—he also began the long road of NATO expansion into Central and Eastern Europe and the exclusion of the USSR/Russia from most European organizations, which eventually contributed to problems with a resurgent Russia during later American presidential administrations. The end of the Cold War, however, did help Bush end Reagan's needless and wasteful fiasco of supporting the Contra rebels against the Sandinista government in Nicaragua.

More regrettably, Bush bailed out Latin American banks as a hidden subsidy to US financial institutions and corporations. At home, Bush began reducing Reagan's massive budget deficits by exchanging income tax increases for three times the amount in defense and discretionary domestic spending reductions.

Domestically, Bush conducted a costly bailout of the savings and loan industry to deal with Reagan's disastrous partial deregulation and enhanced subsidization of that industry. Bush tightened air pollution restrictions, but in a more market-friendly way than usual, and also subsidized nonviable renewable energy technologies. Bush's Americans with Disabilities Act of 1990 seemed compassionate, but the added requirements for accommodating disabled persons may have actually discouraged employers from undertaking the additional expenses to hire them. Finally, Bush continued Reagan's costly War on Drugs; deepened the federal government's role in education; unconstitutionally pardoned Caspar Weinberger, Reagan's secretary of defense; and also pardoned other people involved in the Iran-Contra scandal—perhaps to cover his tracks in that affair while serving as vice president.

9

A Good Fiscal Record Counts

YEARS BEFORE WINNING election to the White House in 1992, Bill Clinton (president from 1993 to 2001) had outlined a more conservative agenda, including welfare reform. He had formed the Democratic Leadership Council, which advocated such policies.[1] Although his wife Hillary had pulled him off that track with her Orwellian and costly healthcare "reform" scheme (which made even Barack Obama's later convoluted healthcare law look efficient) during the first two years of his presidency, Clinton still cut the federal budget significantly during that time, working with a Democratic Congress. He then returned to a more conservative path after his wife's failed healthcare proposal delivered Congress into Republican hands in the 1994 off-year election.

A Good Fiscal Record

Although Bill Clinton was a Democrat, he promised small government and delivered more of it than most of the Republicans we have been discussing. Of post–World War II presidents (Harry Truman was excluded because his budget cuts came after the government had reached an all-time abnormal high of 44 percent of GDP during World War II), Clinton was the champion at slashing federal government spending as a portion of GDP. Dwight Eisenhower was a distant second, and all other presidents of the era, including Ronald Reagan, the king of "small government" hot air, actually increased federal spending as a percentage of GDP. Clinton was the only one of this group of presidents to cut per capita federal spending.[2] He turned a significant annual budget deficit from the Reagan/George H. W. Bush era into surplus by reaching a budget agreement with Republican Senate Majority Leader Trent Lott. If the trend of budget surpluses that Clinton realized had continued, all national debt would have been liquidated by 2013. The budget surpluses did not stay there long, however, as his successor, Republican George W. Bush, spent domestically like a drunken sailor and started two nation-building wars in Iraq and Afghanistan that alone cost $4 to $6 trillion—and the meter is still running—ultimately leading to record deficits.

Republicans will give Newt Gingrich, Republican speaker of the House of Representatives, the lion's share of the credit for this budgetary accomplishment—and he deserves some (unlike Reagan, he was a genuine budget hawk and a much more important Republican historically)—but laws, including the budget, need to be passed by Congress and signed, not vetoed, by the president. Even more important, Clinton—who established reducing the budget deficit as his top priority at considerable political cost to himself—actually cut the budget at a greater rate during the first two years of his presidency, when Democrats controlled Congress and Gingrich was not yet speaker, than in the last six years when Republicans, led by Gingrich, controlled it.[3]

Clinton, to his party's chagrin, abandoned his campaign promise of a massive government "reinvestment" in infrastructure, in order to clean up the Reagan/George H. W. Bush budget deficit mess. Unfortunately, Clinton also had to raise taxes on high-income taxpayers to help remedy the remaining massive deficits, which had been caused by fraudulent tax cuts (tax cuts while increasing spending as a portion of GDP) that Reagan had engineered in the 1980s.[4] However, Clinton's tax increase, done to reassure financial markets of American fiscal responsibility, was less in constant dollars than Reagan's 1982 tax hike (just one of many Reagan tax increases) and also less as a portion of GDP.[5] Clinton had also proposed a middle-class tax cut, which progressives also liked, but which he reluctantly later ditched. He did save an effective tax cut to the poor by enactment of a huge increase in the Earned Income Tax Credit. And unlike Reagan, Clinton cut federal spending as a percentage of GDP, rather than increasing it. Clinton's frugality was even more reassuring to Wall Street, his primary goal in order to spur economic growth, which exceeded the wildest expectations for the remainder of the 1990s. Economic growth was the fastest of the twentieth century. Like Warren Harding in the 1920s and Dwight Eisenhower in the 1950s, Clinton was able to spur a decade of economic growth with a policy of government austerity—confounding the Keynesian theory of using enhanced government spending to prime the pump and get a sugar high of artificial prosperity.

In prior times, for example, during the presidencies of Harding and Coolidge, Republicans genuinely believed in small government but also in being honest about paying for the government that existed. After Reagan's fraudulent tax cuts (cutting taxes but not spending)—which were imitated later by George W. Bush, with Vice President Cheney crowing that Reagan had taught them that budget deficits did not matter—that old-time spending restraint went out the window, thus allowing Republicans the convenient political posture of being for tax cuts and the welfare state at the same time.

During his administration, Clinton's deficit and spending reductions helped create one of the longest periods of economic expansion in American history. Unemployment was the lowest in thirty years, poverty rates rapidly sank, and welfare rolls continued to contract. However, some of the credit should be given to Alan Greenspan, the chairman of the Federal Reserve, for his tight money policies. Yet Greenspan's luster eventually wore off, as his later excessive increases in the money supply led to the over-inflation of the dot-com sector, which led, in part, to a bust and recession in 2001. Later more of the same from Greenspan, in response to that recession, and from Ben Bernanke, his successor, led to over-inflation of the housing sector—a bubble that burst, causing the Great Recession that began in 2008 during the George W. Bush administration.[6]

Reductions in Federal Meddling

In addition to cutting the budget deficit and federal spending per capita and as a percentage of GDP, Clinton also reduced government in other ways. Clinton had been a feverish supporter of welfare reform as governor of Arkansas and had immediately set up a welfare reform study group upon entering the presidency. In 1996, courageously going against most sentiment in his party, Clinton radically reformed welfare by limiting families to five years of assistance and ending federally guaranteed payments to individuals, replacing them with block grants to states[7]—all improvements conservatives had been wanting for years. Clinton thus fulfilled his promise from the presidential campaign in 1992 "to end welfare as we know it"[8] and actually rolled back part of the New Deal, which Ronald Reagan never did. The law also reduced benefits for undocumented immigrants during their first five years in the United States.[9] Finally, the new legal regime stipulated work requirements and mandated that healthy welfare recipients look for work after two years of getting benefits. He also gave businesses a tax credit for hiring people formerly on the welfare rolls.[10]

Clinton also put a high priority on a "Reinventing Government" initiative, and his powerful vice president, Al Gore, spent much of his time shepherding the effort. This project eliminated redundant government programs and streamlined the federal bureaucracy. The initiative saved $157 billion in taxpayer dollars and cut the number of workers on the federal payroll by 350,000.[11] Among post-Truman presidents, Clinton had the largest annualized decrease in civilian federal executive branch employees as a percent of the population. (In contrast, Ronald Reagan, who had an undeserved reputation for cutting the government, was one of only two post-Truman presidents to have increased the same measure, second only to the JFK/LBJ presidency.[12])

Moreover, Clinton went against most in his party again and got the North American Free Trade Agreement (NAFTA) with Mexico and Canada ratified. The agreement removed all trade barriers among the three countries. He deregulated the domestic banking industry, which included removing the artificial and outdated Depression-era Glass-Steagall restriction that separated riskier investment banking from commercial banking.

During the Clinton administration, a law passed preventing Congress from imposing federal mandates on states without funding them.[13] This statute laudably checked Congress's practice of unconstitutionally getting into states' business and not paying for it.

Similarly, Clinton signed an end to the national maximum speed limit of fifty-five miles per hour, which had been instituted by Richard Nixon in an overreaction to the 1973 Arab oil embargo, returning the authority of setting speed limits to the states. The federally mandated speed limit had hurt the economy and saved far less fuel than originally projected.

Although Clinton had promised during his campaign to focus on improving the lagging economy (which he eventually did), because he initially did not have a strong White House chief of staff, he got dragged into what turned out to be the quagmire of the gays in the military issue upon first taking office. Although Clinton, ahead of his time, pushed for gays serving openly in the military, he got severe pushback from the Joint Chiefs of Staff and key congressional leaders, including some Democrats, because he bushwhacked them with no prior notice to lay the groundwork for such dramatic social change. Thus, he was forced to settle for the bizarre "Don't Ask, Don't Tell" compromise, proposed by Colin Powell, chairman of the Joint Chiefs, whereby gays could not serve openly but could not be asked about their sexual orientation if they were able to keep it private. However, if military gays were "outed" or went public, they could be thrown out of the armed forces, and many of them were so tragically dispatched. Yet, although a more deliberate approach to the issue by Clinton might have garnered better results, this halfway and weird compromise did push gay rights down the road a bit, and Clinton should be given credit for it.[14]

Presidential Scandals

Clinton had an excellent fiscal record but was still only an average president. To reach this conclusion, most might think that being evasive to a grand jury, obstructing justice to cover up his marital infidelity with a White House intern, and being impeached for it was what trashed an otherwise good presidential record. Yet the Constitution requires that the standard for impeachment and conviction is having perpetrated "high crimes and misdemeanors." The style committee at the Constitutional Convention removed "against the state" from "high crimes and misdemeanors" phrase, apparently for no substantive reason. Thus, impeachment seems reserved for severe crimes against the state or society, not for personal offenses.

Reinforcing this interpretation, in the debates at that Convention, Alexander Hamilton noted that impeachable offenses "are of a nature which may with peculiar propriety be denominated POLITICAL, as they relate chiefly to injuries done immediately to the society itself" (emphasis in original).[15] In 1974, a congressional committee voted to impeach Richard Nixon but decided not to include Nixon's cheating on his taxes in the articles of impeachent, because although illegal, that behavior was personal, not political.

At worst, any illegal perjury and obstruction of justice by Clinton was also done for personal, not political reasons. Therefore, impeaching Clinton was questionable, especially when he could have been prosecuted for any personal criminal offenses after he left office. In the end, he was eventually disbarred from practicing law for his illicit activities. Thus, although Clinton's potentially illegal behavior was not political, Republican behavior in response to it fell into that category.

Equally relevant in a republic, Ken Starr, the hyper-partisan Republican independent counsel, was guilty of gross prosecutorial misconduct. Although Bill Clinton asked Attorney General Janet Reno to appoint an independent counsel, ultimately a three-judge panel of a federal appeals court—all Republicans—selected Starr as a replacement for the previous such counsel, even though he had a conflict of interest. Starr had earlier filed legal "friend of the court" briefs for the sexual harassment suit by Paula Jones, a former Arkansas state employee, against Bill Clinton.

The independent counsel was originally supposed to be investigating the shady Whitewater land deal, which Hillary Clinton had worked on at the Rose law firm in Little Rock, Arkansas, when Bill Clinton was governor, and the death of Vince Foster, a former colleague of Hillary's at the Rose law firm and Clinton White House aide. To get Clinton's associates in the Whitewater scandal to turn state's evidence, Starr indicted them for crimes for which they had already served time in prison (legal double jeopardy is prohibited by the US Constitution).

However, when Starr's investigation to indict Hillary over her activities at the Rose law firm failed, it then metastasized into a long and costly fishing expedition for any dirt on the Clintons (even reopening an investigation of White House aide Vince Foster's death that had been ruled a suicide by the previous independent counsel) and a purposefully lurid exposé of Clinton's sexual adventures. However, if the secretive Hillary had turned over the embarrassing Rose law records to the *Washington Post*, as all of the president's staff wanted her to do, there would have been no push for an independent counsel, no Ken Starr, and no impeachment of Clinton.

Starr knew through right-wing circles that White House intern Monica Lewinsky was having a sexual affair with Clinton—which could be construed as an immoral act but not an illegal one—and obtained tape recordings of

Lewinsky talking about it. Then, for the legal entrapment of the president to work, Starr had to get Attorney General Janet Reno to expand his mandate to include investigating perjury by the president, a crime that had not yet occurred.

After Starr had successfully gotten his mandate enlarged, he used the president's unrelated deposition in the Paula Jones civil suit against Clinton for sexual harassment (which Clinton could have and should have settled earlier) to try to entrap the president into lying to a grand jury under oath about his affair with Lewinsky. To entrap Clinton, Starr took advantage of the fact that Clinton and Lewinsky, who had nothing to do with the Paula Jones case, had been subpoenaed to testify by Paula Jones's lawyers, who had been apprised of the Lewinsky tapes. Starr tried to detain Lewinsky to gain her cooperation in entrapping Clinton, even though Clinton had not yet committed perjury. Of course, Clinton later took Starr's bait and, despite his lawyer's warning, was evasive about the affair under oath during the deposition; obstructed justice by encouraging Lewinsky to get rid of Clinton's gifts, then under subpoena, by giving them to Clinton's administrative assistant for safekeeping; and then coached the administrative assistant about what to say about the affair.

Starr got Clinton's grand jury testimony, in which eighty questions were about sex and none about Whitewater, publicly released and also issued the Starr report, which contained gratuitous sexual details—all to embarrass Clinton. At Clinton's Senate trial after his impeachment, Starr admitted that he illegally leaked damaging grand jury information to the media but withheld findings when they went in Clinton's favor.[16]

Given Starr's partisan attempt to hound, entrap, and embarrass Clinton at every turn for his sexual irresponsibility, impeachment as a remedy was even less legitimate. And Starr's violation of ethical standards and abuse of prosecutorial authority resounded negatively with the public.

Two-thirds of the American people were against impeachment. At the time of impeachment, Clinton still had an approval rating of 60 percent. The public felt that the scandal did not rise to the level to warrant Clinton being thrown out of office, and the Republican Congress's popularity declined when it tried to do so. Although to most people, Clinton's behavior was tawdry and dishonest and should have been condemned, Hillary still stood by him and most voters wanted the popular Clinton to remain as president. As a result, the Republicans suffered greatly in the November 1998 elections for their anti-Clinton activities. Historically, the party in power usually loses seats in Congress in midterm elections, but in November 1998, the Democrats actually gained seats because the public was fed up with Republican behavior during the Clinton scandal, including the prosecutorial abuse of Ken Starr. As a result of the election losses, Newt Gingrich was tossed out as House Speaker by his own Republican caucus and then resigned his congressional seat. Ironically, the man who had spearheaded the attempt to oust Clinton, even after having several marital affairs himself, was instead thrown out.[17]

Yet unbelievably, despite their election debacle, House Republicans pressed ahead with impeachment in December 1998 anyway. Conservative Republican Senator Richard Shelby (AL), a former prosecutor, found the impeachment case against Clinton to be weak. And Trent Lott, the Republican leader in the Senate, astutely wanted to take a test vote, and if the vote was less than the two-thirds majority needed for conviction—which he had to know it would be—the trial would have been quietly ended. The House Republicans would have none of it. Thus, in January 1999, in a formal vote, the Republican majority in the Senate (55 Republicans) did not get the two-thirds vote needed to convict Clinton, or even get a majority of senators to vote for the same. And the Republicans could have gotten a bipartisan majority to censure Clinton,[18] but they instead wanted it all and failed—ironically, much as Hillary had when failing to compromise on healthcare "reform."

In short, like the corruption scandals in the administrations of Warren Harding and Ulysses S. Grant, of which these presidents had no direct knowledge, Bill Clinton's personal scandal—which did result in potentially illegal personal behavior—did not rise to the level of the constitutional scandals of Iran-Contra during the Reagan administration and Watergate during the Nixon administration. In the latter two scandals, presidents secretly abused presidential power and threatened the republican system of government in doing so. Although Clinton may have committed illegal acts, he did them for personal reasons and not to flagrantly abuse his power.

Clinton also ran into criticism over pardons he made when leaving office, especially of the unconstitutional pardon of Marc Rich—a fugitive indicted for tax evasion—after receiving large contributions from Rich's wife for the Clinton presidential library, Hillary Clinton's senatorial campaign, and furniture for the Clintons' house in New York. Clinton, however, pardoned roughly the same number of people as Jimmy Carter and Ronald Reagan and was exonerated of any criminal wrongdoing in the Marc Rich matter by a federal prosecutor. The president's power to pardon is plenary but should be used only after individuals are convicted of a crime. Clinton's pardon of Rich—like Gerald Ford's pardon of former President Richard Nixon and George H. W. Bush's pardon of Reagan's Secretary of Defense Caspar Weinberger—was unconstitutional because it helped people avoid the stigma of a conviction.

The Constitution does give the president the unconstrained power to pardon people who have committed offenses. Yet Ford's pardon of Nixon and Bush's pardon of Weinberger, both of which were self-serving and unconstitutional, had many more ramifications than Clinton's because they impeded prosecutions in the two worst constitutional scandals in American history, Watergate and Iran-Contra. In fact, some have argued that Ford traded the office of president for a subsequent pardon of Nixon and that Bush pardoned Weinberger because Weinberger could have implicated Bush in the Iran-Contra affair, in which Bush had been more deeply enmeshed than was publicly known. In contrast, Marc Rich was guilty of only mundane crimes of enrichment and would not have implicated Clinton in any wrongdoing.

More Important Foibles

Even more important than Clinton's sex scandal and impeachment were his policy errors. Although Clinton, a politician's politician, governed too much by polls and avoided politically risky stances, one of the big gambles he took was allowing his wife Hillary to send to Congress what Evan Thomas called a "Rube Goldberg" scheme for reforming the healthcare system.[19] According to historian William H. Chafe, after the new president took office, the unelected Hillary Clinton went out of his control. Using a huge task force of thirty-four working groups, she took many months to formulate an overly intricate 1,342-page scheme in secret, which foisted the costs of covering more people with healthcare insurance on businesses and taxpayers, while retaining private insurance and private caregivers. Clinton's entire economic team and his secretary of health, education, and welfare thought that the cumbersome process she set up to concoct her healthcare plan was nutty, and the president's entire administration hated her proposal. Thus, the administration's resulting proposal to change the nation's healthcare system made the subsequent and questionable Obamacare look responsible.

Hillary then refused any compromise on the monstrosity with Congress (the same mistake Woodrow Wilson had made with the post–World War I League of Nations), which had been kept in the dark about the proposal. Although, in principle, healthcare "reform" was supported by 60 percent of the public and proposed compromises in Congress covered between 91 and 95 percent of those needing health insurance, Hillary insisted that Bill Clinton promise to veto any bill providing less than 100-percent coverage— against the advice of his political advisers and likely his better judgment. Fortunately, the Congress nixed Hillary's plan because it was too complex and costly. In Clinton's first two years in office, Hillary had taken a wrecking ball to his presidency.[20]

According to Chafe and based on insiders' accounts, Bill Clinton, contrary to his better judgment against the impending disaster, let Hillary run wild on healthcare because he felt he owed her for being elected president in the first place. She had stood by him during the campaign when accusations of marital infidelity arose, including those surrounding Gennifer Flowers.[21] During the first two years of his presidency, Bill allowed Hillary to be a co-president, which ended in several poor calls on her part. She insisted that her healthcare issue be considered before Bill's longstanding promise to reform welfare. Many Clinton advisers thought that addressing welfare reform first would have given the Clinton administration a quick bipartisan victory and made the passage of her healthcare proposal more likely. Instead, she would have none of it and got none of it.

Also, her nominees for attorney general (Zoe Baird) and deputy attorney general for civil rights (Lani Guinier) flamed out. Furthermore, she infuriated the press by closing them off from the White House press secretary's office, unnecessarily ruining relations with the media for quite some time. Although some financial mismanagement occurred in the White House travel office before the Clintons took power, she fired the entire office and then denied involvement.

Most important, she prevented the White House from releasing documents from her time working at the Rose law firm in Little Rock, Arkansas, while Bill was governor of the state. The Rose papers likely documented her involvement in the shady Whitewater real estate deal, violation of Arkansas conflict-of-interest rules by failing to recuse herself from representing people who had business with the state, overbilling clients, and earning of 1000-percent return in a commodities sweetheart deal. Her failing to release the Rose documents led to a full investigation of the Whitewater affair by the *Washington Post* and *New York Times*, which ultimately led to the appointment of an independent counsel, the prosecutorial abuse of Ken Starr in the Monica Lewinsky affair, and impeachment of the president. Chafe concludes, based on an insider account, that Bill did not override Hillary's horrible decision not to release the Rose documents because "troopergate" had just broken publicly. He was once again humbled in his dealings with her because of reports that, while governor of Arkansas, he had had state troopers procure women for him to have sex with.[22]

Bi-Election Consequences

Clinton's party had a devastatingly bad showing in the 1994 elections after he—against his better instincts and his conservative "New Democrat" agenda —had let his wife propose a failed big government healthcare reform. As a result, Clinton changed course and, with the help of political consultant Dick Morris, returned to being a New Democrat. His now chastened wife faded into the background after dominating the first two years of his presidency, and he contented himself with "triangulation"—that is, coming up with policies in between the Republican congressional opposition and the progressive wing of the Democratic Party—and playing "small ball" by proposing some minor initiatives, most of them not good federal policy. Sometimes, he even stole formerly Republican issues.

Both before and after the Democratic bi-election defeat, Clinton did the following:

- In 1993, even before the bi-election year debacle, he signed the Family Medical Leave Act (FMLA), requiring employers to allow employees to take up to three weeks of unpaid leave to take care of family emergencies. Although this seems like a good idea on the surface, the US

Constitution, which supposedly allows the federal government to assume only powers specifically enumerated in the document, does not mention a federal role in this area. Such laws should be left to the states. Even then, companies could certainly offer such benefits to employees as a recruiting and retention tool, but for government to require it seems to interfere excessively with the employment market; there is also the potential for employees to abuse the practice.

- Micro initiatives for children included guaranteed hospital care for kids of Vietnam veterans born with spina bifida, forty-eight hours of guaranteed hospital time for mothers giving birth, a program for the government to cover children without insurance, quadrupling support for childcare, and hiking Head Start preschool funding by 250 percent. For adult health, Clinton gave women mammograms and instituted programs for Alzheimer's patients.[23]

- Clinton ended the Reagan/Bush era executive orders banning funding for programs on family planning by the US government and international organizations that dispensed information on birth control and abortion. Although the Supreme Court has declared that women have a constitutional right to have abortions, the Constitution does not provide for an enumerated federal role in funding birth control methods or abortions or the dissemination of information about them. That is a role for the states.

- He created AmeriCorps, a domestic equivalent of the Peace Corps, which put young people to work doing community service projects across the nation. Despite the good intent of the organization, it merely interfered with private labor markets. Clinton also meddled with the market by raising the minimum wage, throwing the poorest, most unskilled workers out of jobs when it became too expensive for businesses to hire them.

- Clinton brought the federal government further into education, traditionally a state and local responsibility, by bringing in school uniforms and substantial tax subsidies for college tuition.

- He brought parents V-chips to regulate their children's TV watching.

One of the main problems with most of these micro-initiatives was that the US Constitution did not enumerate a federal role in these areas, and, if done by government at all, they are best left to state and local governments.

Clinton's "tough on crime" stance led to tens of billions of dollars being spent on putting 100,000 more police on the street and on the unfortunate era of mass incarceration, with people jailed for long periods for minor offenses. Of all post-Truman presidents, Clinton had the second greatest annualized increase in spending on public order and safety as a percentage of the federal budget (Nixon's initiation of the "War on Drugs" made him first).[24]

Although the comprehensive Violent Crime Control and Law Enforcement Act of 1994 allowed relief from Ronald Reagan's mandatory minimum prison sentences for certain first-time nonviolent drug offenders, it also established the "three strikes" measure that required mandatory life sentences for convicted violent felons with two or more previous convictions, gave states incentives to lengthen sentences, financed new prisons, criminalized gang membership, funded crime prevention programs, and ended Pell educational grants for prison inmates. As an ex-president, Clinton, who had long touted this crime bill as one of his major accomplishments, repudiated it, saying the law went too far in strengthening sentencing standards, thus contributing to the era of mass incarceration. However, Clinton's Brady Bill, which mandated background checks for new gun ownership and a ban on assault weapons, fit within the literal text of the Constitution's Second Amendment.[25]

In early 1993, after the Branch Davidian religious cult killed four federal agents who were investigating them, the FBI laid siege to them in a house in Waco, Texas. The cult's leader, David Koresh, refused to surrender. Reluctantly, at the request of Attorney General Janet Reno, Clinton ordered a military-style raid on the house using tear gas grenades. Either the grenades or Koresh himself caused a tragic fire that killed eighty cult members, mostly women and children.[26] Unfortunately, the travesty did not end there. In 1995, on the second anniversary of the Waco raid, right-wing militia members Timothy McVeigh and Terry Nichols, to avenge that Clinton administration action, launched a terrorist bombing of the federal building in Oklahoma City, killing 168 people, many of them children at a federal daycare center. Ironically, acting as the nation's "comforter-in-chief" (not a role enumerated for the president in the Constitution), Clinton, after the second tragedy, which was retaliation for the administration's own ill-advised actions, began his comeback as a politician after the 1994 election disaster, which had allowed the Republicans to assume control over both houses of Congress. Clinton also benefited from House Speaker Newt Gingrich, although meaning well in cutting government spending, making tactical political blunders.

Clinton nominated progressive Ruth Bader Ginsburg to the Supreme Court. Sometimes, progressive justices generate better rulings for liberty than conservatives (civil liberties, abortion rights, separation of church and state, etc.) and sometimes not (many economic issues).

An Interventionist Foreign Policy

As governor of Arkansas, Clinton had no prior experience in foreign policy—and it showed. Because the Cold War's demise had taken away any superpower pushback against US military intervention around the world, Clinton ran wild meddling in developing nations. He seemed to agree with Madeleine Albright, his secretary of state, when she asked General Colin Powell, chairman of the Joint Chiefs of Staff, "[W]hat's the point of having this superb military that you're always talking about if we can't use it?" Powell later said, "I thought I would have an aneurysm."[27]

George H. W. Bush had inserted US ground forces into the civil war in Somalia to protect UN food deliveries and was already expanding their mission before he left office. Clinton, early in his first term, decided to take the advice of General Powell, who did not always advocate military restraint, to further expand the mission and to choose sides in the civil war by trying to go after warlord Muhammed Aideed. The "Black Hawk Down" episode, made famous by a later movie, ended up killing US troops and resulted in the ignominious withdrawal of US forces. It was later learned that Osama bin Laden—having taken heart from Ronald Reagan's shameful withdrawal of US forces from Lebanon under fire in the early 1980s after the terrorist bombing of the Marine barracks there—had decided to help push the United States out of Somalia by helping Aideed with attacks against US soldiers.

In Haiti, Clinton sent the USS *Harlan County*, a lightly armed US Navy ship, to Port-au-Prince to pave the way for a return of Jean-Bertrand Aristide, the elected president of Haiti who had been sent into exile by that country's military. Throngs of pistol-wielding Haitians greeted the ship at the dock, yelling, "Somalia, Somalia." As did US ground forces in Somalia, the ship withdrew. This time Secretary of Defense Les Aspin was fired.[28] Later Clinton did begin an invasion of Haiti, which was enough to make its dictator flee. Ostensibly, this action was commenced to restore Aristide, but the case for US intervention was not hurt by the fact that instability in Haiti was causing a refugee migration crisis in Florida, an important state in US presidential elections.

Clinton did learn from the Somali fiasco, but instead of learning to stay out of faraway brushfire wars that did not affect US vital interests, he merely learned to intervene in them without using ground forces. In Bosnia, Kosovo, and Iraq, he used only air power to attempt to gain his objectives. In Bosnia, although he successfully vetoed the lifting of a US arms embargo that would have sent weapons into the civil war there,[29] in 1995, he used the bombing of military targets to strong-arm the Bosnian Serbs to reach the Dayton Peace Accords, ending the civil war there.

In Kosovo in 1999, Clinton waged a "humanitarian war" to attempt to enshrine the new "Responsibility to Protect" (R2P) doctrine into an international norm by preventing "genocide" of the Serbs against the Kosovo Liberation Army (KLA), which some at the US State Department had labeled a terrorist organization. The KLA was composed of Albanians in the Serbian province of Kosovo. The group was fighting a guerrilla war to detach the province from Serbia and was trying to "internationalize" the conflict by attacking the Serbs, in order to get them to launch an over-the-top response, thus bringing a Western response; it worked. The US-led NATO alliance presented Slobodon Milosevic, the Serbian leader, with an ultimatum no nation could possibly accept—to withdraw his forces from Serbia's own province and have them replaced by a NATO peacekeeping force. Because of a reluctance by some members of the US-led coalition to use force in Kosovo, the United States began a gradualist bombing campaign that was reminiscent of LBJ's Rolling Thunder operation in Vietnam. Clinton's bombing made the ethnic cleansing worse by giving the Serbs no reason to restrain themselves against the Kosovar Albanians. They expelled 90 percent of Kosovars into neighboring nations, creating more of a humanitarian crisis than the prior limited ethnic cleansing that the bombing was designed to stop.[30] Although Madeleine Albright, Clinton's secretary of state, claimed before the bombing started that 100,000 Kosovar Albanians had been killed by Serbian ethnic cleansing, only about 4,300 had been killed, most after Clinton started bombing.

NATO was unprepared for the stiff Serb resistance but got lucky when the Russians pulled their diplomatic backing of Serbian dictator Slobodan Milosevic, a major factor leading to Milosevic's withdrawal of forces from the Serbian province of Kosovo. Later, Milosevic was deposed and Kosovo became an independent country.

Clinton's "humanitarian" military interventions usually seemed to have ulterior realpolitik motives (except for the one in Somalia, which was started by George H. W. Bush and simply experienced further nation-building "mission creep" under Clinton). For example, the US interventions in Bosnia and Kosovo seemed designed to make the NATO alliance relevant after its main reason for being—defense against an attack by the Soviet Union and Warsaw Pact—became extinct. NATO needed to remain relevant by expanding its territory and mission (called by the policy's proponents "expand or die") to justify a continued US military presence in Europe after the Cold War ended. Although the NATO Treaty still stipulated an alliance only designed to defend Western European area, the bombing of Bosnia and Kosovo were offensive "out-of-area" missions designed to showcase this unauthorized mission expansion, which also violated international law.

Although George H. W. Bush had promised in writing to then Soviet leader Mikhail Gorbachev, in order to get him to agree to the reunification of Germany, that NATO would not even move its forces into the eastern part of the newly unified state, Clinton began a territorial expansion of the alliance to include Poland, Hungary, and the Czech Republic. Clinton was unenthusiastic about this overseas territorial expansion until he realized that ethnic swing voters, especially Poles, in swing electoral states in the Midwest at home supported it. Subsequently, the alliance has conducted more expansions right up to the Russian border, and George W. Bush told Ukraine and Georgia, countries close to Russia and very important to it, that they could get into NATO. Russia has become nervous; one of the reasons it is helping separatists in eastern Ukraine and has annexed Crimea and its important naval base on the Black Sea is to keep Ukraine out of NATO and to guarantee that it has access to Crimea's base, even if Ukraine has a government unfriendly to Russia. Although Vladimir Putin's takeover of Crimea by force was unacceptable under international law, so was the similar detachment of Serbia's province of Kosovo by US-led NATO using armed force in 1999. Therefore, Clinton's expansion of NATO's territory and mission, and his successors building on this bad precedent to conduct further enlargement, contributed to the creation of an autocratic and more aggressive Russia—a severe unintended consequence.

That ulterior motives usually existed for Clinton's "humanitarian" military interventions is borne out by the one major instance in which Clinton chose not to intervene. In Rwanda, a massive humanitarian crisis emerged. The country was not high on anyone's list of strategic countries and therefore certainly provided no obvious ulterior motives for any US intervention. A slaughter erupted in which the Hutu tribe massacred 500,000 to 1 million other Rwandans, many of them from the rival Tutsi tribe. This bloodbath—a true genocide—made the Balkan wars, in which Clinton intervened, look tame. Yet Bill Clinton, a Democratic president known for proclaiming "humanitarian" purposes for all of his military adventures, stood by and did nothing about the carnage. Thus, the exception proves the rule. The humanitarian rationale for Clinton's interventions (and those of other US presidents) are often bogus; one must usually look deeper to find the real motives of US policymakers.

Republican critics have blamed Clinton for not doing enough to counter the rise of al Qaeda, but he did try to preemptively take down the group. Clinton probably could have done more, but he did attempt to kill or kidnap Osama bin Laden or degrade his operations six times. However, Clinton aborted these efforts because of worries about bad intelligence or the possibility of civilian casualties.[31]

After al Qaeda's bombing of American embassies in Kenya and Tanzania in 1998, Clinton did fire cruise missiles at al Qaeda's training facilities in Afghanistan and what was thought to be, on slim intelligence, an al Qaeda plant in Sudan making substances that could be used as biological weapons. At the time, Republicans criticized Clinton for trying to distract from his upcoming grand jury testimony in the Lewinsky sex scandal. Yet, the cruise missile attack on Afghanistan was timed to kill bin Laden (Clinton's seventh targeting attempt), who US intelligence thought was likely to be attending a meeting in the training camp on a specific date. Bin Laden was at the camp but left an hour before the attack. Many generals and intelligence officials attested to the need for the attack, helping Clinton to win public support for it.

In fact, the sex scandal may have dampened the Clinton administration's response down to just firing cruise missiles, because his major advisers knew that an excessively bold response to the embassy attacks likely would have been ridiculed as a distraction strategy.[32] Thus, the distraction charge seems to lack credibility. In the end, the criticism in the episode should have been that the intelligence was bad in the case of the factory, which apparently had nothing to do with al Qaeda.

George W. Bush has also been accused of not doing enough against bin Laden prior to the 9/11 attacks. However, both presidents probably should be given at least some slack for not realizing that al Qaeda—a small group that had been launching limited attacks overseas on US embassies, American forces, and a US Navy ship—was capable of launching such devastating, high-casualty attacks on America's home territory. Yet for both Clinton and Bush the Younger, warning signs were present before 9/11 of some sort of impending al Qaeda attack.

Also, Clinton, in Operation Desert Fox in 1998, showed his love of aerial bombing by continuing the US war with Saddam Hussein that George H. W. Bush started and George W. Bush would ignominiously finish. Clinton enforced the no-fly zone set up over Iraq's sovereign territory and bombed Iraq for four days. The rationale for the latter was to get Saddam to comply with weapons inspections he had agreed to with George H. W. Bush to end the first Persian Gulf War.

Many presidents have futilely tried to mediate an ultimate peace between the Israelis and Arabs, two parties who do not seem to want to solve the conflict. Clinton was also sucked into this vortex and got burned by going too far in his mediation efforts. Initially, in the fall of 1993, Israeli Prime Minister Yitzhak Rabin called Clinton and informed him of the Oslo agreement between the Israelis and Palestinians, which the United States had had no role in mediating. Nevertheless, Rabin wanted he and Palestinian leader Yasser Arafat to sign the pact at the White House, a limited facilitation role that Clinton appropriately accepted.

Later, in 2000, however, as Clinton's second and final term was drawing to a close, he put on a full-court press to get the Israelis and Arabs to sign a final comprehensive peace deal. Clinton failed and blamed Yasser Arafat for the breakdown in the talks. Yet, the violence in the aftermath of Israeli prime ministerial aspirant Ariel Sharon's visit to an Islamic holy site on the Temple Mount—violating the informal understanding between Jews and Palestinians not to intrude on each other's sacred places—did not make it easy for Arafat to say yes. In addition, the Israelis, too, nixed a final agreement with the Syrians to settle the future of the Golan Heights, despite the surprising flexibility of President Hafez al-Assad of Syria in the negotiations.[33] At any rate, Clinton became too involved in trying to resolve a problem that he had no responsibility to work out and that probably would have cost the United States a lot of money in the future to sponsor a solution. This scenario had already played out in the late 1970s when the United Sates provided billions of dollars in aid to both Israel and Egypt in seeming perpetuity to bribe them to do what was in their best interest anyway: to sign the Camp David accords and the Israeli-Egyptian peace treaty.

The American taxpayer was less fortunate in escaping huge costs for other Clinton foreign policy initiatives. Wallowing in excessive debt, Mexico and its peso faced imminent collapse. Using the flawed logic that is usually dragged out to bail out financial scofflaws, the Clinton administration argued that if it did not provide billions in emergency aid to bail out Mexico's banks, the financial contagion would consume the entire continent and maybe the world. Such arguments were designed to use fear of general economic collapse to motivate a US government bailout of wealthy Wall Street lenders to Mexico and thus ensure that they again would likely make reckless loans in the future. The similarity to arguments in 2008 and 2009 in favor of bailing out equally irresponsible "too-big-to-fail banks" in the United States during the Great Recession should be noted.

Conclusion

Overall, Clinton's haphazard "tilting-at-windmills" foreign policy of conducting numerous, needless small interventions probably takes an otherwise good president—who limited government at home compared to most other recent chief executives—and makes him only an average one. Clinton unnecessarily intervened using military force, or the threat thereof, in conflicts in Bosnia, Kosovo, Somalia, Iraq, and Haiti—none of which affected the vital interests of the United States. Although Clinton allowed his wife Hillary to attempt to pass a complex and costly healthcare "reform" program, which was fortunately rejected by Congress, he cut the federal budget as a portion of GDP more than any post–Truman president, helping to spur a long period of robust economic growth that turned huge Reagan/Bush budget deficits into surpluses; passed welfare reform; and got the North American Free Trade Agreement ratified, at great political cost by going against most of his party.

10

Big Government at Home and Abroad

ALTHOUGH GEORGE W. BUSH lost the popular vote to Al Gore in the 2000 election, the Republican-dominated federal Supreme Court, forgetting its ostensible states' rights orientation and that elections historically have been the purview of the states, made Bush president. The court gave him a win in the electoral college after an election in Florida that statistically was too close to accurately determine the winner. However, Bush did not care about the lack of a mandate from voters and forged ahead with an activist agenda, both at home and abroad.

Bush (president from 2001 to 2009) liked to be known as a "compassionate conservative." This moniker was designed for electoral purposes to show that conservatives could still be concerned about the poor. It really was a new and somewhat more honest euphemism for being a big government conservative (previously, conservatives, such as Newt Gingrich and Ronald Reagan, had claimed they were for small government and yet had given the country big government). Bush more than fulfilled the label. He pursued progressive goals at home and abroad using conservative means.[1] Yet at the same time, Bush, in many respects, did claim to be for reducing government—for example, by backing massive tax cuts.

During the 2000 campaign, Bush claimed to be for small government abroad by objecting to Bill Clinton's nation-building wars and promising a humbler foreign policy. As president, Bush followed the Reagan model, both in image as a rugged Western hombre and in his reckless cowboy behavior overseas. Bush foolishly enmeshed the United States in two overseas military occupations in Afghanistan and Iraq that led to long-term nation-building quagmires, which the US military lost while destabilizing both countries.

Also, like Reagan, Bush cut taxes (even more deeply than Reagan), unnecessarily increased spending on defense and domestic programs significantly, and thus racked up massive budget deficits, thereby ballooning the national public debt. In fact, at the time, Bush spent more on domestic programs than any president since Lyndon Baines Johnson (LBJ). Of post-Truman presidents, Bush was second (behind John F. Kennedy/LBJ) in average annual increase in federal spending as a portion of GDP, first in average annual increase in the budget deficit as a percentage of GDP, and third (behind Ronald Reagan and his father, George H. W. Bush) in annualized growth in debt as a portion of GDP.[2]

Furthermore, excessive monetary expansion during George W. Bush's watch by Alan Greenspan, the Reagan-appointed and long-serving Federal Reserve chairman, and Ben Bernanke, Greenspan's Bush-appointed successor, flowed into the housing industry, led to a bubble that burst, and plunged the world into the greatest recession since the Great Depression in the 1930s. Essentially, this global cataclysm in 2008 started in the United States and was caused by too much borrowing, public and private. In response to the "crisis," the Bush administration, with the help of Bernanke, selectively bailed out or socialized large financial institutions that had acted irresponsibly in the housing market, instead of letting them go out of business, thus ensuring the likelihood of a similar future calamity involving such "too big to fail" giants acting recklessly. To remedy the sickness, the government went back to the cause and added more debt, which had to be accommodated by unprecedentedly large increases in the money supply.[3] Money had to be printed to allow the purchase of government debt.

In addition, many "small government conservatives," who purportedly loved the vision of the nation's founders, strangely supported an unconstitutional, imperial presidency, even though the federal government's overwhelmingly dominant arm was already the Executive Branch. Ninety-eight percent of federal employees work for the president, so the staffs of the congressional and federal judicial branches are merely pimples on the executive branch elephant.

Dick Cheney, Bush's powerful vice president, claimed to be one of those small government conservatives and yet believed in the unitary theory of the executive, which exalted the expansion of executive power, especially during national security crises. In the wake of the 9/11 attacks, Cheney successfully prodded Bush to vastly and unconstitutionally expand executive power as commander-in-chief by authorizing warrantless wiretapping of Americans; the use of secret CIA prisons overseas and the Guantanamo prison in Cuba to circumvent American legal rights and protections of the Geneva Conventions for detainees; the elimination of habeas corpus for prisoners accused of terrorism to challenge their incarceration; the creation of kangaroo military commissions to replace constitutionally guaranteed civilian trials; and the illegal torture of some prisoners.

In most presidential administrations, the expansion of executive power is a byproduct of attempting to achieve the president's policy agenda. In the Bush administration, as author Charlie Savage noted, that expansion seemed to be central objective in itself:

> The unfolding crisis that began with the terrorist attacks of September 11, 2001, provided an enormous opportunity to expand presidential power. As national security concerns rushed to the fore, the Bush-Cheney legal team aggressively seized the opening. A former senior member of the administration legal team who did not want to be identified by name recalled a pervasive post-9/11 sense of masculine bravado and one-upmanship when it came to executive power. A "closed group of like-minded people" were almost in competition with one another, he said, to see who could offer the farthest-reaching claims of what a president could do. In contrast, those government lawyers who were perceived as less passionate about presidential power were derided as "soft" and were often simply cut out of the process.[4]

Finally, members of an administration, who had implied that opponents of the Iraq invasion were unpatriotic, exposed the identity of a CIA covert operative, who was the wife of a war critic. Such exposure can often be dangerous for those operatives. Although not the original leaker of the operative's identity, Lewis "Scooter" Libby, the vice presidential chief of staff, was convicted of perjury and obstruction of justice in the matter. Bush seemed to believe Libby was covering up Cheney's role in the affair; Bush commuted Libby's sentence, so that he never had to spend any time in jail, but refused to pardon him.[5]

So again like Reagan, Bush may have been a conservative, but he was not for small government—either at home or abroad. In fact, despite the fact that Bush was a Republican and thus mouthed the obligatory rhetoric of small government, his policies were very similar to his successor, Barack Obama, who was unabashedly a progressive Democrat. Bush and Obama both undertook huge tax cuts while also carrying out "stimulus" efforts aimed at reviving a stalled economy, which were really just handouts for special interests; bailed out or socialized major companies that were failing (financial and auto industries); advanced federal tentacles further into education; expanded government involvement in the healthcare system; subsidized nonviable renewable energy and increased standards for vehicle fuel economy; spent like drunken sailors on domestic programs; and undermined civil liberties by unconstitutionally conducting warrantless surveillance on Americans, restricting habeas corpus for prisoners without an invasion or insurrection to justify it, using military commissions to restrict defendants' rights, and keeping Guantanamo prison open. Bush and Obama had roughly similar policies toward Iran and North Korea. Probably most important, Bush and Obama both started or escalated needless wars.[6]

The Invasion of Iraq

Bush's unnecessary and ill-fated invasion of Iraq was one of the most serious foreign policy debacles in American history. The invasion and occupation not only ended in a long-term quagmire fighting guerrillas, but so weakened the unpopular Bush in his second term that he was unable to push through Congress what could have been laudable policy initiatives. These proposals were, for example, tax reform and overhaul of the broken immigration and Social Security systems—for the second, a guest worker and amnesty program for illegal immigrants, and for the last, a long-overdue partial privatization proposal. Bush's Secretary of State Colin Powell, Republican House Majority Leader Dick Armey, and Brent Scowcroft, his father's national security advisor, had warned him beforehand that an invasion and occupation of Iraq would suck all the oxygen out of his presidency, would distract from the war on terrorism after 9/11, would make the United States responsible for the future of a shattered country in a deepening bog, would potentially destabilize the entire Mideast region, would prove unpopular globally, and likely would be very costly. Those officials proved to be right on all counts and then some.

Taking Advantage of the 9/11 Attacks

As did his successor Barack Obama—who took advantage of an unrelated economic crisis to justify further federal government intrusion into healthcare—Bush took advantage of post–9/11 public fear and desire for martial revenge to conduct an unrelated invasion of Saddam Hussein's Iraq, which had nothing to do with the September 11 terrorist attacks or the harboring of the attackers (as did Afghanistan). So instead of following his campaign pledge of pursuing a more humble foreign policy, avoiding nation-building, and eschewing overextension abroad[7] (probably just adopted to be different than Bill Clinton's foreign policy, which was heavy on ostensible humanitarian interventions), Bush went wild and used 9/11 as an excuse to invade and conduct nation-building occupations in two Muslim countries. The invasions and occupations of Afghanistan and Iraq increased retaliatory terrorism worldwide and turned into long-term mires that severely overextended the American military and the US budget. Bush's military excursion into Iraq, an unrelated non-Muslim US attack on a Muslim land, actually helped Osama bin Laden by fueling bin Laden's narrative of combatting US aggression in the Middle East and thus generating more funds and fighting recruits for al Qaeda worldwide.

After 9/11, scarce administration attention, intelligence, and defense assets, including specialized troops, were diverted to the invasion of Iraq from capturing or killing bin Laden (he escaped) and neutralizing al Qaeda in Afghanistan.

In reality, though, the 9/11 attacks may have interrupted Bush's plan to settle an old family score with Saddam Hussein. On January 30, 2001, at the first meeting of the National Security Council after Bush took office, the president instructed Secretary of Defense Donald Rumsfeld to review existing military options against Iraq. By the end of July 2001, still before the 9/11 attacks, Rumsfeld was floating the idea of toppling Saddam Hussein. As then National Security Advisor Condoleezza Rice admitted, "Almost from the very beginning, Iraq was a preoccupation of the national security team."

Bush's first secretary of the treasury, Paul O'Neill, similarly disclosed that the administration was determined prior to 9/11 to depose Saddam, and the first major strategic document of the Bush administration claimed the administration's right to engage in preventive war whether the international community approved or not (it does not, because war to prevent amorphous future threats is often abused).[8] O'Neill told the news program *60 Minutes* in 2004, "From the very beginning [of the Bush administration, starting in January 2001], there was a conviction that Saddam Hussein is a bad person and that he needed to go. It was all about finding a way to do it. That was the tone of it. The president saying, 'Go find me a way to do this.'"[9]

On 9/11, at a meeting at the Pentagon only five hours after the hijacked aircraft had hit the building, Rumsfeld brought up attacking Saddam Hussein as well as bin Laden, even though no evidence of Saddam's involvement in the attack existed. On 9/12, Rumsfeld brought up the idea of also attacking Iraq in war cabinet meetings. Also that day, Bush had his famous discussion with Richard Clarke, his counterterrorism adviser, who had insisted that al Qaeda alone was to blame for the attacks, but Bush nevertheless demanded that Clarke "look into Iraq, Saddam."[10]

A few days after 9/11, Rumsfeld and his deputy, Paul Wolfowitz, began making the astounding case for taking out Saddam in Iraq, merely because Iraq had more targets to attack than did the more primitive Afghanistan! And about two weeks after 9/11, Bush instructed Rumsfeld to secretly develop, outside normal government channels, a plan to invade Iraq. Vice President Dick Cheney told Kenneth Adelman, Bush's arms control chief, that the decision to invade Iraq was taken right after 9/11.[11]

Bush administration officials, including Bush himself, deceptively tried to link Saddam to al Qaeda, the 9/11 attackers, and Osama bin Laden. When that preposterous notion began to fall apart—Saddam and bin Laden had disparate worldviews and goals—they began claiming that Saddam had weapons of mass destruction (WMD) and might give them to such terrorists. Vice President Dick Cheney was the most prominent voice arguing that Saddam most assuredly had WMD and would soon get nuclear weapons, but even the more reluctant Secretary of State Powell told the United Nations that "solid intelligence" indicated that Saddam had biological and chemical weapons and was determined to get nuclear weapons.[12] Yet Powell did this knowing that the intelligence was weak. He should have instead resigned, because he had thought invading Iraq was a bad idea. He was right.

After the invasion found no WMD in Iraq and after Bush's chief counter-terrorism adviser, Richard Clarke, went public with Bush's and Cheney's pressure to find a nonexistent link between al Qaeda, the 9/11 attacks, and Saddam, Bush only then fell back on the justification that the invasion would bring democracy to Iraq and foster its adoption throughout the Middle East. Even the allied British government in July 2002, almost a year before the invasion, concluded that Bush had decided to invade but that the case for such action was thin and that the intelligence was being fixed around the policy.

However, contrary to popular belief, Bush did not invent the concept of "preemptive war"; in fact, he did not even practice it. Preemptive war is attacking an enemy when the adversary's attack is imminent. Even those who believed Saddam had WMD did not think an attack by him on the United States was imminent.

Before the invasion, in late December of 2002, as US forces were flooding into the Persian Gulf region, even Bush himself was underwhelmed by the CIA's evidence as to whether Saddam possessed banned WMD; it did not stop him from invading anyway. Shortly before Bush invaded, the UN weapons inspectors said they found no evidence that Iraq had any WMD or had continued or resumed programs to obtain them. Also just prior to the invasion, the International Atomic Energy Agency (IAEA) inspectors had found no evidence that Iraq was "reconstituting its nuclear program."[13] Furthermore, the CIA made public a key assessment that undermined the entire basis for the administration's invasion, but it was only a two-day speed bump on the road to war. When asked by Carl Levin, the top Democrat on the Senate Armed Services Committee, whether Saddam was likely to attack American interests with his presumed chemical or biological weapons, CIA Deputy Director John McLaughlin replied that that was likely to happen only if the United States attacked Iraq first.[14] Furthermore, the US intelligence community's National Intelligence Estimate expressed "low confidence" that Saddam would share WMD with al Qaeda and that any far-fetched probability of such sharing would require him to be under attack and desperate.[15]

Even worse for the administration publicly was that despite the claims of Vice President Cheney that "there is no doubt that Saddam Hussein now has weapons of mass destruction" and "we now know that Saddam has resumed his efforts to acquire nuclear weapons,"[16] no WMD or programs to acquire them were ever found. Then National Security Advisor Condoleezza Rice had implicitly warned of imminent attacks by Iraq with nuclear weapons, saying that the United States might experience a "mushroom cloud" if it did not act against Saddam quickly.[17] In fact, Saddam had given up such weapons programs after international inspectors destroyed his WMD in the early 1990s subsequent to his defeat in the first Gulf War. Yet, US intelligence agencies—not having had anyone inspecting Saddam's WMD programs since UN inspectors had to withdraw late in 1998 in advance of Bill Clinton's bombing attacks on Iraq—just assumed, erroneously as it turned out, that Saddam had continued his WMD programs. To attempt to avert Bush's impending invasion, Saddam had let UN weapons inspectors back into Iraq, but Bush made clear to his invasion sidekick British Prime Minister Tony Blair, in late January 2003, that he was going forward with the invasion no matter what the inspectors found. As noted earlier, however, those international agencies, which inspected Iraq in late 2002 and early 2003, just before the March 2003 US invasion, had reported that no Iraqi WMD programs existed.

Of the "axis of evil" countries, a faux alliance that the Bush administration dreamed up out of thin air to justify his militaristic policies, it was public knowledge that North Korea and Iran were both ahead of Iraq in building nuclear weapons and the missiles to carry them. Instead, Bush decided to deal with North Korea, which probably already had nuclear weapons, gingerly through negotiations, whereas Iraq, which no one thought yet had nuclear weapons, got no respect at all. The administration did not seem to focus on or care what unintended message it was sending to nuclear aspirants like Iran— get nuclear weapons and get them fast.[18]

So rather than a preemptive war to counter a demonstrably imminent attack from an opponent, Bush was fighting a "preventive war," which is frowned on by the international community, because countries can dream up the excuse of preventing this or that vague alleged future threat to justify any invasion or attack. That Bush was doing exactly such threat inflation limited the number of nations that were prepared to help him invade another country for no good reason in violation of international law—thus preventing him from duplicating his father's grand coalition against Saddam in the first Gulf War. And George W. Bush was not even the first president in American history to use the preventive war doctrine—for example, it can be argued that Ronald Reagan did so when he attacked Libya and Grenada in the 1980s and George H. W. Bush also did so when he attacked Panama in 1989.

Why Did Bush Really Invade Iraq?

If most of the major justifications for the ill-advised invasion were debunked, what was the real reason Bush was so eager to take out Saddam Hussein? We may never know for sure. Paul Wolfowitz, the deputy secretary of defense and architect of the war, famously said that the only justification for invading Iraq that everyone could agree on was WMD.[19] This statement implied that the Bush administration wanted to remove Saddam from power and was just looking for any reason to do it. Wolfowitz also seemed to indicate that US military bases in Saudi Arabia, site of some of Islam's holiest sites, were ginning up retaliatory terrorism from bin Laden and other Sunni Islamists and that US bases would be safer in a "liberated" Iraq. Yet Wolfowitz never explained why they would be safer, given that Iraq is home to holy sites of Shi'i Islam.

As for George W. Bush and Cheney, many speculated that the criticism George H. W. Bush and his then Secretary of Defense Cheney had taken among conservatives and others for not removing Saddam during the first Gulf War influenced the decision to undertake the second Gulf War. George W. Bush had always been trying to live up to his famous father's expectations and accomplishments, with some speculating that he wanted to do his father one better in Iraq. Furthermore, after the first Gulf War, George H. W. Bush, his wife Barbara Bush, and George W.'s wife Laura went to Kuwait to take a victory lap; there a sketchy assassination attempt on the former president, supposedly linked to Saddam, was broken up. Even W's closest friends wondered if his motivation to invade Iraq came from an unfinished family vendetta against Saddam.

Negative Consequences of the Iraqi Invasion

Compounding Bush's difficulties from exposure of his deceptive justifications for a war of choice was the abysmal outcome of the campaign. The initial invasion against Saddam's regular forces went swimmingly, because Bush's father had destroyed two-thirds of Saddam's army during the first Gulf War— so even before the junior Bush's invasion, the dictator was little threat to his neighbors. However, Saddam's nasty surprise for Bush the Younger was that he had handed out guns from his sizeable stockpiles to the population to conduct guerrilla warfare against the non-Muslim foreign occupiers.

Since the non-Muslim occupation of Islamic land is a red flag to most Muslims, the resistance became quite spirited and radicalized. Al Qaeda in Iraq— thought to be excessively brutal at the time but which since has morphed into the even more vicious Islamic State of Iraq and Syria (ISIS)—was born to fight against the non-Muslim occupiers and eventually caused a sectarian war in Iraq between the Sunnis and Shia. Bush, ignoring history, was skeptical before the invasion that any ethno-sectarian conflict between groups in Iraq would arise. In fact, during March and April 2004, Bush helped ignite the civil war in Iraq, according to Lt. General Ricardo Sanchez, by making the major strategic error of overruling a Marine commander on the ground, who wanted to avoid alienating the population of Falluja with an all-out assault on the town in retaliation for the killing of four Blackwater private security contractors there. Losing sight of the primary lesson of counterinsurgency war from Vietnam concerning the dangers of alienating the population with the use of excessive firepower, Bush, Cheney, Secretary of Defense Rumsfeld, and John Abizaid, the chief general of the US Central Command, all wanted to "kick ass" to be resolute in the face of the killings.

The overwhelming use of force in Falluja, which killed six hundred civilians, not only alienated the Sunnis but threatened to bring down the Iraqi government—so Bush then aborted the attack. Unbelievably, even after this debacle, in November 2004, right after the American election, Bush resumed the all-out assault on Falluja. Almost the entire population of the city had to flee, the top Sunni political party withdrew from the Iraqi government, and

Sunni leaders encouraged a Sunni boycott of the national elections scheduled for January 2005, which was carried out.

Many US commanders also adopted harsh techniques of collective punishment against Iraqi civilians to isolate or get information on insurgent fighters. US forces surrounded entire towns with dirt walls and barbed wire and then cut off food, water, and electricity for extended periods of time to turn civilians against the insurgents. Such over-the-top methods usually have the opposite effect. Jean Ziegler, the UN's special rapporteur on the right to food, charged that the coalition was "using hunger and deprivation of water as a weapon of war against the civilian population" in a "flagrant violation of international humanitarian law." Furthermore, as in Vietnam, US forces blew up houses and destroyed crops to punish civilians for "allowing" their property to be used to fire on American soldiers. One British officer criticized the general American tendency to use excessive and disproportionate firepower in crowded residential areas.[20] These "bull-in-the-china-shop" methods certainly did not win the hearts and minds of the Sunni population and thus fueled the insurgency. This counterproductive outcome occurred, despite concomitant US aid and reconstruction efforts, because a foreign occupier rarely gets the benefit of the doubt with the local population.

However, US military occupiers eventually were able to take advantage al Qaeda's excessive brutality to pay off Sunni tribes to turn from fighting the United States to fighting the terrorists, who were also led by foreigners. The Bush administration was able to mask this smart, but embarrassing, payoff by claiming that the turnaround was achieved by a troop "surge"—even though the augmented number of American forces in Iraq was no more than had been there some years earlier when violence was rampant. When Sunni violence decreased, Shi'i violence did too.

In an artificial country of three traditionally feuding groups—the Sunnis, the Shia, and the Kurds—which could probably only be held together by the brute force of a dictator, overthrowing that strongman was foolish because the likely result would be chaos. And that's what Bush got, being oblivious to the country's culture and history. The situation was exacerbated by the United States removing tens of thousands of Baath party members from the Iraqi government and disbanding the Iraqi police and army—which rendered many Sunnis with training in arms out of work, angry about it, and willing to join a growing anti-American insurgency. The well-publicized abuse by the foreign occupier of Iraqi prisoners at Abu Ghraib prison and other detention facilities also fueled the rebellion.

Republicans revel in the fact that Bush finally reduced the violence temporarily, after five years of occupation, until Obama later was able to implement Bush's three-year withdrawal plan for US forces. Despite the deep fissures in Iraqi society that were and still are the underlying cause of the violence, Republicans criticized Obama for not negotiating that a small US force be left in Iraq, even though Bush and his generals could not negotiate one in the original withdrawal plan. By then, the Iraqis were simply sick of US occupation.

Of course, Republican arguments are self-serving, because claiming that a small residual US force training the Iraqi military would have continued to ensure long-term stability in a society with deep cleavages (it has not in Afghanistan after the US de-escalation there) puts the blame on Obama instead of Bush for destabilizing Iraq and the entire region with his initial invasion. Furthermore, it took Bush more than four years to learn the primary lesson of Vietnam and institute a counterinsurgency (COIN) strategy that concentrated on the difficult objective of winning the hearts and minds of the Iraqi population, rather than on blasting US enemies to smithereens. Although the COIN strategy was better than his former "bull-in-the-china-shop" strategy and was slightly more likely to have had success, the reduction of violence was always likely to be temporary in a society scarred by such deep ethnosectarian divides.

Furthermore, journalist Matthew Carr mentions other factors that led to the reduction of violence in Iraq besides a more benevolent COIN strategy: the bribing of Sunni tribes to "turn" them from fighting the United States to fighting al Qaeda; the brutal tactics used by al Qaeda that killed many civilians; and the division of Iraq by violence into Sunni and Shi'i ghettos, thus reducing the propensity for further ethnic cleansing by force.[21]

Similarly, Brigadier General Daniel Bolger, who served in both Afghanistan and Iraq, argues that COIN tactics were used in each theater at one time or another but came up short. Bolger reaches essentially the same conclusion as this author in his book, *The Failure of Counterinsurgency: Why Hearts and Minds Are Seldom Won*: even COIN tactics very seldom work; the guerrillas will often just outwait the occupier. Bolger concludes that for such tactics to be successful, the foreign occupier must remain virtually forever; the American public is usually unwilling to commit its military to such an indefinite stay.

In Iraq, Bolger implies that the Sunni Awakening—turning the Sunni tribes from enemies to friends by slathering them with money, guns, public works projects, and promises of government jobs to get them to fight al Qaeda —had more of an effect than the US troop surge. This policy did not win the Iraq war but did give the United States a face-saving way to leave under its own terms. In Afghanistan, the Iraq surge was imitated but had less effect than in Iraq. Bolger correctly concludes, much as the policymakers did after the equally disastrous Vietnam War, that the US military is best at fighting short conventional wars and should thus avoid fighting guerrillas in the future. Bolger also cogently faults the generals for not telling the politicians to simply get out of Afghanistan and Iraq.[22]

Yet Bush's quagmires in Afghanistan and Iraq, especially coming after the US fiasco in Vietnam in the 1960s and 1970s, may have taught potential adversaries that the only way to win against a powerful superpower is to turn any conflict into a drawn-out guerrilla war. Thus, any future US military interventions on the ground may bring forth guerrilla insurgents, which should make US civilian and military leaders leery of conducting such interventions unless American vital interests are at stake. Unfortunately, as time passed, this warning was forgotten after the dismal failure in Vietnam, thereby leading to Bush's quagmires in Afghanistan and Iraq. It is now already being forgotten again, as the United States again reinserts ground forces into Iraq (and also inserts them into Syria) to fight the Islamic State of Iraq and Syria (ISIS).

Bush is even ultimately responsible for the creation and expansion of ISIS, which overran the Sunni areas of Iraq during the subsequent Obama administration. Bush's original invasion led to creation of the al Qaeda in Iraq, ISIS's precursor group, which fought the US occupation. Also, later support for ISIS in Sunni areas of Iraq arose from the persecution of Sunnis by the US-backed sectarian government of Shi'i Prime Minister Nouri al-Maliki, whom Sunnis regarded as more dangerous than even the brutal ISIS. In late 2007, Maliki's foes were plotting to push him out of office, but Bush sent Secretary of State Condoleezza Rice to meddle in the affairs of an ostensible democracy by telling them they would lose American support if they threw out Maliki. Thus, Bush intervened to keep the man in power whose anti-Sunni policies would later spur the expansion of ISIS in retaliation.

Bush's invasion of Iraq eventually got about 4,800 coalition military soldiers killed (of which almost 4,500 were US military personnel) and hundreds of thousands to a million Iraqis (depending on the estimate).[23] However, the instability and continuing civil war unleashed by the US invasion may yet kill many more Iraqis. In addition, after its initial invasion, US forces' refusal to provide the security required by international law resulted in the massive looting of businesses and educational, medical, and cultural institutions, including Iraq's national cultural treasures.

Wider effects of the misadventure in Iraq were felt in the rise of Islamist terrorism worldwide in response to yet another non-Muslim occupation of Islamic soil and in the enhanced power of Iran, America's principal foe in the Middle East, as a result of the elimination of its major regional adversary—an Iraq run by Sunni dictator Saddam Hussein. Now the Iraqi government is run by the Shia, who are clients of Iran. In the wake of the US-trained Iraqi army turning tail and running in the face of the ISIS invasion of Iraq, Baghdad and much of the remainder of Iraq are defended primarily by Iranian-allied and trained Shi'i militias. A smart foreign policy does not start a war that ultimately helps a principal adversary.

As important, Bush's invasion of Iraq also shifted US government attention and effort from the critical need to decimate the main al Qaeda group and capture or kill its leadership. Vital military tools in the war against al Qaeda—for example, special forces and scarce intelligence assets, such as the then limited number of drones—were diverted from Afghanistan and Pakistan to Iraq. And while Bush was distracted by the urgent need to surge troops to get the rampant violence in Iraq under control, the US occupation of Afghanistan began to spin out of control and into a bog. The military made a request for a similar troop surge there, which Bush dumped on his successor.

Because of the diversion of attention and resources to the invasion and occupation of Iraq, Osama bin Laden was not killed until 2011—about ten years after 9/11 and well into the Obama administration. After 9/11, invading Iraq would have been like the United States invading Argentina after the Japanese attack on Pearl Harbor. When a country or group is attacking the United States, that entity should be the intense focus of US security efforts, which should not be hijacked into military misadventures elsewhere.

As of 2015, the 2,300 American deaths in Afghanistan should be added to the more than 4,475 killed in Iraq. The total dead in both conflicts, about 6,800 American lives, is more than twice the number of their almost 3,000 fellow countrymen and women killed on 9/11. The horrible costs of Bush's two military misadventures should also include the far greater number of Afghans and Iraqis killed and the $4 trillion to $6 trillion spent on both wars to date, perhaps as much as almost one-third of the US national debt.

The War on Terror

After the 9/11 attacks, Bush seemed to be warring against everyone but those who had perpetrated the crime. As an indication of the broad war to come, shortly after the attacks, Bush said that his global war on terror "begins with al Qaeda, but it does not end there. It will not end until every terrorist group of global reach has been found, stopped, and defeated."[24] Instead of countering the main al Qaeda group using intelligence, law enforcement, and, if need be, armed action in the shadows using special forces and CIA covert operations, Bush chose to wage the very broad and public cowboy war on terror. He failed to distinguish between groups that focused their attacks on the United States and those that did not, and, as previously noted, even extended the war to countries like Iraq that had nothing to do with 9/11.

A Counterproductive War on Terror

Bush used air attacks on Islamist militants opposing the Pakistani government, thus creating the Pakistani Taliban. The group then attempted to bomb Times Square in New York City. In Yemen, after US airstrikes had already begun, and after a prison break in 2006, al Qaeda's affiliate in the Arabian Peninsula (AQAP) was born. After the demise of the main al Qaeda group in

Afghanistan and Pakistan, AQAP has been considered al Qaeda's most potent regional affiliate. The group then has repeatedly tried to bomb US-bound aircraft, including the attempted underwear bombing.

In Somalia, to counter the Islamic Courts movement, Bush politically and militarily supported an Ethiopian invasion of that country in 2006. Regarded by Somalis as a Christian invasion of a Muslim country, the brutal Ethiopians shot, raped, and tortured Somali civilians and burnt villages.[25] Such atrocities led to the rise of the much more radical al Shabab movement, which took over much of Somalia. The United States then sponsored a Kenyan and Ugandan invasion of Somalia, which has taken back much of the country, at least for the time being. Al Shabab has retaliated with terrorist attacks in these countries and may have the potential to attack in the United States, taking advantage of Somali-Americans returning from the fighting to the Somali community in Minneapolis.

Thus, during the war on terror, terrorism increased worldwide. What's more, Congress never approved attacking anybody but the perpetrators and enablers of the 9/11 attacks—that is, the main al Qaeda group and the Afghan Taliban—so going after these other groups was not only counterproductive but illegal and unconstitutional as well.

Also, because his attention had turned immediately to invading Iraq, Bush turned post–9/11 retaliation on Afghanistan into an ineffectual nation-building occupation that became a drawn-out mire, which then destabilized the country and neighboring Pakistan, a nuclear-weapons state. Initially, Bush only temporarily expelled the Afghan Taliban into Pakistan and failed to crush al Qaeda. According to one US military consultant, "From January 2002 on, we were in the process of snatching defeat from the jaws of victory."[26] Rand Beers, Richard Clarke's successor as Bush's counterterrorism adviser in 2002, quit in disgust and told Clarke that because of the shift toward invading Iraq the United States allowed bin Laden to get away and that the token US occupation force left in Afghanistan allowed the Afghan Taliban to regroup. (The reality was that the US force was enough to be a lightning rod as a "foreign occupier" for the Taliban to use as a recruiting device for a resurgence but too small to be effective in stanching that renaissance.) In 2002, the Pentagon did a study on the initial war in Afghanistan and found that it failed to convert the battlefield triumph into a strategic victory and that it had only been minimally successful in its primary goal of ensuring that al Qaeda could no longer operate in Afghanistan.[27]

Bush foolishly decided on such a long-term occupation in Afghanistan despite three unsuccessful British attempts to subdue Afghanistan in the 1800s and early 1900s and a more recent Soviet failure to do the same in the 1980s, leading the uneasy Condoleezza Rice to say that Afghanistan was "the place where great powers go to die."[28] Such non-Muslim occupation of an Islamic country eventually fueled the resurgence of the Afghan Taliban. The Afghan Taliban, the American enemy, has had a safe haven on the territory of Pakistan, because the Pakistani military, ostensibly a US ally, has played the double game of allowing such a sanctuary, has likely supported the Taliban, and perhaps even hid Osama bin Laden. The Pakistanis have wanted to keep the US client government in Afghanistan, which has been friendly to Pakistan's archrival India, weak, and have desired influence with any post-US Afghan government, whether or not fully controlled by the Afghan Taliban.

The nation-building occupation of Afghanistan and the subsequent attacks on Muslim Pakistan, Yemen, Somalia, and Iraq led Osama bin Laden to gleefully declare publicly that George W. Bush was easy to bait. Bin Laden knew that the rash actions of a superpower would allow him to recruit more radical Islamist fighters and gather more monetary contributions. Also, bin Laden had seen how Ronald Reagan had retreated from Lebanon in early 1984 after the United States had taken casualties from a bombing against the US Marine barracks. Bin Laden thus wanted to lure non-Islamic great powers into quagmires and then expel them for good from Islamic nations. He helped use this method in compelling the Soviet exit from Afghanistan in 1989 and the US withdrawal from Somalia in 1994 in the wake of only a small number of US military casualties. Bin Laden had otherwise tried unsuccessfully to bait Bill Clinton, Bush's predecessor, into such a counterproductive overreaction with attacks on US embassies in Kenya and Tanzania in 1998 and on the USS *Cole* docked in Yemen in 2000. After Bush took office, bin Laden augmented the bait with the 9/11 attacks, and Bush not only took it and conducted an invasion and occupation of Afghanistan, but swallowed it whole by also invading Muslim Iraq.[29] Bush then went even further still by launching drone attacks on Muslim Yemen, Somalia, and Pakistan too.

In contrast to Bush's allegation that the terrorists of al Qaeda "hate our freedoms," bin Laden was very clear that he was attacking the United States because of its policies in the Middle East, especially US troops remaining in Saudi Arabia, his homeland and that of the holiest shrines in the Islamic religion. Non-Muslim forces in Islamic countries regularly rile up Islamist jihadists and even moderate Muslims. The 9/11 attacks were the bait to lure the United States into a bog in a Muslim country and then expel it permanently from the Islamic world. Bin Laden would then later restore the Islamic caliphate or empire that was last seen before the demise of the Ottoman Empire after the end of World War I. Contrary to the hysterical implication of some American hawks, however, bin Laden's pie-in-the-sky objective was only regional, not global, conquest.

And when Bush had turned his attention to preparing for an invasion of Iraq, he bungled a chance to snare bin Laden, who was able to buy his way across the border into Pakistan when Bush relied on Afghan militias to capture him during the initial US attack on Afghanistan after 9/11. At that time, US Marines had landed in Afghanistan, and the Marine commander believed he could rush them to the mountainous Tora Bora region near Pakistan to seal avenues of bin Laden's escape through the mountain passes. The head of CIA operations begged Bush to allow the marines to be so deployed and warned that the United States would lose bin Laden if this action were not taken. However, Bush deferred to Army General Tommy Franks, who, along with Secretary of Defense Rumsfeld, had a political agenda of keeping as few US ground forces in Afghanistan as possible. Because of that economy of effort, Franks decided instead to rely on the Afghans, who pocketed bags of US cash and then let bin Laden escape.[30] This lackadaisical attitude toward snaring bin Laden is striking and may indicate that the Bush administration already had its focus on Iraq. Bin Laden would not be killed for another ten years—during the Obama administration.

"Keeping Us Safe"

Bush and other Republicans took credit for the fact that no 9/11-like terrorist attacks occurred after the catastrophic attack on September 11, 2001. Yet, no other terrorist attack by a small group has ever come close to the casualties inflicted on 9/11, and North America has always had low numbers of terrorist attacks—both before and after 9/11. The United States is far away from the overseas conflicts that spawn terrorism, and extended logistics matters, even for small terrorist groups. In addition, unlike Europe, the United States does not have radicalized Islamist populations to shelter and support such terrorist networks. So statistically, the 9/11 attack should be regarded as an outlier.

Finally, even if the Bush administration had done nothing after 9/11 to beef up American homeland security, air travel would have been much safer on 9/12 and beyond than on 9/11. The prior paradigm was that the crew and passengers on hijacked aircraft should cooperate with the hijackers; the plane would probably end up in Cuba or some other unanticipated destination and the hostages would be released when the hijackers had made their point and got publicity for their cause. After 9/11, crew and passengers, noting that when planes crash into buildings no one survives, became very surly against hijackers; the attempted post–9/11 underwear and shoe bombings of aircraft illustrate this point when the crew or passengers subdued the would-be murderers.

In the post–9/11 world, congratulating Bush for the absence of a rare phenomenon ignores the fact that the most catastrophic terrorist attack by a small group happened on his watch and was probably preventable, according to the bipartisan 9/11 Commission, which investigated the attacks and the Bush administration's response. Richard Clarke, Bush's former top counter-terrorism adviser who had also worked for Bill Clinton, in testifying before the commission, had accused the Bush administration of not taking the threat of terrorism seriously enough prior to 9/11.

All the information needed to discover the September 11 plot and take action to prevent the attacks was in the US intelligence system, but was not recognized or acted upon. George Tenet, Bush's CIA director, rushed to the White House in July 2001, two months before 9/11, with warnings of an imminent "spectacular" terrorist attack and later said that for months before that dark day, the US intelligence system had been "blinking red" about the danger of such an attack. Yet the approval of a long-proposed plan to go after al Qaeda still was not accelerated and thus was too late. In early August 2001, Bush received an intelligence memo titled "Bin Laden determined to strike in US." Even Bush himself later admitted, "I didn't feel that sense of urgency."[31] At minimum, Bush should have ordered intensified intelligence scrutiny of bin Laden and al Qaeda.

In sum, in the almost eight months from Bush's inauguration to the 9/11 attacks, Bush, putting a low priority on pleas from his chief counterterrorism adviser, paid little attention to the rising threat from al Qaeda despite warnings from outgoing Clinton administration officials—instead focusing on the threat of Saddam Hussein and on building a missile defense. However, it was al Qaeda that struck on 9/11, not Saddam, and the group did not use missiles to attack the Pentagon and World Trade Center.

"Reform" of the Intelligence Community

The failure to detect and prevent the 9/11 attacks led to demands to "do something" about the government's poor performance, thereby leading to efforts to reform the intelligence and security services. Of course, in Washington, that meant rearranging boxes on a government organization chart and adding more bureaucracy. The sixteen intelligence agencies in various departments of the federal government were brought under a new office—the Director of National Intelligence (DNI). Existing departments, however, retained budget authority over their intelligence agencies, thus significantly restricting the power of the new DNI bureaucracy. Similarly, twenty-two disparate law enforcement and other miscellaneous agencies were permanently transferred and put under a new Department of Homeland Security (DHS) bureaucracy. Taken together, this was the largest reorganization of the federal bureaucracy since the National Security Act of 1947 at the dawn of the Cold War, which created the Central Intelligence Agency (CIA) and similarly combined the military services under the newly created Department of Defense (DoD) bureaucracy.

Few people in the Bush administration or Congress stopped to ask whether creating new layers of bureaucracy in the intelligence and security worlds was the right way to fight small, nimble terrorist groups. The original governmental response problem on 9/11 was a failure to communicate and cooperate between the CIA and the Federal Bureau of Investigation (FBI); yet the FBI was not affected by the reorganizations and remained in the Department of Justice. Furthermore, the opposite solution to creating new bureaucracies would have made the government more agile—that is, eliminating some intelligence and security agencies, thus reducing bureaucratic coordination problems and improving government responsiveness to terrorist threats.

The Bush administration argued that the reorganizations helped prevent another catastrophic terrorist attack after 9/11, but that cannot be proven since terrorism was a rare phenomenon both before and after 9/11 and because after those attacks, airline travel was much safer anyway because crews and passengers became much more aggressive, thus preventing some terrorism and perhaps deterring other attempts. Furthermore, significant post-"reform" intelligence and security failures continue to occur. For example, the reformed intelligence community failed to predict the rapid takeover of large parts of Iraq by the Islamic State of Iraq and Syria (ISIS) during the Obama administration. Also, within DHS, the Secret Service has had security and sex scandals and the bungling Transportation Security Administration (TSA) has had a poor track record of stopping contraband at airports—tests showed that 96 percent of banned items got through. In short, TSA has become the butt of many jokes by late-night comedians and the public at airports around the country. The DHS and the Secret Service have not fared much better.

Despite their abysmal performance on 9/11, the military services had too much political clout to be "reformed" significantly. By 2001, the US military had long lost sight of its major constitutional responsibility: providing for the common defense of US territory and citizens. Many decades before, it had begun being used almost exclusively as an offensive force to intimidate, attack, and invade other countries—a "power projection" force, to use the Pentagon's euphemism. The macho military culture sees playing defense as wimpy, and instead has acquired a "cult of the offensive." Under George W. Bush's post–9/11 declaration that "offense is the best defense," the military went even more in the wrong direction. If that slogan has some merit, it is only under certain situations against conventional enemies. However, fighting a very public offensive war on terrorism has been a disaster under both George W. Bush and Barack Obama, because terrorists are energized and get more followers and funds in reaction to non-Muslim attacks on or invasions of Muslim countries.

And on 9/11, the military did a lousy job of what should have been job one—defending the country—but that role was considered an uninterest-ing mission left largely to the National Guard. On 9/11, only after the third hijacked aircraft had crashed into the military's headquarters at the Penta-gon—about an hour after the first aircraft hit the World Trade Center—did the Department of Defense get around to scrambling fighters to defend New York and Washington from further attack. And subsequently, even after Bush had ordered that any other wayward civilian aircraft be blown out of the sky, caution, communication difficulties, and an imperfect understanding of the circumstances had delayed engagement orders until the fourth hijacked plane had crashed into a field in Pennsylvania.[32]

The Expansion of Executive Power

Although airport security has long violated the text of the Fourth Amend-ment to the Constitution—because the government does not have probable cause to believe that all air travelers are terrorists—and Bush made the viola-tion worse by creating the TSA, such action was the least of his many abuses of civil liberties.

Bush's powerful vice president, Dick Cheney, believed in the Unitary Theory of the Executive, which promoted a powerful chief executive, and thought that the presidency had been unconstitutionally circumscribed dur-ing the Vietnam and Watergate era and that it should be restored to its former grandeur.[33] In reality, the presidency had been reined in somewhat by Congress, because of executive excesses during that era; this pushback turned out to be only a momentary pause, as the imperial presidency—which since Herbert Hoover, Franklin D. Roosevelt, and Harry Truman had long exceeded the limited role for the president that the founders had envisioned in the nation's Constitution—continued to enlarge its power. Yet Bush, without any prior knowledge of or experience in national policy, relied heavily on Cheney's advice during his first term.

Bush thus expanded the limits of power as commander-in-chief during a crisis that even prior imperial presidents had not claimed. The 9/11 crisis and ensuing national fear about future terrorist attacks gave Bush and Cheney an excuse to expand the role of commander-in-chief much past what the nation's founders had envisioned. To the framers of the Constitution, the president's powers as commander-in-chief were to be narrowly construed—the chief executive was to be merely the leader of troops on the battlefield. Because terrorists could, and did, attack the US homeland, Bush and Cheney felt that the president had the power to exercise such powers at home, as well as abroad; in other words, Bush believed he was not only the commander-in-chief of the military but also of the country.

In their hysteria after the 9/11 attacks, allegedly in order to prevent a second wave of strikes, Bush and Cheney decided to act—that is, vastly expand executive power—and ask permission later. David Addington, a close Cheney adviser, said the administration would "push and push and push until some larger force makes us stop."[34] For example, during the immediate post–9/11 period, in a mini version of Franklin Roosevelt's blanket internment of Japanese-Americans during World War II, Bush and Cheney rounded up about 1,000 Muslims for arrest on immigration violations.

In fact, the Bush administration, unlike other administrations that expanded executive power, had this as a specific goal, not just as a means to other policy ends.[35] Thus, this objective of a more powerful executive led to outrageous claims of presidential aggrandizement—for example, that the president could ignore congressionally passed laws in times of emergency.

The framers would not have approved of this aggregation of executive power in the republic they founded, especially when a small ragtag group such as al Qaeda, who got amazingly and heinously lucky, was unlikely to have the resources to do so again anytime soon. And the "emergency" rationale for this usurpation of power was perhaps disingenuous. As an example of the extent to which Cheney would go to enhance executive power even in the nonsecurity realm, he purposefully refused to turn over information about his energy task force to Congress, even though his executive director of the task force recommended doing so because the committee had nothing to hide.

Unconstitutional Searches

The Fourth Amendment's guarantee to individuals against unreasonable searches and seizures by the government and requirement for a judicially approved warrant for this government surveillance (thus ensuring scrutiny by a competing branch of government as a check on executive power), based on probable cause that a crime has been committed, has no exception for national security. Yet Bush violated the Foreign Intelligence and Surveillance Act of 1978 (FISA) by spying on Americans without a FISA court warrant; got their business information and any "tangible things" without judicial approval, using national security letters issued under the post–9/11 USA PATRIOT Act (Uniting and Strengthening America by Providing Appropriate Tools Required to Intercept and Obstruct Terrorism Act of 2001; a Bush-supported unconstitutional surveillance bonanza for the government); and collected data on phone calls, emails, and other Internet communications of virtually all Americans, violating the prohibition on general search warrants in the Fourth Amendment.

Even some intelligence, Justice Department, and law enforcement officials pushed back at the administration's broad violation of civil liberties. Under the warrantless surveillance program, the administration originally authorized snooping even when both parties to a communication were domestic—not just on any American who was talking to a suspected foreign terrorist overseas—until Michael Hayden, director of the National Security Agency, threatened to go to court if the administration did not limit his spying authority to the latter case. Even that limited warrantless snooping was illegal and unconstitutional.

Furthermore, when a new batch of lawyers arrived at the Justice Department to replace the "go-along" John Yoo, they were appalled at the collection of metadata on emails and other Internet communications of all Americans and wanted the program cancelled. The reaction from Vice President Cheney's office was vituperative, but several Justice Department officials, including the FBI director, threatened to resign unless the program was modified and justified under a different legal theory.[36] The phone metadata program continued without modification and was later exposed by NSA contractor Edward Snowden amid a torrent of public outcry.

Even if one or two terrorist plots were really foiled because of these violations of Americans' constitutional rights—unlikely because, as noted previously, terrorism has always been a low probability in North America, both before and after 9/11—the advent of a police state was a much greater threat to the existence of the republic than the likely small number of deaths from any such attacks.

Rendition and Torture

Because of the post–9/11 crisis, Bush continued Bill Clinton's policy of rendition of terrorism suspects to foreign countries where torture was a routine way to extract information from people. However, Bush went one better than Clinton and created the Guantanamo prison in Cuba and secret CIA prisons overseas in various friendly countries in which illegal torture was practiced on prisoners by US personnel. Bush then had his Justice Department lawyers declare these methods, which had long been nationally and internationally recognized as unlawful, to be legal. The endorsement of such harsh interrogation methods by Bush, Cheney, Rumsfeld, and others at the top of the administration also led to prisoner abuse by the US military at Abu Ghraib prison in Iraq, which merely fueled the insurgency there.

Denial of Habeas Corpus and Jury Trials

The US Constitution says that prisoners held by the government have a right to challenge their detention in front of a judge—the writ of habeas corpus requires the participation of a rival branch of government to check the executive. Only Congress can suspend this right in times of invasion and insurrection. Since 9/11 was neither and the president was not Congress, Bush's effective suspension of habeas corpus for terrorism detainees violated the US Constitution. So for years, the US government has held prisoners indefinitely without a jury trial, which violates the Constitution.

Very few of the prisoners held at Guantanamo have received an indictment by a grand jury (a Fifth Amendment requirement, with the only exception being for US military personnel during wartime) and a speedy jury trial using an impartial jury (a Sixth Amendment requirement with no national security exception). Even the detainees who have not been held indefinitely without any judicial proceeding (just a few of them) have been given only kangaroo military tribunals instead of the required speedy and impartial jury trials. Detainees given military tribunals do not have the same rights as defendants do in a jury trial. In addition, the prosecution, judge, jury, and defense all work for the president—unlike in a jury trial, in which most do not work for the executive branch. Because of the constitutional guarantees of indictment by a grand jury and a speedy and impartial jury trial, with no relevant national security exceptions, military commissions were unconstitutional when Abraham Lincoln convened them during the Civil War, when Franklin D. Roosevelt used them during World War II (even though the Supreme Court, as usual, found a way to bless them), and when George W. Bush used them in the War on Terror.

In fact, the main purpose of using Guantanamo as an offshore prison was so that Bush could escape giving terrorism prisoners either detainee rights under the US Constitution or rights under the Geneva Conventions as prisoners of war (even though Afghanistan had signed those conventions). Treatment of prisoners at Guantanamo and CIA prisons not only besmirched America as a free society but also fueled Islamist radicalism overseas.

Finally, although conservatives often accuse civil libertarians of coddling terrorists, those advocates of individual rights for people accused of any crime are protecting everyone's rights, not just those of terrorists. Everyone in a republic, including those who are accused of committing heinous crimes, deserves legal safeguards. The government can often falsely accuse someone of a crime—either because of a mistake or because of public pressure on prosecutors to make someone pay for a well-publicized atrocious illegality.

And the US government has made mistakes in the War on Terror. Of the prisoners held at Guantanamo, many were captured in Afghanistan because of rewards handed out by American forces there. Yet in a dirt-poor country such as this, a number of people just turned in their neighbors to get what was to them huge reward money. Thus, many of those held at Guantanamo were held for years, even though they were not involved in terrorism. In fact, it is widely accepted that there are still innocent prisoners at Guantanamo who have been detained for years without cause and yet have no prospect of being released anytime soon.

Civil Liberties Violations

Demonstrating how far afield Bush had gone in trampling the nation's cherished civil liberties, even Bush's conservative Attorney General John Ashcroft pushed back on administration policies involving the indefinite detention of detainees at Guantanamo without at least some legal due process; the lack of procedural rights for those tried in front of kangaroo military tribunals; the use of such a military commission, to the exclusion of a civilian court, to try at least one high-profile detainee; and renewal of the NSA domestic surveillance program.

More important, the Supreme Court and Congress started walking back some of Bush's post–9/11 erosion of civil liberties. The Supreme Court demanded that Guantanamo detainees be given at least some right to challenge their detention and that the Geneva Conventions on prisoners rights be applied to al Qaeda detainees. Responding to the court, Congress changed the legal authority for the kangaroo military commissions, but they still lacked the procedural safeguards of civilian courts. Congress ruled out torture but then gave the CIA a loophole under certain circumstances to use some aggressive techniques. Bush then tried to nullify even this conditional congressional limitation when signing the bill by reserving the right as commander-in-chief in an emergency to essentially ignore the law. Later, the Senate Intelligence Committee would say that the value of the intelligence provided by torture had been much exaggerated.

Also, Congress, after complaining vociferously about Bush's warrantless surveillance program, then enshrined it into law and widened it! In sum, Congress and the Supreme Court did not go far enough in insisting on the removal of all of these unconstitutional violations of civil liberties, which make the United States fairly unique in the world.

In fact, in the wake of pushback by Congress and the Supreme Court, Bush realized that some of his national security program—the Iraq War and civil liberties usurpation—likely would not survive into the next presidential administration if he did not trim his sails a bit and consolidate it. He had temporarily stabilized Iraq by bribing opposition fighters and belatedly using a more benign counterinsurgency strategy, so that his successor would not be pressured to withdraw forces faster than in his three-year withdrawal agreement with the Iraqi government. In the agreement, he had negotiated to effect an honorable exit while violence had been lessened. In addition, he had gotten Congress to approve his military tribunals with at least some increased rights for defendants; emptied secret CIA prisons overseas and transferred some prisoners out of Guantanamo with the hope of possibly closing it; scaled back techniques of torture; and gotten Congress to authorize the NSA's warrantless surveillance program.[37] Unfortunately, Bush was largely successful in getting Barack Obama, his successor, to adopt his slightly trimmed program. Only on torture did Obama deviate significantly from Bush's legacy.

Bush's expansion of executive power to usurp civil liberties is one of the worst things he did as president—right up there with getting many American military personnel and innocent Iraqi civilians killed needlessly in a war of choice. The former illustrates how running an aggressive foreign policy will cause the government to grow at home too.

The Relationship with Russia Deteriorates

One of only a few accomplishments Bush achieved during his presidency was a strategic nuclear arms reduction arrangement with Russia to lessen the only existential external threat in American history. Although Bush was leery of Russian leader Vladimir Putin, who had returned autocracy to Russia, he wanted to maintain a good relationship with that country because he astutely believed both nations would need to cooperate to counter a rising China. Russia and the United States each unilaterally announced a reduction of deployed offensive strategic nuclear weapons to levels of the early Cold War but could merely transfer them off deployed status and keep them in storage.

Yet Bush perhaps laid the basis for a future nuclear arms race by abrogating the 1972 Anti-Ballistic Missile (ABM) Treaty,[38] which allowed him to develop and deploy a more limited "Son of Star Wars" antimissile system. Such defenses may seem innocuous but could cause both sides to reverse course in the future, again engaging in a destabilizing buildup of offensive nuclear weapons—especially if Russia believes its smaller deployed nuclear deterrent has been eroded by effective US defenses, which the technologically inferior Russia would not likely possess. At minimum, at some point, US defenses still might cause Russia to bring its stored warheads back to deployed status.

(Barack Obama later reached a binding agreement with Russia to further reduce strategic nuclear weapons, but if future US defenses threaten the smaller Russian nuclear deterrent, Russia could still redeploy some warheads from its reserves or abrogate that binding treaty and launch a buildup of offensive strategic nuclear weapons.)

In terminating the ABM Treaty, Bush did it unilaterally without congressional approval. Although the Constitution requires two-thirds of the US Senate to approve a treaty, it does not comment on the process for terminating the same. Therefore, the only constitutional method of termination would seem to be to substitute a new treaty that nullifies the old one and obtain a two-thirds Senate vote on it.

And Bush undermined the general relationship between Russia and the United States, which has had repercussions down to the present. When Vladimir Putin replaced Boris Yeltsin as president of Russia in 1999, he was not hostile to the United States, even though Bill Clinton already had expanded the NATO alliance into the former Soviet satellite nations of Poland, Hungary, and the Czech Republic. (According to Soviet leader Mikhail Gorbachev, George H. W. Bush had promised him verbally that if the two Germanys would be allowed to reunite, NATO would not expand further east, and Bush did sign an agreement that NATO forces would not be deployed in the old East Germany.) But George W. Bush then opened the floodgates of membership in the alliance to nine more Eastern European countries, including the Baltic states right on the Russian border.

In 2008, Bush also got NATO to promise that Ukraine and Georgia would be admitted in the future. "We agreed today that these countries will become members of NATO," proclaimed the communiqué at the April 2008 NATO summit in Bucharest, Romania. Although Putin had become angry at US policy in 2003 and 2004 when revolutions in Georgia and Ukraine, respectively, installed pro-Western regimes—leading the Russian leader to believe that the United States was trying to encircle Russia—the 2008 NATO promise seemed to further validate this fear and hostility. The expansion and potential further enlargement of an alliance hostile to Russia has eventually led Putin to become nervous and surly.

The United States constantly forgets that the Russians lost twenty-five million people in the most cataclysmic combat in world history on the eastern front during World War II. Even before the German invasion of Russia during World War II, the Mongols, the Swedes, the Prussians, and Napoleon had done so before, because Russia has very few natural defense barriers. Thus, the Russians are very sensitive about maintaining a sphere of influence in Eastern Europe that acts as a security buffer. With the fall of the Warsaw Pact and Soviet Union and NATO expansion, that buffer zone has dwindled dramatically.

In August 2008, likely emboldened by the April 2008 NATO promise that Georgia would be admitted to the alliance, pro-Western Mikheil Saakashvili, the aggressive Georgian president, started a war with Russia; Russia launched a retaliatory incursion into Georgia proper, then withdrew, but it still maintains its Russophilic enclaves in that nation. This war really soured Russia's relations with the United States and the West. When a pro-Russian government in Ukraine was overthrown and replaced by a pro-Western regime in 2014 during the Obama administration, Russia, acting out of weakness, tried to salvage some of Ukraine by annexing Crimea (which houses important Russian naval facilities) and by trying to destabilize eastern Ukraine. All of these actions were a direct result of George W. Bush's prodding NATO—at the alliance's Bucharest summit—to promise Ukraine and Georgia future membership. By essentially occupying parts of Georgia and Ukraine, Russia hopes to prevent these nations' accession to NATO. Historically, Ukraine has been especially important to Russia.

NATO should have been dissolved after the Cold War—not expanded in territory and mission, which could not have but threatened a weakened Russia. Bush is not solely responsible for the deterioration of US-Russian relations since 1999, but he contributed mightily to it. After the Cold War, despite Russia's decline in population, territory, economic power, and global influence, it remains as one of only two nuclear superpowers; that alone is why the erosion of the bilateral relationship is so significant.

Miscellaneous Foreign Policies

Bush, with a reputation as a swaggering cowboy, had some surprising miscellaneous foreign policies, including better relations with Libya, China, Iran, and North Korea, but not Liberia.

- Another of the few genuine accomplishments to which Bush could lay claim during his presidency was a negotiated deal with Libya's strongman Muammar Gaddafi to give up his nuclear program, destroy chemical weapons, and compensate victims of past Libyan terror attacks. In doing so, Bush also exposed the worldwide nuclear proliferation business of Pakistani bombmaker A. Q. Kahn. According to Bush, the agreement with Gaddafi sent a message that "leaders who abandon the pursuit of chemical, biological and nuclear weapons, and the means to deliver them, will find an open path to better relations with the United States and other free nations." Unfortunately, no one told Barack Obama, who ruined this messaging by falling victim to a French scheme to later oust Gaddafi using allied air power, despite Gaddafi's playing ball with the West. Nations aspiring to get such super weapons—such as Iran—might have taken away a different message: get them as fast as possible to try to keep the United States at bay.

- In late March 2001, a couple of months after Bush took office, an American spy aircraft, operating in international waters off the coast of China, was buzzed by a Chinese jet aircraft. In the ensuing collision, the Chinese pilot died and the US plane had to make an emergency landing in China. To get the plane and crew back, the supposedly tough cowboy Bush gave what Vice President Cheney, Secretary of Defense Rumsfeld, and neoconservatives regarded as effectively an apology, even though the collision was caused by the Chinese pilot's reckless behavior.[39]

- During Bush's second term, in the wake of his invasion of Iraq, to mollify European allies that thought his hawkish administration might also attack Iran, his policy toward the latter country became very accommodating—in contrast to the initially harsher policy of his successor, progressive Democrat Barack Obama. Bush permitted the sale to Iran of spare parts for US-made civilian airliners and dropped US opposition to talks for Iran's accession to the World Trade Organization. In contrast, Obama imposed more economic sanctions, escalated them, and only later reached an agreement with Iran to suspend its nuclear program.

- Disregarding evidence that North Korea had helped Syria build a nuclear reactor and past North Korean evasion of agreements restricting its own

nuclear program, Bush signed a deal that would require the hermit kingdom to list all of its nuclear programs, dismantle nuclear facilities, and
allow the reentry of international nuclear inspectors. In return, the United
States would provide fuel for the regime; scale back attempted interdiction of that nation's export of nuclear technology; unfreeze North Korean
money earned in such proliferation, counterfeiting, and drug running;
start talks to renew diplomatic relations; and take North Korea off the list
of nations subject to the Trading with the Enemy Act and remove it from
the list of countries sponsoring terrorism. Although North Korea started
destroying less important nuclear facilities, it provided a pathetically insufficient accounting of its nuclear programs. Yet Bush still removed it
from the list of state sponsors of terror.

- In contrast to his more benevolent policy toward Iran and North Korea, in
2003, Bush helped oust Charles Taylor, the brutal president of Liberia. He
sent in the marines and money to attempt to provide stability in a nation
that had been engulfed in a long-running civil war. What this war had to
do with US security is anyone's guess.

- Bush scrapped the Kyoto climate change treaty, which limited carbon
emissions but excluded developing nations, such as China and India,
which were big carbon emitters. However, this action was not a big departure from the Clinton administration's policy; Clinton had not submitted
the pact for Senate ratification when it became clear that it would be overwhelmingly voted down. Bush's rejection did rile US allies in Europe and
Asia, though. Yet in his last year of office, he became concerned with his
legacy—fearing that people would think he had fiddled while the climate
burned. He realized that the leading Republican and Democratic candidates to succeed him were supporting a cap-and-trade system for carbon
emissions. Under this scheme, a ceiling would be placed on emissions and
greater carbon polluters could buy pollution rights from lesser polluters.
Bush also concluded that he could get credit for starting the ball rolling.
During the 2000 campaign, he had endorsed a cap-and-trade system,
then renounced it upon taking office, only to reverse course again and
start advocating a variant of it during his last year in office. Of course, if

Bush really thought governments were competent enough to effectively coordinate action worldwide to control carbon emissions (a big if), he could have chosen the less intrusive and more efficient carbon tax.

- As one more indication that political labels are not always a good clue to actual policies, Republican George W. Bush was more protectionist in trade than Bill Clinton, his Democratic predecessor. Although supposedly a proponent of free markets, Bush imposed quotas on steel imports of up to 30 percent to win votes in key election states of Ohio and Pennsylvania and also West Virginia.

- Although Bush laudably refused to participate in the new International Court of Justice in The Hague—such international courts are often politicized and subject Americans to lower judicial standards than in the United States—he took things too far by threatening to punish American allies who joined the court.[40]

- To undermine a critic of the Iraq War—a former ambassador who correctly alleged that the Bush administration had embellished intelligence to hype the Iraqi threat—Bush and Cheney aides (perhaps with the foreknowledge of Cheney) leaked the identity of the ambassador's wife, a covert CIA operative, to the media. Such leaks can endanger the lives of such operatives, yet politics trumped such safety considerations in a supposedly security-conscious conservative administration. In the matter, Vice President Cheney's chief aide, Lewis "Scooter" Libby, was convicted of perjury and obstruction of justice. Cheney put such intense pressure on Bush to pardon Libby that even Bush thought it might very well be because the aide was covering up for Cheney; Bush refused the pardon but did commute the aide's two-and-a-half-year prison sentence so that he was not required to go to prison.[41]

Government Economic Intervention and Spending Increases

During Bush's presidency, Alan Greenspan and Ben Bernanke—successive chairmen of the Federal Reserve System appointed by Ronald Reagan and George W. Bush, respectively—flooded the nation's financial system with excessive increases in the money supply. In the late 1990s, Greenspan's increases in the money supply had gone into Internet startup companies, giving the country the dot-com bubble, which burst and led to a recession in 2001. During the George W. Bush administration, Greenspan and Bernanke's similar money-printing spree went into the housing industry, also creating a bubble. People who could not afford houses used the added available credit to take on risky mortgages. Financial institutions took those risky mortgages and repackaged them as risky investments. Then the bubble popped. The housing meltdown triggered a worldwide economic cataclysm called the Great Recession, which was the worst economic downturn since the Great Depression of the 1930s.

Bailing Out the Financial Industry

The attempted cure for the economic catastrophe was colossal government intervention in the economy to shore up companies and financial institutions and to do more of what got the country into the crisis in the first place—turning on the printing presses to increase the money flow. The effort dwarfed any previous government printing spree in American history. Bernanke's printing binge continued into the succeeding administration of Barack Obama, but at this writing, it is still too early to discern what economic sector will experience the next bubble from another economic sugar high.

To deal with the crisis in the financial industry (traditionally regarded by the government as the lifeblood of the economy) induced by reckless behavior on the part of big banks in the housing market, the Bush administration began bailing out "too-big-to-fail" financial institutions. Of course, the US government has been bailing out big financial institutions since the dawn of the republic, allowing them to undertake riskier behavior knowing that they have the government to rescue them when their actions come back to bite them (and everyone else too). Yet government intervention into the market is almost always capricious—and it was in the Bush administration's dealings with these large financial institutions too. The administration allowed Lehman Brothers to fail, while arranging a bailout for Bear Stearns. In the most draconian government intervention into the financial markets since the Great Depression of the 1930s, Bush socialized Freddie Mac and Fannie Mae, private mortgage backers that previously got preferential governmental treatment. Doing that action one better, in an even bigger government intervention into the private sector, he then socialized the giant AIG insurance company with a government takeover. Also, Bush provided the largest industrial bailout in US history for American auto companies, two of which the Obama administration later had the government take over.

All in all, Bush initially allocated more than $700 billion dollars to bail out the financial industry. Bailing out irresponsible large financial institutions, because of excessive fears of economic collapse, merely ensures future economic crises when these "too-big-to-fail" banks undertake further risky behavior, sure that the taxpayers will back up any losses. It is interesting to note that small and medium-sized banks weathered the crisis better, because they had acted more responsibly since they had never received past government bailouts and did not expect any.

Even if several big financial institutions had failed during the housing bust, the largest economy in the world likely would have hiccupped long enough to throw out the dead wood and then would have recovered rapidly through natural processes. Instead, the government—by goosing the economy with fiscal stimulus, bailouts, irresponsible expansion of the money supply, and encouragement of further indebtedness and consumption—likely delayed real economic recovery. The country needed to do the opposite—consume less and pay down excessive public and private debt, which was strangling economic growth. Such excessive debt dragged the economy and later produced the slowest economic recovery from recession in American history.

Fraudulent Tax Cuts

The increasing public debt had been amassed by the trillions Bush spent on needless wars of occupation in Afghanistan and Iraq, domestic spending at a rate not seen since Lyndon B. Johnson's Great Society program, and huge income tax rate cuts—all of which led to record yearly budget deficits and thus massive debt accumulation. Cheney looked to the Reagan model—fraudulent tax cuts because both defense and domestic spending increased—and concluded that budget deficits did not matter. Unlike Reagan, Bush did not surreptitiously later increase taxes in more obscure parts of the tax code. Thus, Bush's budget deficits as a portion of GDP were bigger than even Reagan's.

Yearly federal budget deficits and consequent public debt accumulation do matter, because they hamper economic growth by crowding out necessary private borrowing for business expansion. It is fine to cut taxes, which is always politically easy, but spending cuts, which are politically difficult, must also be made. So fraudulent tax cuts without concomitant spending reductions, such as those of Reagan and Bush, are easy ways for Republican politicians to throw candy to voters to get elected, while slowly and irresponsibly bankrupting the country by adding to mounting deficits and burgeoning national debt. Although claiming to be a "compassionate conservative," Bush reversed Clinton's tax policy—increasing the share of taxes paid by the wealthiest 1 percent of the population and decreasing taxes on the bottom 80 percent—by giving almost half of his massive fraudulent tax cuts to the wealthiest 1 percent, who most likely voted Republican.[42]

Bush not only did not decrease spending, but he spent wildly on defense and domestic programs. Bush used the 9/11 attacks to increase real defense spending by 50 percent during his eight-year administration. Ragtag terrorists are cheap to fight with redirected intelligence assets and inexpensive drone and special forces attacks. Yet Bush spent on expensive defense systems designed to counter great power rivals, which the United States did not have after the Cold War ended. Also, Bush wasted trillions on occupations of choice in Afghanistan and Iraq, which depleted and exhausted expensive military equipment and personnel while making the United States less safe.

Like his successor, Barack Obama, Bush expanded healthcare coverage. He added a huge additional benefit—prescription drugs—to an already financially teetering Medicare system to benefit the wealthiest portion of the population: senior citizens. This policy was another instance that appeared to contradict the "compassionate conservative" president's alleged intent to help the poor. The new benefit cost hundreds of billions of dollars and merely added to the staggering yearly budget deficits and soaring national debt. Passed in late 2003, the new "goodie" bag was designed to help Bush with senior citizens in key states like Florida during his bid for reelection in 2004.[43] Bush did not want another electoral deadlock and near loss like the one in the 2000 election against Al Gore.

Failing to Reform Social Security

In his second term, after he was safely reelected, Bush proposed the modest, but praiseworthy, reform of allowing people to put 2 percent of their Social Security benefits into private retirement accounts. However, Bush should have put a higher priority on fixing the Social Security System, which was (and still is) scheduled to run out of funds because the demographic ratio between payers (workers) and receivers (retirees) was shifting in favor of receivers, as the large Baby Boom generation began coming to retirement age. Thus, Bush should have taken up this issue early during his first term, when his political capital was highest, rather than in the second term, when he was weakened by being a lame duck and because the Iraq War had made him unpopular. But Bush lacked the political courage to make fixing this critical, but politically sensitive, governmental financial problem the focus of his administration when the time was ripe but before his reelection was assured. Instead, his priority was to cut taxes to win votes instead of cutting spending, which usually loses votes.

"No Child Left Behind"

Bush, flouting his party's traditional policy proposal to get rid of the Department of Education, instead vastly expanded the federal role in education, normally a state and local responsibility. In fact, of post-Truman presidents, Bush had the third highest annualized increase in real federal spending on education per pupil, behind the John F. Kennedy/Lyndon Baines Johnson and Eisenhower administrations.[44]

In his program "No Child Left Behind," Bush gave money to schools to close the gap between rich and poor, but in exchange for holding schools accountable with results on standardized tests. If schools did not meet the federally imposed standards, they faced penalties. Neither the right nor the left liked the program, but it passed just after 9/11 because members of Congress idiotically thought they should come together and pass some piece of legislation, no matter how bad it was or how much they disagreed with it.

Welfare at Home and Abroad

Bush channeled government money through religious charities, which some criticized for eroding the barrier between church and state. Also, he initiated a massive program to spend tens of billions of dollars to battle AIDS, malaria, and tuberculosis overseas. Although the cause was worthy, Bush's budget director and other aides were aghast at such extravagant spending, considering the already expensive additional spending required for the "war on terror" and the invasion of Iraq. In addition, Bush started the Millennium Challenge Corporation, which dispensed billions of dollars to developing countries that promised reforms.

Bush, however, did not like foreign aid if it went to international family planning agencies, which he stopped. He also signed executive orders furthering the goals of the anti-abortion lobby.[45] He occasionally vetoed pork-laden farm and water projects bills, but even then was overridden by Congress.[46]

In his largely incompetent response to Hurricane Katrina, Bush slathered the Gulf Coast states with federal money ($126 billion) and tossed states' rights to the wind by demanding that Kathleen Blanco, the Democratic governor of Louisiana, sign a request to bring National Guard troops in the state under federal control. She refused, but Bush instead sent regular army troops anyway to provide humanitarian assistance. Bush had been warned against sending regular army troops by Secretary of Defense Rumsfeld and against federalizing the Louisiana Guard by the general in charge of the National Guard bureau, who correctly believed it would be unconstitutional under those circumstances and would actually hinder relief operations.

Under the Constitution, federal protection can be provided only if states request it, even in the extreme case of internal violence, and the document makes no reference to the federal government protecting or assisting states—by sending troops, federalizing state militias, or otherwise—in time of natural disaster, especially without their consent. Yet politically, Bush needed to appear to be "doing something" about the devastation.

Bush had given positions heading the Federal Emergency Management Agency (FEMA) to political cronies, who mismanaged federal efforts to respond to Katrina.[47] Bush never recovered politically from this fiasco and that of the equally disastrous Iraq invasion.

Regulation

Under Bush a law was passed that was the most significant energy legislation since the oil "crises" of the 1970s and was laced with government intervention. For the first time since 1985, Bush increased the fuel economy standards for autos and light trucks. Also, the bill expanded ethanol production, largely a subsidy for farmers, who are an important Republican constituency. Lastly, the new law ridiculously used government power to phase out incandescent light bulbs. The law was designed to save energy and make the United States more energy independent—a bipartisan goal that can be questioned on the basis of simple economics. Economists generally regard autarky (protectionism) in any good or service as economically inefficient; autarky in energy is no different, because it artificially raises prices. Energy independence will just make energy more expensive, because imported energy, especially oil, is often cheaper than that which is domestically produced.

In the wake of the Enron energy company scandal and a similar one at the company Worldcom, Bush signed the Sarbanes-Oxley law in 2002, which enacted onerous new accounting requirements on corporations, reducing their efficiency. And in a more pro-business stance, Bush reversed Clinton-era policy and allowed logging in formerly protected western forests.

With the death of Chief Justice William H. Rehnquist and the retirement of Sandra Day O'Connor, Bush appointed "conservatives" John Roberts and Samuel Alito, respectively, to replace them. Roberts did not turn out to be so conservative when he found the healthcare program of Barack Obama, Bush's successor, to be constitutional by creatively labeling its requirement for consumers to buy health insurance as a tax. Nowhere in the Constitution does it say the federal government has the power to make people buy a particular product, or even get involved in healthcare. Yet Roberts provided the swing vote needed to keep Obamacare alive.

Conclusion

Lewis L. Gould, who wrote a history of the Republican Party, best succinctly sums up George W. Bush's tenure as president:

> Eight years later they [officials of the Bush administration] had on their record a devastating surprise terrorist attack, an unpopular war, a blundering response to a natural disaster, and governmental policies that had led to a near collapse of the national economy.[48]

Bush can be called many things, but someone who limited government—either domestically or overseas—is not one of them. He, like Ronald Reagan and Richard Nixon, carried an "R" behind his name and so had an easier time of playing the public role of a "conservative." But also like Reagan and Nixon, when one scratches below the surface image to examine his actual policies, the only thing Bush was conserving was the welfare/warfare state. Bush bailed out or socialized industries, further extended the tentacles of the federal government into education, added a massive prescription drug benefit to an already teetering Medicare system, and lavishly slathered federal cash on ethanol, alternative fuels, AIDS programs overseas, and hurricane relief efforts. In fact, at the end of his two terms, he had spent more domestically than any president since Lyndon Johnson.

About Bush's big government conservatism, conservative Fred Barnes gingerly looked on the bright side:

> Many conservatives embrace President Bush, despite his failure to make even a feeble attempt at cutting federal spending.
>
> Make no mistake though, Bush is redefining conservatism for a new era, consciously moving away from certain precepts that have traditionally characterized the conservative movement. Most notably, his championing of results-oriented government . . . breaks from the traditional conservative view, which he characterized succinctly: "basically, the federal government has no role."[49]

Overseas, instead of following a policy of military restraint—which he touted in his campaign for president in 2000 and with which the nation's founders would have agreed—he took advantage of 9/11 to conduct a nation-building bog in Afghanistan and to invade and occupy an unrelated Muslim country, thus leading to another quagmire and a spike in terrorism worldwide. The invasion of Iraq destabilized the entire Persian Gulf region and led to increased Islamist radicalism. Bush also took advantage of 9/11 to restrict the nation's unique civil liberties by rounding up Muslims for arrest on immigration charges, spying on Americans without constitutionally required warrants, detaining many terror suspects indefinitely without trial, creating kangaroo military tribunals to try some terror suspects, and torturing such suspects at Guantanamo and CIA secret prisons around the world. Thus, Bush hardly fulfilled his promises to limit government.

II

Political Rhetoric and Hypocrisy

ALL IS NOT what it first appears to be in presidential history. The public, journalists, and even historians regularly allow politicians, and especially presidents, to define themselves by their own political rhetoric and party affiliation. And political parties in turn define themselves by rhetoric. It is much harder and more work for the public and professional analysts to study the actual policies of presidents, especially when deviations from rhetoric motivate presidents to cover their tracks. However, in reality, the policies of presidents and their governing parties have often diverged from their political rhetoric.

For example, since the early twentieth century, the Republican Party has cultivated the image of promoting limited government (before that, of the two major parties, it was clearly the party of bigger government), but its presidential officeholders have promulgated such policies only in the 1920s during the Harding and Coolidge administrations and only somewhat in the 1950s during the Eisenhower administration. Surprisingly, from the Eisenhower administration on, Republican presidents, compared to Democratic ones, have generally presided over greater average annual increases in the federal government's spending as a percentage of GDP. Furthermore, such greater government spending includes more spending on welfare and social programs as a portion of federal spending by Republican presidents than by Democratic chief executives. Similarly, in the post-Truman era, the Republicans have greatly increased public debt accumulation as a portion of GDP, while Democrats have substantially decreased it.[1]

During the nineteenth century, the Democrats were clearly the party of more limited government, but then became a big government party at the presidential level early in the twentieth century, beginning with Woodrow Wilson and World War I. Yet because Democratic presidents after Harry Truman generally have had a better overall record on the most important measures of limiting government, that reality may very well be the primary reason the economy has performed much better (for individuals and economy-wide) during that period under Democratic chief executives rather than under Republican ones.[2] Fiscally conservative economic policies have given the country better economic performance, but ironically, they have been delivered by a party that cares less about burnishing an image of promoting limited government than its Republican opponent. But because voters often cast their ballots based on images and popular reputations well cultivated by politicians, fiscal conservatives could be voting for the wrong party.

That is not to say that the federal government has not grown, even under recent Democratic presidents. The government has grown even as a percentage of GDP—a very unfavorable development—but surprisingly, it has expanded less under Democratic chief executives than under recent Republican presidents, despite their ample rhetoric to the contrary. So there is enough blame to go around for presidents of both parties.

Our discussion has lauded the limiting of government by five individual presidential administrations—two of them Democrats and three of them Republicans. The Democratic administrations of Jimmy Carter and Bill Clinton spouted conservative rhetoric and in many cases promulgated policies to match—something that has long been forgotten by libertarians and conservatives because of their Democratic Party label. In contrast, if one is examining policies and not rhetoric, in the Republican Party, one has to look back to the Harding/Coolidge administrations of the 1920s and the Eisenhower administration of the 1950s to find presidents who actually limited government. In the last hundred years, the Republican Party has loads of rhetoric on limiting government but only a slightly greater number of presidents than the Democrats with policies that have actually done so. And contrary to popular reputation, in the last six decades, Democratic presidents have actually had better numbers on the major statistics measuring limited government (some of which have been elucidated above).

The evidence shows that most Republican chief executives during the century after Harding and Coolidge have been disappointing in delivering limited government, despite their often intense rhetoric promising to do so. Moderately progressive Republican presidents, such as the administrations of Herbert Hoover and Richard Nixon/Gerald Ford, rapidly expanded government. In Hoover's case especially, he set important bad precedents for enlarging government that were later used as a blueprint by his successor, Democrat Franklin D. Roosevelt, to balloon the federal government's role.

Furthermore, in contrast to their well-cultivated reputations, Ronald Reagan ("Get government off the backs of the people"), George H. W. Bush ("Read my lips, no new taxes"), and George W. Bush ("Compassionate conservative") were big government hawks. Because warfare is the most prominent cause of big government in both American and world history, when conducting excessive military interventions abroad, it is difficult to have small government at home—they did not.

Such conclusions are hard for libertarians, conservatives, and rank-and-file Republicans to accept because they run counter to decades of presidential image-making, which has been absorbed and inculcated by the busy populace, journalists, and even many historians. It does not mean that lovers of limited government should run out and change parties, but what it does mean is that such voters should demand that presidents of both parties adhere in their policies to campaign speeches and other rhetoric extolling and promising limited government. That is, the continuing hypocrisy of promising limited government and then not delivering it should be penalized, not rewarded. Limiting government and letting the private sector flourish are the best ways to promote peace, prosperity, and liberty in the United States.

Notes

Chapter 1. Popular Reputations Depend On Political Rhetoric

1. Woodrow Wilson, *Constitutional Government in the United States* (New York: Columbia University Press, 1908), 59–60.
2. Wilson, *Constitutional Government*, 56.
3. A. Scott Berg, *Wilson* (New York: Berkley Books, 2013), 9–10.
4. James Robenalt, "Warren G. Harding," in *The Presidents and the Constitution*, ed. Ken Gormley (New York: New York University Press, 2016), 371–373; John W. Dean, *Warren G. Harding* (New York: Times Books, 2004), 95.
5. Warren G. Harding, Inaugural Address, March 4, 1921, http://www.presidency.ucsb.edu/ws/?pid=25833.
6. Calvin Coolidge, Third Annual Message, December 8, 1925, http://www.presidency.ucsb.edu/ws/index.php?pid=29566.
7. Herbert Hoover, Inaugural Address, March 4, 1929, https://hoover.archives.gov/info/inauguralspeech.html.
8. Charles Rappleye, *Herbert Hoover in the White House: The Ordeal of the Presidency* (New York: Simon & Schuster, 2016), 455–458.
9. Brion McClanahan, *Nine Presidents Who Screwed Up America and Four Who Tried to Save Her* (Washington, DC: Regnery History, 2016), 76–77.
10. Franklin Delano Roosevelt, First Inaugural Address, March 4, 1933, https://www.archives.gov/education/lessons/fdr-inaugural/.
11. Harry Truman, Annual Message to the Congress on the State of the Union, January 7, 1948, http://www.presidency.ucsb.edu/ws/?pid=13005, and Annual Message to the Congress on the State of the Union, January 5, 1949, http://www.presidency.ucsb.edu/ws/?pid=13293.
12. McClanahan, *Nine Presidents Who Screwed Up America*, 99–100.
13. Richard V. Damms, "Dwight D. Eisenhower," in *The Presidents and the Constitution*, ed. Ken Gormley (New York: New York University Press, 2016), 444–445.
14. John F. Kennedy, Address Accepting the Presidential Nomination Given at the Democratic National Convention in the Los Angeles Memorial Coliseum, July 15, 1960.
15. Robert Dallek, *Lyndon B. Johnson: Portrait of a President* (Oxford: Oxford University Press, 2004), 152–156.
16. McClanahan, *Nine Presidents Who Screwed Up America*, 141.

17. Richard Reeves, *President Nixon: Alone in the White House* (New York: Simon & Schuster, 2001), 112.

18. McClanahan, *Nine Presidents Who Screwed Up America*, 151.

19. John Robert Greene, *The Presidency of Gerald R. Ford* (Lawrence: University Press of Kansas, 1995), 190–192.

20. Burton I. Kaufman and Scott Kaufman, *The Presidency of James Earl Carter Jr.*, 2nd rev. ed. (Lawrence: University Press of Kansas, 2006), 16, 24–25.

21. Kaufman and Kaufman, *The Presidency of James Earl Carter Jr.*, 12–13, 28; John Howard Brown, "Jimmy Carter, Alfred Kahn, and Airline Deregulation: Anatomy of a Political Success," *Independent Review* 19, no. 1 (Summer 2014): 89.

22. Quoted in Steven F. Hayward, *The Age of Reagan: The Conservative Counterrevolution, 1980–1989* (New York: Three Rivers Press, 2009), 4.

23. George H. W. Bush, Address Accepting the Presidential Nomination at the Republican National Convention in New Orleans, August 18, 1988, http://www.presidency.ucsb.edu/ws/?pid=25955; Curt Smith, *George H. W. Bush: Character at the Core* (Lincoln, NE: Potomac Books, 2014), 118–120.

24. Bill Clinton, Democratic Leadership Council Keynote Address, Democratic Leadership Council National Convention, Cleveland, Ohio, May 16, 1991, https://www.c-span.org/video/?17869-1/democratic-leadership-council-keynote-address; John F. Harris, *The Survivor: Bill Clinton in the White House* (New York: Random House, 2005), xv, xxi.

25. George W. Bush, "A Period of Consequences," address given at The Citadel, South Carolina, September 23, 1999, http://www3.citadel.edu/pao/addresses/pres_bush.html.

26. Peter Baker, *Days of Fire: Bush and Cheney in the White House* (New York: Anchor Books, 2014), 49, 51.

27. Benjamin A. Kleinerman, "George W. Bush," in *The Presidents and the Constitution*, ed. Ken Gormley (New York: New York University Press, 2016), 591.

28. T. Becket Adams et al., "The State of Obama's Promises. *Washington Examiner*, January 4, 2016.

29. Mike Kimel and Michael E. Kanell, *Presimetrics: What the Facts Tell Us About How the Presidents Measure Up on the Issues We Care About* (New York: Black Dog & Leventhal, 2010), 38, 46, 51, 54–55.

30. Kimel and Kanell, *Presimetrics*, 38, 51.

31. Phillip G. Payne, *Dead Last: The Public Memory of Warren G. Harding's Scandalous Legacy* (Athens: Ohio University Press, 2009), 8–10, 193.

Chapter 2. Years of Normalcy and Restraint

1. Quoted in Lewis S. Gould, *The Republicans: A History of the Grand Old Party* (Oxford: Oxford University Press, 2014), 160.

2. The White House, Office of Management and Budget, *Summary of Receipts, Outlays, and Surpluses or Deficits: 1789–2021*, https://obamawhitehouse.archives.gov/omb/budget/Historicals.

3. Phillip G. Payne, *Dead Last: The Public Memory of Warren G. Harding's Scandalous Legacy* (Athens: Ohio University Press, 2009), 48.

4. Lewis L. Gould, *The Republicans: A History of the Grand Old Party*, rev. ed. (Oxford: Oxford University Press, 2014), 157–158.

5. David Fromkin, *A Peace to End All Peace: The Fall of the Ottoman Empire and the Creation of the Modern Middle East* (New York: Henry Holt, 2009), 950–951.

6. Adam Tooze, *The Deluge: The Great War, America, and the Remaking of the Global Order, 1916–1931* (New York: Viking, 2014), 407.

7. Amity Shlaes, *Coolidge* (Australia: HarperCollins, 2013), 286, electronic edition.

8. Joan Hoff Wilson, *Herbert Hoover: Forgotten Progressive* (New York: HarperCollins, 1975), 191.

9. John W. Dean, *Warren G. Harding* (New York: Henry Holt, 2004), 129–135.

10. Tooze, *The Deluge*, 402–403.

11. Wilson, *Herbert Hoover*, 183.

12. Ibid., 186.

13. Tooze, *The Deluge*, 440–448, 453–454, 457–459, 461, 472.

14. Ibid., 492–494.

15. John A. Moore, "The Original Supply Siders: Warren Harding and Calvin Coolidge," *The Independent Review* 18, no. 4 (Spring 2014): 600.

16. Wilson, *Herbert Hoover*, 93.

17. Gary M. Pecquet and Clifford F. Thies, "Reputation Overrides Record: How Warren G. Harding Mistakenly Became the 'Worst' President of the United States," *The Independent Review* 21, no. 1 (Summer 2016): 39–40.

18. Moore, "Original Supply Siders," 598.

19. Ibid., 598; Pecquet and Thies, "Reputation Overrides Record," 40.

20. Gould, *The Republicans*, 167.

21. Dean, *Harding*, 105–106; Moore, "Original Supply Siders," 603–604, 608–609, 611.

22. Shlaes, *Coolidge*, 235.

23. Dean, *Harding*, 107–111.

24. Moore, "Original Supply Siders," 610.

25. Pecquet and Thies, "Reputation Overrides Record," 39.

26. Dean, *Harding*, 106–107.

27. Gould, *The Republicans*, 169.

28. Moore, "Original Supply Siders," 605, 609.

29. Gould, *The Republicans*, 175.

30. David Gaffney and Peter Gaffney, *The Presidents* (New York: Hyperion, 2012), 255; Brion McClanahan, *Nine Presidents Who Screwed Up America and Four Who Tried to Save Her* (Washington, DC: Regnery History, 2016), 264.

31. Moore, "Original Supply Siders," 601; Pecquet and Thies, "Reputation Overrides Record," 39.

32. Gould, *The Republicans*, 177–178; Edgar Eugene Robinson and Vaughn Davis Bornet, *Herbert Hoover: President of the United States* (Stanford, CA: Hoover Institution Press, 1975), 125.

33. David Jacobs, "Warren Gamaliel Harding: A Babbitt in the White House," rev. John Milton Cooper, and Michael Harwood, "Calvin Coolidge: The New Englander," rev. Louis L. Gould, both in *American Heritage: The Presidents*, ed. Michael Beschloss (New York: Byron Preiss Books, 2003), 338, 344, 348.

34. Quoted in Dean, *Harding*, 154–155.

35. Michael Gerhardt, *The Forgotten Presidents: Their Untold Constitutional Legacy* (Oxford: Oxford University Press, 2013), 191.

36. Gould, *The Republicans*, 171.

37. Dean, *Harding*, 121–123.

38. Gerhardt, *Forgotten Presidents*, 205.

39. A.J. Langguth, *After Lincoln: How the North Won the Civil War and Lost the Peace* (New York: Simon & Schuster, 2014), 365.

40. Pecquet and Thies, "Reputation Overrides Record," 37–38.

41. Dean, *Harding,* 123–126; Payne, *The Public Memory,* 120–125.

42. Payne, *The Public Memory,* 50, 182.

43. Ibid., 12–13, 103.

44. Ibid., 215.

45. Morton Keller, "Warren G. Harding," in *"To the Best of My Ability": The American Presidents,* ed. James M. McPherson (London: DK Publishing, 2004), 210.

46. Shlaes, *Coolidge,* 282.

47. Pecquet and Thies, "Reputation Overrides Record," 31.

48. Dean, *Harding,* 139–141.

49. Robert Cowley, "Calvin Coolidge," in *"To the Best of My Ability": The American Presidents,* ed. James M. McPherson (London: DK Publishing, 2004), 215.

50. Payne, *The Public Memory,* 62–63, 87.

51. Ibid., 5; Dean, *Harding,* 155–160.

52. Payne, *The Public Memory,* 63.

53. Gould, *The Republicans,* 170.

54. Ibid., 171.

55. Gaffney and Gaffney, *The Presidents,* 255.

56. Gerhardt, *Forgotten Presidents,* 198–199, 201.

57. Payne, *The Public Memory,* 9.

58. Keller, "Warren G. Harding," 209.

59. Dean, *Harding,* 101–102.

60. Cowley, "Calvin Coolidge," 213.

61. Moore, "Original Supply Siders," 604–606, 614–615.

62. Cowley, "Calvin Coolidge," 212, 215–216.

63. Wilson, *Herbert Hoover,* 143; Robinson and Bornet, *Herbert Hoover,* 123.

64. Dean, *Harding,* 111–113.

65. Moore, "Original Supply Siders," 609–610.

66. McClanahan, *Nine Presidents Who Screwed Up America,* 261–262.

67. Gerhardt, *Forgotten Presidents,* 196.

68. Wilson, *Herbert Hoover,* 112–113.

69. Gerhardt, *Forgotten Presidents,* 210–211.

70. Ibid., 210.

71. McClanahan, *Nine Presidents Who Screwed Up America,* 256, 264–265.

72. Shlaes, *Coolidge,* 287.

73. Wilson, *Herbert Hoover,* 94.

74. Gerhardt, *Forgotten Presidents,* 211.

75. McClanahan, *Nine Presidents Who Screwed Up America,* 252–253, 265–267.

76. Robinson and Bornet, *Herbert Hoover,* 59–60, 63–64.

77. Wilson, *Herbert Hoover,* 114–116.

78. Gerhardt, *Forgotten Presidents,* 193; McClanahan, *Nine Presidents Who Screwed Up America,* 253.

79. McClanahan, *Nine Presidents Who Screwed Up America,* 269.

80. Tooze, *The Deluge,* 474.

81. Gould, *The Republicans,* 176.

82. Tooze, *The Deluge,* 404–407, 481–483.

83. Ibid., 435.

Chapter 3. Domestic Troubles But No Foreign Entanglements

1. Quoted in Edgar Eugene Robinson and Vaughn Davis Bornet, *Herbert Hoover: President of the United States* (Stanford, CA: Hoover Institution Press, 1975), 40, 304, 306.

2. Ibid., 40, 51, 67, 74, 303.

3. Lewis L. Gould, *The Republicans: A History of the Grand Old Party* (Oxford: Oxford University Press, 2014), 185.

4. Robinson and Bornet, *Herbert Hoover,* 132, 213.

5. Quoted in ibid., 132.

6. Ibid., 181.

7. Quoted in Joan Hoff Wilson, *Herbert Hoover: Forgotten Progressive* (New York: HarperCollins, 1975), 146.

8. Ibid., 158.

9. Rappleye, *Herbert Hoover in the White House*, 388–392.

10. Robinson and Bornet, *Herbert Hoover*, 71–72, 80–81.

11. Ibid., 165.

12. Ibid., 206–207, 216–217, 252.

13. Ibid., 259.

14. Gould, *The Republicans*, 183.

15. Rappleye, *Herbert Hoover in the White House*, 427.

16. Wilson, *Herbert Hoover*, 155–157; Robinson and Bornet, *Herbert Hoover*, 222.

17. Robinson and Bornet, *Herbert Hoover*, 290–298.

18. Ibid., 223–224.

19. Ibid., 171, 200.

20. Wilson, *Herbert Hoover*, 135.

21. Robinson and Bornet, *Herbert Hoover*, 136–143.

22. Wilson, *Herbert Hoover*, 178–179.

23. Robert Dallek, "Herbert Hoover," in "*To the Best of My Ability*": *The American Presidents*, ed. James M. McPherson (London: DK Publishing, 2004), 219.

24. Wilson, *Herbert Hoover*, 165–166.

25. Robinson and Bornet, *Herbert Hoover*, 257.

26. Quoted in ibid., 183.

27. Rappleye, *Herbert Hoover in the White House*, 356–371.

28. Dallek, "Herbert Hoover," 220–222; Wilson, *Herbert Hoover*, 184–188.

29. Robinson and Bornet, *Herbert Hoover*, 250–251.

30. Saul Brown, "Herbert Clark Hoover: The Great Engineer," rev. Lewis L. Gould, in *American Heritage: The Presidents*, ed. Michael Beschloss (New York: Byron Preiss Books, 2003), 356.

31. Wilson, *Herbert Hoover*, 147–149.

32. Rappleye, *Herbert Hoover in the White House*, 297–310, 331–338.

33. Robinson and Bornet, *Herbert Hoover*, 154.

34. Gould, *The Republicans*, 184–185.

35. Wilson, *Herbert Hoover*, 149–150.

36. Robinson and Bornet, *Herbert Hoover*, 271–272.

37. Wilson, *Herbert Hoover*, 86–87, 98–99, 102, 104–105, 134–135, 137, 140–141, 144, 147.

38. Ibid., 174, 189.

39. Robinson and Bornet, *Herbert Hoover*, 99–100.

40. William E. Leuchtenburg, *Herbert Hoover* (New York: Henry Holt, 2009), 120–122.

41. Wilson, *Herbert Hoover*, 200–202.

42. Robinson and Bornet, *Herbert Hoover*, 103.

43. Wilson, *Herbert Hoover*, 193–194.

44. Ibid., 192–193.

45. Dallek, "Herbert Hoover," 222.

46. Rappleye, *Herbert Hoover in the White House*, 462.

47. Robinson and Bornet, *Herbert Hoover*, 200–201.

48. Wilson, *Herbert Hoover*, 204–208.

49. Quoted in Leuchtenburg, *Herbert Hoover*, 122–125.

50. Ibid., 191–192, 194–196.

51. Robinson and Bornet, *Herbert Hoover*, 106–107.

52. Ibid., 288.

53. Wilson, *Herbert Hoover*, 167.

54. Robinson and Bornet, *Herbert Hoover*, 152–153.

55. Ibid., 230.

56. Ibid., 230–236.

57. Rappleye, *Herbert Hoover in the White House*, 504–524.

58. Wilson, *Herbert Hoover*, 135, 161–162.

59. Ibid., 160–161.

60. Robinson and Bornet, *Herbert Hoover*, 241, 288.

61. Wilson, *Herbert Hoover*, 136–138.

62. Eric Foner and John A. Garraty, *The Reader's Companion to American History* (New York: Houghton Mifflin

Harcourt, 1991), http://www.history
.com.

63. Wilson, *Herbert Hoover*, 135; Robinson and Bornet, *Herbert Hoover*, 53–54, 56–63.

Chapter 4. Smaller Government
at Home and Aboard

1. Herbert S. Parmet, "Dwight D. Eisenhower," in *"To the Best of My Ability": The American Presidents,* ed. James M. McPherson (London: DK Publishing, 2004), 248.
2. Daniel J. Sargent, *A Superpower Transformed: The Remaking of American Foreign Relations in the 1970s* (Oxford: Oxford University Press, 2015), 45.
3. Jim Newton, *Eisenhower: The White House Years* (New York: Anchor Books, 2012).
4. Mike Kimel and Michael E. Kanell, *Presimetrics: What the Facts Tell Us About How the Presidents Measure Up on the Issues We Care About* (New York: Black Dog & Leventhal, 2010), 54–55.
5. Daniel J. Smith and Peter J. Boettke, "An Episodic History of Modern Fed Independence," *The Independent Review* 20, no. 1 (Summer 2015): 101–102,
6. Geoffrey Perret, *Eisenhower* (Holbrook, MA: Adams Media, 1999), 508–509.
7. Ibid., 444–445.
8. Ibid., 449–450, 462–465.
9. Kevin D. Williamson, "Why Like Ike: Conservatives Got Eisenhower Wrong the First Time Around," *National Review* LXV, no. 16 (Sept. 2, 2013): 25–26.
10. Evan Thomas, *Ike's Bluff: President Eisenhower's Secret Battle to Save the World* (New York: Little Brown, 2012).

11. Perret, *Eisenhower*, 457–462, 522–528.
12. Thomas, *Ike's Bluff.*
13. Perret, *Eisenhower*, 450.
14. Michael K. Bohn, *Presidents in Crisis: Tough Decisions Inside the White House from Truman to Obama* (New York: Arcade Publishing, 2015), 41.
15. Thomas, *Ike's Bluff.*
16. Bohn, *Presidents in Crisis*, 46–47.
17. Thomas, *Ike's Bluff.*
18. Perret, *Eisenhower*, 560–563, 565, 578.
19. Thomas, *Ike's Bluff.*
20. Stephen Ambrose, *Eisenhower: Soldier and President* (New York: Simon & Schuster, 1990), 475–476. Citations refer to the 2003 paperback edition.
21. Williamson, "Why Like Ike," 28.
22. Thomas, *Ike's Bluff.*
23. Ibid.
24. Williamson, "Why Like Ike," 25.
25. Newton, *Eisenhower: The White House Years.*
26. Perret, *Eisenhower*, 426–428, 451–455, 566–568.
27. Ibid.
28. Parmet, "Dwight D. Eisenhower," 246–247.
29. Bohn, *Presidents in Crisis*, xxi, 25–27, 31, 32, 36–39.
30. Parmet, "Dwight D. Eisenhower," 246–247.
31. Newton, *Eisenhower: The White House Years.*
32. Ambrose, *Eisenhower: Soldier and President,* 465–469.
33. Perret, *Eisenhower*, 535–539, 569–570.
34. Newton, *Eisenhower: The White House Years.*
35. Ibid.
36. Perret, *Eisenhower*, 476–477, 478–482.
37. Ibid., 485–487.
38. Charles L. Mee, Jr. "Dwight David Eisenhower: I Like Ike," rev. Lewis L. Gould, in *American Heritage: The Presidents,* ed. Michael Beschloss

(New York: Byron Preiss Books, 2003), 393–397.

39. Kimel and Kanell, *Presimetrics*, 38.

40. Gould, *The Republicans*, 196, 212–213, 222–223, 233–234, 240, 255.

41. Williamson, "Why Like Ike," 25; Newton, *Eisenhower: The White House Years.*

42. Thomas, *Ike's Bluff.*

43. Gould, *The Republicans*, 238.

44. Williamson, "Why Like Ike," 25.

45. Ibid.

46. Perret, *Eisenhower*, 421, 487, 509–512, 514–516.

47. Ibid., 491–504.

48. Gould, *The Republicans*, 238–239.

49. Newton, *Eisenhower: The White House Years.*

50. A.J. Langguth, *After Lincoln: How the North Won the Civil War and Lost the Peace* (New York: Simon & Schuster, 2014), 367–368.

51. Gould, *The Republicans*, 239.

52. Lannguth, *After Lincoln*, 368.

53. Perret, *Eisenhower*, 544–554.

54. John Sununu, *The Quiet Man* (New York: Broadside Books, 2015), 343.

55. Perret, *Eisenhower*, 588.

56. Ambrose, *Eisenhower: Soldier and President*, 548.

Chapter 5. Watergate and a More Restrained Foreign Policy

1. Brion McClanahan, *Nine Presidents Who Screwed Up America and Four Who Tried to Save Her* (Washington, DC: Regnery History, 2016), 141.

2. Lewis L. Gould, "Richard Milhous Nixon: The Road to Watergate," and Lewis L. Gould, "Gerald Rudolph Ford: A Time for Healing," both in *American Heritage: The Presidents,* ed. Michael Beschloss (New York: Byron Preiss Books, 2003), 431, 435, 445.

3. Gould, *The Republicans*, 266.

4. Gould, *The Republicans*, 271.

5. John W. Dean, *The Nixon Defense: What He Knew and When He Knew It* (New York: Viking, 2014), 1.

6. McClanahan, *Nine Presidents Who Screwed Up America*, 142.

7. Had the plumbers not been caught at the DNC offices, they planned to burglarize the headquarters of the leading Democratic candidate for president, George McGovern, that same night. Nixon had tried to discredit his feared nemesis, Larry O'Brien, the DNC chairman, by ordering the CIA to dig up dirt on O'Brien. Bob Haldeman, Nixon's White House chief of staff, believed Nixon's vendetta against O'Brien had led to the Watergate break-in. Dean, *The Nixon Defense*, 11–13.

8. Tom Wicker, "Richard M. Nixon," in *"To the Best of My Ability": The American Presidents,* ed. James M. McPherson (London: DK Publishing, 2004), 272.

9. McClanahan, *Nine Presidents Who Screwed Up America*, 156–158.

10. Richard Reeves, *President Nixon: Alone in the White House* (New York: Touchstone Books, 2001), 605; Gould, *The Republicans*, 265.

11. Laura Kalman, "Gerald R. Ford," in *"To the Best of My Ability": The American Presidents,* 275.

12. Gould, *The Republicans*, 282.

13. Kalman, "Gerald R. Ford," 275, 280.

14. Gould, *The Republicans*, 274.

15. John Robert Greene, *The Presidency of Gerald R. Ford* (Lawrence: University Press of Kansas, 1995), 191–192.

16. McClanahan, *Nine Presidents Who Screwed Up America*, 144–145.

17. Ibid, 141, 144, 146.

18. Mike Kimel and Michael E. Kanell, *Presimetrics: What the Facts Tell Us About How the Presidents Measure Up*

on the Issues We Care About (New York: Black Dog & Leventhal, 2010), 134.

19. Gould, *The Republicans*, 267–269.

20. Daniel J. Smith and Peter J. Boettke, "An Episodic History of Modern Fed Independence," *The Independent Review* 20, no. 1 (Summer 2015): 104–106.

21. McClanahan, *Nine Presidents Who Screwed Up America*, 151–153.

22. Daniel L. Sargent, *A Superpower Transformed: The Remaking of American Foreign Relations in the 1970s* (Oxford: Oxford University Press, 2015), 101–130.

23. Smith and Boettke, "An Episodic History," 107.

24. Sargent, *A Superpower Transformed*, 180.

25. Wicker, "Richard M. Nixon," in *"To the Best of My Ability": The American Presidents*, 268–269.

26. Jennifer Steinhauer, "Bipartisan Push Builds to Relax Sentencing Laws," *New York Times*, July 28, 2015.

27. McClanahan, *Nine Presidents Who Screwed Up America*, 144.

28. Smith and Boettke, "An Episodic History," 107.

29. Sargent, *A Superpower Transformed*, 237–238.

30. Ibid., 178–180.

31. Ibid.

32. Kalman, "Gerald R. Ford," 278.

33. Ibid., 275; Greene, *The Presidency of Gerald R. Ford*, 93–95.

34. Gould, *The Republicans*, 262.

35. Benjamin Friedman speaking at a Cato Institute policy forum, "Did the Military Intervention in Libya Succeed?" March 19, 2014.

36. Sargent, *A Superpower Transformed*, 51.

37. Matthew Carr, *Sherman's Ghosts: Soldiers, Civilians, and the American Way of War* (New York: New Press, 2015), 140–144

38. Sargent, *A Superpower Transformed*, 51.

39. Carr, *Sherman's Ghosts*, 140–144.

40. McClanahan, *Nine Presidents Who Screwed Up America*, 154–155.

41. Carl Hulse, "Weighing the Odds in Fight Over Iran Nuclear Deal," *New York Times*, August 25, 2015.

42. Michael K. Bohn, *Presidents in Crisis: Tough Decisions Inside the White House from Truman to Obama* (New York: Arcade Publishing, 2015), 104–105.

43. Tonkin Gulf Resolution, Public Law 88-408, 88th Congress, August 7, 1964; General Records of the United States Government; Record Group 11; National Archives, http://www .ourdocuments.gov/doc.php?doc =98&page=transcript.

44. Sargent, *A Superpower Transformed*, 46.

45. Reeves, *President Nixon*, 104.

46. Ibid.

47. Sargent, *A Superpower Transformed*, 53–58.

48. Ibid., 42–43, 60.

49. Wicker, "Richard M. Nixon," 267.

50. Reeves, *President Nixon*, 486–492.

51. Sargent, *A Superpower Transformed*, 60–62, 214.

52. Ibid., 65–66.

53. Reeves, *President Nixon*, 605–606.

54. Bohn, *Presidents in Crisis*, 95–115; Sargent, *A Superpower Transformed*, 150–151.

55. Sargent, *A Superpower Transformed*, 69–71.

56. Ibid., 82–90.

57. Bohn, *Presidents in Crisis*, xxi, 116–131.

58. Greene, *The Presidency of Gerald R. Ford*, 143–151.

59. War Powers Act, 50 U.S. Code, Chapter 33, War Powers Resolution, Cornell University Law School, https://www.law.cornell.edu/uscode /text/50/chapter-33.

60. Jeffrey Crouch, "Gerald R. Ford," and Scott Kaufman, "Jimmy Carter," both in *The Presidents and the Constitution: A Living History,* ed. Ken Gormley (New York: New York University, 2016), 514–515, 529, 530.

61. Sargent, *A Superpower Transformed,* 185–186.

62. Kalman, "Gerald R. Ford," 280.

63. Sargent, *A Superpower Transformed,* 212–213.

64. Greene, *The Presidency of Gerald R. Ford,* 122–124.

65. Ibid., 124–126.

66. Sargent, *A Superpower Transformed,* 201, 214–216, 219.

67. Ibid., 191.

68. Greene, *The Presidency of Gerald R. Ford,* 112–116.

69. Ibid., 220–222.

70. Ibid., 225.

71. Ibid., 204–208.

Chapter 6: Limited Government Starts to Return

1. Quoted in Thomas O'Neill and William Novak, *Man of the House: The Life and Political Memories of Speaker Tip O'Neill* (New York: Random House, 1987), 297.

2. Lewis L. Gould, "James Earl Carter: Not a Politician," in *American Heritage: The Presidents,* ed. Michael Beschloss (New York: Byron Preiss Books, 2003), 453.

3. Burton I. Kaufman and Scott Kaufman, *The Presidency of James Earl Carter,* 2nd rev. ed. (Lawrence: University Press of Kansas, 2006), 93, 177.

4. Doug Rossinow, *The Reagan Era: A History of the 1980s* (New York: Columbia University Press, 2015), 19.

5. Kaufman and Kaufman, *The Presidency,* 45.

6. Quoted in Daniel J. Sargent, *A Superpower Transformed: The Remaking of American Foreign Relations in the 1970s* (Oxford: Oxford University Press, 2015), 229.

7. Douglas Brinkley, "Jimmy Carter," in *"To the Best of My Ability": The American Presidents,* ed. James M. McPherson (London: DK Publishing, 2004), 284.

8. Quoted in Michael K. Bohn, *Presidents in Crisis: Tough Decisions Inside the White House from Truman to Obama* (New York: Arcade Publishing, 2015), 134.

9. Kaufman and Kaufman, *The Presidency,* 48, 156.

10. Bohn, *Presidents in Crisis,* 132–137

11. War Powers Act, 50 U.S. Code, Chapter 33, War Powers Resolution, Cornell University Law School, https://www.law.cornell.edu/uscode/text/50/chapter-33.

12. Scott Kaufman, "Jimmy Carter," in *The Presidents and the Constitution: A Living History,* ed. Ken Gormley (New York: New York University, 2016), 529–530.

13. Stuart E. Eizenstat, "Jimmy Carter's Unheralded Legacy," *New York Times,* August 25, 2015, A19.

14. Kaufman and Kaufman, *The Presidency,* 193–194, 211–213.

15. Brinkley, "Jimmy Carter," 285–286.

16. Bohn, *Presidents in Crisis,* 138–141, 150–151.

17. Ibid., 151.

18. Ibid., 138–139, 143, 150.

19. Russell Mokhiber and Robert Weissman, "How Wall Street Created a Nation," *Common Dreams,* October 27, 2001, www.commondreams.org/views/2001/10/27/how-wall-street-created-a-nation.

20. Michael Gerhardt, *The Forgotten Presidents: Their Untold Constitutional*

Legacy (Oxford: Oxford University Press, 2013), 228–229.

21. Kaufman, "Jimmy Carter," 528–529.

22. Kaufman and Kaufman, *The Presidency*, 56–57.

23. Gerhardt, *The Forgotten Presidents*, 230, 232.

24. Kaufman and Kaufman, *The Presidency*, 189–191.

25. Gerhardt, *Forgotten Presidents*, 229–230.

26. Kaufman and Kaufman, *The Presidency*, 208–209.

27. Sargent, *A Superpower Transformed*, 253–254.

28. Brinkley, "Jimmy Carter," 283.

29. Sargent, *A Superpower Transformed*, 252–253, 256, 260.

30. Ibid., 257.

31. Rossinow, *The Reagan Era*, 36.

32. Ibid., 38–39.

33. Gerhardt, *Forgotten Presidents*, 228.

34. Quoted in Sargent, *A Superpower Transformed*, 261.

35. Quoted in Kaufman and Kaufman, *The Presidency*, 197.

36. Ibid., 196.

37. Sargent, *A Superpower Transformed*, 2, 286–289.

38. Quoted in Kaufman and Kaufman, *The Presidency*, 198.

39. Ivan Eland, *No War for Oil: U.S. Dependency and the Middle East* (Oakland, CA: The Independent Institute, 2011).

40. Kaufman and Kaufman, *The Presidency*, 110–111.

41. John Howard Brown, "Jimmy Carter, Alfred Kahn, and Airline Deregulation: Anatomy of a Policy Success," *The Independent Review* 19, no. 1 (Summer 2014): 86.

42. Eizenstat, "Jimmy Carter's Unheralded Legacy," A19.

43. Brown, "Jimmy Carter," 85, 90, 92–93, 98.

44. Steven Morrison and Clifford Winston, *The Evolution of the Airline Industry* (Washington, DC: Brookings Institution, 1995).

45. Gerhardt, *Forgotten Presidents*, 231.

46. Gould, *The Republicans*, 289.

47. Ibid., 289.

48. Mike Kimel & Michael E. Kanell, *Presimetrics: What the Facts Tell Us About How the Presidents Measure Up on the Issues We Care About* (New York: Black Dog & Leventhal, 2010), 228.

49. Gerhardt, *Forgotten Presidents*, 222–223.

50. Sargent, *A Superpower Transformed*, 237–238.

51. Ibid., 273, 275.

52. Eizenstat, "Jimmy Carter's Unheralded Legacy," A19.

53. Daniel J. Smith and Peter J. Boettke, "An Episodic History of Modern Fed Independence," *The Independent Review* 20, no. 1 (Summer 2015): 108–109.

54. Ibid., 109.

55. Kaufman and Kaufman, *The Presidency*, 216–217, 222.

56. Rossinow, *The Reagan Era*, 20.

57. Ibid., 35.

58. Quoted in Sargent, *A Superpower Transformed*, 281.

59. Kimel and Kanell, *Presimetrics*, 21, 23, 38, 46, 51, 87, 100, 111, 134

60. Brinkley, "Jimmy Carter," 283.

61. Kaufman and Kaufman, *The Presidency*, 68–69.

62. Ellen Schrecker, ed., *Cold War Triumphalism: The Misuse of History After the Fall of Communism* (New York: New Press, 2004), 15–16.

63. Kaufman and Kaufman, *The Presidency*, 227–228.

64. Ibid., 138.

65. Rossinow, *The Reagan Era*, 18.

66. Kaufman and Kaufman, *The Presidency*, 92–98, 100.
67. Ibid., 123–125.
68. Ibid., 91, 93.
69. Gerhardt, *Forgotten Presidents*, 232–233.
70. Kaufman, "Jimmy Carter" 524–528.
71. Sargent, *A Superpower Transformed*, 292–293.
72. Kimel and Kanell, *Presimetrics*, 97.
73. Kaufman and Kaufman, *The Presidency*, 249–250.
74. Rossinow, *The Reagan Era*, 19.

Chapter 7. Busting the Myths

1. Brion McClanahan, *Nine Presidents Who Screwed Up America and Four Who Tried to Save Her* (Washington, DC: Regnery History, 2016), 253, 271.
2. Doug Rossinow, *The Reagan Era: A History of the 1980s* (New York: Columbia University Press, 2015), 9–10.
3. Quoted in Will Bunch, *Tear Down This Myth: How the Reagan Legacy Has Distorted Our Politics and Haunts Our Future* (New York: Free Press, 2009), 103–104.
4. James T. Patterson, "Ronald Reagan," in *"To the Best of My Ability": The American President,* ed. James M. McPherson (London: DK Publishing, 2004), 294.
5. Gould, *The Republicans*, 303.
6. Michael K. Bohn, *Presidents in Crisis: Tough Decisions Inside the White House from Truman to Obama* (New York: Arcade Publishing, 2015), 162.
7. Ibid., xx.
8. John Samples, *The Struggle to Limit Government* (Washington, DC: Cato Institute, 2010), 150.
9. Patterson, "Ronald Reagan," 288.
10. Rossinow, *The Reagan Era*, 13–14.
11. Ibid., 66–67.
12. Daniel J. Sargent, *A Superpower Transformed: The Remaking of American Foreign Relations in the 1970s* (Oxford: Oxford University Press, 2015), 229.
13. Jon Zobenica, "How Lenin Beat Reagan: The USSR Is Gone—But Its Ethos Lives on at Fox News," *American Conservative* (September/October 2015).
14. Bunch, *Tear Down This Myth*, 26.
15. Victor Sebestyen, *Revolution 1989: The Fall of the Soviet Empire* (New York: Vintage Books, 2009), xx.
16. Rossinow, *The Reagan Era*, 236–239, 270–272.
17. Quoted in Steven F. Hayward, *The Age of Reagan: The Conservative Counterrevolution* (New York: Three Rivers Press, 2009), 251–253, 257–258.
18. Quoted in Rossinow, *The Reagan Era*, 67.
19. Quotes from James Mann, *The Rebellion of Ronald Reagan: A History of the End of the Cold War* (New York: Penguin Books, 2009), 248–251.
20. Ibid., 249.
21. Bunch, *Tear Down This Myth*, 80.
22. Mann, *The Rebellion of Ronald Reagan*, 248–249.
23. Hayward, *The Age of Reagan*, 242–243.
24. Sebestyen, *Revolution 1989*, 54–55, 58.
25. Hayward, *The Age of Reagan*, 244–245.
26. Chris Matthews, *Tip and the Gipper: When Politics Worked* (New York: Simon & Schuster, 2013), 46.
27. Hayward, *The Age of Reagan*, 249–251, 307.
28. Ibid., 310.
29. Rossinow, *The Reagan Era*, 111–113, 276–277.
30. Sebestyen, *Revolution 1989*, 25, 75–77, 194–197, 226–227.
31. Ibid., 155–156.

32. Sargent, *A Superpower Transformed*, 302–306.

33. Sebestyen, *Revolution 1989*, xix, 20.

34. Ibid., 78.

35. Bunch, *Tear Down This Myth*, 26.

36. David A. Stockman, *The Great Deformation: The Corruption of Capitalism in America* (New York: PublicAffairs, 2013), 75.

37. Quoted in Bunch, *Tear Down This Wall*, 82. Knopf does claim that the main effect of Reagan's defense buildup on the USSR was therefore psychological. However, this claim is much harder to prove. Also, Gorbachev abandoned the military defense of illegitimate Eastern European Communist regimes because the sagging Soviet economy would no longer support the cost, not because the Soviets were scared of Reagan.

38. Mann, *The Rebellion of Ronald Reagan*, 247.

39. John H. Sununu, *The Quiet Man: The Indispensable Presidency of George H. W. Bush* (New York: Broadside Books, 2015), 157.

40. Bunch, *Tear Down This Myth*, 83–84.

41. Sebestyen, *Revolution 1989*, 158–159.

42. Lou Cannon, *President Reagan: The Role of a Lifetime* (New York: PublicAffairs, 2000), 760, 763.

43. Quoted in Rossinow, *The Reagan Era*, 109.

44. Hayward, *The Age of Reagan*, 292–298.

45. Sebestyen, *Revolution 1989*, 152–153, 199.

46. Hayward, *The Age of Reagan*, 321.

47. Mann, *The Rebellion of Ronald Reagan*, 263–264.

48. Cannon, *President Reagan*, 761–762.

49. Rossinow, *The Reagan Era*, 101.

50. Hayward, *The Age of Reagan*, 325; Sam Roberts, "NATO War Games Unwittingly Put Soviets on 'Hair Trigger' in '83, Analysis Suggests," *New York Times*, November 9, 2015.

51. Roberts, "NATO War Games."

52. Sebestyen, *Revolution 1989*, 79–94; Roberts, "NATO War Games."

53. Mann, *The Rebellion of Ronald Reagan*, 250–251.

54. Bunch, *Tear Down This Myth*, 25.

55. Quoted in Rossinow, *The Reagan Era*, 78.

56. Hayward, *The Age of Reagan*, 174.

57. Rossinow, *The Reagan Era*, 71–72.

58. Francis A. Boyle, *Destroying Libya and World Order: The Three-Decade U.S. Campaign to Terminate the Qaddafi Revolution* (Atlanta: Clarity Press, 2013), 38–101; Rossinow, *The Reagan Era*, 74, 192.

59. Bohn, *Presidents in Crisis*, 170.

60. Ibid., 169.

61. Ibid., 168–175.

62. Hayward, *The Age of Reagan*, 491.

63. Matthews, *Tip and the Gipper*, 263–268.

64. Ibid., 314–315.

65. Bohn, *The Age of Reagan*, 158–162.

66. Ibid., 158.

67. Quoted in Rossinow, *The Reagan Era*, 115.

68. Quoted in Bunch, *Tear Down This Myth*, 104.

69. Gould, *The Republicans*, 296.

70. Bohn, *Presidents in Crisis*, 163–168.

71. Bohn, *Presidents in Crisis*, 163–168.

72. Quoted in Rossinow, *The Reagan Era*, 275.

73. Ibid., 297.

74. Ivan Eland, *No War for Oil: U.S. Dependency and the Middle East* (Oakland, CA: The Independent Institute, 2011).

75. Quoted in Hayward, *The Age of Reagan*, 50, 528.

76. Ibid., 441.

77. Bunch, *Tear Down This Myth*, 15, 92.

78. Rossinow, *The Reagan Era*, 165–166.

79. Hayward, *The Age of Reagan*, 538, 543.

80. John Ehrman, *The Eighties: America in the Age of Reagan* (New Haven and London: Yale University Press, 2005), 141.

81. Rossinow, *The Reagan Era*, 200.

82. Bohn, *Presidents in Crisis*, 156–157, 174–175.

83. Rossinow, *The Reagan Era*, 181-182.

84. Rossinow, *The Reagan Era*, 181–182, 184–185, 218.

85. Hayward, *The Age of Reagan*, 355–356, 429, 516.

86. Quotes from Secord and North in Rossinow, *The Reagan Era*, 220.

87. Bunch, *Tear Down This Myth*, 18, 109.

88. Rossinow, *The Reagan Era*, 199–200.

89. Lewis L. Gould, "Ronald Wilson Reagan: The Great Communicator," in *American Heritage: The Presidents*, ed. Michael Beschloss (New York: Byron Preiss Books, 2003), 465, 471.

90. Gould, *The Republicans*, 301.

91. Rossinow, *The Reagan Era*, 78.

92. Ibid., 102.

93. Ibid., 266.

94. Ibid., 71.

95. Ehrman, *The Eighties*, 138–139.

96. Rossinow, *The Reagan Era*, 44.

97. Hayward, *The Age of Reagan*, 39.

98. Quoted in Rossinow, *The Reagan Era*, 55.

99. Ibid., 90, 95.

100. Ibid., 31.

101. Ibid., 61.

102. Hayward, *The Age of Reagan*, 154.

103. Ibid., 152.

104. Stockman, *The Great Deformation*, 72–73; Hayward, *The Age of Reagan*, 183.

105. Rossinow, *The Reagan Era*, 54–55.

106. Quoted in Stockman, *The Great Deformation*, 74.

107. Hayward, *The Age of Reagan*, 182–183; Rossinow, *The Reagan Era*, 68–69.

108. Samples, *The Struggle to Limit Government*, 142; Rossinow, *The Reagan Era*, 62.

109. Hayward, *The Age of Reagan*, 182–183, 188.

110. Samples, *The Struggle to Limit Government*, 143–145, 147–148, 153.

111. Rossinow, *The Reagan Era*, 178.

112. Carl Hulse, "Weighing the Odds in Fight Over Iran Nuclear Deal," *New York Times*, August 25, 2015.

113. Bunch, *Tear Down This Myth*, 51, 61.

114. Kimel and Kanell, *Presimetrics*, 100.

115. Hayward, *The Age of Reagan*, 67, 70–71.

116. Rossinow, *The Reagan Era*, 34.

117. Gould, *The Republicans*, 278–279

118. Alan Greenspan, *The Age of Turbulence: Adventures in a New World* (New York: Penguin Press, 2007), 147.

119. Kimel and Kanell, *Presimetrics* 38, 51.

120. Rossinow, *The Reagan Era*, 33–34.

121. CNNMoney.com, "Taxes: What People Forget About Reagan," September 12, 2010, http://money.cnn.com/2010/09/08/news/economy/reagan_years_taxes/#.

122. Bunch, *Tear Down This Myth*, 51, 58–59, 126.

123. Rossinow, *The Reagan Era*, 63.

124. Kimel and Kanell, *Presimetrics*, 42.

125. Samples, *The Struggle to Limit Government*, 131; Ehrman, *The Eighties*, 135–136.

126. William A. Niskanen, *Reaganomics: An Insider's Account of the Policies and the People* (New York: Oxford University Press, 1988), 71.

127. Gould, *The Republicans*, 300.

128. Stockman, *The Great Deformation*, 55.

129. Ehrman, *The Eighties*, 132.

130. Stockman, *The Great Deformation*, 87, 99.

131. Samples, *The Struggle to Limit Government*, 148.
132. Christina D. Romer and David H. Romer, "Do Tax Cuts Starve the Beast? The Effect of Tax Changes on Government Spending," *Brookings Papers on Economic Activity* (Spring 2009), 139–214.
133. Ehrman, *The Eighties*, 54, 56.
134. Hayward, *The Age of Reagan*, 88–89.
135. Stockman, *The Great Deformation*, 105.
136. Ellen Schrecker, ed., *Cold War Triumphalism: The Misuse of History After the Fall of Communism* (New York: New Press, 2004), 131, 135.
137. Kimel and Kanell, *Presimetrics*, 51.
138. Rossinow, *The Reagan Era*, 283.
139. Sununu, *The Quiet Man*, 165.
140. Samples, *The Struggle to Limit Government*, 80, 82.
141. Kimel and Kanell, *Presimetrics*, 38.
142. CNNMoney.com, "Taxes: What People Forget About Reagan."
143. Patterson, "Ronald Reagan," 291.
144. Ibid.
145. Quoted in Bunch, *Tear Down This Myth*, 61, 65–66.
146. Ibid., 63.
147. Hayward, *The Age of Reagan*, 637–638.
148. Kip Viscusi, "The Misspecified Agenda," in *Economic Policy in the 1980s*, ed. Martin Feldstein (Chicago: University of Chicago Press, 1994), 457.
149. Hayward, *The Age of Reagan*, 218.
150. Patterson, "Ronald Reagan," 291; Herbert S. Parmet, "George Bush," in *"To the Best of My Ability": The American Presidents,* ed. James M. McPherson (London: DK Publishing, 2004), 297.
151. Sununu, *The Quiet Man*, 84–86.
152. CNNMoney.com, "Taxes: What People Forget About Reagan."
153. Stockman, *The Great Deformation*, 59, 65.
154. Ehrman, *The Eighties*, 63.
155. Rossinow, *The Reagan Era*, 282.
156. CNNMoney.com, "Taxes: What People Forget About Reagan."
157. Cited by Bunch, *Tear Down This Myth*, 137.
158. Stockman, *The Great Deformation*, 97–98, 105.
159. Daniel L. Smith and Peter J. Boettke, "An Episodic History of Modern Fed Independence," *The Independent Review* 20, no. 1 (Summer 2015): 109–111.
160. Smith and Boettke, "An Episodic History," 112.
161. Bunch, *Tear Down This Myth*, 15.
162. Sununu, *The Quiet Man*, 75, 83.
163. Samples, *The Struggle to Limit Government*, 102.
164. Rossinow, *The Reagan Era*, 52.
165. Hayward, *The Age of Reagan*, 584–585.
166. Samples, *The Struggle to Limit Government*, 118–119.
167. Bunch, *Tear Down This Myth*, 40.
168. All quotes from Hayward, *The Age of Reagan*, 7, 9, 42, 87.
169. Bunch, *Tear Down This Myth*, 17.
170. Ibid., 15.
171. Sununu, *The Quiet Man*, 260.
172. Rossinow, *The Reagan Era*, 122.
173. Nicholas Fandos, "Joe Biden's Role in '90s Crime Law Could Haunt Any Presidential Bid," *New York Times*, August 21, 2015.
174. Rossinow, *The Reagan Era*, 124; Jennifer Steinhauer, "Bipartisan Push Builds to Relax Sentencing Laws," *New York Times*, July 28, 2015.
175. Rossinow, *The Reagan Era*, 5.
176. Hayward, *The Age of Reagan*, 565–567.
177. Quoted in Gould, *The Republicans*, 294–295. Also see Rossinow, *The Reagan Era*, 43.

178. Hayward, *The Age of Reagan*, 410.
179. Rossinow, *The Reagan Era*, 42–43, 163.
180. Hayward, *The Age of Reagan*, 216–217.
181. Ibid., 572–581.
182. Denis P. Doyle and Terry W. Hartle, "The 'Safety Net' after Three Years: Income Maintenance and Redistribution Programs in the Reagan Administration: Education," *AEI Public Policy Week*, December 6, 1983, 27.
183. Samples, *The Struggle to Limit Government*, 110.
184. Rossinow, *The Reagan Era*, 85–86.

Chapter 8. Hawkish Tendencies

1. Timothy Naftali, *George H. W. Bush* (New York: Henry Holt, 2007), 151.
2. Curt Smith, *George H. W. Bush: Character at the Core* (Lincoln, NE: Potomac Books, 2014), 161.
3. John H. Sununu, *The Quiet Man: The Indispensable Presidency of George H. W. Bush* (New York: Broadside Books, 2015), 273–274.
4. David Henderson, "The Myth of Saddam's Oil Stranglehold," in *America Entangled: The Persian Gulf Crisis and Its Consequences*, ed. Ted Galen Carpenter (Washington, DC: Cato Institute, 1991), 41–44.
5. Sununu, *The Quiet Man*, 278–282.
6. Jon Meacham, *Destiny and Power: The American Odyssey of George Herbert Walker Bush* (New York: Random House, 2015), 703–704, 708–713.
7. Michael K. Bohn, *Presidents in Crisis: Tough Decisions Inside the White House from Truman to Obama* (New York: Arcade Publishing, 2015), xxi.
8. Meacham, *Destiny and Power*, 722–723.
9. Doug Rossinow, *The Reagan Era: A History of the 1980s* (New York: Columbia University Press, 2015), 277–279.
10. Sununu, *The Quiet Man*, 284.
11. Ibid., 295–296, 314, 316–317.
12. Smith, *George H. W. Bush*, 163.
13. Matthew Carr, *Sherman's Ghosts: Soldiers, Civilians, and the American Way of War* (New York: New Press, 2015), 202–208.
14. Sununu, *The Quiet Man*, 142.
15. Meacham, *Destiny and Power*, 629.
16. Naftali, *George H. W. Bush*, 66–68.
17. Sununu, *The Quiet Man*, 122–123, 125–126.
18. Herbert S. Parmet, "George Bush," in *"To the Best of My Ability": The American Presidents,* ed. James M. McPherson (London: DK Publishing, 2004), 298–299.
19. Smith, *George H. W. Bush*, 162, 237.
20. Naftali, *George H. W. Bush*, 136.
21. Ibid.
22. Ibid., 66–67.
23. Sununu, *The Quiet Man*, 143–148.
24. Rossinow, *The Reagan Era*, 272.
25. Meacham, *Destiny and Power*, 633, 664, 670, 674–675.
26. Ibid., 665.
27. Naftali, *George H. W. Bush*, 80–82.
28. Rossinow, *The Reagan Era*, 267–268.
29. Carr, *Sherman's Ghosts*, 197–200.
30. Smith, *George H. W. Bush*, 232–233.
31. Lewis L. Gould, "George Herbert Walker Bush: The Last Cold Warrior," in *American Heritage: The Presidents,* ed. Michael Beschloss (New York: Byron Preiss Books, 2003), 479.
32. Sununu, *The Quiet Man*, 76–78.
33. Rossinow, *The Reagan Era*, 265–266.
34. Ibid., 268–269.
35. Sununu, *The Quiet Man*, 334–337.
36. William H. Chafe, *Bill and Hillary: The Politics of the Personal* (New York: Farrar, Straus & Giroux, 2012), 306.
37. Sununu, *The Quiet Man*, 79–80.
38. Ibid., 80–82, 358.
39. Mike Kimel and Michael E. Kanell, *Presimetrics: What the Facts Tell Us*

About How the Presidents Measure Up on the Issues We Care About (New York: Black Dog & Leventhal, 2010), 42.

40. Parmet, "George Bush," in 291.

41. Kimel and Kanell, *Presimetrics*, 38.

42. Sununu, *The Quiet Man*, 198–199, 202–203, 358.

43. Kimel and Kanell, *Presimetrics*, 38.

44. Parmet, "George Bush," 300.

45. Smith, *George H. W. Bush*, 163–164.

46. Gould, *The Republicans*, 311–312.

47. Rossinow, *The Reagan Era* , 258.

48. Gould, *The Republicans*, 313.

49. James T. Patterson, "Ronald Reagan," in *"To the Best of My Ability": The American Presidents,* ed. James M. McPherson (London: DK Publishing, 2004), 291; Parmet, "George Bush," 297.

50. Naftali, *George H. W. Bush*, 140.

51. Sununu, *The Quiet Man*, 75, 83–90.

52. Smith, *George H. W. Bush,* 243.

53. Sununu, *The Quiet Man*, 216.

54. Ibid., 221, 224–225.

55. Naftali, *George H. W. Bush*, 133.

56. Rossinow, *The Reagan Era*, 259.

57. Sununu, *The Quiet Man*, 263–265.

58. Ibid., 348.

59. Rossinow, *The Reagan Era*, 258.

60. Sununu, *The Quiet Man*, 256–259.

61. Ibid., 239–240, 251–252.

62. Ibid., 246.

63. Ibid., 268–269.

64. Rossinow, *The Reagan Era*, 259–260.

65. Sununu, *The Quiet Man*, 267–268.

66. Ibid., 224–224.

67. Gould, *The Republicans*, 315.

68. Smith, *George H. W. Bush*, 237.

69. Naftali, *George H. W. Bush*, 154.

70. Meacham, *Destiny and Power*, 880.

71. Smith, *George H. W. Bush*, 191.

Chapter 9. A Good Fiscal Record Counts

1. John Sununu, *The Quiet Man: The Indispensable Presidency of George H. W. Bush* (New York: Broadside Books, 2015), 375.

2. Mike Kimel and Michael E. Kanell, *Presimetrics: What the Facts Tell Us About How the Presidents Measure Up on the Issues We Care About* (New York: Black Dog & Leventhal, 2010), 32–38.

3. Lewis L. Gould, "William Jefferson Clinton: Prosperity and Turmoil," in *American Heritage: The Presidents,* ed. Michael Beschloss (New York: Byron Preiss Books, 2003), 488; Kimel and Kanell, *Presimetrics*, 37.

4. Evan Thomas, "Bill Clinton," in *"To the Best of My Ability": The American Presidents,* ed. James M. McPherson (London: DK Publishing, 2004), 304.

5. Lewis L. Gould, *The Republicans: A History of the Grand Old Party* (Oxford: Oxford University Press, 2014), 319.

6. Daniel J. Smith and Peter J. Boettke, "An Episodic History of Modern Fed Independence," *The Independent Review* 20, no. 1 (Summer 2015): 112–113.

7. Thomas, "Bill Clinton," 303.

8. John F. Harris, *The Survivor: Bill Clinton in the White House* (New York: Random House, 2005), 231.

9. Gould, *The Republicans*, 324.

10. William H. Chafe, *Bill and Hillary: The Politics of the Personal* (New York: Farrar, Straus & Giroux, 2012), 259–262, 264.

11. Chafe, *Bill and Hillary*, 181.

12. Kimel and Kanell, *Presimetrics*, 98–100.

13. Gould, *The Republicans*, 323.

14. Chafe, *Bill and Hillary*, 164–166.

15. Quoted in Chafe, *Bill and Hillary*, 302–303.

16. Ibid., 274–278, 294–296, 302.

17. Gould, *The Republicans*, 326–327.

18. Chafe, *Bill and Hillary*, 300–301, 308.

19. Thomas, "Bill Clinton," in McPherson, ed., *"To the Best of My Ability,"* 304.

20. Chafe, *Bill and Hillary*, 182–183, 208–209, 212, 213–214, 223–224, 328.

21. Ibid., 210, 213–214, 231.

22. Ibid., 203–204, 216–217.

23. Ibid., 262–263, 266–267, 283.

24. Kimel and Kanell, *Presimetrics*, 167.

25. Nicholas Fandos, "Joe Biden's Role in '90s Crime Law Could Haunt Any Presidential Bid," *New York Times*, August 21, 2015.

26. Chafe, *Bill and Hillary*, 172.

27. Quoted in Harris, *The Survivor*, 50.

28. Chafe, *Bill and Hillary*, 198–199.

29. Carl Hulse, "Weighing the Odds in Fight Over Iran Nuclear Deal," *New York Times*, August 25, 2015.

30. Matthew Carr, *Sherman's Ghosts: Soldiers, Civilians, and the American Way of War* (New York: New Press, 2015), 211–215.

31. Michael K. Bohn, *Presidents in Crisis: Tough Decisions Inside the White House from Truman to Obama* (New York: Arcade Publishing, 2015), 210.

32. Bohn, *Presidents in Crisis*, 204–209.

33. Chafe, *Bill and Hillary*, 315–318.

Chapter 10. Big Government at Home and Abroad

1. Peter Baker, *Days of Fire: Bush and Cheney in the White House* (New York: Anchor Books, 2014), 51.

2. Mike Kimel and Michael E. Kanell, *Presimetrics: What the Facts Tell Us About How the Presidents Measure Up on the Issues We Care About* (New York: Black Dog & Leventhal, 2010), 38, 46, 51.

3. Daniel J. Smith and Peter J. Boettke, "An Episodic History of Modern Fed Independence," *The Independent Review* 20, no. 1 (Summer 2015): 112–114.

4. Charlie Savage, *Takeover: The Return of the Imperial Presidency and the Subversion of American Democracy* (New York: Little, Brown, 2007), 76.

5. Baker, *Days of Fire*, 1–2, 8, 11.

6. Ibid., 644.

7. Ibid., 68.

8. William H. Chafe, "George W. Bush," in *"To the Best of My Ability": The American Presidents*, ed. James M. McPherson (London: DK Publishing, 2004), 310, 312.

9. Michael K. Bohn, *Presidents in Crisis: Tough Decisions Inside the White House from Truman to Obama* (New York: Arcade Publishing, 2015), 229–230.

10. Ibid., 229–230.

11. Quoted in Baker, *Days of Fire*, 91, 109, 129, 144, 160–161, 266.

12. Quoted in Bohn, *Presidents in Crisis*, 231.

13. Elizabeth Holtzman with Cynthia L. Cooper, *The Impeachment of George W. Bush* (New York: Nation Books, 2006), 78–79.

14. Baker, *Days of Fire*, 224.

15. Holtzman, *The Impeachment of George W. Bush*, 63.

16. Ibid., 211–212, 239–240.

17. Ibid., 44.

18. In a private meeting with Secretary of Defense Donald Rumsfeld prior to the clearly impending invasion of Iraq, I asked him to comment on this potentially unintended consequence of the policy, but he could only muster a rambling, incoherent answer.

19. Gould, *The Republicans*, 335.

20. Matthew Carr, *Sherman's Ghosts: Soldiers, Civilians, and the American Way*

of War (New York: New Press, 2015), 223, 226–227.

21. Carr, *Sherman's Ghosts*, 230.

22. Daniel Bolger, *Why We Lost: A General's Inside Account of the Iraq and Afghanistan Wars* (New York: Houghton Mifflin Harcourt, 2014), 268–269, 429–431.

23. Carr, *Sherman's Ghosts*, 230.

24. Quoted in ibid., 217.

25. Ibid., 220.

26. Bohn, *Presidents in Crisis*, 229.

27. Ibid., 231, 233.

28. Quoted in Baker, *Days of Fire*, 144.

29. Bolger, *Why We Lost*, 18–24.

30. Baker, *Days of Fire*, 179–181; Bohn, *Presidents in Crisis*, 228–229.

31. Baker, *Days of Fire*, 108, 113, 115.

32. Bohn, *Presidents in Crisis,* 218–219.

33. Baker, *Days of Fire*, 30.

34. Ibid., 468–469.

35. Benjamin A. Kleinerman, "George W. Bush," in *The Presidents and the Constitution: A Living History*, ed. Ken Gormley (New York: New York University Press, 2016), 590–591.

36. Ibid., 172, 314–318.

37. Ibid., 569–570.

38. Fred Barnes, *Rebel-in-Chief: Inside the Bold and Controversial Presidency*

of George W. Bush (New York: Three Rivers Press, 2006), 23, 201.

39. Ibid., 99–100.

40. William H. Chafe, "George W. Bush," 310.

41. Ibid., 1–2, 280–281, 555–556.

42. Ibid.

43. Gould, *The Republicans*, 337.

44. Kimel and Kanell, *Presimetrics*, 217.

45. William H. Chafe, "George W. Bush," 309.

46. Carl Hulse, "Weighing the Odds in Fight Over Iran Nuclear Deal," *New York Times*, August 25, 2015.

47. Gould, *The Republicans*, 339.

48. Ibid., 348.

49. Barnes, *Rebel-in-Chief,* 202.

Chapter 11: Political Rhetoric and Hypocrisy

1. Mike Kimel and Michael E. Kanell, *Presimetrics: What the Facts Tell Us About How the Presidents Measure Up on the Issues We Care About* (New York: Black Dog & Leventhal, 2010), 38, 51, 111, 134.

2. Ibid., 21, 23, 87, 190, 194.

Bibliography

Adams, T. Becket et al. "The State of Obama's Promises." *Washington Examiner*, January 4, 2016.

Ambrose, Stephen. *Eisenhower: Soldier and President*. New York: Simon & Schuster, 1990. Citations refer to the 2003 paperback edition..

Baker, Peter. *Days of Fire: Bush and Cheney in the White House*. New York: Knopf-Doubleday/Anchor Books, 2014.

Berg, A. Scott. *Wilson*. New York: Berkley Books, 2014.

Bohn, Michael. *Presidents in Crisis: Tough Decisions Inside the White House from Truman to Obama*. New York: Arcade Publishing, 2015.

Bolger, Daniel. *Why We Lost: A General's Inside Account of the Iraq and Afghanistan Wars*. Boston: Houghton Mifflin Harcourt, 2014.

Boyle, Francis A. *Destroying Libya and World Order: The Three-Decade U.S. Campaign to Terminate the Qaddafi Revolution*. Atlanta: Clarity Press, 2013.

Brown, John Howard. "Jimmy Carter, Alfred Kahn, and Airline Deregulation: Anatomy of a Policy Success." *The Independent Review* 19, no. 1 (Summer 2014): 85–99.

Bunch, Will. *Tear Down This Myth: How the Reagan Legacy Has Distorted Our Politics and Haunts Our Future*. New York: Simon & Schuster/Free Press, 2009.

Bush, George H. W. Address Accepting the Presidential Nomination at the Republican National Convention in New Orleans, August 18, 1988. http://www.presidency.ucsb.edu/ws/?pid=25955;

Bush, George W. "A Period of Consequences." Address given at The Citadel, South Carolina, September 23, 1999. http://www3.citadel.edu/pao/addresses/pres_bush.html

Cannon, Lou. *President Reagan: The Role of a Lifetime*. New York: PublicAffairs, 2000.

Carr, Matthew. *Sherman's Ghosts: Soldiers, Civilians, and the American Way of War*. New York: The New Press, 2015.

Chafe, William H. *Bill and Hillary: The Politics of the Personal*. New York: Farrar, Straus and Giroux, 2012.

Clinton, Bill. Democratic Leadership Council Keynote Address. Given at Democratic Leadership Council National Convention, Cleveland, Ohio, May 16, 1991.

Coolidge, Calvin. Third Annual Message, December 8, 1925. http://www.presidency .ucsb.edu/ws/index.php?pid=29566

Crouch, Jeffrey, "Gerald R. Ford." In *The Presidents and the Constitution: A Living History*, edited by Ken Gormley. New York: New York University, 2016.

Dallek, Robert. *Lyndon B. Johnson: Portrait of a President*. Oxford: Oxford University Press, 2004.

Damms, Richard V. "Dwight D. Eisenhower." In *The Presidents and the Constitution: A Living History*, edited by Ken Gormley. New York: New York University Press, 2016.

Dean, John W. *Warren G. Harding: The American Presidents Series: The 29th President, 1921–1923*. New York: Times Books, 2004.

Dean, John W. *The Nixon Defense: What He Knew and When He Knew It*. New York: Viking, 2014.

Doyle, Denis P., and Terry W. Hartle. "The 'Safety Net' after Three Years: Income Maintenance and Redistribution Programs in the Reagan Administration: Education." *AEI Public Policy Week*, December 6, 1983.

Ehrman, John. *The Eighties: America in the Age of Reagan*. New Haven, CT: Yale University Press, 2005.

Eizenstat, Stuart E. "Jimmy Carter's Unheralded Legacy." *New York Times*, August 25, 2015.

Eland, Ivan. *No War for Oil: U.S. Dependency and the Middle East*. Oakland, CA: Independent Institute, 2011.

————. *Recarving Rushmore: Ranking the Presidents on Peace, Prosperity, and Liberty*. Updated edition. Oakland, CA: Independent Institute, 2014.

Fandos, Nicholas. "Joe Biden's Role in '90s Crime Law Could Haunt Any Presidential Bid." *New York Times*, August 21, 2015.

Foner, Eric, and John A. Garraty. *The Reader's Companion to American History*. New York: Houghton Mifflin Harcourt, 1991.

Friedman, Benjamin, "Did the Military Intervention in Libya Succeed?" Address given at Cato Institute Policy Forum, March 19, 2014.

Fromkin, David. *A Peace to End All Peace: The Fall of the Ottoman Empire and the Creation of the Modern Middle East*. New York: Henry Holt, 2009.

Gaffney, David, and Peter Gaffney. *The Presidents*. New York: Hyperion, 2012.

Gerhardt, Michael. *The Forgotten Presidents: Their Untold Constitutional Legacy*. Oxford: Oxford University Press, 2013.

Gould, Lewis L. "Gerald Rudolph Ford: A Time for Healing." In *American Heritage: The Presidents*, edited by Michael Beschloss. New York: Byron Preiss Books, 2003.

———. "James Earl Carter: Not a Politician." In *American Heritage: The Presidents*, edited by Michael Beschloss. New York: Byron Preiss Books, 2003.

———. "Richard Milhous Nixon: The Road to Watergate." In *American Heritage: The Presidents*, edited by Michael Beschloss. New York: Byron Preiss Books, 2003.

———. "Ronald Wilson Reagan: The Great Communicator." In *American Heritage: The Presidents*, edited by Michael Beschloss. New York: Byron Preiss Books, 2003.

———. *The Republicans: A History of the Grand Old Party*. Revised edition. Oxford: Oxford University Press, 2014.

Greene, John Robert. *The Presidency of Gerald R. Ford*. Lawrence, KS: University Press of Kansas, 1995.

Greenspan, Alan. *The Age of Turbulence: Adventures in a New World*. New York: Penguin Press, 2007.

Harding, Warren G. Inaugural Address, March 4, 1921, http://www.presidency.ucsb.edu/ws/?pid=25833.

Harris, John F. *The Survivor: Bill Clinton in the White House*. New York: Random House, 2005.

Hayward, Steven F. *The Age of Reagan: The Conservative Counterrevolution, 1980–1989*. New York: Three Rivers Press, 2009.

Henderson, David. "The Myth of Saddam's Oil Stranglehold." In *America Entangled: The Persian Gulf Crisis and Its Consequences*, edited by Ted Galen Carpenter. Washington, DC: Cato Institute, 1991.

Holtzman, Elizabeth, with Cynthia L. Cooper. *The Impeachment of George W. Bush: A Practical Guide for Concerned Citizens*. New York: Nation Books, 2006.

Hoover, Herbert. Inaugural Address, March 4, 1929, https://hoover.archives.gov/info/inauguralspeech.html.

Hulse, Carl. "Weighing the Odds in Fight Over Iran Nuclear Deal." *New York Times*, August 25, 2015.

Jacobs, David. "Warren Gamaliel Harding: A Babbitt in the White House," rev. John Milton Cooper and Michael Harwood. In *American Heritage: The Presidents*, edited by Michael Beschloss. New York: Byron Preiss Books, 2003.

Kalman, Laura. "Gerald R. Ford." In *"To the Best of My Ability": The American Presidents*, edited by James M. McPherson. London: DK Publishing, 2004.

Kaufman, Burton I., and Scott Kaufman. *The Presidency of James Earl Carter, Jr.*, 2nd rev. ed. Lawrence KS: University Press of Kansas, 2006.

Kaufman, Scott. "Jimmy Carter." In *The Presidents and the Constitution: A Living History*, edited by Ken Gormley. New York: New York University, 2016.

Keller, Morton. "Warren G. Harding." In *"To the Best of My Ability": The American Presidents*, edited by James M. McPherson. London: DK Publishing, 2004.

Kennedy, John F. Address Accepting the Presidential Nomination Given at the Democratic National Convention in the Los Angeles Memorial Coliseum, July 15, 1960.

Kimel, Mike, and Michael Kanell. *Presimetrics: What the Facts Tell Us About How the Presidents Measure Up on the Issues We Care About*. New York: Black Dog & Leventhal, 2010.

Kleinerman, Benjamin A. "George W. Bush." In *The Presidents and the Constitution: A Living History*, edited by Ken Gormley. New York: New York University Press, 2016.

Langguth, A. J. *After Lincoln: How the North Won the Civil War and Lost the Peace*. New York: Simon & Schuster, 2014.

Mann, James. *The Rebellion of Ronald Reagan: A History of the End of the Cold War*. New York: Penguin Books, 2009.

Matthews, Chris. *Tip and the Gipper: When Politics Worked*. New York: Simon & Schuster, 2013.

McClanahan, Brion. *Nine Presidents Who Screwed Up America and Four Who Tried to Save Her*. Washington, DC: Regnery History, 2016.

Meacham, Jon. *Destiny and Power: The American Odyssey of George Herbert Walker Bush*. New York: Random House, 2015.

Mee, Jr., Charles L. "Dwight David Eisenhower: I Like Ike," rev. Lewis L. Gould. In *American Heritage: The Presidents*, edited by Michael Beschloss. New York: Byron Preiss Books, 2003.

Mokhiber, Russell, and Robert Weissman. "How Wall Street Created a Nation." *Common Dreams*, October 27, 2001. www.commondreams.org/views/2001/10/27/how-wall-street-created-nation

Moore, John A. "The Original Supply Siders: Warren Harding and Calvin Coolidge." *The Independent Review* 18, no. 4. Spring 2014.

Morrison, Steven and Winston, Clifford. *The Evolution of the Airline Industry*. Washington, DC: Brookings Institution, 1995.

Naftali, Timothy. *George H. W. Bush*. New York: Henry Holt, 2007.

Newton, Jim. *Eisenhower: The White House Years*. New York: Knopf Doubleday Publishing Group/Anchor Books, 2012.

Niskanen, William A. *Reaganomics: An Insider's Account of the Policies and the People*. New York: Oxford University Press, 1988.

O'Neill, Thomas and William Novak. *Man of the House: The Life and Political Memories of Speaker Tip O'Neill*. New York: Random House, 1987.

Parmet, Herbert S. "Dwight D. Eisenhower." In *"To the Best of My Ability": The American Presidents,* ed. James M. McPherson. London: DK Publishing, 2004.

Patterson, James T. "Ronald Reagan." In *"To the Best of My Ability": The American President,* edited by James M. McPherson. London: DK Publishing, 2004.

Payne, Phillip G. *Dead Last: The Public Memory of Warren G. Harding's Scandalous Legacy.* Athens: Ohio University Press, 2009.

Pecquet Gary M., and Clifford F. Thies. "Reputation Overrides Record." *The Independent Review* 21, no. 1 (Summer 2016): 29–45.

Perret, Geoffrey. *Eisenhower.* Holbrook, MA: Adams Media, 1999.

Rappleye, Charles. *Herbert Hoover in the White House: The Ordeal of the Presidency.* New York: Simon & Schuster, 2016.

Reeves, Richard. *President Nixon: Alone in the White House.* New York: Simon & Schuster/Touchstone Books, 2001.

Robenalt, James. "Warren G. Harding." In *The Presidents and the Constitution: A Living History,* edited by Ken Gormley. New York: New York University Press, 2016.

Roberts, Sam. "NATO War Games Unwittingly Put Soviets and US on 'Hair Trigger' in '83, Analysis Suggests." *New York Times,* November 9, 2015.

Robinson, Edgar Eugene, and Vaughn Davis Bornet. *Herbert Hoover: President of the United States.* Stanford, CA: Hoover Institution Press, 1975.

Romer, Christina D., and David H. Romer. "Do Tax Cuts Starve the Beast? The Effect of Tax Changes on Government Spending." *Brookings Papers on Economic Activity.* Spring 2009.

Roosevelt, Franklin Delano. First Inaugural Address, March 4, 1933, https://www.archives.gov/education/lessons/fdr-inaugural/

Rossinow, Doug. *The Reagan Era: A History of the 1980s.* New York: Columbia University Press, 2015.

Sahadi, Jeanne. "Taxes: What People Forget About Reagan." CNNMoney.com, September 12, 2010.

Samples, John. *The Struggle to Limit Government.* Washington, DC: Cato Institute, 2010.

Sargent, Daniel J. *A Superpower Transformed: The Remaking of American Foreign Relations in the 1970s.* Oxford: Oxford University Press, 2015.

Savage, Charlie. *Takeover: The Return of the Imperial Presidency and the Subversion of American Democracy.* New York: Little, Brown, 2007.

Schrecker, Ellen, ed. *Cold War Triumphalism: The Misuse of History After the Fall of Communism.* New York: The New Press, 2004.

Sebestyen, Victor. *Revolution 1989: The Fall of the Soviet Empire.* New York: Vintage Books, 2009.

Shlaes, Amity. *Coolidge.* Australia: HarperCollins, 2013. Kindle edition.

Smith, Curt. *George H. W. Bush: Character at the Core.* Lincoln, NE: Potomac Books, 2014.

Smith, Daniel J. and Peter J. Boettke. "An Episodic History of Modern Fed Independence." *The Independent Review* 20, no. 1 (Summer 2015) 99–120.

Steinhauer, Jennifer. "Bipartisan Push Builds to Relax Sentencing Laws." *New York Times,* July 28, 2015.

Stockman, David A. *The Great Deformation: The Corruption of Capitalism in America.* New York: PublicAffairs, 2013.

Sununu, John H. *The Quiet Man: The Indispensable Presidency of George H. W. Bush.* New York: Broadside Books, 2015.

The White House, Office of Management and Budget, *Summary of Receipts, Outlays, and Surpluses or Deficits: 1789–2021.* https://obamawhitehouse.archives.gov/omb/budget/Historicals

Thomas, Evan. *Ike's Bluff: President Eisenhower's Secret Battle to Save the World.* New York: Little Brown, 2012.

Tonkin Gulf Resolution, Public Law 88-408, 88th Congress, August 7, 1964; General Records of the United States Government; Record Group 11; National Archives. http://www.ourdocuments.gov/doc.php?doc=98&page=transcript

Tooze, Adam. *The Deluge: The Great War, America, and the Remaking of the Global Order, 1916–1931.* New York: Viking, 2014.

Truman, Harry. Annual Message to the Congress on the State of the Union, January 7, 1948. http://www.presidency.ucsb.edu/ws/?pid=13005

Truman, Harry. Annual Message to the Congress on the State of the Union, January 5, 1949. http://www.presidency.ucsb.edu/ws/?pid=13293

Viscusi, Kip. "The Misspecified Agenda." In *Economic Policy in the 1980s,* edited by Martin Feldstein. Chicago: University of Chicago Press, 1994.

War Powers Act, 50 U.S. Code, Chapter 33, War Powers Resolution, Cornell University Law School, https://www.law.cornell.edu/uscode/text/50/chapter-33

Wicker, Tom. "Richard M. Nixon." In *"To the Best of My Ability": The American Presidents,* edited by James M. McPherson. London: DK Publishing, 2004.

Williamson, Kevin D. "Why Like Ike: Conservatives Got Eisenhower Wrong the First Time Around." *National Review* LXV, no. 16, September 2, 2013.

Wilson, Joan Hoff. *Herbert Hoover: Forgotten Progressive.* New York: HarperCollins, 1975.

Wilson, Woodrow. *Constitutional Government in the United States.* New York: Columbia University Press, 1908.

Zobenica, Jon. "How Lenin Beat Reagan: The USSR Is Gone—But Its Ethos Lives on at Fox News." *American Conservative,* September/October 2015.

Index

About the Author

IVAN ELAND is Senior Fellow and Director of the Center on Peace & Liberty at the Independent Institute. He has been Director of Defense Policy Studies at the Cato Institute, and he spent fifteen years working for Congress on national security issues, including stints as an investigator for the House Foreign Affairs Committee and Principal Defense Analyst at the Congressional Budget Office. He also has served as Evaluator-in-Charge (national security and intelligence) for the US General Accounting Office (now the Government Accountability Office) and has testified on the military and financial aspects of NATO expansion before the Senate Foreign Relations Committee, on the effects of international economic sanctions before that same committee, on CIA oversight before the House Government Reform Committee, and on the creation of the Department of Homeland Security before the Senate Judiciary Committee.

Dr. Eland is the author of *Partitioning for Peace: An Exit Strategy for Iraq*; *Recarving Rushmore: Ranking the Presidents on Peace, Prosperity, and Liberty*; *The Empire Has No Clothes: U.S. Foreign Policy Exposed*; *Putting "Defense" Back into U.S. Defense Policy*; *No War for Oil: U.S. Dependency and the Middle East*; as well as *The Failure of Counterinsurgency: Why Hearts and Minds Are Not Always Won*. He is a contributor to numerous volumes and the author of forty-five in-depth studies on national security issues.

Dr. Eland is a graduate of Iowa State University and received an MBA in applied economics and a PhD in Public Policy from George Washington University.

His articles have appeared in *American Prospect, Arms Control Today, Bulletin of the Atomic Scientists, Emory Law Journal, The Independent Review, Issues in Science and Technology* (National Academy of Sciences), *Mediterranean Quarterly, Middle East and International Review, Middle East Policy, Nexus, Chronicle of Higher Education, American Conservative, International Journal of World Peace*, and *Northwestern Journal of International Affairs*. Dr. Eland's popular writings have appeared in such publications as the *Los Angeles Times, San Francisco Chronicle, USA Today, Houston Chronicle, Dallas Morning News, New York Times, Chicago Sun-Times, San Diego Union-Tribune, Miami Herald, St. Louis Post-Dispatch, Newsday, Sacramento Bee, Orange County Register, Washington Times, Washington Examiner, CNN.com, New York Post, Providence Journal, The Hill*, and *Defense News*. He has appeared on ABC's *World News Tonight*, NPR's *Talk of the Nation*, PBS, Fox News Channel, CNBC, Bloomberg TV, CNN, CNN Crossfire, CNN-fn, C-SPAN, C-SPAN's *Washington Journal*, MSNBC, Canadian Broadcasting Corp. (CBC), Canadian TV (CTV), Radio Free Europe, Voice of America, BBC, France 24, and other local, national, and international TV and radio programs.

Dr. Eland was awarded the Presidential Medal of the President of Italy.

Independent Institute Studies in Political Economy

Independent Institute Studies in Political Economy

INDEPENDENT I N S T I T U T E

100 SWAN WAY, OAKLAND, CA 94621-1428

For further information:

510-632-1366 • orders@independent.org • http://www.independent.org/publications/books/